BIBLICAL LANGUAGES: HEBREW
3

Editors
Stanley E. Porter
Richard S. Hess

Sheffield Academic Press
Sheffield

A Biblical Hebrew Reference Grammar

Christo H.J. van der Merwe
Jackie A. Naudé
Jan H. Kroeze

Biblical Languages: Hebrew
3

Dedicated to Eric Samson.
Without his generous sponsorship of the
Eric Samson Chair for Hebrew Grammar
this project would not have been possible.

Copyright © 1999 Sheffield Academic Press

Published by
Sheffield Academic Press Ltd
Mansion House
19 Kingfield Road
Sheffield S11 9AS
England

Typeset by Sheffield Academic Press
and
Printed on acid-free paper in Great Britain
by Bookcraft Ltd
Midsomer Norton, Bath

British Library Cataloguing in Publication Data

A catalogue record for this book is available
from the British Library

ISBN 1-85075-861-1
1-85075-856-5 pbk

CONTENTS

Foreword

The contents of most modern introductory Biblical Hebrew (= BH) grammars are arranged according to didactic principles. For example, in these grammars the simple forms of the verb are often introduced at the very outset, followed by the simpler forms of the noun. The irregular stems of nouns and verbs are then dealt with bit by bit in the rest of the grammar. Although didactic principles should play a decisive role in structuring an introductory grammar, it often happens that such introductory grammars become the only source of information for second language readers of BH. Apart from the limited data available in these works, tracing in them information on a particular theme can be a very time-consuming process.

The aim of this grammar is to serve as *a reference work at an intermediate level* for exegetes and translators of the Hebrew Bible who have a basic knowledge of BH, but would like to *use and broaden* the knowledge they have acquired in an introductory course. It therefore strives, on the one hand, to systematize as briefly as possible the BH linguistic knowledge that is normally presented in introductory courses. On the other hand, it offers BH information beyond that of introductory courses in areas that are deemed relevant for exegetes and translators. For this reason, unlike an introductory grammar, it is not intended as a manual to be learned systematically. The intention is rather to present information concerning BH systematically for easy reference. It attempts neither to present information in terms of a single linguistic theory nor to be absolutely comprehensive. It also avoids discussing problems regarding the description of BH. It is a grammar trying to offer solutions to users who are not interested in the problems of describing BH. Although most of the examples come from the prose sections of the Bible, this volume represents, to the opinion of the authors, a major part of the BH linguistic information required by an exegete of the *Biblia He-*

braica Stuttgartensia. Footnotes and bibliographical references have been kept to a minimum.

This grammar is a team effort in the true sense of the word. Apart from the three authors, there have also been contributions by the Reverend Wouter van Wyk of the Rand Afrikaans University. Professor Cynthia Miller of the North Carolina State University (USA) and Ms Jackie du Toit of the University of the North provided valuable criticisms of the beta version. In editing the English edition (which was translated by Dr Edwin Hees of the Department of English at the University of Stellenbosch) Ms Helen Efthimiadis of the University of the North made numerous brilliant suggestions which we incorporated.

Although reference grammars are rarely compiled consistently in terms of a single linguistic framework or theory, the process of compiling such a grammar does not occur in a vacuum. In this grammar the following principles were consciously adopted:

1. This grammar is intended for a very specific audience, namely *translators and exegetes of BH texts* who wish to engage critically with existing translations and interpretations of the *Biblia Hebraica Stuttgartensia*.

2. The linguistic information has been structured and presented in such a way as to be accessible to an ordinary interpreter of a BH passage. For this reason (as far as possible) linguistic terms have been used that (1) may be familiar to users and/or (2) they will come across regularly in the type of literature they are going to consult. Thus, for example, the terms perfect, imperfect and waw consecutive imperfect are used (in place of linguistically more accurate terms) because they are used in Holladay's popular dictionary. In 'explaining' the phonological processes that occur in the conjugation of some weak verbal stems, didactic considerations carried more weight than the accurate representation of the diachronic development of a particular form. In this regard our use of the concept 'compensatory lengthening' may be called into question too.

3. More modern and possibly less familiar terms are used only in cases where they make a significant contribution towards a clearer understanding of the BH constructions in the authors' view, e.g. the terms *postconstructus*, fronting, focus particle, discourse marker, adjunct and complement.

4. In Chapter 3 the metalinguistic frame of reference that is relevant to this volume is explained. Although the linguistic structure of English and BH is by no means the same, English examples are used for didactic purposes.

5. The type of information presented must be useful to the above-mentioned audience in their exegesis of the BH text. For this reason a very wide definition of what constitutes the knowledge of a language has been adopted. On the one hand, knowledge of BH includes the ability to understand the organization (grammar) and meaning (semantics) of the language at the level of pronunciation, forms, phrases, clauses, sentences and texts. On the other hand, it also includes the ability to understand the use of the above-mentioned linguistic constructions (pragmatics and sociolinguistics). This volume is fairly traditional in its use (for didactic reasons) of *The Verbs* (Chapter 4), *The Nouns* (Chapter 5) and *The Other Word Classes* (Chapter 6) as three of its major categories at a macro level. At the lower levels, however, where relevant and where possible, the semantics and pragmatics of some constructions are dealt with. In a contemplated next volume most of the categories at the macro level, e.g. inter-sentence relationships, text types, speech acts and sociolinguistic conventions, will not be word-based.

6. Unnecessary detail has been avoided. If constructions with a low frequency have been mentioned for the sake of completeness, they are indicated as seldom or rare. A *glossary* of linguistic terms used here and/or which users of this grammar may encounter in other exegetical works may be found at the back of the grammar.

7. No attempt has been made to be linguistically innovative. Existing knowledge of BH has been incorporated. The grammars of Gesenius–Kautzsch–Cowley (1909), Richter (1978, 1979 and 1980), Waltke and O'Connor (1990) and Joüon–Muraoka (1991) have been used extensively. Nevertheless an attempt has been made throughout to utilize where relevant the findings of recent research in BH for the purposes of this grammar. The sections on construct relationships, pronouns, focus particles, some conjunctions and word order are examples in this regard. Furthermore, the linguistic interests of the authors (interests that range from the works of Noam Chomsky to Simon Dik and Deirdre Wilson) must certainly have played an unconscious role in the writing of this grammar. Even so, a deliberate

attempt has been made to subordinate these interests to the primary purpose of this grammar.

8. English translations of the Hebrew text come mainly from the RSV. In cases where the RSV translation fails to illustrate a grammatical construction under discussion or was too archaic the RSV's translation was modified.

9. The authors want to acknowledge their indebtedness to the tradition of BH grammatical teaching in South Africa. Without it this grammar would not have been possible. Until the beginning of the 1970s B. Gemser's *Hebreeuse Spraakkuns* was used by most institutions where BH was taught. Since then scholars at the different institutions experimented with grammars that they had compiled themselves and distributed in the form of photocopied notes. Such grammars were compiled at the University of the Free State, Potchefstroom University of Christian Higher Education, University of Pretoria, University of South Africa and University of Stellenbosch. These grammars are important forerunners of this reference work and influenced the thoughts of the authors in more than one way.

10. The authors also want to express their appreciation to their mentors and/or other scholars who played a significant role in their careers as Hebrew linguists. *Christo van der Merwe*: Professors F.C. Fensham, W.T. Claassen, W. Richter, W. Gross, F.E. Deist, E. Talstra, Dr. A. Michel and Dr. A. Disse; *Jackie Naudé*: Professors F. du T. Laubscher, P. Nel, H. Borer and J. Oosthuizen; and *Jan Kroeze*: Professors E.J. Smit, H.F. van Rooy, J. Hoftijzer and Dr. P.J.J. van Huyssteen.

11. Steve Barganski of Sheffield Academic Press should be thanked for his contribution to (and patience in) the final editing of this book.

ABBREVIATIONS

A	Adjective
ADV	Adverb
ADVP	Adverbial phrase
AP	Adjective phrase
BH	Biblical Hebrew
BHS	*Biblica Hebraica Stuttgartensia*
c.	common
coh.	cohortative
cop.	copulative
du.	dual
f.	feminine
Hi.	Hiphil
Ho.	Hophal
imp.	imperative
impf.	imperfect
inf. abs.	infinitive absolute
inf. cs.	infinitive construct
juss.	jussive
lit.	literal
m.	masculine
Mp	*Masora parva*
N	Noun
Ni.	Niphal
NP	Noun phrase
P	Preposition

part. act.	participle active
part. pass.	participle passive
part.	participle
pcs.	*postconstructus*
perf.	perfect
Pi.	Piel
pl.	plural
PP	Prepositional phrase
Pu.	Pual
S	Clause
sing.	singular
st. abs.	*status absolutus*
st. cs.	*status constructus*
SVO	Subject–Verb–Object
V	Verb
VP	Verb phrase
VSO	Verb–Subject–Object
wc.+impf.	waw consecutive + imperfect
wc.+perf.	waw consecutive + perfect
WH-interrogative	factual interrogative

Chapter 1

INTRODUCTION

§1. **Biblical Hebrew as a Semitic Language**

BH is the language of the Tanach/Old Testament. It was spoken in Israel from about 1200 BCE to about 400 BCE. Then, under the influence of the Persian empire, Aramaic became the language of Israel. Even so, Hebrew survived as a spoken and written religious language.

The languages that display the same common features as BH (e.g. morphology, syntax and lexicon) are known as the Semitic languages. These languages were spoken by the inhabitants of the Arabian peninsula (central zone) and the fertile region (peripheral zone) which stretched in the form of a crescent from Mesopotamia in the north-east, across Syria and Palestine in the north-west to Ethiopia in the south-west. The Semitic languages also bear similarities to certain language groups in North Africa, for example, Egyptian and Berber. This larger grouping of languages which includes the Semitic languages is currently classified as Afro-Asiatic.

The Semitic languages can be subdivided according to the zones in which they were spoken as follows (the dates next to the languages indicate the earliest writings found in those languages).

1. *East Semitic*

This zone covers the area traditionally known as Mesopotamia. It is possible to distinguish the following languages:

- Old Akkadian (from about 2400 BCE)
- Babylonian in all its stages (from about 1700 BCE)
- Assyrian in all its stages (from about 2000–600 BCE)

2. North-West Semitic

This zone covers the area traditionally known as Syro-Palestine. The earliest languages in this region are:

- Amorite (from about 2000 BCE)
- Ugaritic (from about 1450–1200 BCE)

By 1200 BCE the languages of this group formed Canaanite and Aramaic branches:

- The Canaanite branch included, among others

  Hebrew (from about 1200 BCE)
  Phoenician (from about 1100 BCE)
  Moabite (from about 850 BCE)

- The Aramaic Branch

  Aramaic was spoken in Syria (Aram) from about 800 BCE. Under the Persians it later became the official language of correspondence and common usage in the ancient Near East. The later dialects are usually divided into West Aramaic and East Aramaic. The best known dialect of the West Aramaic group is Jewish-Palestinian Aramaic, in which certain of the Qumran texts, the Targumim (Aramaic paraphrases of the Hebrew Bible), and parts of the Palestinian Talmud were written.

  In the Eastern Aramaic group one finds, *inter alia*, Syriac in which a great deal of Christian literature from 200 to 1200 CE was written.

3. South-West Semitic

The most important languages here are:

- North Arabic (the most important example of which is the language of the Qur'an, from about 600 CE).
- Ethiopian

§2. The Historical Unity and Development of Hebrew

The Hebrew language has remained in many ways the same. The changes that occurred affected mainly the vocabulary and syntax, but not the essential morphological and phonological structure of the language. Hebrew is usually divided into four periods.

1. *Biblical Hebrew (= BH)*

Although BH is regarded by many as a language with its own characteristic features, it is not uniform. It was used over a period of about 1000 years. Any language undergoes changes over such a long period of time. Furthermore, archaization techniques (= application of archaic forms) or modernization techniques (= replacement of older forms by contemporary forms) were sometimes adopted in the writing.

For the sake of convenience BH has been subdivided into smaller categories:

- Classical BH is mainly the language of the prose sections of the pre-exilic periods.
- Late BH is the language of the sections from the postexilic period. Late BH shows similarities to the language of the Qumran texts and the latter is therefore also classified as such by some.

Originally a BH text consisted of consonants only.In order to prevent the eventual complete loss of the correct pronunciation, a group of Jewish scholars began to devise a system of signs (from about 600 CE) to record and standardize the received pronunciation (inasmuch as it was known). They were known as the 'Masoretes' (from the Hebrew word 'masora' which means 'what was handed down').

The work of the Masoretes was continued for many centuries by a large number of scholars. Several systems of vocalization were developed. The system used in printed texts today is known as the Tiberian system and is the product of the work of the Ben Asher family (about 900 CE) in Tiberias. The BH as found in BHS and described in this grammar is, strictly speaking, the Masoretic BH of the Ben Asher family.

2. *Rabbinic Hebrew (Mishnaic Hebrew)*

Although the Jews spoke mainly Aramaic from about 400 BCE onwards, a form of Hebrew survived as a spoken and written language, primarily in the synagogues. This form of Hebrew had its own characteristic features which distinguished it from Biblical Hebrew. It was the language of the Mishnah.

3. *Mediaeval Hebrew*

This was the language used by Jewish scholars and writers in the Arab countries and Europe during the Middle Ages. The fact that this form of the language borrowed heavily from Arabic during this period distinguishes it from Rabbinic Hebrew.

4. *Modern Hebrew (Ivrit/Israeli Hebrew)*

This is the language that was revived from the beginning of this century, especially in the State of Israel. It is a further development of the earlier forms of Hebrew. In 1948 it became one of the official languages of the new State of Israel.

§3. A Short Review of the Grammatical Treatment of Biblical Hebrew

1. *The early Jewish grammarians (1000–1500 CE)*

The earliest signs of the grammatical description of Hebrew may be found in the marginal notes of rabbis in midrashic studies dating from the eighth century CE. Furthermore, the Masoretes, whose work culminated in the tenth century CE, conducted their vocalization of BH texts in terms of a particular oral grammatical tradition.

The first written BH grammars appeared in Spain—a centre of Jewish intellectual activity between 1000 and 1200 CE. They were written in the scientific language of the day, namely Arabic. The Jewish grammarians based their description of Jewish grammar on the model used for the description of Arabic. The fruit of their labours culminated in the works of grammarians such as Abraham ibn Ezra and David Qimhi. At a later stage these works became influential in other European centres as well. For example, Martin Luther would probably have learned BH from David Qimhi's grammar.

2. *Christian BH grammarians since the reformation (1500–1750 CE)*

During the Reformation Christians dominated the study of BH grammar. The linguistic model used then for the description of BH was no longer Arabic but Latin. The study of grammar and the study of rhetoric, formerly seen as one, became two separate disciplines. As the emphasis fell on BH grammar, a wealth of BH rhetorical conventions was lost.

The study of BH grammar flourished in the sixteenth century, especially in humanist circles. Johannes Reuchlin's *Rudimenta linguae hebraicae* (1506) is regarded as one of the influential works of this period. In the seventeenth century, however, humanist interest in BH waned, so that BH was confined to being the handmaiden of theology.

3. *The comparative and historical-comparative BH grammars (1750–1960)*

The most significant BH grammar after Reuchlin's is that of Albert Schultens, entitled *Institutiones* (1737). This work laid the basis for the study of BH as a Semitic language. The main purpose of this BH grammar was to ascertain what light the other Semitic languages could cast on the understanding of BH.

One of the most highly esteemed and most authoritative BH grammars—that of Wilhelm Gesenius—appeared for the first time in 1807. There have been 28 subsequent editions. The last seven were produced by Emile Kautzsch and in 1910 Arthur Cowley produced an English version. *Gesenius' Hebrew Grammar* by Gesenius–Kautzsch–Cowley remains a standard BH reference work to this day.

In the nineteenth century linguists not only devoted much attention to the comparison of languages, but also tried to explain the various degrees of similarity between languages. By paying particular attention to the sequence of sound changes within languages that belong to the same family, sound rules were identified which could then be used to draw up a family tree of a language group. This approach to the study of language is known as historical-comparative linguistics. Carl Brockelmann's *Grundriss der vergleichenden Grammatik der semitischen Sprachen* of 1908–1913 is regarded as a benchmark of Semitic historical-comparative grammar.

As far as BH is concerned, the historical-comparative approach led to the following BH grammars: Friedrich König's comprehensive grammar, *Historisch-kritisches Lehrgebäude der hebräischen Sprache*, which appeared in three volumes between 1881 and 1897, drew on the work of the older Jewish grammars. This work is still highly regarded today. Bauer–Leander's *Historische Grammatik der hebräischen Sprache* (1922) and Bergsträsser's 29th edition of Gesenius were the crowning glory of the attempts at utilizing the principles of the historical-comparative method to describe BH.

Historical-comparative linguistics was particularly useful in providing a framework for studying the phonology and morphology of language. This is one of the reasons the works of Bauer–Leander and Bergsträsser have hardly any description of BH syntax. Syntactic constructions were mostly explained in terms of psychological considerations, as in Brockelmann's *Hebräische Syntax* (1956).

4. *Modern BH grammarians since 1960*

Since the 1920s the historical-comparative method has been superseded by a structuralist approach. According to this approach language is a structural system. It is the relationship between its various components at a particular period in history—the so-called synchronic level—that must be studied separately from the historical development of the language—the so-called diachronic level. Although the structuralist approach to the description of language revolutionized linguistics and led to a host of new theories on language, it did not have an immediate influence on BH grammar. Works such as those by Francis Andersen, *The Sentence in Biblical Hebrew* (1974), and Wolfgang Richter, *Grundlagen einer althebräischen Grammatik* (1978–1980), only relatively recently paved the way in this regard.

The recent grammar by Bruce Waltke and Murphy O'Connor, *An Introduction to Biblical Hebrew Syntax* (1990), describes a large variety of BH syntactic constructions. They use not only broad structural principles for this purpose, but also draw on the more traditional descriptions of BH. In the process of doing so, this work also provides a useful taxonomy of BH constructions, as well as a sound review of current BH grammatical research.

A Grammar of Biblical Hebrew (1991) by Takamitsu Muraoka is a revision of a grammar published in 1923 by Paul Joüon. It is cast in the form of a traditional grammar and explains some BH syntactic constructions psychologically. However, Muraoka specifically attempts to incorporate the insights of grammarians who had published their research results in Modern Hebrew. Some of the categories that he uses, as well as some of the arguments he presents in his grammar, indicate that aspects of the structuralist approach have been adopted in Joüon–Muraoka.

The works of Waltke and O'Connor, and of Joüon–Muraoka are regarded as the standard reference works for the 1990s. This reference grammar draws on both these studies. It must be borne in mind, however, that neither of these grammars utilizes the insights of one of the major trends in structuralist linguistics, the so-called generative approach. Furthermore, both grammars deal with the sentence as the largest unit of linguistic description. This implies a narrow view of the knowledge of a language. Since the 1980s the following have also been regarded as part of the knowledge of a language: the way in which sentences are used to create texts (text linguistic conventions), the conventions relating to the ways people use utterances to execute matters (pragmatic conventions) and the conventions that determine *which* linguistic constructions are adopted by *which* role-playing members of a particular society and *when* they are adopted (sociolinguistic conventions).

Chapter 2

THE HEBREW ALPHABET AND MASORETIC SIGNS

§4. The Alphabet—Consonants

§4.1. *The Form of the Hebrew Consonants*

The Hebrew alphabet consists of 23 characters (some with alternative graphic signs) which represent consonants only. The table below gives the name, form, transliteration and approximate pronunciation of each consonant.

No	Name	Form		Transli-teration	Pronunciation
			Final		
1	aleph	א		/ʾ/	A very light glottal stop corresponding to the Greek *spiritus lenis*. Even before a vowel it is lost to the ear, like the *h* in *hour*.
2	beth	בּ		/b/	bank
		ב		/b/	never
3	gimel	גּ		/g/	go
		ג		/g/	go
4	daleth	דּ		/d/	door
		ד		/d/	door
5	he	ה		/h/	hand
6	waw	ו		/w/	vote
7	zayin	ז		/z/	zone
8	ḥeth	ח		/ḥ/	lo**ch** (velar as in Scots)

No	Name	Form		Transli-teration	Pronunciation
9	ṭeth	ט		/ṭ/	time
10	yod	׳		/y/	year
11	kaph	כ		/k/	keep
		כ	ך	/k/	Bach (palatal as in German)
12	lamedh	ל		/l/	line
13	mem	מ	ם	/m/	main
14	nun	נ	ן	/n/	noon
15	samekh	ס		/s/	silver
16	ayin	ע		/ ʿ /	A hard glottal stop formed at the back of the throat. It may be heard in certain pronunciations of words like *bottle* and *battle* in which the glottal stop replaces the normal *t*.
17	pe	פ		/p/	pay
		פ	ף	/p/	face
18	ṣade	צ	ץ	/ṣ/	cats
19	qoph	ק		/q/	keep
20	resh	ר		/r/	rope
21	sin	שׂ		/ś/	silver
22	shin	שׁ		/š/	shoe
23	taw	ת		/t/	time
		ת		/t/	time

Note the following:

(1) Hebrew is written from right to left and from the top to the bottom of the page.

(2) Transliteration means that a language that has its own distinctive characters is rewritten in the equivalent characters of the Latin or Roman alphabet. In cases where no equivalents exist, special transliteration symbols have been devised with the help of certain diacritical signs, for example, a dot under an h, /ḥ/ (letter 8), an inverted circumflex on an s, /š/ (letter 22).

§4.2. *Special Features of the Hebrew Consonants*

1. *Letters with two forms (the final letters or end consonants)*
Five Hebrew consonants have alternative forms when they appear at the end of a word.

Beginning or middle of the word:

כ/ך (11),   מ (13),   נ (14),   פ/ף (17), צ (18)

End of the word: ך-   ם-   ן-   ף-   ץ-

2. *Letters with two alternative pronunciations*
Six of the Hebrew consonants, namely ב (2), ג (3), ד (4), כ (11), פ (17) and ת (23) are allophones. In other words the same letter is used to indicate either a plosive or a fricative pronunciation.

There is, however, no possibility of confusion as the plosives are marked by a diacritical point, the dagesh. (Cf. §8.2/1.)

ב	ג	ד	כ	פ	ת
b	g	d	k	p	t

The fricatives are written without the dagesh:

ב	ג	ד	כ/ך	פ/ף	ת
v	g	d	Bach	f	t

The fricative pronunciation of ג, ד and ת has fallen out of current use, and they are pronounced like their plosive counterparts.

The distinction between the plosives and the fricatives is clear:

plosives   always contain a dagesh,
            always appear after a consonant,
            usually occur at the beginning of a word;
fricatives always written without the dagesh and
            always occur after a vowel.

Because it is sometimes necessary to refer to these consonants as a group, they are arranged alphabetically and furnished with vowels to form a catchword, namely: *begadkefat*.

3. *Letters with homogeneous pronunciation*

In the following examples various groups of letters are pronounced more or less similarly:

ג	(3)	and	ג		like	g	in	go
ד	(4)	and	ד		like	d	in	**d**oor
ת	(23)	and	ת		like	t	in	time
א	(1)	and	ע	(16)				glottal stop
ב	(2)	and	ו	(6)	like	v	in	never and **v**ote
ח	(8)	and	כ/ך	(11)	like	ch	in	Lo**ch** and Ba**ch**
ט	(9)	and	ת/ט	(23)	like	t	in	time
כ	(11)	and	ק	(19)	like	k	in	**k**eep
ס	(15)	and	שׂ	(21)	like	s	in	**s**ilver

Although these groups of signs have more or less the same pronunciation now, their sound values originally differed (that is, distinctive pronunciations originally existed for all the signs of the alphabet). These differences are reflected in the orthography.

4. *Letters with the same place of articulation*

(i) *Gutturals*

A group of consonants is articulated at the back of the throat, namely: א (1), ה (5), ח (8) and ע (16).

- א must not be confused with the English 'a' or Greek alpha (α). The latter two are vowels, while א is a consonant.

- א and ע are not pronounced at the beginning or at the end of a word.

- In the middle of a word א and ע are pronounced as a glottal stop, made by the complete stoppage of breath in the throat, almost like the 'stop' between the two **e**'s in re-enact.

The consonant ר (20) bears certain similarities to the four gutturals and is usually grouped with them.

Should certain vowel changes become necessary in a word as, for example, when a plural is formed, the deviation from the normal is predictable within this group of consonants, namely:

- When a sound rule requires a vowel to be reduced, the vowel attached to a guttural will be reduced to a half vowel (also referred to as a composite šᵉwâ or ḥāṭēp vowel). (Cf. §5.2/2(iii).)
- When a sound rule requires the doubling of a consonant, this doubling will occur neither with the gutturals nor with resh. (Cf. §8.2/2.)

(ii) *Dentals/Alveolars*

A group of consonants is articulated when the tongue obstructs the air flow against the upper teeth or alveolar ridge:

ד / ד (4), ט (9) and ת / ת (23)
ל (12), נ (14) and ר (20)

- When a word begins with a dental, the deviation from any customary change in this group is predictable, for example, assimilation.[1]
- When a conjugation results in two dentals occurring in immediate succession, the first dental becomes assimilated by the second dental.

5. *Letters articulated in a similar fashion*

(i) *Sibilants*

A group of consonants is formed when the speech canal is narrowed and the air stream is forced through with a hissing sound, namely

שׁ (22), ז (7), ס (15) and שׂ (21)

When a word begins with a hissing sound, the deviation from the customary change in this group is predictable, e.g:

- When a conjugation results in a sibilant occurring immediately after a dental, *metathesis*[2] of the sibilant and the dental occurs.

---

1. Assimilation is a phonological process which usually takes place when one consonant which closes a syllable passes over into another beginning the next syllable, so forming with it a strengthened letter. In this process the sounds of the two consonants are equalized. Note, for example, the case of nasal assimilation in which ten mice is pronounced as tem mice. Assimilation is not restricted to dentals only.

2. *Metathesis* is a phonological process in which two sounds are reversed, e.g. the use of aks instead of ask.

(ii) *Glides*

A group of consonants is formed when the air flow is obstructed to a limited extent, namely

ה (5), ו (6) and י (10)

The obstruction is so limited that these consonants have more in common with vowels than with consonants. The result is that a vowel and the glide immediately following it sometimes become fused, so that the glide becomes associated with specific vowel sounds. (Cf. §5.1.)

ה	e	as in	there
	ey	as in	café
	o	as in	more
	a	as in	father
ו	o	as in	more
	oo	as in	book
י	i	as in	machine
	ey	as in	café
	e	as in	there

In certain cases the א (1) has lost its consonantal character. In such cases א is also associated with specific vocalic sound values:

א	o	as in	more
	a	as in	father
	ey	as in	café

BH was originally written with consonants only. This could easily lead to misinterpretations; for example,

ים could be interpreted as /yām/ (sea) or /yôm/ (day).

In order to ensure that the reader would distinguish between the forms, one of the above-mentioned glides was used with the latter form — namely ו — to indicate the presence of a [ô] vowel between the two consonants: יום. This ensured the reading of the latter form as /yôm/. The form without the glide was read as /yām/.

When the glides (ה, ו and י) and א represent vowels and not consonants, they are called vowel indicators (*matres lectionis*, 'mothers of reading'). (Cf. §5.2/2(i).)

§5. The Alphabet—Vowels

A group of Jewish scholars, the Masoretes, did important work between 600 and 1000 CE in preserving and transmitting the text of the Hebrew Bible. Three groups of Masoretes were active, namely in Babylon, Palestine and Tiberias. Their most important task was transmitting the consonantal text with the utmost accuracy. To ensure that the oral tradition did not weaken further and to combat uncertainty, they devised vowel signs (or points) and added them to the consonantal text. The tradition from Tiberias, the so-called Tiberian vocalization, is used in the BHS.

When the Masoretes introduced the system of vowel signs, BH had already been committed to writing in consonants. The vowel indicators were then added to these. (Cf. §4.2/5(ii).) The text was left unchanged and the vowel signs were simply added to the existing letters. In most cases a vowel sign was placed under a consonant, in one case above the consonant and in others next to the consonant. In BH the consonant is normally read first followed by the vowel accompanying it. (Cf. also §6.2.)

§5.1. *The Form of the Hebrew Vowels*

The signs that represent vowels are given in the table below (always after the letter ט or ה). The combination of vowel signs and vowel indicators is also given.

No	Name	Form	Trans-literation	Sound value (Modern Hebrew)
1	qāmeṣ	טָ	/ā/	father
		טָה, אָ	/â/	
2	pataḥ	טַ	/a/	father
3	ḥātēp pataḥ	טֲ	/ᵃ/	father
4	ḥōlem	טֹ	/ō/	more
		טׂו, טׂה, אׂ	/ô/	
5	qāmeṣ ḥāṭûp	טָ	/o/	hot

No	Name	Form	Trans-literation	Sound value (Modern Hebrew)
6	ḥāṭēp qāmeṣ	חָ	/°/	hot
7	ṣērê	טֵ	/ē/	café[3]
		טִי, טֵה, אֵ	/ê/	
8	sᵉgōl	טֶ	/e/	pen
		טֶי	/ê/	
		טֶה	/ê/	
9	ḥāṭēp sᵉgōl	חֱ	/ᵉ/	pen
10	šûreq	טוּ	/û/	put
11	qibbûṣ	טֻ	/u/	put
12	ḥireq	טִ	/i/	hit
		טִי	/î/	
13	audible šᵉwâ	טְ	/ᵉ/	above

§5.2. The Classification of Vowels and their Characteristics

1. The classification of vowels

It is generally held that the Tiberian vowel system indicated only the sound value or quality of a particular vowel but that it did not give a reliable representation of its length or quantity. The Tiberian vowels are classified phonologically by some grammarians as follows:

(i) *Short vowels*

טִ (2), טָ (5=o), טֶ (8), טֻ (11) and טִ (12)

(ii) *Changeable (ordinary) long vowels*

טָ (1=ā), טֹ (4), טֵ (7)

(iii) *Unchangeable long vowels*

אֵא, טָה (1), טוֹ, טֹה, אֹא (4), טֵי, טֵה, אֵ (7), טֶי, טֶה (8), טוּ (10), טִי (12)

(iv) *Extra short vowels—also referred to as half vowels (Cf. §5.2/2 (iii).)*

חֳ (3), חֱ (6), חֱ (9), טְ (13)

---

3.   In American circles the ṣērê is pronounced as -ey as in they. According to Joüon-Muraoka §6h, the ṣērê must also be pronounced as the -e- in pen.

2. *Characteristics of vowels*

(i) *Vowel indicators* (*matres lectionis*)

It was stated in §4.2.5(ii) that the glides (ה, ו and י) and א could represent consonants as well as specific vowels, i.e. they could be used as vowel indicators; for example:

> ה for /ô/, /â/ and /ê/
> ו for /ô/ and /û/
> י for /î/, /ê/ and /ǝ/

Therefore, in the text vocalized by the Masoretes, the א, ה, ו and י could sometimes represent a consonant and sometimes a vowel. The Masoretes resolved this ambiguity through their vowel system as follows:

- In BH every consonant within a word must be accompanied by a vowel sign except for the final consonant of a word, which does not necessarily have to be accompanied by a vowel sign. When one of these glides represented a consonant, the Masoretes simply placed a vowel sign beneath it.

- Where a glide represented a vowel indicator the Masoretes combined their own vowel sign with the vowel indicator. In other words, when one of these four letters follows another consonant and only one vowel sign accompanies the two characters, the second character is functioning as a vowel indicator.

- א, ה, ו and י are used as vowel indicators solely in combination with specific vowel signs as indicated in §5.1.

Examples:

(1) In the word ראֹשׁ the א is not a consonant. If it were a consonant, then א and שׁ, two consonants, would stand next to each other without being separated by a vowel. This would be unacceptable in BH. (Cf. §7.1/2.) The א must therefore be regarded as a vowel indicator in this case.

(2) The א at the end of a word such as מָצָא may be regarded as a vowel indicator. In מָאַס the א must be understood as a full consonant. Should it be regarded as a vowel indicator, it would mean that two vowels would stand next to each other, which is unacceptable in BH. (Cf. §7.1/2.)

(3) The ה is used as a vowel indicator only at the end of the word, for example, סוּסָה. (Cf. also §9.2.)

(4) In the word אָהַב a vowel follows the ה within a word and thus ה cannot be regarded as a vowel indicator.

(5) There can be no confusion with the ו as a new sign is always created when the vowel and the vowel indicator are joined, namely וֹ and וּ.

The unchangeable long vowels are formed in combination with the vowel indicators. (Cf. §5.2/1(iii).)

(ii) *Full and defective mode of writing*

In some instances a vowel may be represented by two different forms simultaneously. This is due to the fact that vowel signs were added to the text only after it had been fixed in consonants and vowel indicators.

- In some words a vowel indicator was used to refer to a particular vowel even before the Masoretic vocalization. During the vocalization another vowel sign referring to the same vowel was added to the vowel indicator. When a vowel sign is combined with a vowel indicator in this way, one speaks of the 'full mode of writing' or *scriptio plena*.

- If the vowel is written without a vowel indicator, one speaks of the defective mode of writing or *scriptio defectiva*. There is no difference in the pronunciation of the two modes of writing.

The same word can sometimes be written in the full and sometimes in the defective mode of writing, e.g.:

$$\text{קָדוֹשׁ} \quad \text{or} \quad \text{קָדֹשׁ}$$
$$\text{טוֹב} \quad \text{or} \quad \text{טֹב}$$

(iii) *The distribution of the half vowels*

The first vowel of some words is a half vowel, namely an audible šᵉwâ, e.g.:

לְבוּשׁ

It was stated in §4.2/4(i) that a deviation from the customary change is predictable with the gutturals (א, ה, ח and ע). One of the characteristics of the gutturals is that they may not be vocalized with the audible šᵉwâ. Instead of the audible šᵉwa the gutturals are vocalized with ḥāṭēp vowels.

The ḥāṭēp vowels are also half vowels. The Masoretic signs for the ḥāṭēp vowels are a combination of the šᵉwa sign with the pataḥ, the sᵉgōl or the qāmeṣ. This produces the ḥāṭēp vowels, namely:

ḥāṭēp pataḥ	(3)	חֲמוֹר*	>	חֲמוֹר
ḥāṭēp qāmeṣ	(6)	חֳלִי*	>	חֳלִי
ḥāṭēp sᵉgōl	(9)	אֱמֶת*	>	אֱמֶת

The question may arise as to which one of the ḥāṭēp vowels takes the place of the šᵉwâ:

- In the case of the examples above the ḥāṭēp vowel is part of the actual composition of each word and must be learned as such.
- In other cases a sound rule may require the pronunciation of an audible šᵉwâ immediately after a guttural. A ḥāṭēp pataḥ usually replaces the šᵉwâ in such a case.

§6. Diphthongs

Diphthongs are sounds formed when two different vowels are combined into one syllable. In BH diphthongs may be formed in two ways:

§6.1. *With ' after a Vowel*

When ' follows certain vowels, they are pronounced as diphthongs. In the following table the diphthong is written after the consonant ט as an example:

Consonant	Combination	Pronunciation
'	טִי	tie
	טַי	sky
	טוֹי	boy
	טוּי	gluey

Note the following:

- When טַי is followed by a waw as in טַיו*, the construction is pronounced as tâv.

§6.2. *The Transitional Pataḥ or Pataḥ Furtivum*

1. *Characteristics*

The consonants ה, ח and ע are articulated by moving the base of the tongue in the direction of the wall of the throat. This unusual articulation at the end of a closed syllable (cf. §7.1/1) is strenuous. The vowel that produces the least stress on the speech organs in pronouncing ח or ע at the end of a closed syllable is the 'a' (/ā/ or /a/), e.g.

יָדַע and אָח

When one of the other long vowels appears before ה, ח and ע in the last syllable, a transitional vowel or glide element becomes necessary to facilitate pronunciation. In these cases the pataḥ is utilized as the transitional vowel.

Not /rûḥ/ but /ruâḥ/
Not /kōḥ/ but /kōaḥ/

It is important to note that this pataḥ does not begin a new syllable, but only denotes a transition in the current syllable. The combination of the preceding vowel with the pataḥ creates a diphthong before the final consonant.

The *pataḥ furtivum* is written as follows:

רוּחַ and כֹּחַ

Although the pataḥ is written after the final consonant, it is pronounced between this consonant and vowel preceeding it. This pataḥ is called the transitional pataḥ or *pataḥ furtivum* (the pataḥ that slides in).

2. *The distribution of the pataḥ furtivum*

The *pataḥ furtivum* is a pataḥ that occurs at the end of a word when:

- The final consonant of a word is ה, ח and ע and
- the preceding vowel is not a pataḥ or a qāmeṣ, e.g.:

רֵעַ and רוּחַ
but שָׁלַח

Because ע and ח in רֵעַ and רוּחַ were not originally furnished with a pataḥ, the insertion of the *pataḥ furtivum* became necessary. In שָׁלַח, however, the ח is preceded by a pataḥ and the insertion of the pataḥ furtivum is thus unnecessary.

§7. **Syllables and Accents**

§7.1. *Types of Syllables*

1. *Open and closed syllables*
The word *syllable* denotes a combination of consonants and vowels that produces a word or a segment of a word in a single effort of articulation, i.e. the smallest grouping of sounds in a word that can be pronounced as a unit. The following distinctions are usually made with regard to syllables:

- *Open syllables* An open syllable consists of a consonant and a vowel.
- *Closed syllables* A closed syllable consists of a consonant-vowel-consonant.

Open syllable	Closed syllable
go	got
CV	*CVC*
spa	spank
CCV	*CCVCC*
mi-ni	mind-ful
CV–CV	*CVCC–CVC*

2. *Hebrew syllables*
Every language has its own rules according to which vowels and consonants are combined into syllables. In English, for example, a cluster of two consonants commonly occurs at the beginning or end of a syllable, as in **blank** or **art**. The following rules apply to syllables in Hebrew:

(a) A syllable always begins with a consonant. (Cf. §31.1/1 for an exception.)
(b) A syllable may be open or closed.
(c) There are usually no consonant clusters within a syllable, i.e. a syllable begins with only one consonant and a closed syllable ends with only one consonant.

3. *Examples of syllables:*
  (1) One open syllable   לֹא

(2) One closed syllable   בַּת

(3) Two open syllables   סוּסָה > סוּ-סָה

(4) Two syllables, one open and one closed   כָּתַב > כָּ-תַב

§7.2. *Accentuation*

1. *Rules*

The following rules may serve as broad guidelines for accentuation in BH:

(a) In a *word* the accent usually falls on the *final* (ultimate) syllable.

(b) In words with the vowel pattern / - $\bar{\;}$ $\bar{\;}$ /, / - $\bar{\;}$ $\bar{\;}$ /, / - $\bar{\;}$ $\bar{\;}$ / or / - $\bar{\;}$ $\bar{\;}$ / the accent falls on the second-last (penultimate) syllable.

(c) In a *clause* the accent usually falls on the stressed syllable of the last word.

The stressed syllable is referred to as the tone syllable and the two preceding it as the pretonic and the propretonic syllables respectively.

2. *Examples*

The Masoretes designed a system for noting the accentuation of all the words in BH. This complex system is dealt with in §9.5. Where it becomes essential to indicate the accentuation of a particular word, this grammar will use the sign ['] to mark the accented syllable, e.g.:

(1)   שְׁמֹו

(2)   מֶ-לֶךְ

(3)   רְ-שֶׁ-ת

(4)   אָ-מַר

(5)   הֹו-צִי-אָם

3. *Additional or secondary accentuation*

In BH certain words have a secondary accent. Words consisting of three syllables, with the primary accent on the final syllable, often receive a secondary accent on the third to last syllable. The Masoretic sign that indicates secondary accent is a vertical line to the left of the first vowel. This sign is called the meteg (cf. §9.1) and denotes that the word concerned receives a secondary or additional accent, e.g.:

כְּתֻבָה = כֵּ-תֻ-בָֿה

§7.3. *The Distribution of Vowels in Syllables*

There is a clear correlation between the classification of the Masoretic vowel signs and their use in syllables:

(a) Half vowels always occur in open, unaccented syllables, e.g.

שְׁמוֹ   his name

(b) Short vowels usually occur in closed, unaccented syllables, e.g.

מִדְבָּר   desert

(c) Short vowels can also occur in open, accented syllables, e.g.

קַיִן   Cain

(d) Long vowels usually occur in open syllables regardless of whether the syllable is accented or not, e.g.

בָּנָה   he built

(e) Long vowels can also occur in closed, accented syllables, e.g.

מִדְבָּר   desert

§8. Masoretic Signs with a Double Function

§8.1. *The Šᵉwâ*

1. *The audible šᵉwâ*
The šᵉwâ has already been encountered as the sign of the half vowel (§5.2/2(iii)) as in

לְבוּשׁ   garment

This šᵉwâ is called the audible šᵉwâ or *šᵉwâ mobile*. It acts as the 'vowel' of an open syllable.

$$CV = X$$

The distribution of the audible šᵉwâ can be determined as follows:

(a) The šᵉwâ is audible in the first syllable of a word, as in

בְּ-רִית   =   בְּרִית

(b) The šᵉwâ is audible after a syllable with a long vowel, as in:

סוּ-סְ-כֶם   =   סוּסְכֶם

(c) The šᵉwâ is audible after an accented syllable, as in:

כָּ-תְ-בָה   =   כָּתְבָה

Note the following:

(1) Should two audible šᵉwâs be found in two consecutive open syllables, they fuse into one (half-) closed syllable with the vowel / ˘ /, e.g.

כְּשְׁמוּאֵל*   becomes   כִּשְׁמוּאֵל

(2) If the second open syllable begins with the consonant י, the י loses its consonantal value and becomes a vowel indicator, e.g.

בְּיְהוּדָה *   becomes   בִּיהוּדָה

(3) If a guttural with a ḥāṭēp vowel is preceded by an open syllable with an audible šᵉwâ as vowel, this open syllable takes the full vowel corresponding to the ḥāṭēp vowel, e.g.

בְּחֲלוֹם*   becomes   בַּחֲלוֹם

2. *The silent šᵉwâ*

The šᵉwâ is also used for another purpose, namely to note the end of a closed syllable in a word, such as

מִשְׁ-פָּט   =   מִשְׁפָּט

מִדְ-בָּר   =   מִדְבָּר

This šᵉwâ is called the silent šᵉwâ or *šᵉwâ quiescens*. It is an orthographical aid used to indicate a closed syllable and the absence of a vowel in that position.

$$\text{CVC} \quad = \quad \text{XX}$$

The distribution of the silent šᵉwâ can be determined as follows:

(a) The šᵉwâ is usually silent after a short vowel, e.g.

מִדְ-בָּר   =   מִדְבָּר

כָּ-תַבְ-תְּ   =   כָּתַבְתְּ

When a word ends on a closed syllable, the final consonant is usually not accompanied by a Masoretic sign, e.g. כָּתַב. In the following cases, however, a deviation from the norm occurs:

(b) A silent šᵉwâ is usually placed in a final kaph in order to distinguish the latter from a final nun, e.g. הָלַךְ.

(c) A silent šᵉwâ is also placed under a double final taw e.g. אַתְּ. (The doubling of the final taw is simply orthographic. It is not articulated. Words ending with a double consonant are usually written with a single consonant, e.g. עַם 'am< 'amm).

(d) What appears to be a consonant cluster may sometimes be found at the end of a word. The cluster originated from the combination of a closed and an open syllable, with the vowel of the latter syllable having lost its sound. In this case a silent šᵉwâ occurs underneath each of the consonants, e.g. כָּתַבְתְּ.

(e) Furthermore, a sound rule may lead to a silent šᵉwâ appearing after a guttural. In such cases a ḥāṭēp vowel may appear in the place of the silent šᵉwâ, e.g. יֶחֱזַק. (Cf. §5.2/2(iii).)

3. *The medial šᵉwâ*

The medial šᵉwâ is used in syllables in which the vowel is no longer pronounced but in which its effect remains so that the subsequent begadkefat letters do not have a plosive dagesh, e.g.

מַלְכֵי   /malkê/ instead of /malᵉkê/

Historically the word מַלְכֵי derives from מְלָכֵי in which the kaph is preceded by a vowel. In the historical development of this word the vowel became silent and the kaph was pronounced directly after the lamedh. To indicate the original presence of a vowel before the kaph, the Masoretes did not place a plosive dagesh in the begadkefat letter.

The šᵉwâ sign that replaces the original vowel is known as the medial šᵉwâ or the *šᵉwâ medium*. For pronunciation purposes the medial šᵉwâ is a silent šᵉwâ and the begadkefat letter following it a fricative.

§8.2. *The Dagesh*

1. *The plosive dagesh or dagesh lene*

The dagesh has already been encountered as the diacritical point that occurs only in the begadkefat letters and which distinguishes the plosives from the fricatives. (Cf. §4.2/2.) This form of the dagesh is called the plosive dagesh or *dagesh lene* (weak dagesh).

The distribution of the plosive dagesh may be determined as follows:

(a) It usually occurs at the beginning of a word, as in:

בְּרִית   =   בְּ-רִית

(b) It occurs after a closed syllable, as in:

מִדְבָּר   =   מִדְ-בָּר

כְּתַבְתָּ   =   כָּ-תַב-תָּ

2. *The doubling dagesh or dagesh forte*

The dagesh is also used for another purpose, namely to indicate the doubling of a consonant:

הַסּוּס instead of הַס-סוּס		Two closed syllables
עַמּוּד instead of עַמ-מוּד		Two closed syllables
צַדִּיק instead of צַד-דִיק		Two closed syllables

This form of the dagesh is called the doubling dagesh or the *dagesh forte* (strong dagesh). The consonant which is doubled is written once only and then punctuated with the doubling dagesh. The doubled consonant thus simultaneously ends one syllable and begins the next one.

The distribution of the strong dagesh may be determined as follows:

- The dagesh found in consonants that follow a vowel is a doubling dagesh. This vowel is usually short.

צַדִּיק   =   צַד-דִיק

עַמּוּד   =   עַמ-מוּד

The gutturals and ר normally do not double. (Cf. §4.2/4(i).) Under certain conditions which would normally require doubling, the gutturals and ר are therefore not doubled and thus either no changes are made (e.g. נַחַת) or the preceding vowel is changed, for example, בֵּרֵךְ instead of בֵּרֵּךְ*. The former process is called virtual doubling. Since in most cases a so-called short vowel is replaced with a long vowel, the process is also referred to as 'compensatory lengthening'.

3. *The conjunctive dagesh*

When a word ends on an unaccented /ā, â/ or /ê/ and the first syllable of the next word is accented, the first consonant of the second word is written with a conjunctive dagesh as in:

שָׁבִיתָ שֶּׁבִי

שִׂימָה לָּנוּ

This dagesh is called the conjunctive dagesh or the *dagesh conjunctivum*. It is generally understood that this dagesh does not indicate the doubling of the consonant, but it has not been possible to ascertain its precise function as yet.

4. *The disjunctive dagesh*

This dagesh does not indicate the doubling of the consonant, to distinguish the audible šᵉwâ from the silent šᵉwâ as in:

עִקְּבֵי   / 'ikᵉbê/ instead of / 'ikbê/

The distribution of the disjunctive dagesh can be determined as follows: short vowels usually occur in closed, unaccented syllables. (Cf. §7.3.) In some cases a short vowel may appear in an open syllable as in the word עִקְּבֵי. In such cases, when the short vowel is followed by an audible šᵉwâ, confusion could arise concerning the pronunciation of that particular word. A disjunctive dagesh is placed in the consonant between the short vowel and the šᵉwâ sign.

5. *The qenemlui letters*

It sometimes happens that the doubling of the consonant is dropped, as in the ' of

וַיְהִי /wayᵉhî/< וַיְּהִי /wayyᵉhî/

This is due to the fact that the doubling of certain consonants is dropped when they are followed by an audible šᵉwâ. This occurs with ', ו, ל, מ, נ and ק, the so-called qenemlui letters, and the sibilants. (Cf. §4.2/5(i).)

§8.3. *The Qāmeṣ*

1. *Different phonetic values (different pronunciations)*

The qāmeṣ sign indicates two possible sound values.

a as in the English word father
o as in the English word hot

The latter is called the qāmeṣ ḥāṭûp.

2. *Distribution*

The distribution of the qāmeṣ and the qāmeṣ ḥāṭûp can be determined as follows:

(a) The ָ occurring in open or closed accented syllables is the qāmeṣ.

(b) The ָ occurrring in closed, unaccented syllable is the qāmeṣ ḥāṭûp.

(c) Wherever uncertainty may arise concerning the correct interpretation of the ָ , the meteg (cf. §9.1) is used whenever the syllable concerned has a secondary accent and is vocalized with a qāmeṣ.

(d) A ָ followed by a ֳ is read as a qāmeṣ ḥāṭûp, in spite of the fact that it occurs in an open syllable, e.g. פָּעֳלִי /poʿŏlî/.

3. *Examples of distribution*

(1) The first syllable is open and unaccented; the vowel is a qāmeṣ, e.g.

כָּתַב   כָּ-תַב

(2) The last syllable is closed but accented; the vowel is a qāmeṣ, e.g.

מִדְבָּר   מִד-בָּר

(3) The syllable is closed but accented; the vowel is a qāmeṣ, e.g.

אָב   אָב

(4) The first syllable is open and accented; the vowel is a qāmeṣ, e.g.

כָּתְבָה   כָּ-תְ-בָה

(5) The first syllable is closed and unaccented; the vowel is a qāmeṣ ḥāṭûp, e.g.

חָכְמָה   חָכְ-מָה

(6) The penultimate syllable is open and accented; the vowel is a qāmeṣ. The last syllable is closed and unaccented; the vowel is a qāmeṣ ḥāṭûp, e.g.

וַיָּקָם   וַי-יָ-קָם

§8.4. *The ו Sign*

The ו sign can function either as a šûreq or as a double waw. If it appears after a consonant, it is a šûreq (e.g. בָּרוּךְ); if it appears after a short vowel, it is a double waw (צִוָּה). (Cf. §5.2/2(i).)

§9. **Additional Masoretic Signs**

§9.1 *The Meteg*

The meteg ( ) is a small vertical line that is written underneath the consonant and to the left of the vowel (in BHS sometimes to the right of the vowel) with the purpose of indicating a secondary or additional accent in a word. (Cf. §7.2/3.)

The meteg should not be confused with the sillûq, which only appears under the last word of the verse. (Cf. §9.5/2(i).)

One of the orthographic functions of the meteg is to distinguish between the qāmeṣ and qāmeṣ ḥāṭûp. (Cf. §8.3.) The qāmeṣ ḥāṭûp is a short vowel in a closed, unaccented syllable. (Cf. §7.3(iii).) The qāmeṣ, on the other hand, usually appears as a long vowel in an accented syllable. The meteg is used with the qāmeṣ in any position where doubt may arise in order to ensure that it will not be interpreted as a qāmeṣ ḥāṭûp.

אָכְלָה can be interpreted as / 'ākᵉlâ / (she ate) or as / 'oklâ / (food). In order to eliminate confusion the meteg is used in the first instance, namely, אָכְלָה to indicate that ָ is stressed and cannot be interpreted as a qāmeṣ ḥāṭûp. In the latter case ָ occurs in a closed, unaccented syllable. The meteg is absent and it must therefore be interpreted as a qāmeṣ ḥāṭûp.

In this grammar the meteg is used only when a distinction has to be made between qāmeṣ and qāmeṣ ḥāṭûp.

In BHS the meteg is not used consistently.

(a) The qāmeṣ and ṣērē are regularly replaced by half vowels in open pretonic or propretonic syllables. Because the occurrence of the qāmeṣ and ṣērē in these positions would be anomalous, they are usually marked with a meteg, e.g.

אָנֹכִי
בֵּרַכְתַּנִי

(b) Although the principle is not applied consistently, any pretonic or propretonic vowel may be marked with the meteg, e.g.

הוֹשִׁיעֵנִי

(c) Short vowels usually occur in closed syllables before the primary accent. Should this not be the case, the vowel is marked with a meteg, e.g.

תַּעֲמֹד

(d) A short vowel with a meteg in what appears to be a closed syllable is an indication that the normal doubling of the following consonant has been dropped:

הַמְרַגְּלִים instead of   הַמְרַגְלִים

§9.2. *The Mappîq*

In §5.2/2(i) it was stated that the ה could act as a vowel indicator. To ensure that a consonant ה at the end of a word is not accidentally interpreted as a ה used as a vowel indicator, the Masoretes placed a point inside the ה to distinguish it from the ה vowel indicator.

ה consonant:	סוּסָהּ	her horse
	גָּבַהּ	He is high.

This diacritical point is called the mappîq. It must not be confused with the dagesh.

§9.3. *The Maqqēf*

The maqqēf is a hyphen that joins a short word to the word that follows it. The maqqēf is written as follow:

לֹא־דָרְשָׁה   She did not seek.

The two words joined in this way form a single tone unit. The accent then falls on the last part of the unit—usually on the last syllable of that part.

§9.4. *The Sôf Pāsûq*

The sôf pāsûq, which looks like a boldly printed colon [:], is the sign that indicates the end of a verse. It may be compared to a full stop.

§9.5. *The Accent Signs*

1. *Introduction*
In addition to their vowel system, the Masoretes also developed a system of accents.

(i) *Functions*
The accent system indicates:

- the stressed syllable of a word,
- the place where long or short pauses occur in a clause and
- which words belong together.

(ii) *Accents for prose and for poetry*
There are *two* accent systems:

- one for the prose sections and
- one for the poetic books, namely Psalms, Job and Proverbs.

The most important accent signs are, however, more or less the same for both.

(iii) *Conjunctive and disjunctive accents*
Two groups of accent signs may be distinguished, namely *conjunctive* (joining) and *disjunctive* (separating) accents. They are used as follows:

- The accent sign indicates the position of the stressed syllable in a word. In BH the final syllable (and in certain cases also the penultimate) is usually accented. The accent sign is normally placed above or below the first consonant of the accented syllable. In some cases accent signs are placed at the beginning or end of the word — the so-called prepositional and postpositional accents.
- The conjunctive and disjunctive accents often follow each other in a fixed order. The resultant sequence of accents was used to group together the words of the BH text. This grouping of words facilitated the recitation of the Hebrew Bible in the synagogues and was thus similar to punctuation in modern-day publications.

2. *The most important conjunctive and disjunctive accents*
A list of the most important conjunctive and disjunctive accents is given below.

(i) *Prose system*

a. Main *disjunctive* accents

Name	Form	Remarks
sillûq	ְ◌	Identifies the final accented syllable of a verse and with the sôf pāsûq (cf. §9.4) indicates the end of the verse. It is written below the accented syllable.
'atnāḥ	ֱ◌	Indicates the main pause in a verse. It is placed to the left of the vowel in the accented syllable of the word preceding the pause. It divides the verse into two and has the approximate force of a semi-colon.
ṭifḥā'	֖◌	Indicates either the main pause in short verses or the final pause before a sillûq or 'atnāḥ.
zāqēf qāṭôn	֔◌	A long unit with 'atnāḥ as main subdivision is further subdivided by a zāqēf qāṭôn.
s͏ᵉgôltâ' r͏ᶜbî͏ᵃ	֒◌	Postpositional. Indicates the first of two main pauses in a verse. It is written to the left above the last letter of the word preceding the pause.
r͏ᵉbî͏ᵃ	֓◌	Separates zāqēf, s͏ᵉgôltâ' or ṭifḥā' sections. It may also be used to mark the focal point of a clause.

b. Weaker *disjunctive* accents

Name	Form	Remarks
paštā'	֙◌	Postpositional. If the accent does not fall on the final syllable of the word, it is repeated on the accented syllable.
zarqā'	֮◌	Postpositional
gercš	֜◌	

c. Main *conjunctive* accents

Name	Form	Remarks
mûnaḥ	◌	
m͏ᵉhuppāk	◌	
mêr͏ᵉkā'	◌	

d. Less strong *conjunctive* accents

Name	Form	Remarks
tᵉlišā qᵉtannâ	o֑o	Postpositional
'azlā	o֜o	

(ii) *Poetry system*

Main *disjunctive* accents

Name	Form	Remarks
'ôleh wᵉyôrēd	o֫oȯ	Placed on the accented syllable and on the preceding syllable of the word preceding the pause.

3. *Examples of the most common combinations of accent signs*

(1) 'atnāḥ and sillûq

וַיֹּאמֶר אֱלֹהִים יְהִי אוֹר	And God said: Let there be light!
וַיְהִי־אוֹר	And there was light (Gen. 1.3).

(2) mêrᵉkā', tifḥā', mûnaḥ, 'atnāḥ

וַיֹּאמֶר אֱלֹהִים יְהִי אוֹר	And God said: Let there be light! (Gen. 1.3).

(3) mᵉhuppāk, paštā', zāqēf qāṭôn

וַיֹּאמֶר יְהוָה אֶל־קַיִן ...	And the Lord said to Cain ... (Gen. 4.9).

(4) mûnaḥ, zarqā', mûnaḥ, sᵉgôltā'

וַיָּרַח יְהוָה אֶת־רֵיחַ הַנִּיחֹחַ	And the Lord smelled a soothing aroma (Gen. 8.21).

(5) mûnaḥ, rebîᵃ

וַיֹּאמֶר אֱלֹהִים ...	And God said (Gen. 1.24) ...

(6) tᵉlišā qᵉtannâ, 'azlā, gereš

... וַיִּצֶר יְהוָה אֱלֹהִים	And the Lord God formed ... (Gen. 2.19).

§9.6. *The Pausal Forms*

A word that occurs at the end of a verse or section of a verse is pronounced with particular emphasis on the accented syllable. Consequently short vowels in this syllable may lengthen and long vowels

that have been reduced may return to their original form. (Cf. §7.3.)
These forms are known as pausal forms and occur particularly with
the zāqēf qātôn, 'atnāḥ and sillûq.

In the following example, the pataḥ in מַיִם has changed to a qāmeṣ
(מָיִם), at the end of each verse section due to the influence of the
accents 'atnāḥ and sillûq.

וַיֹּאמֶר אֱלֹהִים יְהִי רָקִיעַ בְּתוֹךְ	And then God said: Let there be a
הַמָּיִם וִיהִי מַבְדִּיל בֵּין מַיִם	firmament in the midst of the waters
לָמָיִם	and let it divide the waters from the
	waters (Gen. 1.6).

§9.7. *Kethib and Qere Readings*

The Masoretes sometimes believed that a word should be pronounced differently to its textual rendering. As they did not wish to
alter the text itself, they recorded variant readings in the margin.

Variant readings of certain written textual forms thus appear in the
margins of the BHS. The variant form in the margin is called the qere
reading (from קְרִי—to be read) and the corresponding written form
in the text is referred to as the kethib reading (from כְּתִיב written).
The qere reading was normally preferred to the kethib reading. The
vocalization of the qere reading in the margin was placed below the
kethib form in the text. A small circle above the relevant word in the
text refers to the qere reading in the margin.

For example:

(1) In Ps. 54.7 the form יָשׁוּב is found. According to the Masoretes
one should rather read יָשִׁב at this point, because they vocalize
ישוב in the text as יָשׁוּב. The consonants ישיב are written in the
margin and the assumption is that they should be read with the
vowels under ישוב in the text as יָשִׁב.

(2) Some words are so frequently pronounced differently to the
written text that they are not explained in the margin. The most
important of these is the name of God. In BH God's name is
written as יהוה and is probably pronounced 'Yahweh'. The
word אֲדֹנָי 'my lord' was always read in the place of the name
יהוה. The Masoretes retained the consonants of the name
יהוה—out of respect for the text, but always appended to them
the vowels of the word אֲדֹנָי as an indication of how the word
should be read. This produced the form יְהֹוָה, which the Jews
always pronounced as /ˀdōnāy/ and never as /yᵉhōwâ./

§9.8. *Other Masoretic Markers*

1. *Paragraph markers*

Paragraphs were originally indicated by spaces in the text. Two types of paragraphs may be found:

The 'open' paragraph or petûḥâ that begins on a new line and the 'closed' paragraph or setûmâ that begins later on on the same line which the previous paragraph ended.

Petûḥâ	Setûmâ	
....	....	....
פ	.... ס	.... ס
....	....	....

In BHS (and other printed editions) the letter פ has been inserted in the space to mark a petûḥâ and the letter ס to mark a setûmâ.

2. *Liturgical chapter markers*

The Pentateuch was divided in two different ways for liturgical readings:

(i) *Sēder* (ס in the margin)

According to *Palestinian tradition* the Pentateuch is recited in a cycle of three years. For this purpose it was divided into 154 or 167 segments. Each segment is called a sēder and is marked by a ס in the margin. Different manuscripts, however, vary in the number of sedā-rîm. There are a total of 452 sedārîm.

(ii) *Pārāšāḥ* (פרש in the margin)

According to *Babylonian tradition* the Pentateuch is recited in an annual cycle and is thus divided into *54 parts*. Each part is called a pārāšāḥ and indicated by the letters פרש in the margin.

In BHS the symbols for sēder and pārāšāḥ always appear in the inner margin (i.e. in the middle of the bound book).

3. *Critical signs in the text*

The Masoretes made use of certain critical signs in the text

- to focus attention on the text itself,
- to indicate instances of uncertainty in the correctness of the text,
- to indicate where the text had been improved.

These critical signs could take the following forms:

(i) *Large letters (literae majusculae)*

Some letters were deliberately enlarged when a passage deserved special attention.

שְׁמַ֖ע יִשְׂרָאֵ֑ל   Hear, O Israel: The Lord our God is
יְהֹוָ֥ה אֱלֹהֵ֖ינוּ יְהֹוָ֥ה אֶחָֽד   one Lord (Deut. 6.4).

(ii) *Small letters (literae minusculae)*

Some letters were deliberately decreased in size when the form of the word was not standard. This technique was not adopted by BHS.

(iii) *Dangling letters (literae suspensae)*

Some letters were deliberately written above the line either when there was uncertainty about that particular section or when that section had been improved.

וִיהוֹנָתָ֨ן בֶּן־גֵּרְשֹׁ֜ם בֶּן־מְנַשֶּׁה   and Jonathan, the son of Gershom,
the son of Moses **or** *the son of
Menassah* (Judg. 18.30).

(iv) *The inverted nun (nun inversum)*

An inverted nun was added to a section that did not fit into the context and had to be placed in brackets, as it were.

בִּנְסֹעַ֖ מִן־הַמַּחֲנֶ֑ה׃ ׀ ס   Whenever they set forth from the
35 וַיְהִ֞י בִּנְסֹ֣עַ הָאָרֹן֙   camp 35. And whenever the ark set
וַיֹּ֣אמֶר מֹשֶׁ֔ה ...   out, Moses said ... 36. ... the ten
36 ... רִבְב֖וֹת אַלְפֵ֥י   thousand thousands of Israel ...
יִשְׂרָאֵֽל׃ ׀ פ   (Num. 10.34-36).

(v) *Extraordinary points (puncta extraordinaria)*

Points were placed above doubtful letters.

... וַיֹּאמְר֣וּ אֵלָ֔יו   And they said to him ... (Gen. 18.9).

4. *Critical comments that supplement the text*

(i) *Masoretic endnotes* or *Masora finalis*

Lists were added at the end of every book in the Hebrew Bible (with the exception of 1 Samuel, 1 Kings, Ezra, and 1 Chronicles which originally were paired with 2 Samuel, 2 Kings, Nehemiah and 2 Chronicles respectively). These lists contained information about the number of verses in a book, but could also contain information such as the following:

- The note at the end of Deuteronomy mentions, for example, that the book has 955 verses;

- that the middle-point of the book is עַל־פִּי in 17.10;
- and that there are 31 sedārîm in the book.
- It also states that the Pentateuch consists of 5,845 verses, 158 sedārîm, 79,856 words and 400,945 letters.

These Masoretic comments were a form of quality control against which a new manuscript could be checked.

(ii) *Masoretic marginal notes* or *Masora marginalis*

a. *Masora parva (Mp)*

These marginal notes are also called the *Masora parva* (*Mp*) (or little Masora). Apart from the qere reading (cf. §9.7), the notes contain commentary on the text, non-textual traditions, rare words and the centre of whole books or larger sections. They also contain other statistical information such as the following:

- Words that appear only once in the Hebrew Bible are marked by the letter ל, which is the abbreviation for the Aramaic לֵית / לֵית לָא ('There is no other').

- Words/phrases used twice are marked by ב (the Hebrew notation for the numeral two) and those used three times by ג, etc.

The commentary of the *Masora parva* (*Mp*) is placed in the outer margin of BHS (i.e. on the right-hand side of even-numbered pages and on the left-hand side of odd-numbered pages). It is written mostly in Aramaic.

Small circles written above words in the text identify those portions of the text on which commentary is provided in the Mp on the adjacent line. Should more than one word in the same line be marked by such a circle, points are used to distinguish the marginal notes to the various words. The small numbers in the *Mp* refer to the *Masora magna*.

b. *Masora magna*

The *Masora magna* is not found in the same volume as the BHS text, but is found in a separate volume, the *Massorah gedolah*. The *Masora magna* of a particular text may be accessed by means of the *Masora parva*. A circle above a word refers to the *Masora parva*. A small number in the *Masora parva* refers to the note at the bottom of the page (just above the critical *apparatus*). This note refers to a particular entry in the *Massorah gedolah*.

Chapter 3

WORD, CLAUSE AND TEXT IN BIBLICAL HEBREW: A SURVEY

§10. The Levels of Language Structure

In order to study Biblical Hebrew grammar it is necessary to know the metalanguage (linguistic categories) that provides the means of discussing its language structure. Additionally, some insight is necessary into the various relationships between the elements of language structure. This chapter provides a basic grammatical orientation to these matters. Please note that using English examples does not imply that the structure of English and BH is the same.

Language structure can be described at different levels, namely the phonetic and phonological, morphological, syntactic, semantic and pragmatic, and textual levels.

1. *The phonetic and phonological level*

Speech sounds, used in languages to convey *meaning*, are described on the *phonetic level*. In order to convey meaning, each language must have a system whereby speech sounds are combined. This system of sound-combination is studied at the *phonological level*. §4-9 addressed certain features of the sound aspect of Biblical Hebrew language structure in addition to its form of writing or orthography. Speech sounds were described, classified and transcribed on the phonetic level, while on the phonological level reference was made to certain phonological processes such as assimilation (§4.2/4(ii)) and *metathesis* (§4.2/5(i)).

2. *The morphological level*

A morpheme is the smallest linguistic unit that bears grammatical meaning. Morphemes may be affixes, clitics or words. The structure or form of words is described on the morphological level. Words belong to different classes, called word categories/classes or parts of speech. §11 provides a basic morphological orientation with regard to the different categories of words. Some of these word categories may be inflected. Words are inflected through the addition of affixes (that is, prefixes, infixes and/or suffixes). For example, in BH there are suffixes that indicate that certain nouns are masculine while others are feminine. Furthermore, the possessive pronoun is not independent of the noun to which it relates but is added to the noun in the form of a suffix.

3. *The syntactic level*

The syntactic level describes how words are combined to form phrases, clauses and sentences. In view of the general grammatical orientation, §12 presents a review of the clause and its structure.

4. *The semantic and pragmatic level*

The semantic contribution of a word or construction refers to the minimum contribution that it makes towards an understanding of the context. The following construction indicates *possession*:

> The palace *of* the king.

Pragmatics refers to the conventions according to which speakers belonging to a particular culture *do* various things in particular ways with language. Thus speakers can perform an action with the words that they utter, e.g.

> Look, I *appoint* you to rule over the whole of Egypt.

The role of non-linguistic information such as background information and personal prejudices in the interpretation of sentences is in this way included in the grammatical description of language.

In this grammar a semantic and/or pragmatic level is distinguished only when possible and when relevant for the purposes of this work.

5. *The textual level*

In a written document sentences are usually organized to form larger units or texts. The communicative purpose of a text determines its form and content. A narrative, for example, looks very different from a piece of legislation. For this reason a distinction is made between different *types of texts* (or *discourse types*). The way in which sentences are organized to form coherent texts is also determined by the conventions of a particular society in this respect.

§11. **The Word Categories/Classes in Biblical Hebrew**

Words are divided into the following categories in this grammar:

- Verbs (V)
- Nouns (N)
- Adjectives (A)
- Prepositions (P)
- Conjunctions
- Adverbs (Adv)
- Predicators of existence (existential words)
- Interrogatives
- Discourse markers
- Interjections

§11.1. *Verbs*

Verbs express the action, condition or existence of a person or thing. Verbs may be divided into two syntactic groups, namely transitive (i.e. verbs that take a direct object, e.g. kill) and intransitive (i.e. verbs that do not take a direct object, e.g. sleep). Verbs have the following characteristics:

1. *Modality*
Modality refers to (the orientation of a speaker concerning) the actuality of a process. The following types of modality are important here:

- Indicative

The indicative refers to a fact in the form of a statement or question. This is regarded as the unmarked form, e.g.

> David plays the harp.

- Subjunctive

The subjunctive refers to a wish, expectation, possibility or uncertainty about the actuality of a matter, e.g.

> David *should* play the harp.
> David *can* play the harp now.

Languages sometimes either make use of auxiliary verbs (e.g. should, can) or of specific conjugations to express the subjunctive. BH does not have either auxiliary verbs or specific conjugations to express the subjunctive, but uses the same conjugation forms as the indicative. (Cf. 19.3.)

- Directive

The directive refers to a command, instruction, order, commission, prompting or request, e.g.

>   *Play* the harp.

2. *Time*

Time indicates the temporal aspect of an action, for example, present, future or past, e.g.

>   David *plays* the harp.
>   David *will play* the harp.
>   David *played* the harp.

3. *Aspect*

Aspect indicates whether the action is complete or incomplete. The terms perfect or imperfect (respectively) are sometimes used to denote the aspect of a verb, e.g.

>   God *made* the earth.
>   God (continually) *sustains* creation.

4. *Voice*

Voice indicates the way in which the action of the verb is related to the subject. In the *active* voice the subject performs the action, e.g.

>   David *plays* the harp.

In the *passive* voice the action is orientated towards the subject, e.g.

>   The harp *is played* by David.

5. *Conjugations*

Among the most important conjugations in BH are the following:

- *Perfect form*   כָּתַב   he wrote
- *Imperfect form*   יִכְתֹּב   he will write
- *Imperative form*   כְּתֹב   write!

- *Infinitive construct* כְּתֹב   to write
- *Infinitive absolute* כָּתוֹב
- *Participle* כֹּתֵב   (he is) writing

6. *Congruency features (or agreement markers)*

Congruency features indicate gender (masculine or feminine), number (singular and plural), person (1st, 2nd and 3rd). All the verbal conjugations in BH except the infinitive (which has no congruency features) and participles (with no indication of person) display all these congruency features. Nouns and adjectives do not display person, but determination (definite and indefinite).

7. *Finite/Non-Finite*

A finite verb can be marked for person and may stand on its own in an independent sentence. It indicates formal contrasts in time and mood. Non-finite verbs, contrary to finite verbs, occur only in dependent clauses and lack contrasts in person, time and mood. All BH verb conjugations except the infinitive and participles are finite.

§11.2. *Nouns*

Nouns (*nomen–nomina*) may be divided into the following main classes:

1. *Substantive nouns*

Substantive nouns indicate the names of people, places, things, ideas, conditions, qualities or feelings. The following subcategories are distinguished in BH:

- *Proper nouns* denote the names of a specific person, place or thing, e.g. David, Jerusalem, Passover, etc.
- *Common nouns* are the words used to designate any object, e.g. table, tree, altar, etc.
- *Collective nouns* denote classes or groups made up of many individual members, e.g. herd, cattle, forest, etc.
- *Abstract nouns* are words that refer to qualities, traits or ideas, e.g. love, illness, work, etc.

In BH nouns are qualified in terms of gender (masculine and feminine) and number (singular, plural or dual). A substantive noun may be definite or indefinite. Proper names, pronouns and nouns with the article are regarded as definite nouns.

2. *Pronouns*

A pronoun (*pronomen-pronomina*) is used as a substitute for a noun or noun phrase. A pronoun is not a specific name for an object. Its identification with a particular noun is determined by its position in a sentence or paragraph. Its signification may, however, remain undefined. Pronouns may be classified as follows:

- *Personal* pronouns (subject): I, you, etc.
- *Personal* pronouns (object): me, you, etc.
- *Possessive* pronoun: my, your, his, her [horse], etc.
- *Demonstrative* pronouns: this, that, etc.
- *Interrogative* pronouns: who, what, etc.
- *Relative* pronouns: whose, which, etc.
- *Indefinite* pronouns: everyone, all, etc.
- *Reflexive* pronouns: myself, yourself, etc.[4]
- *Reciprocal* pronouns: each other, one another, etc.

A personal pronoun usually refers to a person or thing that has already been mentioned. Such a person or thing is called the *antecedent* of the pronoun. BH has a set of independent personal pronouns used as the subject of a clause. Personal pronouns as objects and possessive pronouns do not occur as separate words but are to be found in the form of pronominal suffixes affixed to verbs, nouns and other types of words. Reflexive and reciprocal pronouns are *anaphora*, which implies that they must have a fixed antecedent in the same clause (as opposed to the case of personal pronouns), e.g.

> *David* saves *himself* from the hand of Saul, but not
> *David saves *herself* from the hand of Saul.[5]

3. *Numerals*

There are two kinds of numerals:

---

4. BH does not have direct equivalents for the English reciprocal (one another) and reflexive (myself) pronouns. BH uses other means to express them, e.g. the Niphal and Hithpael stem formations. (Cf. §16.3/2(ii) and 16.6/2(i).)

5. The asterisk indicates that this is an ungrammatical sentence. 'Herself' requires a female antecedent in the above-mentioned sentence.

- *Cardinal* numbers indicate a specific amount or quantity, e.g.

  three women

- *Ordinal* numbers indicate sequence or order, e.g.

  in the tenth year on the seventieth day

§11.3. *Adjectives*

An adjective is a word that qualifies a substantive noun, pronoun or substantive (a substantive is any word or group of words that is used grammatically as a substantive noun). In BH the adjective usually agrees with the word it qualifies according to most of its congruency features.

The qualification can be attributive, e.g.

The *good* king

or predicative, e.g.

The king is *good*.

In BH the adjective has no degrees of comparison. The semantic effect normally obtained by means of degrees of comparison is expressed through other constructions.

Although adjectives may be classified as an independent word class, in this grammar they are dealt with as a subcategory of nouns due to their morphological similarities with nouns.

§11.4. *Prepositions*

A preposition is used to join a succeeding noun or a pronoun to another word or group of words. It does it in such a way that the preposition and the subsequent noun or pronoun become directly associated with the remaining words of the clause, e.g.

He places the firewood *on* Isaac's shoulders.
They wandered *around* the city.

Prepositions express position in time or space or any similar abstract relationship.

§11.5. *Conjunctions*

A conjunction joins words, phrases, clauses or sentences in such a way that they form a unit. There are two types of conjunctions.

1. *Co-ordinating conjunctions*

A co-ordinating conjunction joins grammatically equivalent items such as nouns or independent clauses, e.g.

> John walks *and* Mary rides.

2. *Subordinating conjunction*

A subordinating conjunction joins a subordinate clause (i.e. a clause that cannot stand independently) to the main clause.

> You are cursed, *because of* what you did.

§11.6. *Adverbs*

An adverb (*adverbium*) is used to qualify an adjective, a verb or another adverb with respect to time, manner, place, e.g.

> You are *still* speaking to the king.
> You speak *little*.
> You speak *outside*.

These adverbs are called *ordinary adverbs* in this grammar. Adverbs can also qualify clauses, e.g.

> *Truly*, Sarah will bear a son.

Such adverbs will be called *modal words* here. Some adverbs place the focus on the item or clause that follows them. The referent for these adverbs is a qualification or limitation of another referent, e.g.

> Let me speak *just* this once.

This class is called *focus particles*. Words expressing the *negative* are also regarded as adverbs in this grammar.

§11.7. *Predicators of Existence*

BH has predicators of existence that express the existence or non-existence of (mostly) an impersonal object; they can be translated as *there is/there is not*, e.g.

> *There is* wheat in Egypt.
> *There are no* people to cultivate the land.

§11.8. *Interrogatives*

Apart from the interrogative pronouns that mark factual questions, BH has an interrogative that marks clauses requiring a yes-no answer. This interrogative has no lexical equivalent in English.

§11.9. *Discourse Markers*

BH speakers use discourse markers to comment on the content of a sentence (or sentences) from the perspective of a meta-level. In this way the sentence or sentences are anchored in the discourse. These discourse markers always precede the sentence(s) to which they refer. It often draws attention to the contents of the succeeding sentence(s), affording that sentence(s) greater prominence within its larger context, e.g.

> *Look*, I am going to do something.

§11.10. *Interjections*

An interjection is an expression inserted between the other words of a sentence but which has no grammatical link to them. Often it indicates some sudden emotional reaction, e.g. *Ah, Oh, Alas.*

§12. **The Clause in Biblical Hebrew**

§12.1. *The Clause: A Definition*

A clause is a meaningful series of words that has at least a subject and a predicate. Since a clause is built up from words and a formal relationship/coherence hold between these words, a clause is a unit that can be analysed structurally.

§12.2. *The Syntactical Units of the Clause*

Words may be grouped together into larger units known as phrases. The following kinds of phrases are important here:

- *Noun phrase* (NP)   the boys
- *Verb phrase* (VP)   ate the bread
- *Adverbial phrase* (AP)   when they walked
- *Prepositional phrase* (PP)   to the fields

§12.3. *The Relationships between the Syntactical Units of the Clause*

All clauses are built up of phrases that have a particular relationship with one another. The simplest clause or sentence (S)[6] can be divided into a noun phrase (NP) and a verb phrase (VP).

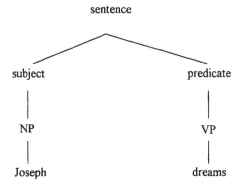

This diagram represents the most basic relationship. It corresponds to the traditional division of the clause and/or sentence into subject and predicate. The predicate may be used with a direct object, for example,

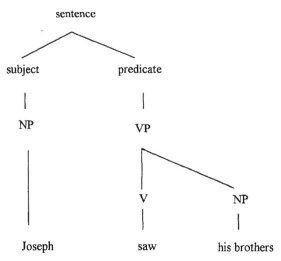

or an indirect object, for example,

6. The convention to refer to the highest node in a tree diagram as 'sentence' is retained here.

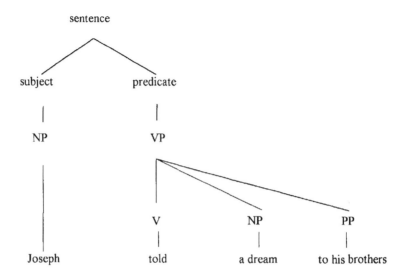

The type and number of phrases selected by a verb (V) are determined by the nature of the verb. Intransitive verbs do not select any phrases.

> [Jacob] sleeps Ø (Ø = nothing).

Transitive verbs may take a noun phrase (NP), a prepositional phrase (PP) or a clause (S), respectively.

> [Joseph] relates *a dream* (NP).
> [Jacob] lives *in Canaan* (PP).
> [Joseph] knows that the Lord will help him (S).

Ditransitive (doubly transitive) verbs take a noun phrase (NP) and a prepositional phrase (PP) or two noun phrases (NPs), respectively.

> [Jacob] gives bread (NP) to his sons (PP).
> [Jacob] gives his sons (NP) bread (NP).

Should any of these phrases be omitted, the clause would be incomplete. These phrases are obligatory parts of the clause and are known as *complements*. In contrast to complements, there are other, optional phrases in a clause, which may be omitted, as in the case of the prepositional phrase in the following sentence:

> Jacob sleeps *in Bethel* (PP).

These phrases are known as *adjuncts*.

The subject in the first sentence above may also be expanded. A noun phrase (NP) may be extended by an article or a prepositional phrase.

> *The* man dreams.
> The man *in the tent* dreams.

In principle, the noun phrase (NP) may be extended infinitely through recursive processes, i.e. processes that can be applied infinitely in number. The following are examples of such processes.

- Co-ordination

  > Joseph *and* Rebecca dream.

- Adjectival qualification

  > The *handsome* man dreams.

- Apposition

  > Jacob, *the traitor*, dreams.

- Qualification by means of a relative pronoun

  > Jacob, *who lived in Canaan*, dreams.

- Qualification by means of a construct relationship

  > The son *of Jacob* dreams.

A noun phrase (NP) can thus be extended. Similarly, prepositional phrases (PP) and adjective phrases (AP) can be extended.

> Jacob gives bread to his hungry sons *who are watching over his sheep*.

> The charming, *handsome* man dreams.

§12.4. *Typical Characteristics of BH Clauses*

Typical features of BH syntax are the following:

1. *Absent subject*

The pronominal subject may be absent in certain cases. In such cases a trace of the subject has remained and must be assumed. The following form is thus a complete clause even though no visible subject exists:

כָּתַב
wrote–[he]
he wrote

2. *Free inversion of the subject, or any other constituent*

BH is often regarded as a so-called VSO (= **V**erb, **S**ubject, **O**bject) language, i.e. the verb normally preceeds the subject and object of a clause. However, free inversion means that the subject (or any other constituent) can be placed either before or after the verb phrase, e.g.

(1)   כָּתַב אָב
wrote–[he] father
a father wrote

(2)   אָב כָּתַב
a father wrote–[he]
a father wrote

Although the sequence in (2) is not predicate (verb) followed by subject, it still forms a clause. This process can, however, have semantic implications. (Cf. §46-47.)

3. *Nominal clause (or verbless clause)*

These are clauses in BH that do not contain a finite form of the verb. The English copulative verb 'is' must be added to them to facilitate translation.

Jacob [is] old.
Jacob [is] a farmer.
Jacob [is] in the tent.

In such clauses the non-verbal complement forms the predicate. A nominal clause therefore consists of: Subject + Predicate and thus does form a clause.

§12.5. *Types of Sentences*

The following types of sentences may be identified in BH:

1. *Simple sentence*

- Nominal sentence (Cf. §12.4.)
- Verbal sentence, e.g.

Statements

> He gave bread to the boy.

Interrogative sentence[7]

Factual (also referred to as WH-questions)

> Who buys wheat?

Questions expecting a yes/no answer (also referred to as polar questions)

> Did you buy wheat?

Commands

> Pick it up!/You may not pick it up.
> You must pick it up/You must not pick it up.
> Let us pick it up/Let us not pick it up.

2. *Extended sentence*

The extension forms part of the main clause and expands a part of the clause, for example, the subject or the object of the clause. In the next clause the subordinate clause is an extension of the subject, the NP, Jacob.

> Jacob, *who lives in Canaan,* loved Joseph.

3. *Complex sentence*

Complex sentences consist of one or more clauses related to the so-called main clause.

- Co-ordinating clause

> At first Joseph was strict with his brothers, *then he treated them well.*

- Subordinate clause

> *When Joseph saw his brothers,* he immediately recognized them.

A basic difference between subordinate and co-ordinate clauses is that speakers normally do not carry out speech acts in subordinate clauses. In other words, a speaker does not make a statement, pose a

---

7.   Questions are not necessarily posed by means of interrogative sentences, e.g. in the case of rhetorical questions. In such cases a question like 'Were you not the one who bought the wheat?' can be used to say, 'You were, indeed, the one who bought the wheat'.

question or make an appeal in a subordinate clause. Examples of sub-ordinate clauses in BH are:

- *Conditional clauses* (syntactical composition: *Protasis* + *Apodosis*)

    If you believe, you will receive mercy.

- *Circumstantial* clause

    When he was old, he returned.

The subordinate clauses above, also called *supplement* clauses, are distinguished from subordinate clauses that can act as complements in a clause, for example, as its subject or object. These so-called *complement* clauses are more integrally linked to their main clauses than the supplement clauses, e.g.

    God sees *that you love him* (object).
    To give (subject) is your duty.

§13. The Text in Biblical Hebrew

Clause and sentences are used to create texts. This usually occurs by means of utilizing conventions regarding cohesion and rhetorical organization.

1. *Cohesion*
Every language community has its own conventions that determine the form that their texts should take in order to be understood as coherent texts. This includes conventions regarding the manner in which semantic links are made between the relevant people and things in a text, e.g.

- *Reference* to people and things. In English a text initially refers to persons by mentioning their names and positions, e.g. Elijah, man of God. Subsequently only their names will often be used, i.e. Elijah. In BH, however, the person's name and position will often be repeated regularly.

- The *use of pronouns*. In BH texts the name of a person will be used explicitly much more often than it would in English. The direct translation of Gen. 41.15-16 reads 'And Pharaoh said to Joseph ... and Joseph answered *Pharaoh*'. In English, the second explicit reference to Pharaoh would be replaced with a pronoun: '... and Joseph answered *him*'.

2. *Rhetorical organization*

Sentences are organized to form texts. The rhetorical organization of texts is not always the same, however. That is why different types of texts may be distinguished:

- Narrative texts
- Descriptive texts
- Argumentative/discursive texts
- Prescriptive or instructional texts.

Naturally, a mixture of the different kinds of texts may also occur.

Language communities have various conventions that govern the way different types of texts are begun, the way they proceed, and the way they are concluded. This is why these conventions are regarded as part of the 'organizational' structure of a language. For example, narrative texts in BH often concludes with a summary of the narrative, namely 'And so this (or that) happened'.

Chapter 4

THE VERB

§14. Review

BH verbs can be derived from a stem or root consisting of three consonants. These roots never occur on their own in BH texts but are always provided with affixes (that is, prefixes, infixes and/or suffixes) which indicate that they belong to:

- A specific *stem formation* (also referred to as a *verbal stem*). For example, in the *Qal* the root כתב is vocalized with the vowel pattern / ָ ַ /, also known as an infix. The verb is then read as כָּתַב. If the same root begins with a ה prefix and has the infix / ִי ַ /, i.e. הִכְתִּיב, one knows that is a *Hiphil* stem formation. There are seven main stem formations in BH:

    Qal, Niphal, Piel, Pual, Hithpael, Hiphil and *Hophal*.

- A particular *conjugation* of a stem formation. For example, the ־תִּי suffix of the word כָּתַבְתִּי indicates the perfect form of a verb; while the ־י prefix of the word יִכְתֹּב indicates the imperfect form. The following conjugations are found in BH:

    Perfect, Imperfect, Imperative, Jussive, Cohortative,
    Infinitive Construct, Infinitive Absolute and *Participle*.

- A specific feature or mark of congruency (*person, gender, number*, where applicable) in the conjugation. For example, in the perfect and the imperfect the suffixes and prefixes are used to indicate a difference in person (subject of the verb). The congruency features distinguished in BH are the following:

	Singular	Plural
3rd person	he, she	they (m. and f.)
2nd person	you (m. and f.)	you (m. and f.)
1st person	I	we

These sets of affixes are usually clearly discernible in the regular stems. In other words it is usually easy to recognize the stem (or root), stem formation and conjugation of a particular verb form. In the so-called irregular stems, however, a whole range of phonological processes must be considered, which makes it more difficult to recognize the stem and/or stem formation. These processes are related to the phonetic features of the *irregular stems*.

In English a graphic unit never comprises more than one lexical item or word. This is not the case in BH. Not only is the subject part of the verb, but a verb can also contain a pronominal suffix that refers to the object of the verb. This suffix is a separate lexical item and has nothing to do with the verbal system as such. Yet the suffix influences the vocalization of the verb—a factor that has to be taken into account in order to understand the vocalization of a verb.

In BH there are also certain *verb chains and sequences* associated with the perfect, imperfect and imperative forms. In describing the meaning of these sequences the context or discourse must be taken into account more systematically than with the other conjugations.

Each of the above features of the BH verb will be discussed in the ensuing sections.

§15. The Morphology of the Basic Paradigm

Seeing that, morphologically speaking, the Qal paradigm has the simplest form and is normally the first to be learnt, it will be used to describe the basic morphology of the BH verb.

§15.1. *The Perfect Form (= Suffix Conjugation or Qatal)*[8]

Perfect forms[9] refer, broadly speaking, to complete events or facts that often can be translated with the past tense. (Cf. §19.2.) The perfect has the following forms:

כָּתַב	3 m. sing.	he wrote
כָּתְבָה	3 f. sing.	she wrote
כָּתַבְתָּ	2 m. sing.	you (m.) wrote
כָּתַבְתְּ	2 f. sing.	you (f.) wrote

---

8. The reason for referring to the same form by three different terms is explained in §19.1.

9. Unless stated otherwise, in this study perfect refers only to the perfect forms of a BH verb.

כָּתַבְתִּי	1 sing.	I wrote
כָּתְבוּ	3 pl.	they wrote
כְּתַבְתֶּם	2 m. pl.	you (m. pl.) wrote
כְּתַבְתֶּן	2 f. pl.	you (f. pl.) wrote
כָּתַבְנוּ	1 pl.	we wrote

Note the following characteristics:

(1) Person is indicated by means of suffixes. Although there is no suffix in the 3 masculine singular, the infix sufficiently identifies it as a Qal perfect.

(2) In the case of the 1 singular, 1 plural and 3 plural no distinction is made between the masculine and feminine forms.

(3) The suffix of the perfect is either consonantal, e.g. כָּתַבְתִּי, or vocalic, e.g. כָּתְבוּ.

(4) The vowel pattern of the Qal perfect is / - - /. However, the following exceptions are to be found:

a. before vocalic suffixes the / - / becomes an audible šᵉwâ (/ - /) due to the fact that vocalic suffixes are always accented. The / - / changes in the syllable nearest to a changeable vowel due to the accent shift produced by the addition of the suffix, for example, כָּתַב plus הָ- becomes כָּתְבָה and not כָּתַבָה. (Cf. §7.3/(i).)

b. The consonantal suffixes תֶּם- 2 masculine plural and תֶּן — 2 feminine plural carry the emphasis and consequently the first syllable loses its accent. The / - / in the first syllable is reduced to the audible šᵉwâ. (Cf. §7.3/(i).)

(5) In the 3 feminine singular and 3 plural forms the / - / acquires a meteg which indicates that the syllable carries an additional accent and that / - / must be read as /ā/. (Cf. §9.1.)

(6) Whenever the perfect form is preceded by a waw it may be a waw consecutive or waw copulative. (Cf. §21.1 and 21.4.)

§15.2. *The Imperfect Form (= Prefix Conjugation or Yiqtol Form)*

Imperfect[10] forms refer, broadly speaking, to incomplete events that often could be translated with the present or future tense. (Cf. §19.3.)

The imperfect has the following forms:

יִכְתֹּב	3 m. sing.	he will write
תִּכְתֹּב	3 f. sing.	she will write
תִּכְתֹּב	2 m. sing.	you (m.) will write
תִּכְתְּבִי	2 f. sing.	you (f.) will write
אֶכְתֹּב	1 sing.	I will write
יִכְתְּבוּ	3 m. pl.	they (m.) will write
תִּכְתֹּבְנָה	3 f. pl.	they (f.) will write
תִּכְתְּבוּ	2 m. pl.	you (m. pl.) will write
תִּכְתֹּבְנָה	2 f. pl.	you (f. pl.) will write
נִכְתֹּב	1 pl.	we will write

Note the following characteristics:

(1) Person is indicated by means of prefixes as well as by suffixes in certain cases.

(2) The prefix forms a closed syllable with the first stem consonant, and the vowel pattern of the Qal imperfect is usually / ־ ־ /.

a. Before consonantal suffixes the / ־ / remains unchanged, e.g. תִּכְתֹּבְנָה.

b. Before vocalic suffixes the / ־ / becomes an audible šᵉwâ, e.g. תִּכְתְּבוּ.

(3) On a morphological level, no distinction is made between masculine and feminine forms in the case of the 1 singular and the 1 plural.

(4) The 2 masculine singular and the 3 feminine singular have the same morphological form. The context in which the words are used always provides clues towards making the necessary distinction. The same applies to the 2 feminine plural and 3 feminine plural forms.

(5) A distinction is made between a masculine and a feminine form in the third person.

---

10. Unless stated otherwise, in this study 'imperfect' refers only to the imperfect *forms* of a BH verb.

(6) Whenever the imperfect form is preceeded by a waw it may be a waw consecutive or waw copulative. (Cf. §21.1 and 21.)

§15.3. *The Imperative Form*

The meaning of the imperative can broadly be described as a direct command to the 2nd person. (Cf. §19.4.) For indirect commands in the 1st person and the 3rd person the cohortative and jussive forms (respectively) are used. The following imperative forms can be distinguished:

כְּתֹב	2 m. sing.	(You) write!
כִּתְבִי	2 f. sing.	(You) write!
כִּתְבוּ	2 m. pl.	(You) write!
כְּתֹבְנָה	2 f. pl.	(You) write!

Note the following characteristics:

(1) The forms of the imperative are the same as the imperfect 2nd person without the prefix, for example, תִּכְתְּבִי 'you will write' minus the prefix is כְּתֹבִי 'write!'

(2) There is an / ִ / vowel in the imperative feminine singular and masculine plural. It results from the fusion of two audible šᵉwâs, e.g. כְּתֹבִי > כְּתְבִי > תִּכְתְּבִי

§15.4. *The Cohortative Form*

The meaning of the cohortative can broadly be described as an indirect command to the 1st person. (Cf. §19.3.) In the cohortative the suffix ָה is added to the imperfect of the 1st person. The final stem vowel which occurs before this vocalic suffix is reduced. This phenomenon is found in every stem formation with the exception of the Hiphil where the / ִ / occurring before the vowel suffix is retained. (Cf. §16.7.)

אֶכְתְּבָה	1 sing.	Let me write
נִכְתְּבָה	1 pl.	Let us write

§15.5. *The Jussive Form*

The meaning of the jussive can broadly be described as an indirect command to the 3rd person. The jussive form is also used with אַל in negative commands to the 2nd person. (Cf. §19.4.) The jussive often appears as a shortened form of the imperfect. However, this shortened form can only be found in certain cases as, for example, in the

Hiphil where the / ־ / of the conjugation forms without suffixes is 'shortened' to / ־ /. (Cf. §16.7/1.) The shortened form also occurs with II waw / II yod (cf. §18.8/3) and III he verbs. (Cf. §18.5/4 for these so-called apocopated forms.)

יִכְתֹּב	3 m. sing.	Let him/may he write
תִּכְתֹּב	3 f. sing.	Let her/may she write
יִכְתְּבוּ	3 m. pl.	Let them/may they (m.) write
תִּכְתֹּבְנָה	3 f. pl.	Let them/may they (f.) write

§15.6. *The Infinitive Construct (= Declinable Infinitive)*

In BH a distinction is made between two infinitive forms, namely the infinitive construct or declinable infinitive and the infinitive absolute or undeclinable infinitive. The infinitive construct is a verbal noun that expresses action without referring to the time or person. (Cf. §20.1.)

כְּתֹב	unmarked	to write

Note the following characteristics:

   (1) The infinitive construct usually has the same form as the masculine singular imperative.

   (2) The infinitive construct is often used with a pronominal suffix or a preposition. (Cf. §17.5.)

§15.7. *The Infinitive Absolute (= Undeclinable Infinitive)*

The infinitive absolute has the following form:

כָּתוֹב	unmarked	to write

Note the following characteristics:

   (1) The infinitive absolute is usually characterized by a / וֹ / in the final syllable. (Cf. §20.2.)

   (2) The infinitive absolute does not decline.

§15.8. *The Participle*

In BH the participle is a verbal adjective that functions as a verb, noun or adjective. (Cf. §20.3.) The participle has the following forms:

כֹּתֵב	m. sing.	writing
כֹּתֶבֶת	f. sing.	writing

| כֹּתְבִים | m. pl. | writing |
| כֹּתְבוֹת | f. pl. | writing |

Note the following characteristics:

(1) The nominal grammatical morphemes added to the participle correspond with those used for the adjective. (Cf. §30.1.)

(2) כֹּתְבָה is also used for the feminine singular participle, but does not occur frequently.

§16. The Stem Formations

§16.1. *The Names of the Stem Formations*

The Qal stem formation is the simplest, requiring only the verb stem for its various forms / conjugations. The other stem formations are morphological extensions of this stem. These extended forms may express various semantic associations with the Qal such as passive, causative, etc. This semantic relationship with the Qal must not, however, be taken for granted. Each stem formation should rather be regarded as an independent form, the meaning of which must be learned separately. The 3rd masculine singular perfect of the stem פָּעַל has been used as a pattern to illustrate the so-called derived or extended stem formations. Hence the paradigm:

Qal	פָּעַל	Piel	פִּעֵל	Hiphil	הִפְעִיל
Niphal	נִפְעַל	Pual	פֻּעַל	Hophal	הָפְעַל
		Hithpael	הִתְפַּעֵל		

The idea that the more complex stem formations are derivations of the Qal led grammarians to assume that the Qal forms also reflect the most basic meaning of a verb and that the meanings of the other stem formations could thus be derived from it. Although this is often the case, recent research has clearly indicated that this assumption is untenable. This is one of the reasons why the above system is no longer used in some more recent BH grammars. Cf. also Richter (1978: 73).

The following system may also be used for denoting the stem formations:

G	= Qal
D	= Piel and Pual
Dt	= Hithpael

H   = Hiphil and Hophal
N   = Niphal

In this grammar the traditional categories will be used.

§16.2. *Morphology and Semantics of the Qal*

1. *Morphology*

The morphology of the Qal stem formation has already been dealt with in §15. Table 1 provides a summary of the complete paradigm of the Qal stem formation.

(i) Table 1. *The paradigm of the Qal stem formation*

		QAL		
		ā-a	*ā-e*	*ā-ō*
Perf. sing.	3 m.	כָּתַב	כָּבֵד	קָטֹן
	3 f.	כָּתְבָה	כָּבְדָה	קָטְנָה
	2 m.	כָּתַבְתָּ	כָּבַדְתָּ	קָטֹנְתָּ
	2 f.	כָּתַבְתְּ	כָּבַדְתְּ	קָטֹנְתְּ
	1.	כָּתַבְתִּי	כָּבַדְתִּי	קָטֹנְתִּי
Perf. pl.	3.	כָּתְבוּ	כָּבְדוּ	קָטְנוּ
	2 m.	כְּתַבְתֶּם	כְּבַדְתֶּם	קְטָנְתֶּם
	2 f.	כְּתַבְתֶּן	כְּבַדְתֶּן	קְטָנְתֶּן
	1.	כָּתַבְנוּ	כָּבַדְנוּ	קָטֹנּוּ
Impf. sing.	3 m.	יִכְתֹּב	יִכְבַּד	יִקְטֹן
	3 f.	תִּכְתֹּב	תִּכְבַּד	תִּקְטֹן
	2 m.	תִּכְתֹּב	תִּכְבַּד	תִּקְטֹן
	2 f.	תִּכְתְּבִי	תִּכְבְּדִי	תִּקְטְנִי
	1.	אֶכְתֹּב	אֶכְבַּד	אֶקְטֹן
Impf. pl.	3 m.	יִכְתְּבוּ	יִכְבְּדוּ	יִקְטְנוּ
	3 f.	תִּכְתֹּבְנָה	תִּכְבַּדְנָה	תִּקְטֹנָּה
	2 m.	תִּכְתְּבוּ	תִּכְבְּדוּ	תִּקְטְנוּ
	2 f.	תִּכְתֹּבְנָה	תִּכְבַּדְנָה	תִּקְטֹנָּה
	1.	נִכְתֹּב	נִכְבַּד	נִקְטֹן
Imp. sing.	2 m.	כְּתֹב	כְּבַד	קְטֹן
	2 f.	כִּתְבִי	כִּבְדִי	קְטְנִי

QAL			ā-e	ā-ō
		ā-a		
Imp. pl.	2 m.	כִּתְבוּ	כִּבְדוּ	קִטְנוּ
	2 f.	כְּתֹבְנָה	כְּבַדְנָה	קְטַנָּה
Coh. sing.	1.	אֶכְתְּבָה	אֶכְבְּדָה	אֶקְטְנָה
Juss. sing.	3 m.	יִכְתֹּב	יִכְבַּד	יִקְטֹן
Inf. cs.		כְּתֹב	כְּבַד	קְטֹן
Inf. abs.		כָּתוֹב	כָּבוֹד	קָטוֹן
Part. act.		כֹּתֵב	כָּבֵד	קָטֹן
Part. pass.		כָּתוּב		

(ii) The most important *morphological features of the Qal* are:

a. In the perfect the vowel pattern is / -- / (כָּתַב)[11]

   or / -- / (כָּבֵד)

   or / -- / (קָטֹן).

   - Before the vocalic suffixes the / - /, / - /, / - / in the second stem syllable are reduced to an audible šᵉwâ. (Cf. §8.1/1.) (כָּתְבָה, קָטְנָה, כָּבְדָה)
   - The consonantal suffixes תֶם- 2 masculine plural and תֶן- 2 feminine plural draw the accent to themselves. The first syllable consequently loses its accent. The / - / in the first syllable is reduced to an audible šᵉwâ (כְּתַבְתֶּם).

b. In the imperfect the vowel pattern is / -- / (יִכְתֹּב) or / -- / (יִלְמַד).[12]

   - The / - / becomes an audible šᵉwâ before vocalic suffixes (תִּכְתְּבוּ).

c. In the imperative and infinitive construct the vowel pattern is / - - / (כְּתֹב).

d. In the participle the vowel in the first syllable is / - / (כֹּתֵב).

e. The cohortative form occurs in the singular and plural of the 1st person. It is formed by adding the ה- suffix to the imperfect 1 singular (אֶכְתְּבָה) and plural (נִכְתְּבָה).

---

11. The vowels / -- / used for the 3 masculine singular are known as the *stem vowels* of the perfect. In the imperfect only the vowel in the second syllable, e.g. the / - / of the Qal imperfect, is regarded as a stem vowel.

12. The prefix, i.e. the consonant and the vowel added to the stem, is also called a *preformative*.

f. The jussive form is a shortened version of the imperfect form. However, this shortened (apocopated) form is often not recognisable, e.g. the jussive and imperfect form of כתב is the same, viz. יִכְתֹּב. In contrast, cf. §18.5/4.

g. In a waw consecutive + imperfect construction (cf. §21.1) the 'imperfect' is in reality not an imperfect form, but this shortened (jussive) form. In some cases, however, this jussive form may change as well. This is due to a shift of accent caused by the addition of the ִ֯. (Cf. §18.8/3(ii)h. and 18.8/3(v)f.)

Note the following:

(1) The difference discernable in the vocalic form of the above verb stems is analogous to the division of verbs into two syntactic groups, namely transitive—the qātal and yiqtōl patterns, and intransitive—the qātēl (e.g. כָּבֵד he was heavy) and qātōl (e.g. קָטֹן he was small) patterns with their corresponding yiqtal forms (e.g. יִכְבַּד and יִקְטַן). In the Qal certain verbs have both a qātēl and a qātal form and are accordingly both transitive or intransitive respectively.

<table>
<tr><td align="right">לָבֵשׁ יְהוָה עֹז</td><td>The Lord is *robed* in majesty (Ps. 93.1).</td></tr>
<tr><td align="right">אֲשֶׁר לָבַשׁ בְּבֹאוֹ אֶל־הַקֹּדֶשׁ</td><td>which he *put on* when he went into the holy sanctuary (Lev. 16.23).</td></tr>
</table>

(2) Certain transitive yiqtal forms also exist, e.g. רכב (ride), למד (learn) and שׁכב (lie).

There is considerable evidence that a Qal passive form also existed in a pre-Masoretic BH phase. However, the Masoretes only acknowledged the active Qal. The only Qal passive form that still occurs fairly regularly in BH is the Qal passive participle. Cf. Waltke and O'Connor §22.6 and Siebesma (1991) for a more complete discussion of the Qal passive hypothesis.

2. *Semantics*

The Qal stem formation has no specific meaning *per se*. Verbs occurring in this stem formation can, at most, be divided into the following semantic categories:

(i) *Action* verbs in which the subject performs some or other action. These verbs are referred to as fientive verbs.

(ii) *Stative* verbs express the condition or state of the subject, e.g. 'he was heavy'; 'he was small'.

§16.3. *Morphology and Semantics of the Niphal*

1. *Morphology*

(i) Table 2. *The paradigm of the Niphal*

NIPHAL			
		Singular	*Plural*
Perf.	*3 m.*	נִכְתַּב	נִכְתְּבוּ
	3 f.	נִכְתְּבָה	נִכְתְּבוּ
	2 m.	נִכְתַּבְתָּ	נִכְתַּבְתֶּם
	2 f.	נִכְתַּבְתְּ	נִכְתַּבְתֶּן
	1	נִכְתַּבְתִּי	נִכְתַּבְנוּ
Impf.	*3 m.*	יִכָּתֵב	יִכָּתְבוּ
	3 f.	תִּכָּתֵב	תִּכָּתַבְנָה
	2 m.	תִּכָּתֵב	תִּכָּתְבוּ
	2 f.	תִּכָּתְבִי	תִּכָּתַבְנָה
	1	אֶכָּתֵב	נִכָּתֵב
Imp.	*m.*	הִכָּתֵב	הִכָּתְבוּ
	f.	הִכָּתְבִי	הִכָּתַבְנָה
Coh.		אֶכָּתְבָה	
Juss.		יִכָּתֵב	
Inf. cs.		הִכָּתֵב	
Inf. abs.		נִכְתֹב / הִכָּתֵב	
Part.		נִכְתָּב	

(ii) The most important *morphological features of the Niphal* are:

a. In the perfect -נ is prefixed to the stem. This prefix forms a closed syllable with the first stem consonant. The vowel pattern is / ִ - ַ / (נִכְתַּב).

  • With the vocalic suffixes the second stem vowel is reduced (נִכְתְּבוּ).

- With the consonantal suffixes both stem vowels are retained (נִכְתַּבְתִּי).

b. In the imperfect the vowel pattern is / - ֲ - / (יִכָּתֵב).

- The first consonant of the stem doubles. The doubling occurs as a result of the assimilation of the nun of the Niphal with the first stem consonant (יִכָּתֵב).
- With vocalic suffixes the / ֵ / is reduced to / ְ / (תִּכָּתְבִי).
- With consonantal suffixes the / ֵ / changes to / ֵ / (תִּכָּתַבְנָה).

c. The prefix in the imperative and infinitive construct is הִ- (הִכָּתֵב).

d. The participle is similar in appearance to the perfect 3 masculine singular. However, the stem vowel of the participle is / ָ / (נִכְתָּב) and not / ַ /(נִכְתַּב).

2. *Semantics*

About 60% of the verb stems that have a Niphal form are semantically related to the Qal form of the verb stem. However, 10% are semantically related to stems in the Piel, and 10% to stems in the Hiphil; while 10% have no semantic relationship to any other active stem formation. (For more statistics, cf. Siebesma 1991: 92-96).

The semantic relationships most often realized are:

(i) the *passive* (mostly of the Qal)

כָּל־מְלָאכָה	No work shall *be done* on them
לֹא־יֵעָשֶׂה בָהֶם	(Exod. 12.16).

(ii) the *reflexive* (mostly of the Qal)
Within this category, also called the *double status Niphal* because the subject of the verb is both the agent and the patient, it is possible to distinguish between

a. *ordinary reflexive*

וְאִנָּקְמָה מֵאוֹיְבָי	And I will *avenge myself* on my foes (Isa. 1.24).

b. and *reciprocal*

וְכִי־יִנָּצוּ אֲנָשִׁים	When men *strive with one another* (Exod. 21.22).

(iii) Some verbs occur *in the Niphal, but not in the Qal, and then express an active meaning of the verb,* e.g. נִלְחַם (he fought), נִסְתַּר (he crept away), נִמְלַט (he slipped away).

§16.4. *Morphology and Semantics of the Piel*

1. *Morphology*

(i) Table 3. *The paradigm of the Piel*

PIEL			
		Singular	*Plural*
Perf.	*3 m.*	כִּתֵּב	כִּתְּבוּ
	3 f.	כִּתְּבָה	כִּתְּבוּ
	2 m.	כִּתַּבְתָּ	כִּתַּבְתֶּם
	2 f.	כִּתַּבְתְּ	כִּתַּבְתֶּן
	1	כִּתַּבְתִּי	כִּתַּבְנוּ
Impf.	*3 m.*	יְכַתֵּב	יְכַתְּבוּ
	3 f.	תְּכַתֵּב	תְּכַתֵּבְנָה
	2 m.	תְּכַתֵּב	תְּכַתְּבוּ
	2 f.	תְּכַתְּבִי	תְּכַתֵּבְנָה
	1	אֲכַתֵּב	נְכַתֵּב
Imp.	*m.*	כַּתֵּב	כַּתְּבוּ
	f.	כַּתְּבִי	כַּתֵּבְנָה
Coh.		אֲכַתְּבָה	
Juss.		יְכַתֵּב	
Inf. cs.		כַּתֵּב	
Inf. Abs.		כַּתֵּב / כַּתּוֹב	
Part.		מְכַתֵּב	

(ii) The most important *morphological features of the Piel* are:

a. The doubling of the second stem consonant (כִּתֵּב, יְכַתֵּב).

b. In the perfect the stem vowel of the first syllable is / - / (כִּתֵּב).

c. In the perfect 3 masculine singular the second stem vowel is usually / - / (כִּתֵּב), but it may sometimes also be / - / (לִמַּד). In the rest of the perfect paradigm it is / - / (כִּתַּבְנוּ).

- Before vocalic suffixes the second stem vowel reduces to / - / (כִּתְּבוּ).
- Before consonantal suffixes the vowel pattern is / - - / (כִּתַּבְנוּ).

d. In the imperfect the preformative vowel is / ֵ / (תִּכְתֹּב) and the vowel
pattern is / ִ ְ ֹ / (יִכְתֹּב).

- Before vocalic suffixes the second stem vowel reduces to / ְ /
(תִּכְתְּבוּ).
- Before consonantal suffixes the vowel pattern remains / ִ ְ ֹ /
(תִּכְתֹּבְנָה).

e. In the imperfect 1 common singular the preformative vowel is
/ ֶ / (אֶכְתֹּב) and not / ֵ /.

f. In the imperative and the infinitive construct the vowel pattern is
/ ְ ֹ /(כְּתֹב).

g. In the participle the preformative is -מְ (מְכַתֵּב).

2. Semantics

All the verbs that occur in the Qal stem formation do not necessarily
have conjugations in the Piel. Similarly all the verbs occurring in the
Piel stem formation do not necessarily have conjugations in the Qal,
e.g. דִּבֶּר (he spoke) and בִּקֵּשׁ (he sought). Should a verb occur both in
the Qal and the Piel, there may be a correspondence of meaning.
However, the nature of this correspondence differs from case to
case.

(i) *Factitive*

In some cases the Piel is used to express the factitive/causative sense
of verbs that occur in the Qal. The Piel indicates the cause that
places an object in the condition to which the Qal form (with a stative meaning) of the same stem refers, e.g.

וְאִם־בְּנֵי עַמּוֹן יֶחֶזְקוּ מִמְּךָ	Qal: And if the Ammonites *are* too *strong* for you (2 Sam. 10.11).
אֲשֶׁר־חִזְּקוּ אֶת־יָדָיו לַהֲרֹג אֶת־אֶחָיו׃	Piel: who *strengthened* his hands to slay his brothers (Judg. 9.24)

Note that the Hiphil also has a causative function. However, it differs from that of the Piel. (Cf. §16.7/2.)

(ii) *Resultative*

The Qal may describe the verb as a process that occurs, while the
Piel describes the result of that process.

אִם פָּרַשְׂתָּ אֵלָיו כַּפֶּךָ	Qal: If you *stretch out* your hands to-ward him (Job 11.13).
פֵּרַשְׂתִּי יָדַי כָּל־הַיּוֹם	Piel: I *spread out* my hands all the day (Isa. 65.2).

The nature of this semantic difference between the Qal and Piel form of a verb is difficult to determine and is sometimes difficult to reflect in English.

(iii) *Denominative*

The Piel refers to the action of the official referred to in the noun with the same stem consonants, for example, the verb כֹּהֵן (he was a priest) refers to the action of the official to which the noun כֹּהֵן (priest) refers. (Cf. also Waltke and O'Connor §24.4.)

וְכִהֵן לִי He may serve me *as priest* (Exod. 40.13).

The Piel must be regarded as an *independent stem formation*, the meaning of which must be determined independently. There may be a similarity with Qal, but this cannot be taken for granted.

§16.5. *Morphology and Semantics of the Pual*

1. *Morphology*

(i) Table 4. *The paradigm of the Pual*

PUAL				
		Singular		*Plural*
Perf.	3 m.	כֻּתַּב		כֻּתְּבוּ
	3 f.	כֻּתְּבָה		כֻּתְּבוּ
	2 m.	כֻּתַּבְתָּ		כֻּתַּבְתֶּם
	2 f.	כֻּתַּבְתְּ		כֻּתַּבְתֶּן
	1	כֻּתַּבְתִּי		כֻּתַּבְנוּ
Impf.	3 m.	יְכֻתַּב		יְכֻתְּבוּ
	3 f.	תְּכֻתַּב		תְּכֻתַּבְנָה
	2 m.	תְּכֻתַּב		תְּכֻתְּבוּ
	2 f.	תְּכֻתְּבִי		תְּכֻתַּבְנָה
	1	אֲכֻתַּב		נְכֻתַּב
Juss.		יְכֻתַּב		
Inf. cs.				
Inf. abs.		כֻּתַּב		
Part.		מְכֻתָּב		

(ii) The most important *morphological features of the Pual* are:

a. The doubling of the second stem consonant and the vowel / ֻ / below the first consonant of the stem (יְכֻתַּב‎, כֻּתַּב‎).

b. In the perfect the vowel pattern is / ֻ ַ / (כֻּתַּב‎).

c. In the imperfect the vowel pattern is / ְ ֻ ַ / (יְכֻתַּב‎).

> • With consonantal suffixes the / ְ ֻ ַ / pattern is retained (תְּכֻתַּבְנָה‎), but with vocalic suffixes the / ַ / changes to / ְ / (תְּכֻתְּבוּ‎).

d. No imperative forms occur in the Pual.

e. In the participle the prefix is מְ‎ and the vowel pattern / ֻ ָ / (מְכֻתָּב‎).

Note that 40% of all Pual forms in the Hebrew Bible are *participles*.

2. *Semantics*

(i) The Pual is in all respects the *passive of the Piel*.

וַיְבַקְשׁוּ שְׁלֹשָׁה־יָמִים וְלֹא מְצָאֻהוּ	Piel: For three days they *sought* him, but did not find him (2 Kgs 2.17).
וַיְבֻקַּשׁ הַדָּבָר	Pual: When the *affair was investigated*, ... (Est. 2.23).

(ii) In certain cases the *passive voice of the Piel* may be expressed by the Niphal.

כָּבְדָה מְאֹד יַד הָאֱלֹהִים שָׁם	Qal: The hand of God *was* very *heavy* there (1 Sam. 5.11).
כִּי־מְכַבְּדַי אֲכַבֵּד	Piel: For I *will honour* those who honour me (1 Sam. 2.30).
וְעַל־פְּנֵי כָל־הָעָם אֶכָּבֵד	Niphal: And I will *be glorified* before all the people (Lev. 10.3).

§16.6. *Morphology and Semantics of the Hithpael*

1. *Morphology*

(i) Table 5. *The paradigm of the Hithpael*

HITHPAEL			
		Singular	Plural
Perf.	3 m.	הִתְכַּתֵּב	הִתְכַּתְּבוּ
	3 f.	הִתְכַּתְּבָה	הִתְכַּתְּבוּ
	2 m.	הִתְכַּתַּבְתָּ	הִתְכַּתַּבְתֶּם
	2 f.	הִתְכַּתַּבְתְּ	הִתְכַּתַּבְתֶּן
	1	הִתְכַּתַּבְתִּי	הִתְכַּתַּבְנוּ

HITHPAEL			
		Singular	*Plural*
Impf.	3 m.	יִתְכַּתֵּב	יִתְכַּתְּבוּ
	3 f.	תִּתְכַּתֵּב	תִּתְכַּתֵּבְנָה
	2 m.	תִּתְכַּתֵּב	תִּתְכַּתְּבוּ
	2 f.	תִּתְכַּתְּבִי	תִּתְכַּתֵּבְנָה
	1	אֶתְכַּתֵּב	נִתְכַּתֵּב
Imp.	m.	הִתְכַּתֵּב	הִתְכַּתְּבוּ
	f.	הִתְכַּתְּבִי	הִתְכַּתֵּבְנָה
Coh.		אֶתְכַּתְּבָה	
Juss.		יִתְכַּתֵּב	
Inf. cs.		הִתְכַּתֵּב	
Inf. Abs.		הִתְכַּתֵּב	
Part.		מִתְכַּתֵּב	

(ii) The most important *morphological features of the Hithpael* are:

a. The doubling of the middle stem consonant and the preformative -תְ-
throughout all its conjugations (הִתְכַּתֵּב).

b. In the perfect the preformative -הִת (הִתְכַּתֵּב).

c. In the perfect the vowel pattern is / -ַ- / (הִתְכַּתֵּב).
   - Before consonantal suffixes the / -ַ / changes to / -ַ / (הִתְכַּתַּבְנוּ).
   - Before vocalic suffixes the / -ַ / is reduced to / - / (הִתְכַּתְּבוּ).

d. In the imperfect the preformative is -יִת (יִתְכַּתֵּב), -תִּת, (תִּתְכַּתֵּב) etc.

e. In the imperative the preformative is -הִת (הִתְכַּתֵּב).

f. In the participle the preformative is -מִת (מִתְכַּתֵּב).

Note the following:

(1) When a verb beginning with a sibilant is conjugated in the Hithpael, *metathesis* occurs between the sibilant and the ת of the הת / ית prefix, for example, הִתְשַׁמֵּר* becomes הִשְׁתַּמֵּר (guard yourself against or refrain from). (Cf. §4.2/5(i).)

(2) When the first stem consonant is צ, *metathesis* as well as assimilation takes place, for example, הִתְצַדֵּק becomes הִצְתַּדֵּק* as a result of *metathesis* and הִצְתַּדֵּק* becomes הִצְטַדֵּק (justify yourself) as a result of assimilation. (Cf. §4.2/4(ii).)

(3) When a verb beginning with a ת, ד or ט is conjugated in the Hithpael, the ת of the הת prefix assimilates, i.e. תְתְדַּבֵּר* becomes תִדַּבֵּר.

(4) Other patterns of the Hithpael also occur without another stem formation being constituted, e.g. Hithpoel, Hithpalel, Hithpolal, Hithpalpel. (Cf. Waltke and O'Connor §26.1.1.)

2. Semantics

(i) The Hithpael usually indicates a *reflexive or reciprocal* action.

וְהִתְקַדִּשְׁתֶּם וִהְיִיתֶם קְדֹשִׁים   *Consecrate yourselves* and be holy (Lev. 11.44).

(ii) The Hithpael also sometimes simply indicates *an active meaning* of the verb.

הִתְפַּלֵּל בְּעַד־עֲבָדֶיךָ   *Pray* for your servants (1 Sam. 12.19).

The Hithpael must be regarded as an *independent stem formation*, the meaning of which must be learned separately. (Cf. Waltke and O'Connor §26.2-4 and Joüon–Muraoka §53i.)

§16.7. *Morphology and Semantics of the Hiphil*

1. *Morphology*

(i) Table 6. *The paradigm of the Hiphil*

HIPHIL			
		Singular	*Plural*
Perf.	*3 m.*	הִכְתִּיב	הִכְתִּיבוּ
	3 f.	הִכְתִּיבָה	הִכְתִּיבוּ
	2 m.	הִכְתַּבְתָּ	הִכְתַּבְתֶּם
	2 f.	הִכְתַּבְתְּ	הִכְתַּבְתֶּן
	1	הִכְתַּבְתִּי	הִכְתַּבְנוּ
Impf.	*3 m.*	יַכְתִּיב	יַכְתִּיבוּ
	3 f.	תַּכְתִּיב	תַּכְתֵּבְנָה
	2 m.	תַּכְתִּיב	תַּכְתִּיבוּ
	2 f.	תַּכְתִּיבִי	תַּכְתֵּבְנָה
	1	אַכְתִּיב	נַכְתִּיב

HIPHIL			
		Singular	*Plural*
Imp.	m.	הַכְתֵּב	הַכְתִּיבוּ
	f.	הַכְתִּיבִי	הַכְתֵּבְנָה
Coh.		אַכְתִּיבָה	
Juss.		יַכְתֵּב	
Inf. cs.		הַכְתִּיב	
Inf. abs.		הַכְתֵּב	
Part.		מַכְתִּיב	

(ii) The most important *morphological features of the Hiphil* are:

a. In the perfect the prefix is הִ- (הִכְתִּיב). This prefix forms a closed syllable with the first stem consonant.

b. In the perfect the vowel pattern is / ִ - ִ - / (הִכְתִּיב).

  • With the vocalic suffixes the unchangeable long second vowel of the stem vowel, / ִי / (הִכְתִּיבָה), is retained.

  • With the consonantal suffixes, however, the second stem vowel is / ַ / (הִכְתַּבְתָּ).

c. In the imperfect the vowel of the preformative is / ַ /. The ה preformative, however, falls away completely (תַּכְתִּיב).

  • In the imperfect the vowel pattern is / ַ - ִ - / (תַּכְתִּיב).

  • With consonantal suffixes the stem vowel / ִי / changes to / ֵ / (תַּכְתֵּבְנָה).

  • With vowel suffixes the vowel pattern remains unaltered (תַּכְתִּיבוּ).

d. In the imperative feminine singular, masculine plural and feminine plural, and the infinitive construct the preformative is הַ- and the stem vowel / ִי / (הַכְתִּיב, הַכְתִּיבוּ).

e. In the infinitive absolute and imperative masculine singular the stem vowel is / ֵ / (הַכְתֵּב).

f. In the jussive form the stem vowel / ִי / changes to / ֵ / (תַּכְתֵּב). As opposed to the other stem formations, the shorter form of the jussive is thus always readily recognizable.

g. In the participle the preformative is מַ- and the stem vowel / ִי / (מַכְתִּיב).

Note the following: the Hiphil is the only stem formation in which the forms of the imperative masculine singular and the infinitive construct differ.

2. *Semantics*

(i) *Causative*

a. The Hiphil stem formation mostly indicates the *causative sense* of verbs occuring in the Qal. (Cf. Waltke and O'Connor §27 and Joüon–Muraoka §54.) In other words, the subject of the stem in the Hiphil causes the object of that verb to act as subject in the idea expressed by the stem.

וְאֵלֶּה אֲשֶׁר־נָחֲלוּ בְּנֵי־יִשְׂרָאֵל	Qal: These are the inheritances which the people of Israel *received* (Josh. 14.1).
כִּי אַתָּה תַּנְחִיל אֶת־הָעָם הַזֶּה אֶת־הָאָרֶץ	Hiphil: For you shall *cause* this people *to inherit* the land (Josh. 1.6).

In Josh. 1.6 'people' is grammatically the object of the Hiphil form of נחל. Semantically, however, it is also the subject or doer of the verb, i.e. it is the 'people' who inherit.

b. The Hiphil may also be used to express the causative of verbs that occur in the *Niphal*.

וַאֲשֶׁר נִשְׁבַּע־לִי	Niphal: And who *swore* to me (Gen. 24.7)
כַּאֲשֶׁר הִשְׁבִּיעֶךָ	Hiphil: As he *made* you *swear* (Gen. 50.6).

(ii) A causative link between the Qal and the Hiphil *cannot always be deduced from the translation* of a verb, for example, Qal: פָּקַד (he visited) *versus* Hiphil: הִפְקִיד (he appointed).

(iii) Some verbs occur *in the Hiphil*, without any conjugations in the Qal, e.g. הִשְׁלִיךְ (he threw), הִשְׁכִּים (he rose early) and הִשְׁמִיד (he eradicated).

Note the following:

(1) The factitive expressed by *the Piel* also has a *causative nuance*.

בְּנוֹ קִדְּשׁוּ	They consecrated his son [lit. *his son* they *caused to be holy*] (1 Sam. 7.1).

(2) When a verb is used in the Piel, it indicates an action that leads to an object ending up in a certain condition. That object does not *do* the action referred to by the verb.

The Hiphil must be regarded as an independent stem formation, the meaning of which must be learned separately.

§16.8. *Morphology and Semantics of the Hophal*

1. *Morphology*

(i) Table 7. *The paradigm of the Hophal*

HOPHAL		Singular	Plural
Perf.	3 m.	הָכְתַּב	הָכְתְּבוּ
	3 f.	הָכְתְּבָה	הָכְתְּבוּ
	2 m.	הָכְתַּבְתָּ	הָכְתַּבְתֶּם
	2 f.	הָכְתַּבְתְּ	הָכְתַּבְתֶּן
	1	הָכְתַּבְתִּי	הָכְתַּבְנוּ
Impf.	3 m.	יָכְתַּב	יָכְתְּבוּ
	3 f.	תָּכְתַּב	תָּכְתַּבְנָה
	2 m.	תָּכְתַּב	תָּכְתְּבוּ
	2 f.	תָּכְתְּבִי	תָּכְתַּבְנָה
	1	אָכְתַּב	נָכְתַּב
Imp.	m.		
	f.		
Coh.			
Juss.		יָכְתַּב	
Inf. cs.			
Inf. abs.		הָכְתֵּב	
Part.		מָכְתָּב	

(ii) The most important *morphological features of the Hophal* are:

a. In the perfect the preformative is -הָ. This prefix forms a closed syllable with the first stem consonant (הָכְתַּב).

b. In the perfect the vowel pattern is / ָ ַ / (הָכְתַּב).

- With vocalic suffixes the / ָ / changes to / ָ / (הָכְתְבוּ).

c. In the imperfect the vowel of the preformative is / ָ / (a qāmeṣ ḥaṭûp), but the preformative -הָ falls away (תָכְתַב, יָכְתַב).

d. In the imperfect the vowel pattern is / ָ ַ / (יָכְתַב).

- With vocalic suffixes the / ַ / changes to / ְ / (יָכְתְבוּ).

e. In the participle the prefix is -מָ and the stem vowel / ָ / (מָכְתָב).

2. Semantics

(i) The primary function of the Hophal stem formation is to express *the passive sense of the Hiphil.*

וַתַּשְׁכִּבֵהוּ בְּחֵיקָהּ	Hiphil: And *laid* him in her bosom (1 Kgs 3.20).
וְהֻשְׁכַּב בְּתוֹךְ עֲרֵלִים	Hophal: And he shall *be laid* among the uncircumcized (Ezek. 32.32).

(ii) In certain cases the passive sense of the Hiphil may be expressed *by the Niphal.*

אִם־לֹא תַשְׁמִידוּ הַחֵרֶם מִקִּרְבְּכֶם	Hiphil: ... Unless you *destroy* the devoted things from among you (Josh. 7.12).
וְנִשְׁמַדְתִּי אֲנִי וּבֵיתִי	Niphal: And I shall be destroyed, both I and my household (Gen. 34.30).

§16.9. Table 8. *The Stem Formations: the Complete Paradigm*

	QAL	NI.	PI.	PU.	HTP.	HI.	HO.
Sing.				*Perfect form*			
3 m.	כָּתַב	נִכְתַּב	כִּתֵּב	כֻּתַּב	הִתְכַּתֵּב	הִכְתִּיב	הָכְתַּב
3 f.	כָּתְבָה	נִכְתְּבָה	כִּתְּבָה	כֻּתְּבָה	הִתְכַּתְּבָה	הִכְתִּיבָה	הָכְתְּבָה
2 m.	כָּתַבְתָּ	נִכְתַּבְתָּ	כִּתַּבְתָּ	כֻּתַּבְתָּ	הִתְכַּתַּבְתָּ	הִכְתַּבְתָּ	הָכְתַּבְתָּ
2 f.	כָּתַבְתְּ	נִכְתַּבְתְּ	כִּתַּבְתְּ	כֻּתַּבְתְּ	הִתְכַּתַּבְתְּ	הִכְתַּבְתְּ	הָכְתַּבְתְּ
1 c.	כָּתַבְתִּי	נִכְתַּבְתִּי	כִּתַּבְתִּי	כֻּתַּבְתִּי	הִתְכַּתַּבְתִּי	הִכְתַּבְתִּי	הָכְתַּבְתִּי
Pl.							
3 c.	כָּתְבוּ	נִכְתְּבוּ	כִּתְּבוּ	כֻּתְּבוּ	הִתְכַּתְּבוּ	הִכְתִּיבוּ	הָכְתְּבוּ
2 m.	כְּתַבְתֶּם	נִכְתַּבְתֶּם	כִּתַּבְתֶּם	כֻּתַּבְתֶּם	הִתְכַּתַּבְתֶּם	הִכְתַּבְתֶּם	הָכְתַּבְתֶּם

	QAL	NI.	PI.	PU.	HTP.	HI.	HO.
Pl.	Perfect form						
2 f.	כְּתַבְתֶּן	נִכְתַּבְתֶּן	כִּתַּבְתֶּן	כֻּתַּבְתֶּן	הִתְכַּתַּבְתֶּן	הִכְתַּבְתֶּן	הָכְתַּבְתֶּן
1 c.	כָּתַבְנוּ	נִכְתַּבְנוּ	כִּתַּבְנוּ	כֻּתַּבְנוּ	הִתְכַּתַּבְנוּ	הִכְתַּבְנוּ	הָכְתַּבְנוּ
Sing.	Imperfect form						
3 m.	יִכְתֹּב	יִכָּתֵב	יְכַתֵּב	יְכֻתַּב	יִתְכַּתֵּב	יַכְתִּיב	יָכְתַּב
3 f.	תִּכְתֹּב	תִּכָּתֵב	תְּכַתֵּב	תְּכֻתַּב	תִּתְכַּתֵּב	תַּכְתִּיב	תָּכְתַּב
2 m.	תִּכְתֹּב	תִּכָּתֵב	תְּכַתֵּב	תְּכֻתַּב	תִּתְכַּתֵּב	תַּכְתִּיב	תָּכְתַּב
2 f.	תִּכְתְּבִי	תִּכָּתְבִי	תְּכַתְּבִי	תְּכֻתְּבִי	תִּתְכַּתְּבִי	תַּכְתִּיבִי	תָּכְתְּבִי
1 c.	אֶכְתֹּב	אֶכָּתֵב	אֲכַתֵּב	אֲכֻתַּב	אֶתְכַּתֵּב	אַכְתִּיב	אָכְתַּב
Pl.							
3 m.	יִכְתְּבוּ	יִכָּתְבוּ	יְכַתְּבוּ	יְכֻתְּבוּ	יִתְכַּתְּבוּ	יַכְתִּיבוּ	יָכְתְּבוּ
3 f.	תִּכְתֹּבְנָה	תִּכָּתַבְנָה	תְּכַתֵּבְנָה	תְּכֻתַּבְנָה	תִּתְכַּתֵּבְנָה	תַּכְתֵּבְנָה	תָּכְתַּבְנָה
2 m.	תִּכְתְּבוּ	תִּכָּתְבוּ	תְּכַתְּבוּ	תְּכֻתְּבוּ	תִּתְכַּתְּבוּ	תַּכְתִּיבוּ	תָּכְתְּבוּ
2 f.	תִּכְתֹּבְנָה	תִּכָּתַבְנָה	תְּכַתֵּבְנָה	תְּכֻתַּבְנָה	תִּתְכַּתֵּבְנָה	תַּכְתֵּבְנָה	תָּכְתַּבְנָה
1.	נִכְתֹּב	נִכָּתֵב	נְכַתֵּב	נְכֻתַּב	נִתְכַּתֵּב	נַכְתִּיב	נָכְתַּב
Sing.	Imperative form						
2 m.	כְּתֹב	הִכָּתֵב	כַּתֵּב		הִתְכַּתֵּב	הַכְתֵּב	
2 f.	כִּתְבִי	הִכָּתְבִי	כַּתְּבִי		הִתְכַּתְּבִי	הַכְתִּיבִי	
Pl.							
2 m.	כִּתְבוּ	הִכָּתְבוּ	כַּתְּבוּ		הִתְכַּתְּבוּ	הַכְתִּיבוּ	
2 f	כְּתֹבְנָה	הִכָּתַבְנָה	כַּתֵּבְנָה		הִתְכַּתֵּבְנָה	הַכְתֵּבְנָה	
Sing.	Cohortative form						
1.	אֶכְתְּבָה	אֶכָּתְבָה	אֲכַתְּבָה		אֶתְכַּתְּבָה	אַכְתִּיבָה	
Sing.	Jussive form						
3 m.	יִכְתֹּב	יִכָּתֵב	יְכַתֵּב	יְכֻתַּב	יִתְכַּתֵּב	יַכְתֵּב	יָכְתַּב
	Infinitive						
cs.	כְּתֹב	הִכָּתֵב	כַּתֵּב		הִתְכַּתֵּב	הַכְתִּיב	
abs.	כָּתוֹב	נִכְתֹּב	כַּתֵּב	כֻּתֹּב	הִתְכַּתֵּב	הַכְתֵּב	הָכְתֵּב

	QAL	NI.	PI.	PU.	HTP.	HI.	HO.
	Participle						
act.	כֹּתֵב	נִכְתָּב	מְכַתֵּב		מִתְכַּתֵּב	מַכְתִּיב	
pass.	כָּתוּב			מְכֻתָּב			מָכְתָּב

§17. Pronominal Suffixes Added to Verbs

§17.1. *Introduction*

In BH the definite object of a clause is usually preceded by the so-called accusative/object marker אֵת/אֶת־. Should this object be pronominalized, i.e. should the noun be replaced with a pronoun, the pronoun may be added either to the אֵת or to the verb of the clause. These two forms are variants and there is no difference in meaning between them.

וְהִכְרַתִּי **אֹתוֹ** מִקֶּרֶב עַמּוֹ	And I will cut *him* off from among his people (Lev. 20.4).
וְהִכְרַתִּיו מִתּוֹךְ עַמִּי	And I will cut *him* off from the midst of my people (Ezek. 14.8).

There is basically one set of suffixes that is added to the perfect, imperfect and imperative. This set of suffixes, which is used in all stem formations, appears in the table below:

1 sing.	נִי-	me	*1 pl.*	נוּ-	us
2 m. sing.	ךָ-	you	*2 m. pl.*	כֶם-	you
2 f. sing.	ךְ-	you	*2 f. pl.*	כֶן-	you
3 m. sing.	הוּ- \ וֹ	him	*3 m. pl.*	ם- / הֶם-	them
3 f. sing.	הָ- \ הָ- / הָ-	her	*3 f. pl.*	ן- / הֶן-	them

The addition of the pronominal suffixes to verbs results in accent shifts and vowel changes within the verbs.

The following variables must be taken into account:

(a) Whether the verbs end in a consonant or a vowel.

(b) Verbs that end in consonants take a connecting vowel.

(c) Perfect forms take / ֵ / or / ַ / and imperfect as well as imperative forms take / $\dot{}$ / or / $\dot{}$ / as the connecting vowel. The suffixes כֶם-, כֶן- and ךָ-, however, do not take a connecting vowel.

(d) Suffixes are light or heavy. The heavy consonantal suffixes כֶם-, כֶן-, הֶם- and הֶן- always attract the accent to themselves resulting in the reduction of the changeable long vowels in preceding syllables.

(e) The so-called 'energic' nun suffix sometimes occurs with imperfect forms and imperatives. It has no semantic value.

§17.2. *Suffixes Added to Perfect Forms (Cf. §15.1.)*

1. *Perfect forms ending in vowels*

(i) List of forms

a. The following perfect forms *usually* end in a vowel:

שָׁמַרְתִּי , שָׁמְרוּ , שָׁמַרְנוּ

b. The following perfect forms *are adapted* to end in a vowel:

- The תְּ ending of the 2 feminine singular becomes תִּי, i.e. שָׁמַרְתִּי instead of שָׁמַרְתְּ. This form thus has the same appearance as the 1 singular.

- The final nun and mem of the 2 feminine and masculine plural fall away and the / $\dot{}$ / is replaced with וּ, for example, שְׁמַרְתּוּ instead of שְׁמַרְתֶּם and שְׁמַרְתֶּן.

c. The following perfect forms *usually* end in a vowel *but are adapted* to end in a consonant:

- The הָ- ending of the 3 feminine singular is replaced by ת-. Normal vowel changes that accompany the addition of an element such as a suffix occur, for example, שְׁמָרַת- instead of שָׁמְרָה.

- The תָּ- ending of the 2 masculine singular contracts to תְּ-, for example, שְׁמַרְתְּ- instead of שָׁמַרְתָּ.

(ii) The most general *vowel changes*

a. When one of the pronominal suffixes is added to a perfect that ends in a vowel, the / $\dot{}$ / in the first open syllable is reduced to / $\dot{}$ /, e.g.

שָׁמַרְנוּ plus suffix is: -שְׁמַרְנוּ

b. If the second syllable is open, the original stem vowel / ִ / is revived and changes to / ָ /, e.g.

שָׁמְרוּ plus suffix is: ‑שְׁמָרוּ

c. If the first syllable is closed, its vowel does not change, e.g.

בְּקֶשׁוּנִי

d. If there is an unchangeable long vowel in the second open syllable, no vowel change occurs, e.g.

הִכְרִיתוּנִי

(iii) *Set of suffixes* that is added
The so-called basic set. (Cf. §17.1.)

2. *Perfect forms ending in consonants*

(i) *List* of forms

a. The following perfect forms *usually* end in a consonant:

שָׁמַר

b. The following perfect forms *are constructed* to end in a consonant:

- The הָ‑ ending of the 3 feminine singular is replaced by ‑תְ. Normal vowel changes which accompany the addition of an element such as a suffix occur, for example, שְׁמָרַת‑ instead of שָׁמְרָה.

- The תָּ‑ ending of the 2 masculine singular contracts to ‑תְּ, for example, שְׁמַרְתְּ‑ instead of שָׁמַרְתָּ.

(ii) The most basic *vowel changes*
The vowel changes are similar to those of the forms ending in vowels, e.g.

שָׁמַר plus suffix is: ‑שְׁמָר

(iii) *Set of suffixes* added to perfect forms ending in consonants

1 sing.	נִי‑	me	1 pl.	נוּ‑	us
2 m. sing.	ךָ‑	you	2 m. pl.	כֶם‑	you
2 f. sing.	ךְ‑ ךְ‑	you	2 f. pl.	כֶן‑	you
3 m. sing.	וֹ‑ / הוּ‑	him	3 m. pl.	ם‑	them
3 f. sing.	הָ‑	her	3 f. pl.	ן‑	them

3. *Summary of all the perfect forms to which pronominal suffixes can be added*

1 sing.	שְׁמַרְתִּי-	1 pl.	שְׁמַרְנוּ-
2 m. sing.	שְׁמַרְתָּ-	2 m. pl.	שְׁמַרְתּוּ-
2 f. sing.	שְׁמַרְתִּי-	2 f. pl.	שְׁמַרְתּוּ-
3 m. sing.	שְׁמָר-	3 m. pl.	שְׁמָרוּ-
3 f. sing.	שְׁמָרַת-	3 f. pl.	שְׁמָרוּ-

§17.3. *Suffixes Added to Imperfect Forms (Cf. §15.2.)*

1. *Imperfect forms ending in vowels*

(i) *List* of forms

Forms that normally end in a vowel:

תִּכְתֹּבְנָה, תִּכְתְּבוּ, יִכְתְּבוּ, תִּכְתְּבִי

(ii) The most basic *vowel changes*

Since the forms to which the suffixes are added contain virtually no changeable vowels, relatively few changes occur when the pronominal suffixes are added. Sometimes וּ is written as / ֻ /, e.g.

וַיְבַקֻשֵׁהוּ instead of וַיְבַקְשׁוּהוּ

(iii) *Set of suffixes* that may be added

This set is the same as the basic set in §17.1.

2. *Imperfect forms ending in consonants*

(i) *List* of forms

Forms that *usually* end in a consonant:

נִכְתֹּב, אֶכְתֹּב, תִּכְתֹּב, יִכְתֹּב

(ii) The most general *vowel changes*

a. The changeable stem vowel, / ֹ / changes to a šᵉwâ in open syllables, e.g.

יִשְׁמְרֵנִי instead of יִשְׁמֹרֵנִי

b. Before the suffixes -ךָ, -כֶם and -כֶן the / ֹ / changes to / ָ /, e.g.

יִשְׁמָרְכֶם instead of יִשְׁמֹרְכֶם

(iii) Set of suffixes *added to imperfect forms ending in consonants*
This set looks virtually like the set given in §17.2/2(iii). The connecting vowels here, however, are / ֶ / and / ֵ /. A partial *set of variant suffixes* also exists in which a nun is inserted between the basic set and the verb. The nun always assimilates with the suffix. The following two sets of suffixes may thus be added to imperfect forms ending in consonants:

1 sing.	נִי֝	נִּ֝י	1 pl.	נוּ֝	נוּ֝
2 m. sing.	ךָ֝	ךְָּ	2 m. pl.	כֶם֝	
2 f. sing.	ךְ֝		2 f. pl.	כֶן֝	
3 m. sing.	הוּ֝	נּוּ֝	3 m. pl.	ם֝	
3 f. sing.	הָ֝ ‏ הָ֝	נָּה֝	3 f. pl.	ן֝	

Note the following:

(1) The unusual dagesh in the kaph of the 2 masculine singular, ךְָּ, reflects the nun that has assimilated with the 2 masculine singular suffix.

(2) The 3 masculine singular and the 1 plural of the alternative suffixes with the assimilated nun look alike.

(3) These suffixes are not added to imperfect forms prefixed with the waw consecutive.

(4) In poetry the pronominal suffixes מוֹ- and מוֹ- are sometimes used for the 3 masculine plural.

(5) A connecting syllable with a nun (the energic nun) is sometimes placed before the singular suffixes, e.g. יַעֲבְרֶנְהוּ (Jer. 5.22).

§17.4. *Suffixes Added to Imperative Forms (Cf. §15.3.)*

Since the form of the imperative is derived from the imperfect, the imperative takes the same connecting vowels and undergoes the same vowel changes as the imperfect forms.

Note however that the masculine singular form to which the suffix is added is קָטְל and not קְטֹל.

§17.5. *Suffixes Added to Infinitives (Cf. §15.5.)*

The infinitive construct takes the set of pronominal suffixes normally added to nouns, namely:

1 sing.	־ִי	me	*1 pl.*	־ֵנוּ	us
2 m. sing.	־ְךָ	you	*2 m. pl.*	־ְכֶם	you
2 f. sing.	־ֵךְ	you	*2 f. pl.*	־ְכֶן	you
3 m. sing.	־וֹ	him	*3 m. pl.*	־ָם	them
3 f. sing.	־ָהּ	her	*3 f. pl.*	־ָן	them

Note the following:

(1) The *verbal* suffix is used only in the first person, e.g. קָטְלֵנִי (to kill me) and קָטְלִי (my killing).

(2) The form of the infinitive to which suffixes are added is קָטְל־ and not קְטֹל.

(3) Sometimes the form of the infinitive to which suffixes are added is קְטֹל־, e.g. נִפְלוֹ (2 Sam. 1.10). At other times the form is קָטָל־ and not קָטְל־, e.g. אָכָלְךָ (Gen. 2.17).

§18. The Morphology of the Irregular (or Weak) Verbs

§18.1. *The Notation of Irregular Verbs*

Irregular or weak verbs are verbs that deviate in their conjugations from the pattern of the regular or strong verb which has been dealt with so far (§16). The deviations occur only in certain groups of verbs. Even so weak verbs do not conjugate erratically, but according to rules determined by the phonetic features of one or more of their stem consonants. The following system of notation has been introduced when referring to specific types of the weak verb:

The three consonants that comprise most of the verb roots in BH are numbered from right to left either with the consonants of the פעל verb stem or with Roman numerals. The position of a weak consonant as the first, second of third consonant of a particular verb stem is indicated either by means of the consonants פעל or by means of a Roman numeral, e.g.

	TRADITIONAL VERB SYSTEM			MODERN ALTERNATIVE			
ל	ע	פ	*Verb stem*	III	II	I	*Numerical*
ר	מ	ע	pe guttural	ר	מ	ע	I guttural
ל	א	שׁ	ayin guttural	ל	א	שׁ	II guttural
ח	ל	שׁ	lamedh guttural	ח	ל	שׁ	III guttural
ל	כ	א	pe aleph	ל	כ	א	I aleph
א	צ	מ	lamedh aleph	א	צ	מ	III aleph
ה	נ	ב	lamedh he	ה	נ	ב	III he
ל	פ	נ	pe nun	ל	פ	נ	I nun
כ	שׁ	י	pe waw / pe yod	כ	שׁ	י	I waw / I yod
ם	ו	ק	ayin waw	ם	ו	ק	II waw
ם	י	שׁ	ayin yod	ם	י	שׁ	II yod
ב	ב	ס	ayin ayin	ב	ב	ס	Double II or geminate

Hes and alephs, which are not pronounced, behave differently from the other gutturals. (Cf. §4.2/5(ii) and 5.2/2.) He in position III is not usually pronounced while aleph is not pronounced in positions I and III. For this reason a distinction is made between aleph and he as gutturals and:

- I aleph -,
- III aleph -,
- III he verbs.

Resh, which is not a guttural, reacts like a guttural, whether in positions I, II or III. (Cf. §4.2/4.)

It often happens that a verb stem has two irregular consonants, e.g.

נָכָה (he hit)

There are also a few verbs that occur frequently and which are irregular in all respects. The way in which they conjugate cannot be determined solely by the phonetic features of their particular consonants.

היה (is), חיה (live), חוה (bend), נתן (give), לקח (take) and הלך (go).

§18.2. *The Gutturals*[13]

1. *General rules that apply to gutturals*

a. After gutturals audible šᵉwâs are replaced by ḥāṭēp vowels. (Cf. §5.2/2(iii).)

עֲמֹד	instead of	עְמֹד
שָׁחֲטוּ	instead of	שָׁחְטוּ

b. A guttural may be followed by a silent šᵉwâ which is often replaced by a ḥāṭēp vowel corresponding to the preceding full vowel. (Cf. §8.1/2.)

הֶעֱמִיד	instead of	הֶעְמִיד
יַעֲמֹד	instead of	יַעְמֹד

c. Gutturals and resh (normally) cannot be doubled. If a guttural is supposed to be doubled, '*compensatory lengthening*' often occurs in the preceding syllable. (Cf. §8.2/2.)

בֵּרֵךְ	instead of	בֶּרֵךְ
יְבָרֵךְ	instead of	יְבַרֵךְ
בֹּחַר	instead of	בֹּחֵר

2. *I Guttural*

(i) Table 9. *I Guttural*

	QAL	QAL	NI.	HI.	HO.
Gloss	stand	become strong			
Sing.	*Perfect form*				
3 m.	עָמַד	חָזַק	נֶעֱמַד	הֶעֱמִיד	הָעֳמַד
3 f.	עָמְדָה	חָזְקָה	נֶעֶמְדָה	הֶעֱמִידָה	הָעֳמְדָה
2 m.	עָמַדְתָּ	normal	נֶעֱמַדְתָּ	הֶעֱמַדְתָּ	הָעֳמַדְתָּ
2 f.	עָמַדְתְּ		נֶעֱמַדְתְּ	הֶעֱמַדְתְּ	הָעֳמַדְתְּ
1 c.	עָמַדְתִּי		נֶעֱמַדְתִּי	הֶעֱמַדְתִּי	הָעֳמַדְתִּי
Pl.					
3 c.	עָמְדוּ		נֶעֶמְדוּ	הֶעֱמִידוּ	הָעֳמְדוּ
2 m.	עֲמַדְתֶּם		נֶעֱמַדְתֶּם	הֶעֱמַדְתֶּם	הָעֳמַדְתֶּם

13. For a more complete description of the morphology of the gutturals, cf. Joüon–Muraoka §67-70.

	QAL	QAL	NI.	HI.	HO.
Pl.			*Perfect form*		
2 f.	עֲמַדְתֶּן		נֶעֱמַדְתֶּן	הׇעֳמַדְתֶּן	הׇעֳמַדְתֶּן
1 c.	עָמַדְנוּ		נֶעֱמַדְנוּ	הֶעֱמַדְנוּ	הׇעֳמַדְנוּ
Sing.			*Imperfect form*		
3 m.	יַעֲמֹד	יֶחֱזַק	יֵעָמֵד	יַעֲמִיד	יׇעֳמַד
3 f.	תַּעֲמֹד	תֶּחֱזַק	תֵּעָמֵד	תַּעֲמִיד	תׇּעֳמַד
2 m.	תַּעֲמֹד	תֶּחֱזַק	תֵּעָמֵד	תַּעֲמִיד	תׇּעֳמַד
2 f.	תַּעַמְדִי	תֶּחֶזְקִי	תֵּעָמְדִי	תַּעֲמִידִי	תׇּעֳמְדִי
1 c.	אֶעֱמֹד	אֶחֱזַק	אֵעָמֵד	אַעֲמִיד	אׇעֳמַד
Pl.					
3 c.	יַעַמְדוּ	יֶחֶזְקוּ	יֵעָמְדוּ	יַעֲמִידוּ	יׇעׇמְדוּ
3 f.	תַּעֲמֹדְנָה	תֶּחֱזַקְנָה	תֵּעָמַדְנָה	תַּעֲמֵדְנָה	תׇּעֳמַדְנָה
2 m.	תַּעַמְדוּ	תֶּחֶזְקוּ	תֵּעָמְדוּ	תַּעֲמִידוּ	תׇּעׇמְדוּ
2 f.	תַּעֲמֹדְנָה	תֶּחֱזַקְנָה	תֵּעָמַדְנָה	תַּעֲמֵדְנָה	תׇּעֳמַדְנָה
1 c.	נַעֲמֹד	נֶחֱזַק	נֵעָמֵד	נַעֲמִיד	נׇעֳמַד
Sing.			*Imperative form*		
2 m.	עֲמֹד	חֲזַק	הֵעָמֵד	הַעֲמֵד	
2 f.	עִמְדִי	חִזְקִי	הֵעָמְדִי	הַעֲמִידִי	
Pl.					
2 m.	עִמְדוּ	חִזְקוּ	הֵעָמְדוּ	הַעֲמִידוּ	
2 f.	עֲמֹדְנָה	חֲזַקְנָה	הֵעָמַדְנָה	הַעֲמֵדְנָה	
Sing.			*Cohortative form*		
	אֶעֱמִידָה			אַעֲמִידָה	
Sing.			*Jussive form*		
	יַעֲמֹד	יֶחֱזַק		יַעֲמֵד	
			Infinitive		
cs.	עֲמֹד	חֲזֹק	הֵעָמֵד	הַעֲמִיד	הׇעֳמֵד
abs.	עָמוֹד	חָזוֹק	נַעֲמוֹד	הַעֲמֵד	הׇעֳמֵד
			Participle		
act.	עֹמֵד	חָזֵק	נֶעֱמָד	מַעֲמִיד	מׇעֳמָד
pass.	עָמוּד				

(ii) *Qal*

a. In the perfect most conjugations are like those of the strong verbs. The only difference is that the audible š°wâ under the guttural becomes a ḥāṭep vowel in the 2 masculine and feminine plural. (Cf. §5.2/2(iii).)

עֲמַדְתֶּן   instead of   עְמַדְתֶּן

b. In the imperfect

· the preformative vowel of the imperfect, / ṣ /, is replaced with / ṣ /

יַעֲמֹד   instead of   יַעְמֹד

· and the silent š°wâ after the I guttural is always replaced by a ḥāṭep vowel.

יַעֲמֹד   instead of   יַעְמֹד

· When a vocalic suffix is added, the final stem vowel is reduced. As a result, a hypothetical form arises in which the ḥāṭep vowel is followed by an audible š°wâ. The ḥāṭep vowel and the audible š°wâ then fuse (into one syllable with the full vowel corresponding to the ḥāṭep).

יַעַמְדוּ   instead of   יַעֲמְדוּ

· In the first person the / ṣ / is retained. It is not replaced with / ṣ /.

אֶעֱמֹד   instead of   אֶעְמֹד

c. In verbs beginning with ח the vowel of the preformative is / ṣ / and not / ṣ /. The ḥāṭep, which replaces the silent š°wâ after the guttural in some cases, is then a ḥāṭep s°gōl.

יֶחֱזַק   instead of   יַחְזַק

d. In some I aleph verbs, for example, אהב and אסף, the vowel of the preformative is / ṣ / instead of / ṣ /.

יֶאֱסֹף   instead of   יַאְסֹף

· If a vocalic suffix is added to these forms in the imperfect, the / ṣ / becomes a / ṣ /. In the process the / ṣ / vowel of the preformative also assimilates into a / ṣ /. In other words, the following process occurs: יַאֶסְפוּ > יֶאֱסְפוּ > יֶאַסְפוּ.

יַאַסְפוּ   instead of   יֶאַסְפוּ

(iii) *Niphal*

a. In the perfect the preformative is -נֶ and not -נִ. A ḥāṭēp segōl sometimes occurs in the place of the silent šᵉwâ after the guttural.

נֶעֱמַד   instead of   נִעְמַד

- When a vocalic suffix is added the last stem vowel is reduced. A hypothetical form is then created in which the ḥāṭēp vowel is followed by an audible šᵉwâ. The ḥāṭēp vowel and the audible šᵉwâ then fuse (into a single syllable with the full vowel of the ḥāṭēp). Here it is a segōl.

נֶעֶמְדוּ   instead of   נֶעֱמְדוּ

b. In the imperfect and imperative the vowel of the preformative / ִ / changes to / ֵ / as a result of 'compensatory lengthening'. (Cf. §8.2/2.) The vowel pattern is then / ֵ ֲ ֵ /.

יֵעֲמֵד   instead of   יִעְמֵד

הֵעָמֵד   instead of   הִעְמֵד

(iv) *Piel, Pual and Hitpael*

I guttural verb stems in these stem formations are conjugated like regular verb stems.

(v) *Hiphil*

a. In the perfect

- the vowel of the preformative is / ֶ / and not / ִ /.

הֶעֱמִיד   instead of   הִעְמִיד

- A ḥāṭēp segōl occurs in the place of the silent šᵉwâ after the guttural.

הֶעֱמִיד   instead of   הֶעְמִיד

b. In the imperfect

- the vowel of the preformative (/ ַ /) is the same as that of the strong verbs (תַּעֲמִיד).
- A ḥāṭēp pataḥ sometimes occurs instead of the silent šᵉwâ after the guttural.

תַּעֲמִיד   instead of   תַּעְמִיד

(vi) *Hophal*

In the perfect and the imperfect the vowel of the preformative / ָ / is the same as that of the strong verb verbs, but a ḥāṭēp qāmeṣ occurs instead of the silent šᵉwâ after the guttural.

הָעֳמַד instead of הָעֲמַד

יָעֳמַד instead of יַעֲמַד

3. *II Guttural*

(i) Table 10. *II Guttural*

	QAL	NI.	PI.	PU.	HTP.
Gloss	slaughter		bless		
Sing.			*Perfect form*		
3 m.	שָׁחַט	נִשְׁחַט	בֵּרַךְ	בֹּרַךְ	הִתְבָּרַךְ
3 f.	שָׁחֲטָה	נִשְׁחֲטָה	בֵּרְכָה	בֹּרְכָה	הִתְבָּרְכָה
2 m.	שָׁחַטְתָּ	נִשְׁחַטְתָּ	בֵּרַכְתָּ	בֹּרַכְתָּ	הִתְבָּרַכְתָּ
2 f.	שָׁחַטְתְּ	נִשְׁחַטְתְּ	בֵּרַכְתְּ	בֹּרַכְתְּ	הִתְבָּרַכְתְּ
1 c.	שָׁחַטְתִּי	נִשְׁחַטְתִּי	בֵּרַכְתִּי	בֹּרַכְתִּי	הִתְבָּרַכְתִּי
Pl.					
3 c.	שָׁחֲטוּ	נִשְׁחֲטוּ	בֵּרְכוּ	בֹּרְכוּ	הִתְבָּרְכוּ
2 m.	שְׁחַטְתֶּם	נִשְׁחַטְתֶּם	בֵּרַכְתֶּם	בֹּרַכְתֶּם	הִתְבָּרַכְתֶּם
2 f.	שְׁחַטְתֶּן	נִשְׁחַטְתֶּן	בֵּרַכְתֶּן	בֹּרַכְתֶּן	הִתְבָּרַכְתֶּן
1 c.	שָׁחַטְנוּ	נִשְׁחַטְנוּ	בֵּרַכְנוּ	בֹּרַכְנוּ	הִתְבָּרַכְנוּ
Sing.			*Imperfect form*		
3 m.	יִשְׁחַט	יִשָּׁחֵט	יְבָרֵךְ	יְבֹרַךְ	יִתְבָּרֵךְ
3 f.	תִּשְׁחַט	תִּשָּׁחֵט	תְּבָרֵךְ	תְּבֹרַךְ	תִּתְבָּרֵךְ
2 m.	תִּשְׁחַט	תִּשָּׁחֵט	תְּבָרֵךְ	תְּבֹרַךְ	תִּתְבָּרֵךְ
2 f.	תִּשְׁחֲטִי	תִּשָּׁחֲטִי	תְּבָרְכִי	תְּבֹרְכִי	תִּתְבָּרְכִי
1 c.	אֶשְׁחַט	אֶשָּׁחֵט	אֲבָרֵךְ	אֲבֹרַךְ	אֶתְבָּרֵךְ
Pl.					
3 c.	יִשְׁחֲטוּ	יִשָּׁחֲטוּ	יְבָרְכוּ	יְבֹרְכוּ	יִתְבָּרְכוּ
3 f.	תִּשְׁחַטְנָה	תִּשָּׁחַטְנָה	תְּבָרֵכְנָה	תְּבֹרַכְנָה	תִּתְבָּרֵכְנָה
2 m.	תִּשְׁחֲטוּ	תִּשָּׁחֲטוּ	תְּבָרְכוּ	תְּבֹרְכוּ	תִּתְבָּרְכוּ
2 f.	תִּשְׁחַטְנָה	תִּשָּׁחַטְנָה	תְּבָרֵכְנָה	תְּבֹרַכְנָה	תִּתְבָּרֵכְנָה
1 c.	נִשְׁחַט	נִשָּׁחֵט	נְבָרֵךְ	נְבֹרַךְ	נִתְבָּרֵךְ
Sing.			*Imperative form*		
2 m.	שְׁחַט	הִשָּׁחֵט	בָּרֵךְ		הִתְבָּרֵךְ
2 f.	שַׁחֲטִי	הִשָּׁחֲטִי	בָּרְכִי		הִתְבָּרְכִי
Pl.					
2 m.	שַׁחֲטוּ	הִשָּׁחֲטוּ	בָּרְכוּ		הִתְבָּרְכוּ
2 f.	שְׁחַטְנָה	הִשָּׁחַטְנָה	בָּרֵכְנָה		הִתְבָּרֵכְנָה

	QAL	*NI.*	*PI.*	*PU.*	*HTP.*
Sing.	*Cohortative form*				
	אֶשְׁחֲטָה	אֶשָּׁחֲטָה	אֲבָרְכָה		אֶתְבָּרְכָה
Sing.	*Jussive form*				
	יִשְׁחַט	יִשָּׁחֵט	יְבָרֵךְ		
	Infinitive				
cs.	שְׁחֹט	הִשָּׁחֵט	בָּרֵךְ		הִתְבָּרֵךְ
abs.	שָׁחוֹט	נִשְׁחוֹט	בָּרֵךְ		הִתְבָּרֵךְ
			בָּרֹךְ		
	Participle				
	שֹׁחֵט	נִשְׁחָט	מְבָרֵךְ	מְבֹרָךְ	מִתְבָּרֵךְ
act.	שָׁחוּט				
pass.					

(ii) *Qal*

a. In the perfect most of the conjugations are like those of the strong verbs. The only difference is that the audible / ֲ / under the guttural becomes a ḥāṭēp vowel with the vocalic suffixes.

  שָׁחֲטוּ instead of שָׁחְטוּ

b. In the imperfect the expected vowel after the guttural is replaced with a / ַ / in an accented closed syllable. The vowel pattern is then / ִ ַ ַ /.

  יִשְׁחַט instead of יִשְׁחֹט

c. The / ַ / after the infinitive is, however, retained.

  שְׁחַט instead of שְׁחֹט

d. In the inflection of the Qal imperative the / ֲ / shifts to a position after the first consonant.

  שַׁחֲטוּ instead of שְׁחֲטוּ

(iii) *Piel, Pual and Hitpael*

In the II guttural and II resh verbs the middle consonant (normally) cannot double and 'compensatory lengthening' occurs.

- In the Piel perfect the / ִ / changes to a / ֵ / and the vowel pattern is / ֵ ַ /.

  בֵּרַךְ instead of בִּרַךְ

- In the Piel imperfect the / ֱ / changes to a / ֲ / and the vowel pattern is / ְ ֲ ֵ /.

       יְבָרֵךְ   instead of   יְבַרֵךְ

- In the Pual perfect the / ֻ / changes to a / ֳ / and the vowel pattern is / ֹ ַ /.

       בֹּרַךְ   instead of   בֻּרַךְ

(iv) *Hiphil and Hophal*

The II guttural verbs conjugate like the strong verbs.

4. *III Guttural*

(i) Table 11. *III Guttural*

	QAL	NI.	PI.	PU.	HTP.	HI.	HO.
Gloss	send						
Sing.				*Perfect form*			
3 m.	שָׁלַח	נִשְׁלַח	שִׁלַּח	שֻׁלַּח	הִתְפַּתַּח	הִשְׁלִיחַ	הָשְׁלַח
3 f.	שָׁלְחָה	נִשְׁלְחָה	שִׁלְּחָה	שֻׁלְּחָה	הִתְפַּתְּחָה	הִשְׁלִיחָה	הָשְׁלְחָה
2 m.	שָׁלַחְתָּ	נִשְׁלַחְתָּ	שִׁלַּחְתָּ	שֻׁלַּחְתָּ	הִתְפַּתַּחְתָּ	הִשְׁלַחְתָּ	הָשְׁלַחְתָּ
2 f.	שָׁלַחַתְּ	נִשְׁלַחַתְּ	שִׁלַּחַתְּ	שֻׁלַּחַתְּ	הִתְפַּתַּחַתְּ	הִשְׁלַחַתְּ	הָשְׁלַחַתְּ
1 c.	שָׁלַחְתִּי	נִשְׁלַחְתִּי	שִׁלַּחְתִּי	שֻׁלַּחְתִּי	הִתְפַּתַּחְתִּי	הִשְׁלַחְתִּי	הָשְׁלַחְתִּי
Pl.							
3 c.	שָׁלְחוּ	נִשְׁלְחוּ	שִׁלְּחוּ	שֻׁלְּחוּ	הִתְפַּתְּחוּ	הִשְׁלִיחוּ	הָשְׁלְחוּ
2 m.	שְׁלַחְתֶּם	נִשְׁלַחְתֶּם	שִׁלַּחְתֶּם	שֻׁלַּחְתֶּם	הִתְפַּתַּחְתֶּם	הִשְׁלַחְתֶּם	הָשְׁלַחְתֶּם
2 f.	שְׁלַחְתֶּן	נִשְׁלַחְתֶּן	שִׁלַּחְתֶּן	שֻׁלַּחְתֶּן	הִתְפַּתַּחְתֶּן	הִשְׁלַחְתֶּן	הָשְׁלַחְתֶּן
1 c.	שָׁלַחְנוּ	נִשְׁלַחְנוּ	שִׁלַּחְנוּ	שֻׁלַּחְנוּ	הִתְפַּתַּחְנוּ	הִשְׁלַחְנוּ	הָשְׁלַחְנוּ
Sing.				*Imperfect form*			
3 m.	יִשְׁלַח	יִשָּׁלַח	יְשַׁלַּח	יְשֻׁלַּח	יִתְפַּתַּח	יַשְׁלִיחַ	יָשְׁלַח
3 f.	תִּשְׁלַח	תִּשָּׁלַח	תְּשַׁלַּח	תְּשֻׁלַּח	תִּתְפַּתַּח	תַּשְׁלִיחַ	תָּשְׁלַח
2 m.	תִּשְׁלַח	תִּשָּׁלַח	תְּשַׁלַּח	תְּשֻׁלַּח	תִּתְפַּתַּח	תַּשְׁלִיחַ	תָּשְׁלַח
2 f.	תִּשְׁלְחִי	תִּשָּׁלְחִי	תְּשַׁלְּחִי	תְּשֻׁלְּחִי	תִּתְפַּתְּחִי	תַּשְׁלִיחִי	תָּשְׁלְחִי
1 c.	אֶשְׁלַח	אֶשָּׁלַח	אֲשַׁלַּח	אֲשֻׁלַּח	אֶתְפַּתַּח	אַשְׁלִיחַ	אָשְׁלַח

	QAL	NI.	PI.	PU.	HTP.	HI.	HO.
Pl.	*Imperfect form*						
3 c.	יִשְׁלְחוּ	יִשָּׁלְחוּ	יְשַׁלְּחוּ	יְשֻׁלְּחוּ	יִתְפַּתְּחוּ	יַשְׁלִיחוּ	יָשְׁלְחוּ
3 f.	תִּשְׁלַחְנָה	תִּשָּׁלַחְנָה	תְּשַׁלַּחְנָה	תְּשֻׁלַּחְנָה	תִּתְפַּתַּחְנָה	תַּשְׁלַחְנָה	תָּשְׁלַחְנָה
2 m.	תִּשְׁלְחוּ	תִּשָּׁלְחוּ	תְּשַׁלְּחוּ	תְּשֻׁלְּחוּ	תִּתְפַּתְּחוּ	תַּשְׁלִיחוּ	תָּשְׁלְחוּ
2 f.	תִּשְׁלַחְנָה	תִּשָּׁלַחְנָה	תְּשַׁלַּחְנָה	תְּשֻׁלַּחְנָה	תִּתְפַּתַּחְנָה	תַּשְׁלַחְנָה	תָּשְׁלַחְנָה
1 c.	נִשְׁלַח	נִשָּׁלַח	נְשַׁלַּח	נְשֻׁלַּח	נִתְפַּתַּח	נַשְׁלִיחַ	נָשְׁלַח
Sing.	*Imperative form*						
2 m.	שְׁלַח	הִשָּׁלַח	שַׁלַּח		הִתְפַּתַּח	הַשְׁלַח	
2 f.	שִׁלְחִי	הִשָּׁלְחִי	שַׁלְּחִי		הִתְפַּתְּחִי	הַשְׁלִיחִי	
Pl.							
2 m.	שִׁלְחוּ	הִשָּׁלְחוּ	שַׁלְּחוּ		הִתְפַּתְּחוּ	הַשְׁלִיחוּ	
2 f.	שְׁלַחְנָה	הִשָּׁלַחְנָה	שַׁלַּחְנָה		הִתְפַּתַּחְנָה	הַשְׁלַחְנָה	
Sing.	*Cohortative form*						
	אֶשְׁלְחָה	אֶשָּׁלְחָה	אֲשַׁלְּחָה		אֶתְפַּתְּחָה	אַשְׁלִיחָה	
Sing.	*Jussive form*						
	יִשְׁלַח	יִשָּׁלַח	יְשַׁלַּח		יִתְפַּתַּח	יַשְׁלַח	
	Infinitive						
cs.	שְׁלֹחַ	הִשָּׁלַח	שַׁלַּח		הִתְפַּתַּח	הַשְׁלִיחַ	הָשְׁלַח
abs.	שָׁלוֹחַ	נִשְׁלֹחַ	שַׁלֵּחַ		הִתְפַּתֵּחַ	הַשְׁלֵחַ	הָשְׁלֵחַ
	Participle						
act.	שֹׁלֵחַ		מְשַׁלֵּחַ		מִתְפַּתֵּחַ	מַשְׁלִיחַ	
pass.	שָׁלוּחַ	נִשְׁלָח		מְשֻׁלָּח			מָשְׁלָח

(ii) *The following rules apply to all the stem formations*:

a. In a syllable that ends in a guttural the vowel is usually / ַ /. It replaces the expected vowel.

        שָׁלַח   instead of   שָׁלֵח

- The same process occurs if a consonantal suffix is added (שְׁלַחְתֶּן).

b. With zero or vocalic suffixes, if the expected vowel in a syllable that ends in a guttural is a / ִי /, / וּ / or / וֹ / (i.e. unchangeably long), or if it is a /ֵ/ or /ֶ/, it is not replaced with a /ֶ/. A transitional pataḥ is placed between the normal stem vowel and the guttural. (Cf. §6.2.)

שֶׁלַח	instead of	שֶׁלַח
יַשְׁלִיחַ	instead of	יַשְׁלִיחַ

c. In the perfect 2 feminine singular the silent šᵉwâ under the guttural is replaced with a /ֶ/.

שָׁלַחְתְּ	instead of	שָׁלַחְתְּ

d. In the imperfect the stem vowel before the consonantal suffixes is /ֶ/.

תִּשְׁמַעְנָה	instead of	תִּשְׁמַעְנָה
תַּשְׁמַעְנָה	instead of	תַּשְׁמֵעְנָה

e. In the participle the feminine singlar does not have the expected /ֶ ֶ/ pattern. Its vowel pattern is /ֵ ֶ/.

שָׁמַעַת	instead of	שֹׁמַעַת

§18.3. *The I Aleph That is Not Pronounced*

In BH the א has a very weak consonantal character. At the end of a closed syllable the א has become silent. (Cf. §4.2/5(ii).) The preceding short vowel changes to compensate for the loss of the א.

This phenomenon is limited to the Qal imperfect form of only five verbs, namely אָכַל (he ate), אָמַר (he said), אָבַד (he perished), אָבָה (he was willing), אָפָה (he baked).[14] The verbs אָחַז (he held fast), אָהַב (he loved) and אָסַף (he collected) also have I aleph variants in addition to the usual forms for I guttural verbs (§18.1 and 18.2), for example, I gutturals such as יֶאֱהַב (Prov. 3.12) and I aleph such as וְאֹהַב (Mal. 1.2).

a. The usual vowel of the preformative /ֶ/ becomes /ֹ/.

יֹאמַר	instead of	יֶאֱמֹר

b. With the imperfect preformative of the 1 singular the א of the verb stem has fallen away in writing.

אֹמַר	instead of	אֶאֱמֹר

c. In the second syllable the usual stem vowel /ֹ/ is replaced with /ֵ/ or /ֶ/. The latter is usually the pausal form.

יֹאמֵר	instead of	יֹאמֹר

---

14. For a more complete discussion, cf. Joüon–Muraoka §73.

יֵאכֵל   instead of   יַאְכֹל

d. All the other forms of the I aleph verbs are regular. The infinitive construct of the verb stem אמר with the preposition ל is, however, an exception.

לֵאמֹר   instead of   לֶאֱמֹר

e. The waw consecutive + imperfect of אמר is also an exception. The / ֵ / in the second syllable changes to / ֶ /, due to the accent shift. With the pausal forms (cf. §9.6), the / ֵ / vowel returns.

וַיֹּאמֶר   instead of   וַיֹּאמֵר

§18.4. *The III Aleph That Is Not Pronounced*

1. *Introduction*

In BH the א has a very weak consonantal character. At the end of a closed syllable the א often becomes silent. (Cf. §4.2/5(ii) and 5.2/2(i).) To compensate for the loss of the א the preceding short vowels are changed. Although the א looks like a vowel indicator in this case, it is actually a silent consonant that appears with a changed vowel. At the beginning of a syllable, however, the א retains its consonantal character.

The above implies that the aleph is not pronounced when a verb ends on the aleph or when a III aleph appears before a consonantal suffix (namely the ־תִי, ־תָ, ־תְ, ־נוּ of a perfect, the ־נָה and ־ן of an imperfect), for example, הִמְצִיא (but הִמְצִיאוּ).

2. Table 12. *III aleph verbs*

	QAL	NI.	PI.	PU.	HTP.	HI.	HO.
Gloss.	find						
Sing.	*Perfect form*						
3 m.	מָצָא	נִמְצָא	מִצֵּא	מֻצָּא	הִתְמַצֵּא	הִמְצִיא	הֻמְצָא
3 f.	מָצְאָה	נִמְצְאָה	מִצְּאָה	מֻצְּאָה	הִתְמַצְּאָה	הִמְצִיאָה	הֻמְצְאָה
2 m.	מָצָאתָ	נִמְצֵאתָ	מִצֵּאתָ	מֻצֵּאתָ	הִתְמַצֵּאתָ	הִמְצֵאתָ	הֻמְצֵאתָ
2 f.	מָצָאת	נִמְצֵאת	מִצֵּאת	מֻצֵּאת	הִתְמַצֵּאת	הִמְצֵאת	הֻמְצֵאת
1 c.	מָצָאתִי	נִמְצֵאתִי	מִצֵּאתִי	מֻצֵּאתִי	הִתְמַצֵּאתִי	הִמְצֵאתִי	הֻמְצֵאתִי
3 c.	מָצְאוּ	נִמְצְאוּ	מִצְּאוּ	מֻצְּאוּ	הִתְמַצְּאוּ	הִמְצִיאוּ	הֻמְצְאוּ
2 m.	מְצָאתֶם	נִמְצֵאתֶם	מִצֵּאתֶם	מֻצֵּאתֶם	הִתְמַצֵּאתֶם	הִמְצֵאתֶם	הֻמְצֵאתֶם

	QAL	NI.	PI.	PU.	HTP.	HI.	HO.
Pl.				*Perfect form*			
2 f.	מְצָאתֶן	נִמְצֵאתֶן	מִצֵּאתֶן	מֻצֵּאתֶן	הִתְמַצֵּאתֶן	הִמְצֵאתֶן	הָמְצֵאתֶן
1 c.	מָצָאנוּ	נִמְצֵאנוּ	מִצֵּאנוּ	מֻצֵּאנוּ	הִתְמַצֵּאנוּ	הִמְצֵאנוּ	הָמְצֵאנוּ
Sing.				*Imperfect form*			
3 m.	יִמְצָא	יִמָּצֵא	יְמַצֵּא	יְמֻצָּא	יִתְמַצֵּא	יַמְצִיא	יֻמְצָא
3 f.	תִּמְצָא	תִּמָּצֵא	תְּמַצֵּא	תְּמֻצָּא	תִּתְמַצֵּא	תַּמְצִיא	תֻּמְצָא
2 m.	תִּמְצָא	תִּמָּצֵא	תְּמַצֵּא	תְּמֻצָּא	תִּתְמַצֵּא	תַּמְצִיא	תֻּמְצָא
2 f.	תִּמְצְאִי	תִּמָּצְאִי	תְּמַצְּאִי	תְּמֻצְּאִי	תִּתְמַצְּאִי	תַּמְצִיאִי	תֻּמְצְאִי
1 c.	אֶמְצָא	אֶמָּצֵא	אֲמַצֵּא	אֲמֻצָּא	אֶתְמַצֵּא	אַמְצִיא	אֻמְצָא
Pl.							
3 c.	יִמְצְאוּ	יִמָּצְאוּ	יְמַצְּאוּ	יְמֻצְּאוּ	יִתְמַצְּאוּ	יַמְצִיאוּ	יֻמְצְאוּ
3 f.	תִּמְצֶאנָה	תִּמָּצֶאנָה	תְּמַצֶּאנָה	תְּמֻצֶּאנָה	תִּתְמַצֶּאנָה	תַּמְצֶאנָה	תֻּמְצֶאנָה
2 m.	תִּמְצְאוּ	תִּמָּצְאוּ	תְּמַצְּאוּ	תְּמֻצְּאוּ	תִּתְמַצְּאוּ	תַּמְצִיאוּ	תֻּמְצְאוּ
2 f.	תִּמְצֶאנָה	תִּמָּצֶאנָה	תְּמַצֶּאנָה	תְּמֻצֶּאנָה	תִּתְמַצֶּאנָה	תַּמְצֶאנָה	תֻּמְצֶאנָה
1.	נִמְצָא	נִמָּצֵא	נְמַצֵּא	נְמֻצָּא	נִתְמַצֵּא	נַמְצִיא	נֻמְצָא
Sing.				*Imperative form*			
2 m.	מְצָא	הִמָּצֵא	מַצֵּא		הִתְמַצֵּא	הַמְצֵא	
2 f.	מִצְאִי	הִמָּצְאִי	מַצְּאִי		הִתְמַצְּאִי	הַמְצִיאִי	
Pl.							
2 m.	מִצְאוּ	הִמָּצְאוּ	מַצְּאוּ		הִתְמַצְּאוּ	הַמְצִיאוּ	
2 f.	מְצֶאנָה	הִמָּצֶאנָה	מַצֶּאנָה		הִתְמַצֶּאנָה	הַמְצֶאנָה	
Sing.				*Cohortative form*			
1.	אֶמְצְאָה	אֶמָּצְאָה				אַמְצִיאָה	
Sing.				*Jussive form*			
3 m.	יִמְצָא	יִמָּצֵא				יַמְצֵא	
				Infinitive			
cs.	מְצֹא	הִמָּצֵא	מַצֵּא		הִתְמַצֵּא	הַמְצִיא	הָמְצָא
abs.	מָצוֹא	נִמְצֹא	מַצֵּא		הִתְמַצֵּא	הַמְצֵא	הָמְצֵא

	QAL	NI.	PI.	PU.	HTP.	HI.	HO.
	Participle						
act.	מֹצֵא	נִמְצָא	מְמַצֵּא		מִתְמַצֵּא	מַמְצִיא	
pass.	מָצוּא			מְמֻצָּא			מָמְצָא

3. *General characteristics*

a. Where there are no suffixes the א becomes silent. An / $\underline{\;}$ / before the א changes to / $\overline{\;}$ /.

מָצָא   instead of   מָצֵא

b. Where there are vocalic suffixes, the א functions as a consonant and the verb stem conjugates regularly (הִמְצִיאוּ).

c. Where there are consonantal suffixes the א becomes silent and the Qal perfect and imperfect take an / $\text{א}\overline{\;}$ / (מְצָאתָ, מְצָאתֶם),

   - the perfect of *all the other* stem formations takes an / $\text{א}\overline{\;}$ / (נִמְצֵאתָ, הִמְצֵאתָ), and
   - the imperfect of *all the other* stem formations takes an / $\text{א}\overline{\;}$ / (תִּמְצֶאנָה, תַּמְצֶאנָה) vowel.

In other words:

   - In the Niphal / $\underline{\;}$ / is used where one would expect / $\overline{\;}$ /.

   נִמְצֵאתָ   instead of   נִמְצָאתָ

   - In the Hiphil / $\underline{\;}$ / is used where one would expect / $\overline{\;}$ /.

   הִמְצֵאתָ   instead of   הִמְצִיאתָ

   - The Hiphil 3 singular masculine form is regular, however (e.g. הִמְצִיא).

d. The vowels of the Qal infinitive construct look just like those of a regular verb stem.

מְצֹא   instead of   מְצֵא

e. In stative verbs with / $\overline{\;}\;\overline{\;}$ / (cf. §16.2) the / $\overline{\;}$ / in the Qal perfect is retained (מָלֵאתִי, מָלֵא).

f. The א sometimes falls away.

מָלֵתִי   instead of   מָלֵאתִי

g. As many of the conjugations of the III he and III aleph verbs sound identical, some III he verbs are vocalized as the III aleph and *vice versa*, e.g.

- the III he verb אָתָה (to come) sometimes looks like the verb stem אתא in the Qal perfect 3 masculine singular

  אָתָא   instead of   אָתָה

- the III aleph verb כלא (to restrain) looks like the verb כלה (be finished) in the Qal perfect 1 singular

  כָּלִאתִי   as   בָּנִיתִי
          instead of   כָּלָאתִי

§18.5. *The III He Verbs*

1. *Introduction*

The term III he refers specifically to verbs in the Qal perfect 3 masculine singular that end in a ה vowel indicator, for example, שָׁתָה 'to drink', etc. At an early stage of the language these verbs ended in a yod or waw. In other words they were originally III yod and III waw verbs. These consonants fell away either through elision or were retained as vowel indicators before consonantal suffixes. Verbs that originally ended in he and reflect the consonantal character of the he with a mappîq (e.g. גבַהּ 'be high') are not recognized as III he verbs.

2. Table 13. *III he verbs*

	QAL	NI.	PI.	PU.	HTP.	HI.	HO.
Gloss	reveal						
Sing.	*Perfect form*						
3 m.	גָּלָה	נִגְלָה	גִּלָּה	גֻּלָּה	הִתְגַּלָּה	הִגְלָה	הָגְלָה
3 f.	גָּלְתָה	נִגְלְתָה	גִּלְּתָה	גֻּלְּתָה	הִתְגַּלְּתָה	הִגְלְתָה	הָגְלְתָה
2 m.	גָּלִיתָ	נִגְלֵיתָ	גִּלִּיתָ	גֻּלֵּיתָ	הִתְגַּלִּיתָ	הִגְלֵיתָ	הָגְלֵיתָ
2 f.	גָּלִית	נִגְלֵית	גִּלִּית	גֻּלֵּית	הִתְגַּלִּית	הִגְלֵית	הָגְלֵית
1 c.	גָּלִיתִי	נִגְלֵיתִי	גִּלִּיתִי	גֻּלֵּיתִי	הִתְגַּלִּיתִי	הִגְלֵיתִי	הָגְלֵיתִי
Pl.							
3 c.	גָּלוּ	נִגְלוּ	גִּלּוּ	גֻּלּוּ	הִתְגַּלּוּ	הִגְלוּ	הָגְלוּ
2 m.	גְּלִיתֶם	נִגְלֵיתֶם	גִּלִּיתֶם	גֻּלֵּיתֶם	הִתְגַּלִּיתֶם	הִגְלֵיתֶם	הָגְלֵיתֶם
2 f.	גְּלִיתֶן	נִגְלֵיתֶן	גִּלִּיתֶן	גֻּלֵּיתֶן	הִתְגַּלִּיתֶן	הִגְלֵיתֶן	הָגְלֵיתֶן
1 c.	גָּלִינוּ	נִגְלֵינוּ	גִּלִּינוּ	גֻּלֵּינוּ	הִתְגַּלִּינוּ	הִגְלֵינוּ	הָגְלֵינוּ

	QAL	NI.	PI.	PU.	HTP.	HI.	HO.
Sing.	Imperfect form						
3 m.	יִגְלֶה	יִגָּלֶה	יְגַלֶּה	יְגֻלֶּה	יִתְגַּלֶּה	יַגְלֶה	יָגְלֶה
3 f.	תִּגְלֶה	תִּגָּלֶה	תְּגַלֶּה	תְּגֻלֶּה	תִּתְגַּלֶּה	תַּגְלֶה	תָּגְלֶה
2 m.	תִּגְלֶה	תִּגָּלֶה	תְּגַלֶּה	תְּגֻלֶּה	תִּתְגַּלֶּה	תַּגְלֶה	תָּגְלֶה
2 f.	תִּגְלִי	תִּגָּלִי	תְּגַלִּי	תְּגֻלִּי	תִּתְגַּלִּי	תַּגְלִי	תָּגְלִי
1 c.	אֶגְלֶה	אֶגָּלֶה	אֲגַלֶּה	אֲגֻלֶּה	אֶתְגַּלֶּה	אַגְלֶה	אָגְלֶה
Pl.							
3 c.	יִגְלוּ	יִגָּלוּ	יְגַלּוּ	יְגֻלּוּ	יִתְגַּלּוּ	יַגְלוּ	יָגְלוּ
3 f.	תִּגְלֶינָה	תִּגָּלֶינָה	תְּגַלֶּינָה	תְּגֻלֶּינָה	תִּתְגַּלֶּינָה	תַּגְלֶינָה	תָּגְלֶינָה
2 m.	תִּגְלוּ	תִּגָּלוּ	תְּגַלּוּ	תְּגֻלּוּ	תִּתְגַּלּוּ	תַּגְלוּ	תָּגְלוּ
2 f.	תִּגְלֶינָה	תִּגָּלֶינָה	תְּגַלֶּינָה	תְּגֻלֶּינָה	תִּתְגַּלֶּינָה	תַּגְלֶינָה	תָּגְלֶינָה
1.	נִגְלֶה	נִגָּלֶה	נְגַלֶּה	נְגֻלֶּה	נִתְגַּלֶּה	נַגְלֶה	נָגְלֶה
Sing.	Imperative form						
2 m.	גְּלֵה	הִגָּלֵה	גַּלֵּה		הִתְגַּלֵּה	הַגְלֵה	
2 f.	גְּלִי	הִגָּלִי	גַּלִּי		הִתְגַּלִּי	הַגְלִי	
Pl.							
2 m.	גְּלוּ	הִגָּלוּ	גַּלּוּ		הִתְגַּלּוּ	הַגְלוּ	
2 f.	גְּלֶינָה	הִגָּלֶינָה	גַּלֶּינָה		הִתְגַּלֶּינָה	הַגְלֶינָה	
Sing.	Jussive form						
	יִגֶל	יִגָּל	יְגַל		יִתְגַּל	יֶגֶל	
	Infinitive						
cs.	גְּלוֹת	הִגָּלוֹת	גַּלּוֹת	גֻּלּוֹת	הִתְגַּלּוֹת	הַגְלוֹת	הָגְלוֹת
abs.	גָּלֹה	נִגְלֹה	גַּלֹּה	גֻּלֹּה	הִתְגַּלֵּה	הַגְלֵה	הָגְלֵה
	Participle						
act.	גֹּלֶה	נִגְלֶה	מְגַלֶּה		מִתְגַּלֶּה	מַגְלֶה	
pass.	גָּלוּי			מְגֻלֶּה			מָגְלֶה

3. *General characteristics*

A particular systemization is evident in all the conjugations of the III he verbs. This systematization can best be appreciated if all the conjugations are arranged according to their suffixes.

(i) In forms where *no suffix* is added, the endings are as follows:

a. The perfect ends in הָ-.

Qal	גָּלָה
Ni.	נִגְלָה
Pi.	גִּלָּה
Hi.	הִגְלָה

b. The imperfect ends in הֶ-.

Qal	יִגְלֶה
Ni.	יִגָּלֶה
Hi.	יַגְלֶה

c. The imperative ends in הֵ-.

Qal	גְּלֵה
Ni.	הִגָּלֵה
Hi.	הַגְלֵה

d. The infinitive ends in וֹת-.

Qal	גְּלוֹת
Ni.	הִגָּלוֹת
Pi.	גַּלּוֹת
Hi.	הַגְלוֹת

e. The masculine singular participle ends in הֶ-. The construct form of the participle ends in הֵ-.

Qal	בֹּנֶה
Ni.	נִגְלֶה
Hi.	מַבְנֶה

(ii) Forms in which *a suffix beginning with a vowel* is added:

a. With all the stem formations the 3 feminine singular form of the perfect is formed by replacing the final ה with an older feminine ת ending and then adding the suffix הָ-.

בָּנְתָה   instead of   בָּנְהָ

b. In all the other cases the III he and the preceding vowel or audible šᵉwâ fall away and the suffix is added immediately after the second stem consonant.

גְּלוֹ   instead of   גְּלָהוּ

c. The object suffixes (cf. §17) are also added directly after the second stem consonant.

גְּלָנִי   and   גְּלָה

(iii) In forms where *a suffix beginning with a consonant* is added, the original ʾ replaces the ה. The ʾ fuses with the preceding vowel resulting in the following connecting vowels:

a. The Qal, Piel, Hiphil and Hithpael have / ʾ- / as connecting vowel.

Qal	גָּלִיתָ
Hi.	הִגְלִיתָ

b. The perfect of the Niphal, Pual and Hophal have / ʾ- / as connecting vowel.

Ni.	נִבְנֵיתָ
Pu.	בֻּנֵּיתָ
Ho.	הֻבְנֵיתָ

c. In the imperfect and imperative of all the stem formations the connecting vowel is / ʾ- / (בְּנֶינָה, תִּבְנֶינָה).

4. *The apocopated forms of the III he verbs*
An accent shift normally takes place in the jussive and waw consecutive + imperfect forms. In the III he verbs this shift results in the he falling away, i.e. apocope takes place, for example, יִגְלֶה is shortened to יִגֶל. A list of the most common 'short' forms, i.e. jussives or waw consecutive + imperfect is given below. Note that the 3rd person short form of a particular verb can differ from that of its 2nd person.

a. In the Qal there are four apocopated forms.

	Long	and	*Short*
3 m. sing.	יֵשֵׁבֶה		וַיֵּשֶׁב
3 m. sing.	יִבְכֶּה		וַיֵּבְךְּ
3 m. sing.	יִרְבֶּה		וַיִּרֶב
2 m. sing.	תִּפְנֶה		וַתֵּפֶן

b. III he verbs that have a guttural as the first or second stem consonant
in the Qal, have their own apocopated forms.

	Long	and	*Short*
3 m. sing.	יַעֲלֶה		וַיַּעַל
3 m. sing.	יֶחֱרֶה		וַיִּחַר
3 m. sing.	יִרְאֶה		וַיַּרְא
2 m. sing.	תִּרְאֶה		וַתֵּרְא

c. The Niphal stem formation has one apocopated form.

תִּגָּלֶה   and   תִּגָּל

d. The Piel stem formation has one apocopated form.

2 m. sing.	יְכַלֶּה	and	וַיְכַל

e. The Hiphil stem formation has two apocopated forms.

3 m. sing.	יַשְׁקֶה		וַיַּשְׁקְ
3 m. sing.	יַרְבֶּה		וַיֶּרֶב

f. III he verbs that have a guttural as first stem consonant in the Hiphil
also have another apocopated form.

יַעֲלֶה   and   וַיַּעַל

§18.6. *The I Nun Verbs*

1. *Introduction*

When a nun appears at the end of a closed syllable, it often assimilates with the next consonant. (Cf. §4.2/4(ii).)

2. Table 14. *I nun verbs*

	QAL	*QAL*	*NI.*	*PI.*	*HTP.*	*HI.*	*HO.*
Gloss	fall	approach					
Sing.	Perfect form						
3 m.	נָפַל	נָגַשׁ	נִגַּשׁ	regular	regular	הִגִּישׁ	הֻגַּשׁ
3 f.	נָפְלָה	נָגְשָׁה	נִגְּשָׁה			הִגִּישָׁה	הֻגְּשָׁה
2 m.	נָפַלְתָּ	נָגַשְׁתָּ	נִגַּשְׁתָּ			הִגַּשְׁתָּ	הֻגַּשְׁתָּ
2 f.	נָפַלְתְּ	נָגַשְׁתְּ	נִגַּשְׁתְּ			הִגַּשְׁתְּ	הֻגַּשְׁתְּ
1 c.	נָפַלְתִּי	נָגַשְׁתִּי	נִגַּשְׁתִּי			הִגַּשְׁתִּי	הֻגַּשְׁתִּי

	QAL	QAL	NI.	PI.	HTP.	HI.	HO.
Pl.				Perfect form			
3 c.	נָפְלוּ	נִגְּשׁוּ	נִגְּשׁוּ			הֻגְּשׁוּ	הֻגְּשׁוּ
2 m.	נְפַלְתֶּם	נִגַּשְׁתֶּם	נִגַּשְׁתֶּם			הֻגַּשְׁתֶּם	הֻגַּשְׁתֶּם
2 f.	נְפַלְתֶּן	נִגַּשְׁתֶּן	נִגַּשְׁתֶּן			הֻגַּשְׁתֶּן	הֻגַּשְׁתֶּן
1 c.	נָפַלְנוּ	נִגַּשְׁנוּ	נִגַּשְׁנוּ			הֻגַּשְׁנוּ	הֻגַּשְׁנוּ
Sing.				Imperfect form			
3 m.	יִפֹּל	יִגַּשׁ	יִנָּגֵשׁ			יַגִּישׁ	יֻגַּשׁ
3 f.	תִּפֹּל	תִּגַּשׁ	תִּנָּגֵשׁ			תַּגִּישׁ	תֻּגַּשׁ
2 m.	תִּפֹּל	תִּגַּשׁ	תִּנָּגֵשׁ			תַּגִּישׁ	תֻּגַּשׁ
2 f.	תִּפְּלִי	תִּגְּשִׁי	תִּנָּגְשִׁי			תַּגִּישִׁי	תֻּגְּשִׁי
1 c.	אֶפֹּל	אֶגַּשׁ	אֶנָּגֵשׁ			אַגִּישׁ	אֻגַּשׁ
Pl.							
3 c.	יִפְּלוּ	יִגְּשׁוּ	יִנָּגְשׁוּ			יַגִּישׁוּ	יֻגְּשׁוּ
3 f.	תִּפֹּלְנָה	תִּגַּשְׁנָה	תִּנָּגַשְׁנָה			תַּגֵּשְׁנָה	תֻּגַּשְׁנָה
2 m.	תִּפְּלוּ	תִּגְּשׁוּ	תִּנָּגְשׁוּ			תַּגִּישׁוּ	תֻּגְּשׁוּ
2 f.	תִּפֹּלְנָה	תִּגַּשְׁנָה	תִּנָּגַשְׁנָה			תַּגֵּשְׁנָה	תֻּגַּשְׁנָה
1 c.	נִפֹּל	נִגַּשׁ	נִנָּגֵשׁ			נַגִּישׁ	נֻגַּשׁ
Sing.				Imperative form			
2 m.	נְפֹל	גַּשׁ	הִנָּגֵשׁ			הַגֵּשׁ	
2 f.	נִפְלִי	גְּשִׁי	הִנָּגְשִׁי			הַגִּישִׁי	
Pl.							
2 m.	נִפְלוּ	גְּשׁוּ	הִנָּגְשׁוּ			הַגִּישׁוּ	
2 f.	נְפֹלְנָה	גַּשְׁנָה	הִנָּגַשְׁנָה			הַגֵּשְׁנָה	
Sing.				Cohortative form			
	אֶפְּלָה	אֶגְּשָׁה				אַגִּישָׁה	
Sing.				Jussive form			
	יִפֹּל	יִגַּשׁ				יַגֵּשׁ	

	QAL	QAL	NI.	PI.	HTP.	HI.	HO.
	Infinitive						
cs.	נְפֹל	גֶּשֶׁת	הִנָּגֵשׁ			הַגִּישׁ	הֻגַּשׁ
abs.	נָפוֹל	נָגוֹשׁ	הִנָּגֹשׁ			הַגֵּשׁ	הֻגֵּשׁ
	Participle						
act.	נֹפֵל	נֹגֵשׁ	נִגָּשׁ			מַגִּישׁ	
pass.		נָגוּשׁ					מֻגָּשׁ

3. General characteristics

a. In stem formations and conjugations that have a preformative, the first nun often assimilates with the next consonant which then doubles as a result.

יִצֹּר   instead of   יִנְצֹר

b. If the second consonant of the verb stem is a guttural, no assimilation occurs.

יִנְחַם   instead of   יִחַם

c. The distinction between the / - / and the / - / in the Qal imperfect has an important effect on the imperative and the infinitive construct.

- Verbs with / - / in the imperfect have a regular imperative and infinitive construct.

נְפֹל   from   יִנְפֹּל

- Verbs with / - / in the imperfect have an imperative without the nun.

גַּשׁ   from   יִגַּשׁ

- Their infinitive construct forms also have no nun but they do take a ת suffix. The infinitive construct formed has a / - - / vowel pattern which is typical of segholates.

גֶּשֶׁת   instead of   נְגֹשׁ

When a pronominal suffix is added to these infinitives, they usually manifest a / - / like segholates with an i-stem, e.g. גִּשְׁתִּי. (Cf. §27.3/4.)

d. In the Niphal, assimilation of the first nun occurs in the perfect, participle and infinitive construct in addition to the usual forms of assimilation, e.g. נִגַּשׁ. (Cf. §4.2/4.)

e. No assimilation occurs in any of the Piel, Pual and Hithpael conjugations. Here the I nun verb stem conjugates like a regular strong verb, e.g. נִבֵּל.

f. Assimilation occurs in all the forms of the Hiphil, e.g. הִגִּישׁ, יַגִּישׁ.

g. Assimilation occurs in all the forms of the Hophal. Furthermore, the vowel of the preformative is / ֻ / and not / ֳ /.

הֻגַּשׁ   instead of   הֻנְגַּשׁ

§18.7. *The I Yod and I Waw Verbs*

1. *Introduction*

These two classes must be considered together because of their historical development.

Old-Hebrew	יטב*	ושב*
BH (Qal perfect)	יטב	ישב
BH (Hiphil perfect)	היטיב	הושיב

The Old Hebrew verb ושב* became ישב in the Qal perfect of BH, but the historical distinction between יטב and ושב can still be seen in the Hiphil. In the following discussion a distinction will be made between verbs that were original I yod verbs, such as יטב and verbs which were original I waw verbs, such as ישב.

2. Table 15. *I waw and I yod verbs*

	QAL	QAL	NI.	HI.	HO.	QAL	HI.
			I waw			I yod	
Gloss	sit	take possession				be good	
Sing.				*Perfect form*			
3 m.	יָשַׁב	יָרַשׁ	נוֹשַׁב	הוֹשִׁיב	הוּשַׁב	יָטַב	הֵיטִיב
3 f.	יָשְׁבָה	יָרְשָׁה	נוֹשְׁבָה	הוֹשִׁיבָה	הוּשְׁבָה	יָטְבָה	הֵיטִיבָה
2 m.	יָשַׁבְתָּ	יָרַשְׁתָּ	נוֹשַׁבְתָּ	הוֹשַׁבְתָּ	הוּשַׁבְתָּ	יָטַבְתָּ	הֵיטַבְתָּ
2 f.	regular	regular	נוֹשַׁבְתְּ	הוֹשַׁבְתְּ	הוּשַׁבְתְּ	regular	הֵיטַבְתְּ
1 c.			נוֹשַׁבְתִּי	הוֹשַׁבְתִּי	הוּשַׁבְתִּי		הֵיטַבְתִּי

	QAL	QAL	NI.	HI.	HO.	QAL	HI.
			I waw			I yod	
Pl.			*Perfect form*				
3 c.			נוֹשְׁבוּ	הוֹשִׁיבוּ	הוּשְׁבוּ		הֵיטִיבוּ
2 m.			נוֹשַׁבְתֶּם	הוֹשַׁבְתֶּם	הוּשַׁבְתֶּם		הֵיטַבְתֶּם
2 f.			נוֹשַׁבְתֶּן	הוֹשַׁבְתֶּן	הוּשַׁבְתֶּן		הֵיטַבְתֶּן
1 c.			נוֹשַׁבְנוּ	הוֹשַׁבְנוּ	הוּשַׁבְנוּ		הֵיטַבְנוּ
Sing.			*Imperfect form*				
3 m.	יֵשֵׁב	יִירַשׁ	יִוָּשֵׁב	יוֹשִׁיב	יוּשַׁב	יִיטַב	יֵיטִיב
3 f.	תֵּשֵׁב	תִּירַשׁ	תִּוָּשֵׁב	תּוֹשִׁיב	תּוּשַׁב	תִּיטַב	תֵּיטִיב
2 m.	תֵּשֵׁב	תִּירַשׁ	תִּוָּשֵׁב	תּוֹשִׁיב	תּוּשַׁב	תִּיטַב	תֵּיטִיב
2 f.	תֵּשְׁבִי	תִּירְשִׁי	תִּוָּשְׁבִי	תּוֹשִׁיבִי	תּוּשְׁבִי	תִּיטְבִי	תֵּיטִיבִי
1 c.	אֵשֵׁב	אִירַשׁ	אִוָּשֵׁב	אוֹשִׁיב	אוּשַׁב	אִיטַב	אֵיטִיב
Pl.							
3 c.	יֵשְׁבוּ	יִירְשׁוּ	יִוָּשְׁבוּ	יוֹשִׁיבוּ	יוּשְׁבוּ	יִיטְבוּ	יֵיטִיבוּ
3 f.	תֵּשַׁבְנָה	תִּירַשְׁנָה	תִּוָּשַׁבְנָה	תּוֹשֵׁבְנָה	תּוּשַׁבְנָה	תִּיטַבְנָה	תֵּיטַבְנָה
2 m.	תֵּשְׁבוּ	תִּירְשׁוּ	תִּוָּשְׁבוּ	תּוֹשִׁיבוּ	תּוּשְׁבוּ	תִּיטְבוּ	תֵּיטִיבוּ
2 f.	תֵּשַׁבְנָה	תִּירַשְׁנָה	תִּוָּשַׁבְנָה	תּוֹשֵׁבְנָה	תּוּשַׁבְנָה	תִּיטַבְנָה	תֵּיטַבְנָה
1 c.	נֵשֵׁב	נִירַשׁ	נִוָּשֵׁב	נוֹשִׁיב	נוּשַׁב	נִיטַב	נֵיטִיב
Sing.			*Imperative form*				
2 m.	שֵׁב	רַשׁ	הִוָּשֵׁב	הוֹשֵׁב			הֵיטֵב
2 f.	שְׁבִי	רְשִׁי	הִוָּשְׁבִי	הוֹשִׁיבִי			הֵיטִיבִי
Pl.							
2 m.	שְׁבוּ	רְשׁוּ	הִוָּשְׁבוּ	הוֹשִׁיבוּ			הֵיטִיבוּ
2 f.	שֵׁבְנָה	רַשְׁנָה	הִוָּשַׁבְנָה	הוֹשֵׁבְנָה			הֵיטַבְנָה
Sing.			*Cohortative form*				
	אֵשְׁבָה	אִירְשָׁה					
Sing.			*Jussive form*				
	יֵשֵׁב			יוֹשֵׁב		יִיטַב	יֵיטֵב

	QAL	QAL	NI.	HI.	HO.	QAL	HI.
	I waw					I yod	
	Infinitive						
cs.	שֶׁבֶת	רֶשֶׁת	הִוָּשֵׁב	הוֹשִׁיב	הוּשַׁב	יְטֹב	הֵיטִיב
abs.	יָשׁוֹב	יָרוֹשׁ	הִוָּשֵׁב	הוֹשֵׁב		יָטוֹב	הֵיטֵב
	Participle						
act.	יֹשֵׁב	יֹרֵשׁ		מוֹשִׁיב		יֹטֵב	מֵיטִיב
pass.	יָשׁוֹב	יָרוֹשׁ	נוֹשָׁב		מוּשָׁב	יָטוֹב	

3. *Original I yod verbs*

Note that only seven verbs that belong to this category occur in the Bible, namely יבשׁ (dry up), ינק (suckle), ישׁר (be honest), יטב (be good), יקץ (be awake), ילל (scream), and ימן (go to the right).[15] If the yod were to appear at the end of a closed syllable under normal circumstances, i.e by analogy with the regular verb, it would function as a vowel indicator. (Cf. §5.2/2(i).)

a. A characteristic of this verb stem is that the I yod is retained in all the conjugations; cf. the Qal imperfect 3 masculine singular.

        יִיטַב   instead of   יְטַב

b. In the Hiphil perfect the vowel of the preformative / - / is replaced with / - /.

        הֵיטִיב   instead of   הִיטִיב

c. In the Hiphil imperfect and participle the usual vowel of the preformative / - / becomes / - /.

        יֵיטִיב   instead of   יַיְטִיב
        מֵיטִיב   instead of   מַיְטִיב

4. *Original I waw*

Original I waw verbs include ישׁב (sit), ילד (give birth), ירד (go down), ידע (know) and יצא (go out). In conjugating these verbs the original waw is sometimes retained, but each stem formation will be considered separately.

---

15. Cf. Joüon–Muraoka §76.

(i) *Qal (with an active meaning)*

a. In the perfect the I waw is replaced by a yod. In other respects this verb stem conjugates regularly.

יָשַׁב   instead of   וְשַׁב

b. Fusion of the imperfect preformative and the waw of the verb stem leads to the vowel of the preformative / - / changing to / - /.

יֵשֵׁב   instead of   יִוְשֵׁב

c. The stem vowel of the imperfect is / - / and not / - /.

יֵשֵׁב   instead of   יֵשַׁב

d. When the waw consecutive is added to the Qal imperfect, the / - / vowel in the last syllable changes to / - / due to the accent shift that accompanies the addition of the conjunction.

וַיֵּשֶׁב   instead of   וַיֵּשֵׁב

e. In the imperative the ו falls away.

שֵׁב   instead of   וְשֵׁב

f. In the infinitive construct the ו falls away, but a ת suffix is added to the remaining consonants. These consonants are vocalized as follows: / - - /.

שֶׁבֶת   instead of   וְשֵׁב

The infinitive construct with a pronominal suffix behaves like a typical segholate with an i-stem, e.g. שִׁבְתִּי. (Cf. §27.3.)

(ii) *Qal (with a stative meaning)*

In the imperfect of these forms the י of the verb stem, which has replaced the ו, does not fuse with the preformative.

יִירָא   instead of   יִוְרָא

Note the following:

(1) The imperfect and infinitive construct of the stative verb יָכֹל (he is able), which occurs only in the Qal, are completely irregular. They conjugate as if they are Hophal imperfect forms, e.g.

Perfect	יָכֹל
Imperfect	יוּכַל
Infinitive construct	יְכֹלֶת

(2) With the exception of the Qal perfect, the verb הָלַךְ conjugates in the Qal and the Hiphil stem formations like a typical original I waw verb. (Cf. Table 20.)

(3) In some of the I yod verbs where the middle consonant is a צ, the yod assimilates when it appears at the end of a closed syllable, just like the I nun verbs. There are only six such verbs in the Hebrew Bible, namely יצב (take a position), יצק (cast), יצע (spread out), יצת (set alight), יצג (place), יצר (form, make). (Cf. Joüon–Muraoka §77.) Note that יצא (go out) is not regarded as part of this group. (Cf. Joüon–Muraoka §75g.)

(4) The verb ידע (know) which has both an original I waw and a guttural as third stem consonant, has a / ֵ ַ / vowel pattern in the Qal imperfect. The / ַ / before the guttural is also observable in the imperative and infinitive construct, e.g.

Qal imperfect	יֵדַע
Qal imperative	דַּע
Qal infinitive construct	דַּעַת

(iii) *Niphal*

The original waw is retained in all the conjugations of the Niphal stem formation.

a. The waw of the verb stem is retained as a vowel indicator in the perfect and participle.

נוֹלַד   instead of   נִוְלַד

b. The waw of the verb stem is retained as a consonant in the imperfect, imperative, infinitive construct and infinitive absolute, e.g. יִוָּשֵׁב.

c. The imperfect 1 singular, however, takes a / ֵ / instead of a / ָ / vowel in the preformative.

אִוָּשֵׁב   instead of   אָוְּשֵׁב

(iv) *Piel, Pual and Hithpael*

In these stem formations the I waw verbs conjugate like the regular verbs.

a. In the Piel and Pual a consonantal yod appears as first stem consonant, e.g. יִלְּדָה, יִשֵּׁב.

b. In the Hithpael the original waw is usually retained as a consonant, e.g. יִתְוַכָּח.

(v) *Hiphil and Hophal*

The 'original' I waw is retained here. In the Hiphil the waw is retained as a וֹ vowel indicator and in the Hophal as a וּ vowel indicator, e.g. הוֹשַׁב ,הוֹשִׁיב.

5. *Mixed forms*

A number of I yod verbs do not conjugate consistently either as original I yod or original I waw verbs. They have conjugation forms that correspond with both these groups. In the Qal stem formation these verbs usually follow the pattern of the original I yod verbs. In the remaining stem formations they usually follow the pattern of the original I waw, e.g.

Qal perfect	יָירַשׁ
Qal imperative	רֵשׁ
Qal infinitive construct	רֶשֶׁת
Hiphil perfect	הוֹרִישׁ

§18.8. *The II Waw and II Yod Verbs*

1. *Introduction*

The weak consonantal character of the waw and the yod (cf. §4.2/5(ii) and §5.2/2(ii)) may also be observed in verbs with waw and yod as middle consonants. The waw and yod have fallen out of the written form in certain cases, while in other cases they function as vowel indicators.

2. Table 16. *II waw and II yod verbs*

	QAL	QAL	QAL	NI.	HI.	HO.	QAL
	II waw						II yod
Gloss	get up	die	be ashamed				put down
Sing.	*Perfect form*						
3 m.	קָם	מֵת	בּוֹשׁ	נָקוֹם	הֵקִים	הוּקַם	שָׂם
3 f.	קָמָה	מֵתָה	בּוֹשָׁה	נָקוֹמָה	הֵקִימָה	הוּקְמָה	שָׂמָה
2 m.	קַמְתָּ	מַתָּה	בֹּשְׁתָּ	נְקוּמֹתָ	הֲקִימוֹתָ	הוּקַמְתָּ	שַׂמְתָּ
2 f.	קַמְתְּ	מַתְּ	בֹּשְׁתְּ	נְקוּמֹת	הֲקִימוֹת	הוּקַמְתְּ	שַׂמְתְּ
1 c.	קַמְתִּי	מַתִּי	בֹּשְׁתִּי	נְקוּמֹתִי	הֲקִימוֹתִי	הוּקַמְתִּי	שַׂמְתִּי

	QAL	QAL	QAL	NI.	HI.	HO.	QAL
	II waw						II yod
Pl.	Perfect form						
3 c.	קָמוּ	מֵתוּ	בּוֹשׁוּ	נָקוֹמוּ	הֵקִימוּ	הוּקְמוּ	שָׂמוּ
2 m.	קַמְתֶּם	מַתֶּם	בָּשְׁתֶּם	נְקוֹמֹתֶם	הֲקִימוֹתֶם	הוּקַמְתֶּם	שַׂמְתֶּם
2 f.	קַמְתֶּן	מַתֶּן	בָּשְׁתֶּן	נְקוֹמֹתֶן	הֲקִימֹתֶן	הוּקַמְתֶּן	שַׂמְתֶּן
1 c.	קַמְנוּ	מַתְנוּ	בֹּשְׁנוּ	נְקוֹמוֹנוּ	הֲקִימוֹנוּ	הוּקַמְנוּ	שַׂמְנוּ
Sing.	Imperfect form						
3 m.	יָקוּם	יָמוּת	יֵבוֹשׁ	יִקּוֹם	יָקִים	יוּקַם	יָשִׂים
3 f.	תָּקוּם	תָּמוּת	תֵּבוֹשׁ	תִּקּוֹם	תָּקִים	תּוּקַם	תָּשִׂים
2 m.	תָּקוּם	תָּמוּת	תֵּבוֹשׁ	תִּקּוֹם	תָּקִים	תּוּקַם	תָּשִׂים
2 f.	תָּקוּמִי	תָּמוּתִי	תֵּבוֹשִׁי	תִּקּוֹמִי	תָּקִימִי	תּוּקְמִי	תָּשִׂימִי
1 c.	אָקוּם	אָמוּת	אֵבוֹשׁ	אֶקּוֹם	אָקִים	אוּקַם	אָשִׂים
Pl.							
3 c.	יָקוּמוּ	יָמוּתוּ	יֵבוֹשׁוּ	יִקּוֹמוּ	יָקִימוּ	יוּקְמוּ	יָשִׂימוּ
3 f.	תְּקוּמֶינָה	תְּמוּתֶינָה	תֵּבוֹשְׁנָה		תְּקִימֶינָה תָּקֵמְנָה	תּוּקַמְנָה	תְּשִׂימֶינָה
2 m.	תָּקוּמוּ	תָּמוּתוּ	תֵּבוֹשׁוּ	תִּקּוֹמוּ	תָּקִימוּ	תּוּקְמוּ	תָּשִׂימוּ
2 f.	תְּקוּמֶינָה	תְּמוּתֶינָה	תֵּבוֹשְׁנָה		תְּקִימֶינָה תָּקֵמְנָה	תּוּקַמְנָה	תְּשִׂימֶינָה
1 c.	נָקוּם	נָמוּת	נֵבוֹשׁ	נִקּוֹם	נָקִים	נוּקַם	נָשִׂים
Sing.	Imperative form						
2 m.	קוּם	מֻת	בּוֹשׁ	הִקּוֹם	הָקֵם		שִׂים
2 f.	קוּמִי	מוּתִי	בּוֹשִׁי	הִקּוֹמִי	הָקִימִי		שִׂימִי
Pl.							
2 m.	קוּמוּ	מוּתוּ	בּוֹשׁוּ	הִקּוֹמוּ	הָקִימוּ		שִׂימוּ
2 f.	קֹמְנָה	מוּתֶנָה	בּוֹשֶׁנָה	הִקָּמְנָה	הָקֵמְנָה		
Sing.	Cohortative form						
	אָקוּמָה	אָמוּתָה	אֵבוֹשָׁה		אָקִימָה		אָשִׂימָה

	QAL	QAL	QAL	NI.	HI.	HO.	QAL
			II waw				II yod
Sing.				Jussive form			
	יָקֹם	יָמֹת	יֵבוֹשׁ		יָקֵם		יָשֵׂם
				Infinitive			
cs.	קוֹם	מוֹת	בּוֹשׁ	הִקּוֹם	הָקִים	הוּקַם	שִׂים
abs.	קוֹם	מוֹת	בּוֹשׁ	הִקּוֹם	הָקֵם	הוּקֵם	שׂוֹם
				Participle			
act.	קָם	מֵת	בּוֹשׁ	נָקוֹם	מֵקִים	מוּקָם	שָׂם
pass.	קוּם						

3. General features

(i) General

a. In the stem syllable (i.e. the syllable that begins with the first stem consonant) the waw or yod falls way or functions as a vowel indicator, e.g. קָם and מֵת, קוּם and מוֹתּ.

b. A connecting vowel occurs before the consonantal suffixes.

- In the perfect it is / וֹ /

         הֲקִימוֹתִי   instead of   הֲקִימְתִי

- and in the imperfect it is / ֶּ- /.

         תְּקוּמֶינָה   instead of   תָּקוּמְנָה

c. The vowel of the prefix is long and is found in an open syllable. This long vowel reduces should a connecting vowel occur in the verb.

         הֲקִימוֹתִי   instead of   הֲקִימוֹתִי
         תְּקוּמֶינָה   instead of   תָּקוּמֶינָה

d. The II yod verbs are, *with the exception of the Qal imperfect, imperative and infinitive construct*, identical to the II waw verbs in all respects, e.g. קָם and שָׂם.

- In these exceptions the yod, instead of the waw, functions as a vowel indicator (as the only distinguishing feature of II yod verbs), e.g. קָם and קוּם תָּקָם, but שָׂם and תָּשִׂים.

Note the following:

(1) The II yod verbs are considerably fewer in number than the II waw verbs. The II yod verbs that occur most frequently are דִּין (judge), בִּין (understand), גִּיל (shudder), רִיב (strive), שִׁיר (sing) and שִׁית (put down).

(2) Certain II waw verbs retain the characteristics of verbs having three stem consonants, namely גּוע (dwindle away), צוה (command), קוה (hope), היה (be) and חיה (live).

(ii) *Qal*

a. In the perfect 3 masculine singular and the 3 feminine singular forms the waw and yod have fallen away in the stem syllable, e.g. קָם and קָמָה.

- A long vowel occurs before vocalic suffixes and forms without suffixes, e.g. קָם and קָמָה.

- This long vowel changes before consonantal suffixes, e.g. קַמְתָּ and שַׂמְתָּ.

b. The vowels of the stative perfect form correspond to the vowels in the second syllable of verbs with three stem consonants, e.g. מֵת as קָ-טֵל, בּושׁ as כָּ-בֵד.

c. When the normal suffixes of the perfect are added to verbs such as מֵת, the / ֵ / is replaced by / ַ /, e.g. מַתָּה as קָמְתָּ. (The ת doubles because the verb stem ends on a ת and the suffix begins with a ת.) In stative verbs such as בּושׁ, however, the / ֵ / is retained (בֹּשְׁתָּ).

d. In the imperfect the vowel of the preformative is / ָ / instead of / ִ /.

תָּקוּם	instead of	תִּקוּם
תָּשִׂים	instead of	תִּשִׂים

e. In the imperative and infinitive construct

- the II waw verbs take / וּ / as stem vowel, e.g. קוּם and קוּמִי and
- the II yod verbs take / ִי / as stem vowel, e.g. שִׂים and שִׂימִי.

f. The stem vowel of the infinitive absolute is / וֹ / like that of the regular verbs, e.g. קוֹם as כָּתוֹב.

g. In the jussive

- the long / וּ / of the II waw changes to / ָ /.

תָּקָם	instead of	תָּקוּם

- the / ִי / of the II yod changes to / ֵ /.

תָּשֵׂם   instead of   תָּשִׂים

h. In the waw consecutive + imperfect

• the / ֹ /of the II waw changes to / ֹ / (qāmeṣ ḥāṭûp).

וַתָּקָם   instead of   וַתָּקוּם

• the / ֵ / of the II yod changes to / ֶ /.

וַתָּשֶׂם   instead of   וַתָּשֵׂם

i. The masculine singular participle and the perfect 3 masculine singular are identical in form, viz. קָם. Although the corresponding
feminine forms also seem to be identical, the accent in the perfect
falls on the first syllable (קָ֫מָה) while it falls on the final syllable in
the participle (קָמָ֫ה).

(iii) *Niphal*

a. Since the preformative in the perfect does not form a closed syllable
with the first stem consonant, the preformative is -נָ and not -נִ.

נָקוֹם   instead of   נִקוֹם

b. The stem vowel of the perfect is / וֹ / (נָקוֹם) or / וֹ / (נְקוּמֹתִי) and not
/ ַ / (קַם).

• With the consonantal suffixes the connecting vowel / ֹ / is
inserted between the suffix and the final stem consonant. As a
result of the accompanying accent shift, the preformative / ַ / is
reduced to / ְ /.

נָקוּמֹתִי*   instead of   נָקוּמֹתִי*
נְקוּמֹתִי   instead of   נָקוּמֹתִי*

c. The imperfect is highly irregular. The vowel of the preformative is / ִ /.
The next consonant doubles and the waw functions as the vowel
indicator / וֹ /, e.g. יִקּוֹם as יִכָּתֵב.

(iv) *Piel, Pual and Hithpael and Polel, Polal and Hithpolel*

Instead of the Piel, Pual and Hithpael stem formations, the II waw
and II yod verbs have a Polel, Polal and Hithpolel stem formation,
respectively. It is clear from the names of these stem formations that
the final stem consonant is repeated. The conjugation of verbs in
these stem formations is otherwise regular.

Table 17. *Polel, Polal and Hithpolel*

	POLEL	POLAL	HITHPOLEL
Sing.	Perfect form		
3 m.	קוֹמֵם	קוֹמַם	הִתְקוֹמֵם
3 f.	קוֹמֵמָה	(קוֹמֲמָה)	(הִתְקוֹמֲמָה)
2 m.	קוֹמַמְתָּ	קוֹמַמְתָּ	הִתְקוֹמַמְתָּ
2 f.	(קוֹמַמְתְּ)	(קוֹמַמְתְּ)	(הִתְקוֹמַמְתְּ)
1 c.	קוֹמַמְתִּי	קוֹמַמְתִּי	הִתְקוֹמַמְתִּי
Pl.			
3 c.	קוֹמֵמוּ	קוֹמֲמוּ	הִתְקוֹמֲמוּ
2 m.	(קוֹמַמְתֶּם)	(קוֹמַמְתֶּם)	(הִתְקוֹמַמְתֶּם)
2 f.	קוֹמַמְתֶּן	קוֹמַמְתֶּן	הִתְקוֹמַמְתֶּן
1 c.	(קוֹמַמְנוּ)	(קוֹמַמְנוּ)	(הִתְקוֹמַמְנוּ)
Sing.	Imperfect form		
3 m.	יְקוֹמֵם	יְקוֹמַם	יִתְקוֹמֵם
3 f.	תְּקוֹמֵם	(תְּקוֹמַם)	תִּתְקוֹמֵם
2 m.	תְּקוֹמֵם	תְּקוֹמַם	תִּתְקוֹמֵם
2 f.	(תְּקוֹמֲמִי)	תְּקוֹמֲמִי	תִּתְקוֹמֲמִי
1 c.	אֲקוֹמֵם	אֲקוֹמַם	אֶתְקוֹמֵם
Pl.			
3 c.	יְקוֹמֲמוּ	יְקוֹמֲמוּ	יִתְקוֹמֲמוּ
3 f.	תְּקוֹמֵמְנָה	תְּקוֹמַמְנָה	תִּתְקוֹמֵמְנָה
2 m.	תְּקוֹמֲמוּ	(תְּקוֹמֲמוּ)	תִּתְקוֹמֲמוּ
2 f.	תְּקוֹמֵמְנָה	תְּקוֹמַמְנָה	תִּתְקוֹמֵמְנָה
1 c.	נְקוֹמֵם	(נְקוֹמַם)	(נִתְקוֹמֵם)
Sing.	Imperative form		
2 m.	קוֹמֵם		
2 f.	(קוֹמֲמִי)		
Pl.			
2 m.	קוֹמֲמוּ		

	POLEL	*POLAL*	*HITHPOLEL*
Pl.	*Imperative form*		
2 f.	(קוֹמֵמְנָה)		
	Infinitive		
cs.	קוֹמֵם		
abs.			
	Participle		
act.	מְקוֹמֵם		
pass.		מְקוֹמָם	

General features of the Polel, Polal and Hithpolal and the similarities between them.

a. In the perfect
- only a -הֹת is added before the forms of the Polel to form the Hithpolel.
- the Polal can be distinguished from the Polel only in the 3 masculine singular.
- before vocalic suffixes the two matching consonants are separated with a ḥāṭēp vowel rather than with an audible šᵉwâ.

b. In the imperfect the Polel conjugates regularly.
- In the imperfect of the Hithpolel a -הֹת prefix replaces the ׳ preformative of the Polel.
- In the imperfect of the Polal a / ◌ / occurs in the place of the Polel's / ◌ /.

c. The forms of the imperative, infinitive and participle are derived in the usual way.

(v) *Hiphil*

a. In the Hiphil perfect and imperfect the waw falls away and a vowel indicator / ׳ / occurs in the stem syllable.

הֵקִים   instead of   הֵקוּם

b. In the perfect the vowel of the preformative is / ◌ / instead of / ◌ /.

הֵקִים   instead of   הִקִים

- The preformative vowel is reduced when a connecting vowel is inserted later in the verb, e.g. הֲקִימֹתָ.

c. In the imperfect the vowel of the preformative is / ֶ / instead of
/ ָ /.

        תְּקִים   instead of   תָּקִים

• The vowel of the preformative is reduced when a connecting
vowel is used later in the verb, e.g. תְּקִימֶינָה.

d. The preformative vowel of the participle is / ְ / and not / ָ /.

        מְקִים   instead of   מַקִים

e. In the jussive form the stem vowel in the second syllable / י ִ /
changes to / ָ /.

        תָּקֵם   instead of   תָּקִים

f. In the waw consecutive + imperfect the / ָ / mentioned above
changes to / ֶ / due to the accent shift that accompanies the waw
consecutive + imperfect.

        וַתָּקֶם   instead of   וַתָּקֵם

• Should the II waw verb end with a guttural or resh, the stem
vowel / ֶ / changes to / ָ /.

        וַיָּסַר   instead of   וַיָּסָר

g. The preformative vowel of the imperative is also / ֶ /. The
imperative and infinitive construct may also be derived in the usual
way, e.g. הָקֵם.

(vi) *Hophal*

In the perfect and imperfect / ו / functions as the vowel for the preformative instead of / ָ /.

        הוּקַם   instead of   הָקַם
        יוּקַם   instead of   יָקַם

§18.9. *The Geminate Verbs*

1. *Introduction*

The term geminate verbs refers to verbs that have identical second
and third stem consonants, e.g. סבב (surround), בזז (capture). They
bear certain similarities to the II waw verbs. The features of the
geminate verbs in the Qal, Niphal, Hiphil and Hophal stem formations may be systematically described as follows:

(a) A connecting vowel occurs before the consonantal suffix. In
the perfect it is / ו / and in the imperfect it is / י ֶ /.

(b) The preformative vowel in an open syllable is long.

(c) The long vowel is reduced if a connecting vowel occurs in the verb.

(d) In the conjugations that have no suffixes, the third stem consonant usually falls away, while the middle consonant usually doubles in forms which have either vocalic or consonantal suffixes. (The first two stem consonants constitute the stem syllable.)

(e) The accent usually falls on the stem syllable. When a connecting vowel is added, this vowel is usually accented.
In a closed unaccented syllable a vowel change occurs, for example, / - / becomes / - / and / י / becomes / - /.

2. Table 18. *Geminate verbs*

	QAL	QAL	QAL	NI.	HI.	HI.	HO.
Gloss	sur-round	sur-round	be swift				
Sing.				*Perfect form*			
3 m.	סַב	סָבַב	קַל	נָסַב	הֵסַב	הֵסֵב	הוּסַב
3 f.	סַבָּה	סָבְבָה סָבֲבָה	קַלָּה	נָסַבָּה	הֵסַבָּה	הֵסֵבָּה	הוּסַבָּה
2 m.	סַבּוֹתָ		קַלּוֹתָ	נְסַבּוֹתָ	הֲסִבּוֹתָ		הוּסַבּוֹתָ
2 f.	סַבּוֹת		קַלּוֹת	נְסַבּוֹת	הֲסִבּוֹת		הוּסַבּוֹת
1 c.	סַבּוֹתִי		קַלּוֹתִי	נְסַבּוֹתִי	הֲסִבּוֹתִי		הוּסַבּוֹתִי
Pl.							
3 c.	סַבּוּ	סָבֲבוּ סָבְבוּ	קַלּוּ	נָסַבּוּ	הֵסַבּוּ		
2 m.	סַבּוֹתֶם		קַלּוֹתֶם	נְסַבּוֹתֶם	הֲסִבּוֹתֶם		הוּסַבּוֹתֶם
2 f.	סַבּוֹתֶן		קַלּוֹתֶן	נְסַבּוֹתֶן	הֲסִבּוֹתֶן		הוּסַבּוֹתֶן
1 c.	סַבּוֹנוּ		קַלּוֹנוּ	נְסַבּוֹנוּ	הֲסִבּוֹנוּ		הוּסַבּוֹנוּ
Sing.				*Imperfect form*			
3 m.	יָסֹב	יִסֹּב	יֵקַל	יִסֹּב	יָסֵב	יָסֵב	יוּסַב יִסַּב
3 f.	תָּסֹב	תִּסֹּב	תֵּקַל	תִּסֹּב	תָּסֵב		תּוּסַב
2 m.	תָּסֹב	תִּסֹּב	תֵּקַל	תִּסֹּב	תָּסֵב		תּוּסַב
2 f.	תָּסֹבִּי	תִּסֹּבִּי	תֵּקַלִּי	תִּסֹּבִּי	תָּסֵבִּי		תּוּסַבִּי
1 c.	אָסֹב	אֶסֹּב	אֵקַל	אֶסֹּב	אָסֵב		אוּסַב

	QAL	QAL	QAL	NI.	HI.	HI.	HO.
Pl.	Imperfect form						
3 c.	יָסֹבּוּ	יִסְבוּ	יֵקַלּוּ	יִסַּבּוּ	יָסֵבּוּ	יָסֵבּוּ	יוּסַבּוּ
3 f.	תְּסֻבֶּינָה	תִּסֹבְנָה	תְּקַלֶּינָה	תִּסַּבֶּינָה	תְּסִבֶּינָה		תּוּסַבֶּינָה
2 m.	תָּסֹבּוּ	תִּסְבוּ	תֵּקַלּוּ	תִּסַּבּוּ	תָּסֵבּוּ		תּוּסַבּוּ
2 f.	תְּסֻבֶּינָה	תִּסֹבְנָה	תְּקַלֶּינָה	תִּסַּבֶּינָה	תְּסִבֶּינָה		תּוּסַבֶּינָה
1 c.	נָסֹב	נִסֹב	נֵקַל	נִסַּב	נָסֵב		נוּסַב
Sing.	Imperative form						
2 m.	סֹב			הִסַּב	הָסֵב		
2 f.	סֹבִּי			הִסַּבִּי	הָסֵבִּי		
Pl.							
2 m.	סֹבּוּ			הִסַּבּוּ	הָסֵבּוּ		
2 f.	סֻבֶּינָה			הִסַּבֶּינָה	הֲסִבֶּינָה		
Sing.	Cohortative form						
	אָסֹבָּה	אֶסֹבָּה	אֶקַלָּה				
Sing.	Jussive form						
	יָסֹב	יִסֹב	יֵקַל	יִסַּב	יָסֵב		
	Infinitive						
cs.	סֹב		קַל	הִסַּב	הָסֵב		
abs.	סָבוֹב		קָלוֹל	הִסּוֹב	הָסֵב		
	Participle						
act.	סֹבֵב	סוֹבֵב	קַל	נָסָב	מֵסֵב		מוּסָב
pass.		סָבוּב					

3. General characteristics

(i) Qal

A clear distinction must be made between the forms of geminate verbs that have an active meaning and those that have a stative meaning. Here are some of the verbs that occur frequently.

Statives		Actives	
חָתַת	to be destroyed	אָרַר	to curse
מָרַר	to be bitter	בָּלַל	to mix

Statives		Actives	
קָלַל	to be quick	גָּלַל	to roll away
רָעַע	to be bad	מָדַד	to measure
שָׁמֵם	to be desolate	סָבַב	to surround
		שָׁדַד	to destroy

Qal with active meaning

a. In the Qal perfect 3 masculine singular, 3 feminine singular and 3 plural variants occur according to rule, viz. the identical second and third consonants may be visibly repeated (סָבְבָה or סָבְבָה). However, the repetition may also be indicated by means of a dāḡeš in the second consonant (סָבָּה).

   - Sometimes the third consonant falls away and sometimes it is retained, e.g. סָבַב and סַב.

b. In the Qal imperfect the vowel of the preformative is / ָ / and / ֹ / occurs in the stem syllable, e.g. תָּסֹב as תָּקוּם. This conjugation corresponds with that of the II waw verbs.

   - Variants that conjugate like I nun verbs also occur, e.g. תִּסֹב as תִּפֹּל.

c. The accent shift that accompanies the waw consecutive + imperfect results in the / ֹ / of the imperfect changing to / ָ /.

$$\text{וַתָּסָב} \quad \text{instead of} \quad \text{וַתָּסֹב}$$

d. The imperative, infinitive construct and participle may be derived regularly, e.g. סֹב.

Qal with a stative meaning

a. The third consonant falls away in:

   - the perfect 3 masculine singular, the masculine singular participle

$$\text{תַּם} \quad \text{instead of} \quad \text{תָּמַם}$$

   - the imperative

$$\text{תַּם} \quad \text{instead of} \quad \text{תְּמַם}$$

   - and the infinitive

$$\text{תַּם} \quad \text{instead of} \quad \text{תְּמַם}$$

b. The preformative vowel of the imperfect is / ִ / and not / ָ /. An / ַ / also occurs in the stem syllable.

$$\text{יִתַּם} \quad \text{instead of} \quad \text{יִתַּם}$$

(ii) *Niphal*

a. In the Niphal the geminate root always occurs in its shortened form,
   e.g. נָסַבָּה not נְסַבְבָה.

b. The preformative vowel of the perfect and participle changes to
   / ַ /.

נָסַב	instead of	נסַב
נָסָב	instead of	נסָב

c. The stem vowel of the imperfect, imperative and infinitive is
   / ַ /.

חִסַּב	instead of	תִסֵב

(iii) *Piel, Pual and Hithpael / Poel, Poal and Hithpoel*

Geminate verbs have Poel, Poal and Hithpoel stem formations
instead of the Piel, Pual, Hithpael respectively. The former stem
formations are characterized by the vowel indicator / וֹ / between the
first and second stem consonants.

a. The conjugation of verbs in these formations is identical in all
   respects to the Polel, Polal and Hithpolel stem formations of the II
   waw verbs. (Cf. §18.8.)
   - Poel perfect 3 masculine singular, e.g. סוֹבֵב.
   - Poel imperfect 3 masculine singular, e.g. יְסוֹבֵב.

b. The following forms may also be derived regularly:
   - Poel imperative masculine singular, e.g. סוֹבֵב.
   - Poel infinitive construct, e.g. סוֹבֵב.
   - Poel participle, e.g. מְסוֹבֵב.

c. Some geminate verbs have either regular Piel forms or conjugations
   that duplicate the first two stem consonants instead of a Poel stem
   formation. The duplicated stem formations are called the Pilpel and
   Hithpalpel.
   - Piel perfect 3 masculine singular, e.g. גִּלֵּל.
   - Pilpel perfect 1 singular, e.g. גִּלְגַּלְתִּי.
   - Hithpalpel perfect 3 masculine plural, e.g. הִתְגַּלְגָּלוּ.

(iv) *Hiphil*

a. The stem vowel of all Hiphil conjugations is / ַ /.

יַסֵב	instead of	יָסִיב
מֵסֵב	instead of	מֵסִיב

b. The preformative vowel of the perfect changes to / - /.

הֻסַב   instead of   הֵסַב

c. The preformative vowel of the imperfect, infinitive construct and imperative, / - /, changes to / - /.

יֻסַב   instead of   יָסֵב

הֻסֵב   instead of   הָסֵב

d. When a suffix that begins with a consonant is added, the stem vowel of the imperfect changes to / - /.

הֲסִבּוֹנוּ   instead of   הֵסַבּוֹנוּ

e. The forms of the imperative and infinitive may be derived regularly, e.g. הָסֵב.

f. The preformative vowel of the participle is / - / and not / - /.

מֵסַב   instead of   מַסֵב

g. The accent shift that accompanies the waw consecutive + imperfect leads to the / - / in the final syllable changing to / - / in the Hiphil.

וַיָּסֶךְ   instead of   וַיָּסֵךְ

h. In verbs with a guttural as second and third stem consonants:

- the / - / before the final guttural in the 3 masculine singular is replaced by a / - /.

הֵרַע   instead of   הֵרֵע

- 'Compensatory lengthening' occurs in conjugations where the guttural is meant to double. The / - / changes to / - /.

הֲרֵעוֹתָ   instead of   הַרֵעוֹתָ

(v) Hophal

The Hophal is formed by analogy with the II waw verbs

a. Perfect, e.g. הוּסַב as הוּקַם.

b. Imperfect, e.g. יוּסַב as יוּקַם.

c. Infinitive construct, e.g. הוּסֵב as הוּקֵם.

d. Participle, e.g. מוּסָב as מוּקָם.

§18.10. *Verbs with More than One Irregular Consonant*

1. The following types occur fairly frequently:

I aleph and III he, e.g.	אבה	willing	(Cf. Table 19a.)
I nun and III aleph, e.g.	נשא	raise up/carry	(Cf. Table 19b.)
I waw and III he, e.g.	ירה	shoot	(Cf. Table 19c.)
I waw and III aleph, e.g.	יצא	go out	(Cf. Table 19d.)
I yod and III aleph, e.g.	ירא	fear	(Cf. Table 19e.)
II guttural and III he, e.g.	ראה	see	(Cf. Table 19f.)
II waw and III aleph, e.g.	בוא	come	(Cf. Table 19g.)
I nun and III he, e.g.	נטה	stretch out	(Cf. Table 19h.)

2. Table 19a. *I aleph and III he*

	QAL	NI.	PI.	PU.	HI.	HO.
Perf.	אָבָה					
Impf.	יֹאבֶה					
Juss.	יֹאבֶה					
Wc.+impf.	וַיֹּאבֶה					
Imp.						
Inf. cs.						
Inf. abs.						
Part.	אֹבִים					

3. Table 19b. *I nun and III aleph*

	QAL	NI.	PI.	PU.	HI.	HO.
Perf.	נָשָׂא	נִשָּׂא			הִשִּׂיא	
Impf.	יִשָּׂא	As	III aleph	verb stem	יַשִּׂיא	
Juss.	יִשָּׂא				יַשֵּׂא	
Wc.+impf.	וַיִּשָּׂא				וַיַּשֵּׂא	
Imp.	שָׂא				הַשִּׂא	
Inf. cs.	שְׂאֵת				הַשִּׂיא	
Inf. abs.	נָשׂוֹא				הַשֵּׂא	
Part.	נֹשֵׂא				מַשִּׂיא	

4. Table 19c. *I waw and III he*

	QAL	NI.	PI.	PU.	HI.	HO.
Perf.	יָרָה				הוֹרָה	
Impf.		יִיָּרֶה			יוֹרֶה	
Juss.					יוֹר	
Wc.+impf.					וַיּוֹר	
Imp.	יְרֵה					
Inf. cs.						
Inf. abs.	יָרֹה					
Part.	יָרֶה				מוֹרֶה	

5. Table 19d. *I waw and III aleph*

	QAL	NI.	PI.	PU.	HI.	HO.
Perf.	יָצָא				הוֹצִיא	הוּצָא
Impf.	יֵצֵא				יוֹצִיא	יוּצָא
Juss.	יֵצֵא				יוֹצֵא	
Wc.+impf.	וַיֵּצֵא				וַיּוֹצֵא	וַיּוּצָא
Imp.	צֵא				הוֹצֵא	
Inf. cs.	צֵאת				הוֹצִיא	הוּצָא
Inf. abs.	יָצוֹא				הוֹצֵא	
Part.	יֹצֵא				מוֹצִיא	מוּצָא

6. Table 19e. *I yod and III aleph*

	QAL	NI.	PI.	PU.	HI.	HO.
Perf.	יָרֵא					
Impf.	יִירָא	חֵוָרֵא				
Juss.	יִירָא					
Wc.+impf.	וַיִּירָא					
Imp.	יְרָא					
Part.	יָרֵא					

7. Table 19f. *II guttural and III he* (ראה *vs.* ירא)

	QAL	NI.	PI.	PU.	HI.	HO.
Perf.	רָאָה				הֶרְאָה	
Impf.	יִרְאֶה				יַרְאֶה	
Juss.	יֵרֶא				יַרְא	
Wc.+impf.	וַיִּרְאֶה וַתֵּרֶא וַיִּרְא				וַיַּרְאֶה וַיַּרְא	
Imp.	רְאֵה					
Inf. cs.	רְאוֹת				הַרְאוֹת	
Inf. abs.	רָאֹה					
Part.	רֹאֶה				מַרְאֶה	

8. Table 19g. *II waw and III aleph*

	QAL	NI.	PI.	PU.	HI.	HO.
Perf.	בָּא				הֵבִיא	הוּבָא
Impf.	יָבֹא				יָבִיא	יוּבָא
Juss.	יָבֹא				יָבֵא	
Wc.+impf.	וַיָּבֹא				וַיָּבֵא	וַיּוּבָא
Imp.	בֹּא				הָבֵא	
Inf. cs.	בֹּא				הָבִיא	הוּבָא
Inf. abs.	בּוֹא				הָבֵא	
Part.	בָּא				מֵבִיא	מוּבָא

9. Table 19h. *I nun and III he*

	QAL	NI.	PI.	PU.	HI.	HO.
Perf.	נָטָה				הִטָּה	הֻטָּה
Impf.	יִטֶּה				יַטֶּה	יֻטֶּה
Juss	יֵט				יֵט	
Wc.+impf.	וַיֵּט				וַיֵּט	וַיֵּט
Imp.	נְטֵה				הַטֵּה	
Inf. abs.	נָטֹה				הַטֵּה	הֻטָּה

	QAL	NI.	PI.	PU.	HI.	HO.
Inf. cs.	נְטוֹת				הַטּוֹת	הָטּוֹת
Part.	נֹטֶה				מַטֶּה	מֻטֶּה

§18.11. *Others:* הָלַךְ *and* לָקַח, נָתַן, חָוָה, חָיָה, הָיָה

1. Table 20. הָלַךְ *and* לָקַח, נָתַן, חָיָה, הָיָה

	QAL		QAL	NI.	QAL pass.	QAL	NI.	QAL
Sing.	*Perfect form*							
3 m.	הָיָה	חָיָה	נָתַן	נִתַּן	נֻתַּן	לָקַח	נִלְקַח	הָלַךְ
3 f.	הָיְתָה	as	נָתְנָה	נִתְּנָה		לָקְחָה	נִלְקְחָה	regu-
2 m.	הָיִיתָ	היה	נָתַתָּ	נִתַּתָּ	-	לָקַחְתָּ	נִלְקַחְתָּ	lar
2 f.	הָיִית		נָתַתְּ	נִתַּתְּ	-	regu-	נִלְקַחְתְּ	
1 c.	הָיִיתִי		נָתַתִּי	נִתַּתִּי	-	lar	נִלְקַחְתִּי	
Pl.								
3 c.	הָיוּ		נָתְנוּ	נִתְּנוּ	-		נִלְקְחוּ	
2 m.	הֱיִיתֶם		נְתַתֶּם	נִתַּתֶּם	-	..	נִלְקַחְתֶּם	
2 f.	הֱיִיתֶן		נְתַתֶּן	נִתַּתֶּן	-		-	
1 c.	הָיִינוּ		נָתַנּוּ	נִתַּנּוּ	-		נִלְקַחְנוּ	
Sing.	*Imperfect form*							
3 m.	יִהְיֶה		יִתֵּן	יִנָּתֵן	יֻתַּן	יִקַּח	יִלָּקַח	יֵלֵךְ
3 f.	תִּהְיֶה		תִּתֵּן	תִּנָּתֵן	תֻּתַּן	תִּקַּח	תִּלָּקַח	תֵּלֵךְ
2 m.	תִּהְיֶה		תִּתֵּן	תִּנָּתֵן	תֻּתַּן	תִּקַּח	תִּלָּקַח	תֵּלֵךְ
2 f.	תִּהְיִי		תִּתְּנִי	תִּנָּתְנִי	תֻּתְּנִי	תִּקְּחִי	תִּלָּקְחִי	תֵּלְכִי
1 c.	אֶהְיֶה		אֶתֵּן	אֶנָּתֵן	אֻתַּן	אֶקַּח	אֶלָּקַח	אֵלֵךְ
Pl.								
3 c.	יִהְיוּ		יִתְּנוּ	יִנָּתְנוּ	יֻתְּנוּ	יִקְּחוּ	יִלָּקְחוּ	יֵלְכוּ
3 f.	תִּהְיֶינָה		תִּתֵּנָּה		-	תִּקַּחְנָה-		תֵּלַכְנָה
2 m.	תִּהְיוּ		תִּתְּנוּ	תִּנָּתְנוּ	תֻּתְּנוּ	תִּקְּחוּ	תִּלָּקְחוּ	תֵּלְכוּ
2 f.	תִּהְיֶינָה		תִּתֵּנָּה		-	תִּקַּחְנָה-		תֵּלַכְנָה
1 c.	נִהְיֶה		נִתֵּן	נִנָּתֵן	נֻתַּן	נִקַּח	נִלָּקַח	נֵלֵךְ

	QAL		QAL	NI.	QAL pass.	QAL	NI.	QAL
Sing.	*Imperative form*							
2 m.	הֱיֵה		תֵן	הִנָּתֵן	absent	קַח	הִלָּקַח	לֵךְ
2 f.	הֲיִי		תְּנִי	הִנָּתְנִי		קְחִי	הִלָּקְחִי	לְכִי
Pl.								
2 m.	הֱיוּ		תְּנוּ	הִנָּתְנוּ		קְחוּ	הִלָּקְחוּ	לְכוּ
2 f.			תֵּנָּה			קַחְנָה	הִלָּחְנָה	לֵכְנָה
Sing.	*Cohortative form*							
			אֶתְּנָה			אֶקְחָה		אֵלְכָה
Sing.	*Jussive form*							
	יְהִי		יִתֵּן			יִקַּח		
	Infinitive							
cs.	הֱיוֹת		תֵּת	הִנָּתֵן		קַחַת	הִלָּקַח	לֶכֶת
abs.			נָתוֹן	הִנָּתֹן		לָקוֹחַ	הִלָּקֹחַ	הָלוֹךְ
	Participle							
act.			נֹתֵן			לֹקֵחַ		הֹלֵךְ
pass.			נָתוּן	נִתָּן		לָקוּחַ	נִלְקָח	

2. הָיָה *and* חָיָה *(Table 20)*

Apart from the conjugation patterns normally associated with I and III gutturals, this verb stem also has several unique features.

a. / ֱ / is found with the I guttural where one would expect / ֲ /.

הֱיִיתֶם	instead of	הֲיִיתֶם
הֱיוֹת	instead of	הֲיוֹת

b. In the imperfect the vowel of the preformative is not influenced by the I guttural.

יִהְיֶה	instead of	יֶהְיֶה

c. The II yod never becomes a vowel indicator except in the case of (short) jussive forms.

יְהִי	instead of	יִהְיֶה

3. חוה

For a very long time הִשְׁתַּחֲוָה was regarded as a Hithpael form of שׁחה in which *metathesis* had occurred. However, research into Ugaritic, a Semitic language closely related to BH, has clearly indicated that it is a relic from an earlier stage of the language. One is here dealing with a verb stem חוה that is used in a stem formation to which a /hišt-/ or /yišt/ syllable is added. Only one verb stem occurs in this stem formation, namely חוה. The most common meaning of this verb stem is 'to bow'. This stem formation is called the Hištafel.

The following Hištafel forms of חוה occur the most:

	Perf.	*Impf.*	*Imp.*	*Part.*	*Inf. cs.*
3 m. sing.	הִשְׁתַּחֲוָה	יִשְׁתַּחֲוֶה			
2 m. sing.	הִשְׁתַּחֲוִיתָ	תִּשְׁתַּחֲוֶה			
1 sing.	הִשְׁתַּחֲוֵיתִי	אֶשְׁתַּחֲוֶה			
3 m. pl.	הִשְׁתַּחֲווּ	יִשְׁתַּחֲווּ			
2 m. pl.	הִשְׁתַּחֲוִיתֶם	תִּשְׁתַּחֲווּ	הִשְׁתַּחֲווּ		
1 pl.	הִשְׁתַּחֲוִינוּ	נִשְׁתַּחֲוֶה			
					הִשְׁתַּחֲוֹת
m. sing.				מִשְׁתַּחֲוֶה	
m. pl.				מִשְׁתַּחֲוִים	

The waw consecutive + imperfect is formed by adding the conjunction -וַ to the imperfect forms, in which case the first consonant doubles. The following are the forms for the 3 masculine singular and 2 masculine singular:

*וַיִּשְׁתַּחֲוֶה	וַיִּשְׁתַּחוּ	'and he bowed'
*וַתִּשְׁתַּחֲוֶה	וַתִּשְׁתַּחוּ	'and you bowed'

4. נתן *(Table 20)*

a. The perfect conjugates regularly. Note that the final nun assimilates with the ת of the suffixes.

נָתַתָּ   instead of   נָתַנְתָּ

b. The stem vowel of the imperfect is / ֵ / as though this were a I waw verb stem.

יִתֵּן   instead of   יִנְתֵּן

In addition to the assimilation of the first nun, the final nun also assimilates with the subsequent consonantal suffix, נָתַתֶּם and תִּתְּנִי.

c. In the infinitive construct and imperative the I nun of the verb stem falls way (or it may be derived regularly from the imperfect).

     תֵּת instead of   נְתֹן

d. נתן also has conjugations in the Hophal imperfect. However, these forms are traditionally interpreted as passive imperfect forms of the Qal stem formation, e.g. יֻתַּן. (Cf. Joüon–Muraoka §58a and 72i.) Table 20 reflects the traditional interpretation.

e. The infinitive construct is formed with a ת suffix.

 • The infinitive construct looks like a typical monosyllabic noun, e.g. תֵּת. (Cf. §27.4.) When the pronominal suffix is added to the infinitive it has an i-stem, e.g. תִּתִּי.

5. לקח *(Table 20)*

לקח behaves as if it were a I nun verb:

a. The perfect paradigm conjugates normally, e.g. לָקַח and לָקַחְתִּי.

b. In the imperfect conjugation the ל assimilates, like the I nun, with the subsequent consonant, e.g. יִקַּח and אֶקַּח.

c. The imperative is derived regularly from the imperfect.

     קַח instead of   לְקֹח

d. In the infinitive construct the ל of the verb stem falls away, and a suffix ת is added. לקח then looks like a typical segholate noun with a guttural as middle consonant. (Cf. §27.3.)

     קַחַת instead of   לְקֹח

e. לקח also has conjugations in the Pual imperfect. However, these forms have been interpreted traditionally as Qal passive imperfect forms, e.g. יֻקַּח.

6. הלך *(Table 20)*

a. The perfect paradigm conjugates as expected, e.g. הָלַךְ and הָלַכְתָּ.

b. With the exception of the Qal perfect הלך conjugates in the Qal and Hiphil like a typical I waw verb.

 • The imperfect forms look like I waw verbs, e.g. יֵלֵךְ as יֵשֵׁב.

 • In the imperative the ה of the verb stem falls away, e.g. לֵךְ and לְכִי.

• In the infinitive the ה of the verb stem falls away, and a suffix ת is added, e.g. לְכָת. לֶכֶת then has the appearance of a typical segholate noun. (Cf. §27.3.)

§19. **The Syntax and Semantics of the Finite Verb Forms**

§19.1. *The Problematics of the BH Verbal System*

1. *A tense or time system*

When a language possesses the *grammatical means* of referring to *moments in time*, we say that that language has a *tense system*. For example, in English we speak of a present, past and future tense of the verb.

> (1) She comes.
> She came.
> She will come.

The word 'come' conjugates in the *past tense* ('came'), while the *future tense* makes use of an auxiliary ('will'). Such a tense system can be very sophisticated: it may have a variety of different forms that refer to different moments in the past as is the case of English, for example, with its *simple past, present perfect* and *pluperfect*:

> (2) I saw him.
> I have seen him.
> I had seen him.

Each of the above sentences is indicative of a particular moment in the past. In contrast to English, the tense system of other languages may be much simpler, as is the case with Afrikaans that has no grammatical means of differentiating between the *simple past*, the *present perfect* and the *pluperfect*. In other words, the English sentences above will have no direct Afrikaans equivalent in translation. The particular moment in the past to which the translation of the Afrikaans, 'Ek het hom gesien', refers must therefore be determined from its greater context.

2. *Aspect system*

Not all languages possess a grammatically realized tense system. In some languages verbs conjugate primarily to indicate whether an action is complete or incomplete. Languages which have the *grammatical* means of indicating that an *action is complete or incomplete* are described as having an *aspect system*. Consider the following example. In answer to the question:

(3)   What did you do last night?

one could answer:

> I finished reading my book; or
> I was reading my book.

In Russian one would use in the equivalent of *I finished reading my book* the perfect form of the verb 'read' instead of the lexeme 'finished' to indicate that the action has been completed.

3. *Time and aspect in BH*

Various opinions exist as to whether BH has a tense or an aspect system. Older Jewish grammarians, like the more recent grammarians who adopt their point of view, are of the opinion that the BH verb system is primarily a tense system. The *perfect* (cf. §15.1) thus refers to *past time* and the *imperfect* (cf. §15.1) to the *present and future*.[16]

In the previous century the study of the BH verb was freed from its 'time' straightjacket. According to this new interpretation of the perfect and the imperfect forms, they did not refer primarily to moments in time, but to the *aspect* of the verbs. According to this interpretation the perfect and imperfect as semantic categories refer to two extremes in terms of which all actions can be described. By using the perfect speakers describe an action from their perspective as completed. By using the imperfect speakers represent an action as incomplete or being in the process of completion. This explains why BH speakers can use an imperfect, which should refer to future events in terms of the tense system, to refer to a habitual action in the past, e.g.

> וְכֵן יַעֲשֶׂה שָׁנָה בְשָׁנָה   This is what *he used to do* year by
> year (1 Sam. 1.7).

The dilemma with the perfect and the imperfect aspectual categories is that, as with the temporal categories, they do not cover all the nuances that can be expressed by the perfect and the imperfect

---

16. Joüon–Muraoka §111a uses, 'for want of better terms, the common and disparate terms *perfect* and *future*, which at least have the advantage of being short and of reflecting the reality in the majority of cases'.

forms. These terms, which were intended to refer to the aspectual functions of BH verbs, became so entrenched that they are still used today to refer to the forms themselves. Terms such as suffix conjugation and prefix conjugation as well as *qatal* and *yiqtol* were therefore introduced with the specific purpose of preventing possible misunderstandings in this regard. In this grammar the terms perfect and imperfect will be retained because they still occur in most of the popular dictionaries. Note, however, that perfect and imperfect refer here to *the forms* of verbs and *not* to their *functions*.

No attempt will be made to account for the BH verb in terms of any one specific theory. The following distinctions with regard to the perfect and imperfect will serve as the points of departure in this grammar:

- (a) Any semantic functions mentioned here have a bearing only on free-standing perfect and imperfect forms. (For the functions of verb sequences such as waw consecutive + imperfect and waw consecutive + perfect, cf. §21.)

- (b) The interwovenness of aspect and time is a feature of many languages (Lyons 1968: 317).[17]

- (c) The following distinction is made with respect to time (with a few exceptions):

Perfect	= past time
Imperfect	= non-past time

The conjugations in BH do not distinguish between different moments in past time (e.g. the ordinary past, the distant past and the perfect) or between the present time, the future and modality. These distinctions, which naturally appear in the translations of a BH text in tense languages such as English, are exclusively determined by the context and the lexical signification of the verb.

- (d) The aspectual distinctions with regard to complete and non-complete actions correlate more or less with the above

---

17. Buth (1992: 95) quotes Greenberg (1966) in this regard. According to Greenberg one of the phenomena found in all languages which have verbs that conjugate is that these verbs always have 'a tense-aspect-mood signification'.

distinction (with some exceptions), namely[18]

Perfect	= past time	= completed action[19]
Imperfect	= non-past time	= non-complete action

(e) The exceptions,[20] which do not correlate with the above scheme, constitute a clearly distinguishable class in connection with: verbs that express some or other condition, for example, stative and passive, expressions involving performative language acts,[21] and certain conjunctions.

(f) It is not clear whether in BH it is time that assumes aspect, or aspect that assumes time.

(g) BH speakers and narrators had a choice of describing either the aspect or the time of an action. They apparently also had a choice with respect to the perspective from which they described an action. This could be done from the perspective of the narrator or the narrator could present the action from the perspective of his characters. In the latter case it is sometimes difficult to translate the perfect with the past tense and the imperfect with the present or future tense. (Cf. §19.2/1 and 19.3/1.)

§19.2. *The Perfect Form (Suffix Conjugation, Qatal)*

Perfect forms refer, broadly speaking, to complete events or facts that often can be translated with the past tense.

18. According to Buth (1992: 95) the perfect marks the 'definite tense-aspect' which normally refers to '*definite* events (that is, past or perfective or decisive or contrary to the fact)' as opposed to the imperfect which marks the 'indefinite tense-aspect' and refers to 'indefinite events (future or imperfective or potential or repetitive)'.

19. 'Complete' here refers to actions that have been completed or finalized and not to the totality of the action, as in Waltke and O'Connor §30 and 31.

20. It may be theoretically possible to explain these exceptions in terms of a sophisticated aspect theory, which attaches a great deal of importance to the speaker's presentation of events as perfective versus non-perfective, or definitive versus non-definitive. These explanations are not presented here for didactic reasons.

21. A performative action occurs when speakers perform an action by virtue of what they say, e.g. רְאֵה נָתַתִּי אֹתְךָ עַל כָּל־אֶרֶץ מִצְרָיִם 'See, I appoint you over all the land of Egypt' (Gen. 41.41).

1. *The perfect form indicates that actions, processes and events have already been completed in the past.*

(i) In most cases events are presented from the perspective of the narrator and can be translated with *the past tense*.

a. Simple past

וְלַחֹשֶׁךְ קָרָא לָיְלָה

And the darkness he *called* Night (Gen. 1.5).

b. Immediate past ('present perfect')

וַיֹּאמֶר מֶה עָשִׂיתָ

And he said, 'What *have* you *done?*' (Gen. 4.10).

c. Distant past ('pluperfect')

לֹא־יָדַע יַעֲקֹב
כִּי רָחֵל גְּנָבָתַם

Jacob did not know that Rachel *had stolen* them (Gen. 31.32).

(ii) Events in the past and/or completed events *that are described from the (time or aspectual) perspective of the characters* can be translated with the past tense.

לֹא אֹכַל עַד אִם־דִּבַּרְתִּי דְּבָרָי

I will not eat until I *have told* my message (Gen. 24.33).

(iii) *Hypothetical conditions or unrealizable wishes* make no reference to actual past events. From the perspective of the characters or the hypothetical world, however, events in the past are involved.[22]

לוּ־מַתְנוּ בְּאֶרֶץ מִצְרַיִם

Would that we *had died* in the land of Egypt (Num. 14.2).

לוּ הַחֲיִתֶם אוֹתָם
לֹא הָרַגְתִּי אֶתְכֶם:

If you *had saved them alive*, I would not slay you (Judg. 8.19).

2. *The perfect form can express a state of affairs or a condition.*

A state of affairs or a condition is usually expressed through a stative or passive verb. A stative verb cannot express a 'once-off,' completed action. It always carries a certain element of duration. The translation is determined by the context. In *dialogue* it is usually

22. Sometimes a perfect is used in the *protasis* of a real condition, where one would have expected an imperfect. Cf. 2 Kgs 7.4 and Deut. 21.14. For an extensive discussion of the use of verb forms in conditional clauses, cf. Joüon–Muraoka §167g.

translated with the present tense. In *narrative* it is usually translated with the past tense.

וַיֹּאמֶר הִנֵּה־נָא זָקַנְתִּי	And he said, 'Look, I *am old*' (Gen. 27.2).
וַתַּעַשׂ אִמּוֹ מַטְעַמִּים כַּאֲשֶׁר אָהֵב אָבִיו:	And his mother prepared savoury food, such as his father *loved*. (Gen. 27.14).

3. *The perfect form can indicate a performative action.*
A performative action is an action that occurs by means of speaking.

נְתַתִּי אֹתְךָ עַל כָּל־אֶרֶץ מִצְרָיִם	I *appoint* you over all the land of Egypt (Gen. 41.41).

4. *The perfect can indicate actions, events and/or facts that are not time-bound.*
Traditionally this was known as the *gnomic perfect* (rare).

וְתֹר וְסוּס וְעָגוּר שָׁמְרוּ אֶת־עֵת בֹּאָנָה	And the turtledove, swallow, and crane *keep* the time of their coming (Jer. 8.7).

5. *Rare uses*

(i) In prayers in which it is clear that a request is being made (the so-called *precative perfective*). The perfect is used in this way approximately 20 times in the Hebrew Bible, exclusively in the Psalms.

הוֹשִׁיעֵנִי מִפִּי אַרְיֵה וּמִקַּרְנֵי רֵמִים עֲנִיתָנִי:	Rescue me from the mouth of the lion, *save* me from the horns of the wild oxen! (Ps. 22.22).

(ii) *As a rhetorical means* of presenting future events as if they have already happened. This use of the perfect is often called the *prophetic perfect*.

לָכֵן גָּלָה עַמִּי מִבְּלִי־דָעַת	Therefore my people *will go into exile* for want of knowledge (Isa. 5.13).

§19.3. *The Imperfect form (Prefix Conjugation, Yiqtol)*

Imperfect forms refer, broadly speaking, to incomplete events that can often be translated with the present or future tense.

1. *The imperfect form usually indicates that events will occur in the future as definite events or as expectations.*

(i) In most cases the verb is translated with a *future tense*.

כִּי בְּיוֹם אֲכָלְךָ מִמֶּנּוּ	For in the day that you eat of it you
מוֹת תָּמוּת:	*shall die* (Gen. 2.17).

(ii) The events can be described as *'future' events from the character's perspective.*

וַיֵּלֶךְ הָאִישׁ ... לָגוּר בַּאֲשֶׁר	And the man departed ... to live
יִמְצָא	where he *could find* (a place) (Judg. 17.8).

2. *The imperfect form expresses actions and events in the past which continue for shorter or longer periods — usually after words such as:*

(i) טֶרֶם (-בְּ)[23] (Cf. §41.2/2.)

וּלְיוֹסֵף יֻלַּד שְׁנֵי בָנִים	And Joseph had two sons—*before* the
בְּטֶרֶם תָּבוֹא שְׁנַת הָרָעָב	year of famine *came* (Gen. 41.50).

(ii) עַד (Cf. §39.18.)

וַיִּדֹּם הַשֶּׁמֶשׁ ... עַד־יִקֹּם	And the sun stood still ... *until* the
גּוֹי אֹיְבָיו	nation *took vengeance* on its enemies (Josh. 10.13).

(iii) אָז (Cf. §40.4 and §41.2/1.)

אָז יַעֲלֶה חֲזָאֵל מֶלֶךְ אֲרָם	*At that time* Hazael, king of Syria, *went up* (2 Kgs 12.18).

There are several instances where אָז is followed by a perfect, e.g. Judg. 8.3. (Cf. also Revell 1989: 11 in this regard.)

3. *The imperfect form expresses actions and events in the present.*
This aspect of an action is usually expressed by means of participles. The imperfect that refers to *present continuous* ('present incomplete') actions is usually used *where a question is being posed.*

וַיִּשְׁאָלֵהוּ הָאִישׁ לֵאמֹר	And the man asked him, 'What *are*
מַה־תְּבַקֵּשׁ:	you *seeking?*' (Gen. 37.15).

---

23. טֶרֶם is not necessarily a conjunction. It can also function as an adverb. It must then be translated as 'not yet' and can be followed by a perfect or imperfect. When טֶרֶם is a conjunction, it may be preceded by the preposition בְּ and translated with 'before that'. In such cases it must be followed by an imperfect. (Cf. §41.2/2.)

This use of the imperfect occurs otherwise rarely in expressions that refer to actions in the past tense. One could also construe it as a stylistic method used to enliven a narrative. It may be compared to the phenomenon of suddenly switching from the past to the present tense in English.

וְהִנֵּה תְסֻבֶּינָה אֲלֻמֹּתֵיכֶם	And behold, your sheaves gather round (mine) (Gen. 37.7).

4. *The imperfect form indicates habitual actions.*

(i) Such habitual actions refer most often *to repeated and infinite actions*. In *narratives* they are usually embedded in the context of events that happened in the past.

וְכֵן יַעֲשֶׂה שָׁנָה בְשָׁנָה	And this is what *he used to do* year by year (1 Sam. 1.7).

(ii) The imperfect can also refer to *a habit* that prevailed at the time of the narrator's statement and must thus be translated in the present tense.

עַל־כֵּן לֹא־יֹאכְלוּ בְנֵי־יִשְׂרָאֵל אֶת־גִּיד הַנָּשֶׁה	Therefore the Israelites *do* not *eat* the sinew of the hip (Gen. 32.33).

5. *The imperfect form indicates certain modalities (or non-indicatives).*

BH does not have modal auxiliary verbs such as *can/could*, *shall*, *would*, *will*, *may*, etc. The root of the concept 'modality' lies in the distinction made between the form of the indicative, subjunctive and optative 'moods' of Greek and Latin verbs. Each one of these modalities refers to a certain subjective judgement regarding the actuality of an event. The indicative refers to a certain reality (factual event) and is regarded as the unmarked form, for example, 'Peter sings well'. The subjunctive and optative, on the other hand, refer to fictitious events. An event is fictitious if a speaker is not certain about the actuality of the events referred to, for example, 'Peter should (be able to) sing well'. A speaker is sometimes uncertain about the relationship between a subject and its predicate, for example, the sentence 'Peter may sing now' indicates that the speaker does not know whether Peter is actually going to sing. For this reason all directive actions, i.e. commands, instructions, orders, etc., are also classified as expressions of modality.

The imperfect can be used to indicates one of the following modalities:

(i) The *possibility or potential* of events

כָּל־מָקוֹם אֲשֶׁר תִּדְרֹךְ כַּף־רַגְלְכֶם בּוֹ	Every place that the sole of your foot *will tread* upon (Josh. 1.3).
אֵיכָה אֶשָּׂא לְבַדִּי טָרְחֲכֶם	How *can* I alone *bear* your burden? (Deut. 1.12).
כִּי יִפְגָּשְׁךָ עֵשָׂו אָחִי ...	If Esau my brother *meets* you, ... (Gen. 32.18).

(ii) The *(un)desirability of events*

לָמָּה תֵלַכְנָה עִמִּי	Why *do* you *want to go* with me? (Ruth 1.11).
מִפְּנֵי שֵׂיבָה תָּקוּם	You *ought to rise* up before the hoary head (Lev. 19.32).

(iii) *Direct directives*

A directive is a speech act by which speakers want to make their listeners do something, e.g. an order, request, summons. Direct directives also involve the desirability of events, but the speakers indicate explicitly that they wish their listeners to adjust their behaviour accordingly. Directives in BH are usually marked morphologically as cohortative, imperative or jussive. Note, however, that in BH the imperfect is used with לֹא to express an (absolute) prohibition (you *must* not...). As opposed to that אַל is used with the jussive to express the nuance of a temporally binding prohibition ('you should not...'). (Cf. §19.4/2.)

לֹא תִרְצָח	You shall not kill (Exod. 20.13).

6. *Problem cases*

There are a number of instances, especially in the poetic sections, where the imperfect form is used where one would have expected a perfect form.

וַיַּרְעֵם בַּשָּׁמַיִם יְהוָה וְעֶלְיוֹן יִתֵּן קֹלוֹ	And the Lord also thundered in the heavens, and the Most High *uttered* his *voice* (Ps. 18.14).
צָרָה וְיָגוֹן אֶמְצָא:	I *found* distress and anguish (Ps. 116.3).

§19.4. *The Imperative, Cohortative and Jussive Forms*

1. *The directive forms and the particle* נָא-

The suffix נָא- may be added to all the directive forms and usually
follows them. *Inter alia*, it expresses a *polite request* and may be
translated with 'please'.[24] (Cf. 45.5/1(i).)

אִמְרִי־נָא אֲחֹתִי אָתְּ *Please* say you are my sister (Gen.
12.13).

Sometimes it may even be left untranslated.

וַיהוָה אָמַר אֶל־אַבְרָם ... And the Lord said to Abram ... Lift
שָׂא נָא עֵינֶיךָ up your eyes ... (Gen. 13.14).

In negative requests the particle נָא- is usually placed after the
negative.

אַל־נָא תִקְבְּרֵנִי בְּמִצְרָיִם *Please* do not bury me in Egypt
(Gen. 42.29).

In courteous requests that are connected to some condition, the נָא-
may be placed directly after the particle אִם in the *protasis*.

אִם־נָא מָצָאתִי חֵן בְּעֵינֶיךָ If now I have found favor with you,
וְעָשִׂיתָ לִּי אוֹת then show me a sign (Judg. 6.17).

2. *The imperative form*

Imperative form refers predominantly to direct positive commands or
instructions in the 2nd person. For the forms of the imperative, cf.
§15.3. For a series of commands, cf. §21.5.

   In all the stem formations an הָ- suffix may be added to the
imperative masculine singular. Traditionally the resultant command
forms are known as emphatic imperatives. The semantic function of
this הָ- suffix is, however, unknown. As a result of the suffix the final
stem vowel of the imperative is reduced. In the case of the Qal stem
formation the two consecutive audible šᵉwâs fuse, e.g.

מִכְרָה כַיּוֹם אֶת־בְּכֹרָתְךָ לִי First *sell* me your birthright (Gen.
25.31).

---

24. According to some grammarians נָא- expresses the relationship of logical
cause and effect between sentences. (Cf. Lambdin §102 and 136.)

(i) *Directives*

The following types of directives may be expressed by the imperative. Only the context can decide on the type of directive involved in each case.

a. Command

שִׂים־נָא יָדְךָ תַּחַת יְרֵכִי

Put your hand under my thigh (Gen. 24.2).

b. Permission

וַיֹּאמֶר פַּרְעֹה עֲלֵה
וּקְבֹר אֶת־אָבִיךָ

('Now therefore let me go up, so that I may bury my father: then I will return'.) And Pharaoh answered, '*Go up*, and bury your father' (Gen. 50.6).

c. Request

תְּנָה־נָּא לָהֶם כִּכַּר־כֶּסֶף

Please *give* them a talent of silver (2 Kgs 5.22).

d. Invitation

וַיֹּאמֶר לָה בֹעַז לְעֵת הָאֹכֶל
גֹּשִׁי הֲלֹם

And at mealtime Boaz said to her, '*Come* over here' (Ruth 2.14).

(ii) *Wishes* (in the sense of blessings)

אֲחֹתֵנוּ אַתְּ הֲיִי לְאַלְפֵי רְבָבָה

Our sister, *may* you *multiply* to thousands of ten thousands (Gen. 24.60).

Note the following:

(1) The imperative form is never used in a negative command. In order to express a negative command in the 2nd person, the negative אַל is used with the jussive form of the 2nd person.

וְיָד אַל־תִּשְׁלְחוּ־בוֹ

But do not lay a hand upon him (Gen. 37.22).

(2) To express an absolute prohibition in the 2nd person, the negative לֹא is used with the imperfect.

לֹא תִרְצָח

You *shall not kill* (Exod. 20.13).

3. *The cohortative form*

The cohortative is primarily an indirect command to the 1st person. The negative used with the cohortative is אַל. (Cf. §15.4 for the forms of the cohortative.)

(i) *Directives*
a. Exhortation

נֵלְכָה אַחֲרֵי אֱלֹהִים אֲחֵרִים   *Let* us *go after* other gods (Deut. 13.3).

b. Request

אֵלְכָה־נָּא הַשָּׂדֶה   *Let* me *go* to the field (Ruth 2.2).

(ii) *Wishes* (rare)

וְאָמַרְתָּ אֹכְלָה בָשָׂר   And you will say: 'I *want to eat* meat' (Deut. 12.20).

(iii) *Declaration of intent* (rare)

אֵלְכָה וְאֶרְאֶנּוּ   I *will go* and see him (Gen. 45.28).

4. *The jussive form*

The jussive is an indirect command to the 3rd (and sometimes the 2nd) person. The negative used with the jussive is אַל.

(i) *Directives*

In classical BH the so-called neutral imperfects—i.e. those cases in which no formal distinction can be made between the *imperfect* and the *jussive*—may have a directive function and then often stand in first place in a clause. They may be preceded by אַל, and/or followed by וְ-נָ.[25]

תְּחַטְּאֵנִי בְאֵזוֹב וְאֶטְהָר   *Purge* me with hyssop, and I shall be clean (Ps. 51.9).

יֵלֶךְ־נָא אֲדֹנָי בְּקִרְבֵּנוּ   *Let* the Lord *go* in our midst (Exod. 34:9)

The following types of directives can be expressed by the jussive form. Only the context can give an indication as to which type of directive is involved in each case.

a. Command

יְהִי אוֹר   *Let* there *be* light (Gen. 1.3).

b. Request

אִתִּי יַעֲבֹר כִּמְהָם   *Let* Chimham *go* over *with* me (2 Sam. 19.39).

---

25. Cf. also Revell (1989: 13-17) for a fuller discussion in this regard.

c. Invitation

יַעֲבָר־נָא אֲדֹנִי לִפְנֵי עַבְדּוֹ

Let my lord *pass on* before his servant (Gen. 33.14).

(ii) *Wishes*

יְחִי הַמֶּלֶךְ

Long live the king! (1 Sam. 10.24).

§20. **The Syntax and Semantics of the Non-finite Verb Forms**

Non-finite verb forms are verb forms that are not marked in terms of person (e.g. participles), or in terms of person, gender and number (e.g. the infinitive).

§20.1. *The Infinitive Construct (Ordinary Infinitive)*

1. *Introduction*

The infinitive expresses an action without referring to person, gender, number or tense. For this reason the infinitive may not be used independently as the main verb of a clause. An infinitive almost always occurs in relation to another verb. In BH a distinction is made between the ordinary infinitive and the absolute infinitive, called the *infinitive construct* and the *infinitive absolute*, respectively. The latter differs from the *infinitive construct* in that it does not conjugate.

A characteristic of the infinitive construct forms in BH is that in some respects they act syntactically like nouns.

(1) They are similar to nouns in that they may be governed by prepositions, e.g.

וַיְהִי כְמָלְכוֹ הִכָּה
אֶת־כָּל־בֵּית יָרָבְעָם

And as soon as he [Baasha] was king, he killed all the house of Jeroboam (1 Kgs 15.29).

and they also take pronominal suffixes (Cf. §17.5.)

(2) The infinitive construct forms differ from nouns in that they do not take *gender and number morphemes*. They may express actions and states (as finite verbs do) too.

(3) In BH the infinitive construct, unlike finite verbs, is not *negated* by לֹא but by בְּלִי, בִּלְתִּי or לְבִלְתִּי.

הֲמִן־הָעֵץ אֲשֶׁר צִוִּיתִיךָ לְבִלְתִּי
אֲכָל־מִמֶּנּוּ אָכָלְתָּ

Have you eaten of the tree of which I commanded you *not* to eat? (Gen. 3.11).

Semantically speaking the infinitive has no function in itself. The functions of an infinitive refer either to the syntactic function that it fulfils in a clause, or to the semantic relationship between itself and the finite verb. This relationship is often governed by means of a preposition.

2. *The infinitive is used in the place of a noun or as a noun (often as the subject of a clause).*

(i) *Without the preposition* לְ

רַב־לָכֶם שֶׁבֶת בָּהָר הַזֶּה	You have stayed long enough at this mountain [lit. enough for you *to stay* on this mountain] (Deut. 1.6).
טוֹב תִּתִּי אֹתָהּ לָךְ	It is good that I give her to you [lit. good is *my giving* her to you] (Gen. 29.19).

(ii) *With the preposition* לְ

If the infinitive is part of a section of the clause that forms *the subject* of a *verbal clause*, it is usually preceded by the preposition לְ. (Cf. Joüon–Muraoka §124b.)

וְאִם רַע בְּעֵינֵיכֶם לַעֲבֹד אֶת־יהוה	And if it is wrong in your eyes *to serve* the Lord, ... (Josh. 24.15).

3. *The infinitive as part of the predicate*

(i) After *verbs of observation or cognition.* The infinitive construct refers to the content of a mental process.

לֹא אֵדַע צֵאת וָבֹא	I do not know what *to do* [lit. *whether to go out or to come in*] (1 Kgs 3.7).

(ii) After verbs that select an infinitive *as complement* (to complete the verb), e.g. חלל (Hiph: to begin), יסף (Hiph: to continue), חדל (to stop), יכל (to be capable of), אבה (to be willing).

לֹא נוּכַל דַּבֵּר אֵלֶיךָ	We are not able *to speak* to you (Gen. 24.50).

(iii) After finite verbs (especially in the Hiphil and Piel stem formations) which, when they are translated into English, acquire an adverbial connotation. *The infinitive construct takes on the function of the main verb of the sentence in this case.*

וַתֵּרַע לַעֲשׂוֹת	And you *have done* evil (1 Kgs 14.9).
מַדּוּעַ מִהַרְתֶּן בֹּא הַיּוֹם	Why *have* you *come* so soon today? [lit. Why have you made haste to come today?] (Exod. 2.18).

(iv) The infinitive construct refers to the *purpose* of the action expressed by the finite verb. The finite verb is often a *verb of movement.*

וַיֵּרֶד יְהוָה לִרְאֹת אֶת־הָעִיר	And the Lord came down *to see* the city (Gen. 11.5).

(v) The infinitive construct *specifies* the *manner or method* in which the finite verb is executed, or can / may be executed.

כִּי תִשְׁמַע בְּקוֹל יְהוָה אֱלֹהֶיךָ לִשְׁמֹר אֶת־כָּל־מִצְוֹתָיו	If you obey the voice of the Lord your God, *keeping* all his commandments (Deut. 13.19).

(vi) The infinitive construct expresses the *outcome or consequence* of the finite verb.

לַעֲשׂוֹת הָרַע בְּעֵינֵי יְהוָה לְהַכְעִיסוֹ	... doing what was evil in the LORD's sight *and so provoking him to anger* (Deut. 9.18).

(vii) After the verb הָיָה a לְ followed by an infinitive construct functions as the predicate of the clause and bears the *connotation of imminence* (about to happen).

וַיְהִי הַשֶּׁמֶשׁ לָבוֹא	And then, as the sun was *on the point of setting* (Gen. 15.12).

4. *The infinitive construct form* לֵאמֹר *usually acts as a complementizer marking reported speech.*[26]

Significant of the form of לֵאמֹר is that it is not according to what one would expect the infinitive construct of a I aleph root to be, namely לֶאֱמֹר, in analogy to לֶאֱכֹל.(Cf. §18.3.)

---

26. For an exhaustive discussion on the use of לֵאמֹר and other speech frames of reported speech in BH, cf. Miller (1996).

(i) In contrast to speech frames (or dialogue introducers) like the finite forms of אמר that usually mark reported speech in dialogues, for example,

<table>
<tr><td dir="rtl">וַיֹּאמֶר אֲבִימֶלֶךְ אֶל־אַבְרָהָם
מָה רָאִיתָ כִּי עָשִׂיתָ אֶת־הַדָּבָר הַזֶּה:
וַיֹּאמֶר אַבְרָהָם כִּי אָמַרְתִּי ...</td><td>And Abimelech *said* to Abraham, 'What were you thinking of, that you did this thing?' Abraham *said*, 'Because I thought ... (Gen. 20:10-11).</td></tr>
</table>

לֵאמֹר is predominantly used to *mark reported speech* in the following contexts:

a. *where no dialogue* is involved,

<table>
<tr><td dir="rtl">וַיַּגֵּד שָׁפָן הַסֹּפֵר לַמֶּלֶךְ לֵאמֹר
סֵפֶר נָתַן לִי חִלְקִיָּה הַכֹּהֵן</td><td>Shaphan the secretary informed the king, 'The priest Hilkiah has given me a book' (2 Kgs 22:10).</td></tr>
<tr><td dir="rtl">וַיִּשְׁמַע הָעָם הַחֹנִים לֵאמֹר
קָשַׁר זִמְרִי וְגַם הִכָּה אֶת־הַמֶּלֶךְ</td><td>And the troops who were encamped heard the following information (lit. heard saying), 'Zimri has conspired, and he has killed the king' (1 Kgs 16.16).</td></tr>
</table>

b. or where *the matrix verb is not a verb of speaking*.

<table>
<tr><td dir="rtl">וַיָּבֹאוּ כָל־מִצְרַיִם אֶל־יוֹסֵף לֵאמֹר
הָבָה־לָּנוּ לֶחֶם</td><td>All the Egyptians came to Joseph, saying, 'Give us food!' (Gen. 47.15).</td></tr>
</table>

(ii) Although in the above-mentioned cases לֵאמֹר has lost its normal function as an infinitive, it does not mean that לֵאמֹר cannot be used as an infinitive at all. In other words, it may also have one of the uses listed in §20.1/3. However, such use of לֵאמֹר is, in comparison to its use as complementizer, relatively infrequent.

<table>
<tr><td dir="rtl">וַיֹּסֶף עוֹד אַבְנֵר לֵאמֹר אֶל־עֲשָׂהאֵל
סוּר לָךְ</td><td>Abner *said again* to Asahel, 'Turn away from following me' (2 Sam. 2.22).</td></tr>
</table>

5. *The infinitive construct forms part of an adverbial clause or phrase governed by a preposition. The construction reflects the moment in time at which the events indicated by the finite verb occur.*
The specific moment in time proposed here is indicated, *inter alia*, by the preposition used.

(i) When used with the preposition בְּ, the action implied by the infinitive construct is *simultaneous* with that of the main clause. Simultaneous in the sense that the action referred to by the בְּ + infinitive construction constitutes a stretch of time within which the action in the main clause takes place. This construction can be translated 'as', 'when' or 'while'. (Cf. §39.6/2.)

וַיְהִי בְּנָסְעָם מִקֶּדֶם   *And as they migrated from the East,*
וַיִּמְצְאוּ בִקְעָה בְּאֶרֶץ שִׁנְעָר   they came about a plain in the land of
וַיֵּשְׁבוּ שָׁם   Shinar and settled there (Gen. 11.2).

(ii) When used with the preposition כְּ, the action of the infinitive construct occurs *just before* the events described in the main clause. This construction can be translated with 'the moment when' or 'as soon as'. (Cf. §39.10/3 and §44.5/1(i)b.)

וַיְהִי כְמָלְכוֹ הִכָּה אֶת־כָּל־בֵּית   *And as soon as he [Baasha] was*
יָרָבְעָם   *king,* he killed all the house of
     Jeroboam (1 Kgs 15.29).

(iii) When the preposition עַד is used, then the action of the main clause occurs *in the period extending to* the events described by the infinitive construct. The construction may be translated 'until'. (Cf. §39.18/2.)

עַד־בֹּאֲכֶם עַד־הַמָּקוֹם הַזֶּה   *Until you came* to this place (Deut. 1.31).

(iv) When the preposition אַחֲרֵי is used, then the action in the main clause occurs *after* the events in the infinitive construct. The construction may be translated 'after'. (Cf. §39.2/2.)

אַחֲרֵי הַכֹּתוֹ אֵת סִיחֹן ...   *After* he had defeated Sihon, ... (Deut. 1.4).

(v) The preposition מִן is used when the action of the main clause occurs *from the inception of* the events implied by the infinitive construct. The construction may be translated with 'from (the time) when'. (Cf. §39.14/2.)

מֵהָחֵל חֶרְמֵשׁ בַּקָּמָה   Begin to count the seven weeks *from*
תָּחֵל לִסְפֹּר שִׁבְעָה שָׁבֻעוֹת: *the time you first put the sickle to the*
     standing grain (Deut. 16.9).

§20.2. *The Infinitive Absolute*

The infinitive absolute differs completely from the infinitive construct in terms of form and function. In contrast to the infinitive construct, the infinitive absolute in BH cannot be combined with any other grammatical or lexical morpheme. In other words, the infinitive absolute cannot be governed by a preposition. It also cannot take a pronominal suffix.

The various semantic functions of the infinitive absolute are related to specific syntactic constructions. The semantic functions differentiated here are ordered according to the syntactic constructions in which the infinitive absolute occurs.

1. *Infinitive absolute of root X + verb of root X (e.g.* כָּתוֹב כָּתַב*) or verb + infinitive absolute (e.g.* כָּתַב כָּתוֹב*).*
This syntactic construction is occasioned by the collocation of an infinitive absolute and a verb of the same stem and stem formation. The stem formations of the infinitive absolute and the finite verb, however, may sometimes differ.

Cases in which the infinitive absolute precedes the finite verb (perfect or imperfect) are more common than those in which the infinitive absolute follows the finite verb. Note that when the infinitive absolute is used with a waw consecutive + imperfect, imperative or participle, the infinitive absolute is placed after the particular verb in question. The Hithpael of the infinitive absolute also appears only after the finite form of the verb.

This construction usually intensifies the verbal idea. In this way BH speakers/narrators *express their conviction of the verity of their statements regarding an action.* When a speaker has used this construction, a listener would not be able to claim at a later date that the speakers had not expressed themself clearly enough.

(i) In *statements* speakers commit themselves to the *verity* of what they say, predict or promise will happen. Sometimes the statements refer to what has already happened.

a. In many cases the infinitive absolute construction can be translated by the adverbs 'surely', 'definitely'.

מוֹת תָּמוּת אָתָּה   You shall *surely die* (Gen. 20.7).

b. In other cases the nature or scope of the verbal idea is defined more clearly. There are several options for translating this construction:

אָמוֹר אָמַרְתִּי בֵּיתְךָ וּבֵית   I *stated expressly* that your house and
אָבִיךָ יִתְהַלְּכוּ לְפָנַי   your father's house will serve before
עַד־עוֹלָם   me for all time (1 Sam. 2.30).

כִּי־בָרֵךְ אֲבָרֶכְךָ   I will *bless* you *richly* (Gen. 22.17).

מִכֹּל עֵץ־הַגָּן אָכֹל תֹּאכֵל   You may *freely eat* of every tree of the garden (Gen. 2.16).

(ii) By uttering *instructions and requests* speakers commit themselves to *the fact that they want to have an instruction, request or wish carried out*.

סָקוֹל יִסָּקֵל הַשּׁוֹר   The ox *shall be stoned* (Exod. 21.28).

(iii) In *(rhetorical) questions* speakers express their commitment to the *factual nature* of a state of affairs. Their listeners can only assent to the opinions/views expressed.

הֶאָכוֹל אָכַלְנוּ מִן־הַמֶּלֶךְ   Have we *eaten at all* at the king's expense? (2 Sam. 19.43).

(iv) In the *protasis* of a condition a speaker sometimes uses the infinitive absolute to indicate that the events referred to in the *apodosis* shall/must/can occur *should the listener or speaker be convinced of the factual nature of the events in the protasis*.

אִם־נָתֹן תִּתֵּן אֶת־הָעָם הַזֶּה   If you will *indeed give* this people
בְּיָדִי וְהַחֲרַמְתִּי אֶת־עָרֵיהֶם   into my hand, then I will utterly destroy their cities (Num. 21.2).

Sometimes the *protasis* expresses an unlikely possibility and thus requires considerable persuasion from the speaker.

אִם־הִפָּקֵד יִפָּקֵד וְהָיְתָה נַפְשְׁךָ   If *by any means* he *be missing*, you
תַּחַת נַפְשׁוֹ   will pay for it with your life [lit. your life shall be for his life] (1 Kgs 20.39).

2. *Verb* + *infinitive absolute* + *infinitive absolute*

(i) *Main verb X* + *infinitive absolute X* + *infinitive absolute Y*

The stem X is often הלך or another verb of movement.

a. This construction usually expresses the *simultaneous nature* of two actions / deeds. The main verb refers to a motion to a certain place. The stem of this main verb is repeated in the infinitive absolute with the infinitive absolute form of the second action that occurs simultaneously with it.

וַיֵּלֶךְ הָלוֹךְ וְאָכֹל   And he went on, *eating as he went* (Judg. 14.9).

וַיֵּצֵא יָצוֹא וָשׁוֹב   And it went *to and fro* (Gen. 8.7).

b. The stem הלך often expresses a figurative movement, so that the expression indicates *progression in time* rather than physical movement.

וַיֵּלֶךְ דָּוִד הָלוֹךְ וְגָדוֹל   And David became *greater and greater* (2 Sam. 5.10).

c. In certain cases the stem x is not a verb of motion, but the construction reflects the same kind of simultaneity as described in the cases above.

וַיַּכֵּהוּ הָאִישׁ הַכֵּה וּפָצֹעַ   And the man struck him, *striking and wounding* him (1 Kgs 20.37).

(ii) *Main verb Y* + *infinitive absolute of* הלך + *infinitive absolute Y* (rare)

a. The infinitive absolute of הלך *vividly* expresses the *gradual progression* of the main verb. The stem of the main verb is repeated in the infinitive absolute after the infinitive absolute הלוך.

וַיָּשֻׁבוּ הַמַּיִם מֵעַל הָאָרֶץ הָלוֹךְ וָשׁוֹב   And the waters *gradually* receded from the earth (Gen. 8.3).

b. In certain cases the stem of the main verb differs from that of the second infinitive absolute. In other words, *main verb X* + *infinitive absolute* הלוך + *infinitive absolute Y.*

וְהַמַּיִם הָיוּ הָלוֹךְ וְחָסוֹר עַד הַחֹדֶשׁ הָעֲשִׂירִי   And the waters *continued to abate* until the tenth month (Gen. 8.5).

3. *The infinitive absolute as adverbial modification of the verb where the nature of the adverbial modification is determined by the lexical value of the stem that is in the infinitive absolute.*

Two constructions are important here:

(i) *Infinitive absolute of root X* + *infinitive absolute of root Y*

בַּיּוֹם הַהוּא אָקִים אֶל־עֵלִי אֵת כָּל־אֲשֶׁר דִּבַּרְתִּי אֶל־בֵּיתוֹ הָחֵל וְכַלֵּה   On that day I will fulfil against Eli all that I have spoken concerning his house, *from beginning to end* (1 Sam. 3.12).

(ii) *The infinitive absolute used on its own as adverb to the main verb*

This infinitive absolute is usually in the Hiphil, e.g. הֵיטֵב (well, thoroughly), הַרְבֵּה (many), הַשְׁכֵּם (early), הַרְחֵק (far).

וְדָרַשְׁתָּ ... הֵיטֵב   And you shall *inquire* ... *diligently* (Deut. 13.15).

4. *The infinitive absolute used in the place of other verb forms*

(i) The infinitive absolute is sometimes used in the place of a finite verb *without* waw (usually in utterances of direct speech).

It is *not clear* why the speaker has used the infinitive absolute in the instances below.

a. In the place of an imperative

הָלוֹךְ וְדִבַּרְתָּ אֶל־דָּוִד   *Go* and say to David (2 Sam. 24.12).

b. In the place of an imperfect

כֹּה אָמַר יְהוָה אָכֹל וְהוֹתֵר   Thus says the Lord: They *shall eat* and have some left (2 Kgs 4.43).

c. In the place of a perfect

עָשֹׂה אֵלֶּה לָךְ בִּזְנוֹתֵךְ   (They) have *brought* this *upon* you, because you played the harlot (Ezek. 23.30).

(ii) The infinitive absolute can be used in the place of a finite verb *with* waw. (Cf. §21.1.)

As in the case of §20.2/4(i)), it is not clear why the speaker/narrator has used an infinitive absolute form here. The fact that the texts below originate mostly from the later books of the Hebrew Bible may indicate a particular development in BH. According to Rubenstein (1952: 362-367) this is related to the disappearance of the waw consecutive in late BH as the infinitive absolute always occurs where one would expect a waw consecutive form.

a. After a perfect

כִּי־צַמְתֶּם וְסָפוֹד   When you *fast and mourn* (Zech. 7.5).

b. After an imperfect

שָׂדוֹת בַּכֶּסֶף יִקְנוּ וְכָתוֹב בַּסֵּפֶר   Fields shall be bought for money, and deeds *shall be signed* (Jer. 32.44).

c. After a waw consecutive + imperfect

וַיַּרְא פַּרְעֹה ... וְהַכְבֵּד אֶת־לִבּוֹ   When Pharaoh saw ... he *hardened* his heart (Exod. 8.11).

(iii) The infinitive absolute is used *in the place of an infinitive construct* (rare)

וַיֵּשֶׁב הָעָם לֶאֱכֹל וְשָׁתוֹ

And the people sat down to eat *and drink* (Exod. 32.6).

§20.3. *The Participle*

The participle is by definition a verbal adjective. Syntactically the participle in BH functions as a verb, noun or adjective.

1. *If the participle functions as a verb, it indicates the following types of action:*

(i) *Continuous action* (in the past, present or future)

וַיִּשָּׂא עֵינָיו וַיַּרְא וְהִנֵּה שְׁלֹשָׁה
אֲנָשִׁים נִצָּבִים עָלָיו

And he lifted up his eyes and looked, and behold, three men stood in front of him [lit. *were standing* over him] (Gen. 18.2).

וִיהוֹנָתָן וַאֲחִימַעַץ עֹמְדִים
בְּעֵין־רֹגֵל וְהָלְכָה
הַשִּׁפְחָה וְהִגִּידָה לָהֶם

Now Jonathan and Ahimaaz *were waiting* at Enrogel; a maidservant used to go and tell them (2 Sam. 17.17).

(ii) *Imminent action* (on the point of occurring)

הִנֵּה אָנֹכִי עֹשֶׂה דָבָר בְּיִשְׂרָאֵל

I am *about* to do a thing in Israel (1 Sam. 3.11).

Note the following:

(1) A participle is always negated by אֵין.

אֵינֶנִּי נֹתֵן לָכֶם תֶּבֶן׃

I *will not give* you straw (Exod. 5.10).

(2) The participle agrees in gender and number with its subject. When it is used with a particular direct object, the latter is marked with an object marker.

אֶת־אַחַי אָנֹכִי מְבַקֵּשׁ

I am seeking *my brothers* (Gen. 37.16).

(3) The syntactic ordering of a clause with a participle as verb is normally subject + verb + other phrases. Placing the object at the beginning of a clause, as in the above example from Gen. 37.16, may have semantic implications. (Cf. §46-47.)

2. *If the participle functions as a noun, it displays all the characteristics of a noun, namely:*

(i) The *status absolutus* form (Cf. §25.2.)

שֹׁפְטִים וְשֹׁטְרִים תִּתֶּן־לְךָ

You shall appoint *judges and officers* (Deut. 16.18).

(ii) The *status constructus* form (Cf. §25.1.)

כִּי עַתָּה יָדַעְתִּי
כִּי־יְרֵא אֱלֹהִים אַתָּה

For now I know that you fear God [lit you are *a fearer of* God] (Gen. 22.12).

(iii) With a *suffix*

אַיֵּה אֱלוֹהַּ עֹשָׂי

Where is God my *Maker?* (Job 35.10).

3. *If the participle functions as an adjective, it agrees in number, gender and definiteness with the noun.*

כִּי יְהוָה אֱלֹהֶיךָ אֵשׁ אֹכְלָה הוּא

For the Lord your God is *a devouring fire* (Deut. 4.24).

When used like this the participle is often translated in English as a relative clause.

וְהָיָה הָעַלְמָה הַיֹּצֵאת לִשְׁאֹב

And let it be the young woman *who comes out to draw* (Gen. 24.43).

כִּי יְהוָה אֱלֹהֶיךָ מְבִיאֲךָ
אֶל־אֶרֶץ טוֹבָה אֶרֶץ נַחֲלֵי מָיִם
עֲיָנֹת וּתְהֹמֹת יֹצְאִים בַּבִּקְעָה
וּבָהָר

For the Lord your God is bringing you into a good land, a land of brooks of water, of fountains and springs, *flowing forth in valleys and hills* (Deut. 8.7).

§21. Verb Chains and Sequences

§21.1. *Introduction*

Verb chains are constituted by finite verbs that are preceded by a waw. It, however, applies only to cases in which the conjunction waw is joined directly to the verb in the perfect, imperfect, imperative, jussive or cohortative form. Two types of waws can be distinguished, viz. the ordinary or waw copulative and the waw consecutive. Vocalizing the waw in cases where the (short form of the) imperfect form is involved, requires -וַ with the doubling of the following consonant. The resulting *waw consecutive + imperfect* (wc.+impf.) construction has a particular semantic (and pragmatic) function. (Cf. §21.2.) Under specific conditions (often recognizable on account of its accentuation) a -ן + perfect form may constitute a *waw consecutive + perfect construction* (wc.+perf.) that has a function similar to that of the waw consecutive + imperfect.[27] (Cf. §21.3.)

Some verb chains constitute what is called a *verb sequence.* Introductory grammars often distinguish between the following 'sequences':

perfect	+	wc.+ impf.	Consecutive events in the past
imperfect	+	wc.+ perf.	Consecutive events in the future
directive	+	wc.+ perf.	Consecutive commands
imperfect	+	waw cop. + impf.	Purpose
directive	+	waw cop. + impf.	Purpose

Grammarians agree, however, that the above scheme can be refined. A variety of other factors and problems are involved in identifying verb sequences and their respective functions. This would require a far more nuanced scheme than the one given above.

In determining the *semantic function* of verb sequences (i.e. waw consecutive + imperfect and waw consecutive + perfect) the following inverted pairs are important, broadly speaking:

| x perfect | + wc. + impf. |
| imperfect | + wc. + perf. |

The x refers to the phrase that precedes the perfect, making the point that no *separate perfect (i.e. a perfect without some linguistic item preceding it)* + waw consecutive + imperfect occurs in BH *narrations.*

The following assumptions will be adopted in this grammar:

(a) In interpreting verb chains a distinction must be made between narration (also referred to as discursive speech) and dialogue (also referred to as direct speech). One might expect narrations to be syntactically 'impoverished' and to concentrate on events in the past. They would thus have a relatively small variety of syntactic constructions. As opposed to that, dia-

---

27. Take note that waw consecutive + imperfect and waw consecutive + perfect refer to *the names* of two constructions. In more recent publications they are also referred to as *wayyiqtol* and *weqatalti* constructions.

logue, which often involves all the temporal spheres, is usually syntactically 'rich'.

(b) A distinction is also made between poetic and non-poetic texts. The syntax of poetic texts often reflects a certain correspondence with dialogue.

(c) The waw consecutive + imperfect construction has a unique meaning which, while it often corresponds semantically to the perfect, differs syntactically and text grammatically from it.[28]

(d) On analogy to the waw consecutive + imperfect, the waw consecutive + perfect construction also acquired a distinctive syntactic and pragmatic (in particular, a text grammatical) meaning. This in turn differs from that of an imperfect with a long form.

§21.2. *Waw Consecutive + Imperfect (Short Form)*

A waw consecutive + imperfect does not necessarily succeed a clause with a perfect form of the verb. It may succeed a clause that has a participle or imperfect form as main verb. It may also follow a nominal clause or a clause with an infinitive absolute. It does not simply continue the meaning of the preceding verbs, but must be understood as follows:

1. *Waw consecutive + imperfect bears reference to the same temporal spheres and aspects as a perfect form but it is also characterized by 'progression'.*

(i) The following *temporal spheres* may be distinguished:

a. *Events* in the *past and/or completed* events

וְהָאָדָם יָדַע אֶת־חַוָּה אִשְׁתּוֹ	Now Adam knew Eve his wife, and
וַתַּהַר וַתֵּלֶד אֶת־קַיִן	*she conceived and bore* Cain (Gen. 4.1).

b. *A state of affairs or a condition* (usually expressed by a stative or a passive verb).

וַתִּמָּלֵא אַרְצוֹ סוּסִים ...	And his land *is filled* with horses ...
וַתִּמָּלֵא אַרְצוֹ אֱלִילִים	and his land *is filled* with idols (Isa. 2.7-8).

---

28. For a hypothesis on how the wc. + impf. came to have a meaning similar to that of the perfect, cf. Buth 1992: 104.

(ii) The following types of *progression* may be distinguished in narrations:

a. Sequence in time (most common)

וְהָאָדָם יָדַע אֶת־חַוָּה אִשְׁתּוֹ וַתַּהַר וַתֵּלֶד אֶת־קַיִן	Now Adam knew Eve his wife, and *she conceived and bore* Cain (Gen. 4.1).

b. Logical sequence
Consequence

וַיְהִי יְהוָה אֶת־יוֹסֵף וַיְהִי אִישׁ מַצְלִיחַ	And the Lord was with Joseph, and he *became a successful man* (Gen. 39.2).

Contrast

וַיָּקֻמוּ כָל־בָּנָיו לְנַחֲמוֹ וַיְמָאֵן לְהִתְנַחֵם	And all his sons ... rose up to comfort him; *but he refused* to be comforted (Gen. 37.35).

(iii) The waw consecutive + imperfect is used when *the consecution of two events is emphasized.*

קוֹלִי אֶל־יְהוָה אֶקְרָא וַיַּעֲנֵנִי	I cry aloud to the Lord, and *he answers* me (Ps. 3.5).

2. *Waw consecutive + imperfect can introduce a new narrative or section of a narrative*

(i) When a waw consecutive + imperfect introduces a new narrative, it is usually accompanied by *an introduction of the characters of the new story and a change of location.* A change in time is hardly ever involved. *Verbs of motion and communication occur regularly.* (Cf. Schneider 1993: 66-67.)

וַיֹּאמֶר יְהוָה אֶל־אַבְרָם לֶךְ־לְךָ מֵאַרְצְךָ	Now the Lord said to Abram: 'Go from your country' (Gen. 12.1).

(ii) When a *temporal indication* is involved, it is usually preceded by וַיְהִי. However, this new section follows as a rule on preceding events. In other words, an entirely new narrative is seldom introduced like this. (Cf. also §44.5.)

a. The backbone of the narrative is then introduced *by a subsequent waw consecutive + imperfect form.*

וַיְהִי בָּעֵת הַהִוא וַיֹּאמֶר אֲבִימֶלֶךְ	And at that time Abimelech *said*: (Gen. 21.22).

b. A *nominal clause, a perfect or an x perfect may be inserted* between the temporal indication and the waw consecutive + imperfect to give more *background information.*

<table>
<tr><td dir="rtl">וַיְהִי אַחַר הַדְּבָרִים הָאֵלֶּה</td><td>And some time after this, *the butler*</td></tr>
<tr><td dir="rtl">חָטְאוּ מַשְׁקֵה מֶלֶךְ־מִצְרַיִם</td><td>*of the king of Egypt and his baker*</td></tr>
<tr><td dir="rtl">וְהָאֹפֶה לַאֲדֹנֵיהֶם לְמֶלֶךְ</td><td>*offended their lord the king of Egypt.*</td></tr>
<tr><td dir="rtl">מִצְרָיִם: וַיִּקְצֹף פַּרְעֹה</td><td>And Pharaoh was angry (Gen. 40.1-2).</td></tr>
</table>

c. The waw consecutive + imperfect can also introduce the *backbone* of the narrative after a temporal indication that is not introduced by וַיְהִי (rare).

<table>
<tr><td dir="rtl">בַּיּוֹם הַשְּׁלִישִׁי</td><td>On the third day Abraham *lifted up*</td></tr>
<tr><td dir="rtl">וַיִּשָּׂא אַבְרָהָם אֶת־עֵינָיו</td><td>*his eyes* and *saw* the place afar off</td></tr>
<tr><td dir="rtl">וַיַּרְא אֶת־הַמָּקוֹם מֵרָחֹק:</td><td>(Gen. 22.4).</td></tr>
</table>

Note the following:

> The backbone of a narrative is not only indicated by waw consecutive + imperfect. The 'interruption' of a waw consecutive + imperfect series is sometimes necessitated by BH syntax, for example, where a conjunction, negative adverb, relative pronoun and words such as הִנֵּה and (וְ)עַתָּה are used. These cases must therefore be distinguished from those in which a waw consecutive + imperfect sequence—and thus the flow of the narrative—is interrupted with a specific semantic-pragmatic purpose. (Cf. §47.)

3. *Speakers can use waw consecutive + imperfect to control the flow of their narratives. The backbone of the narrative thus does not have to correlate with the actual course of events in time.*

In the process the following semantic relationships are possible:

(i) *Summary*

<table>
<tr><td dir="rtl">וַיְכֻלּוּ הַשָּׁמַיִם וְהָאָרֶץ</td><td>*Thus* the heavens and the earth *were finished* (Gen. 2.1).</td></tr>
</table>

(ii) *Closer definition*

<table>
<tr><td dir="rtl">וַתִּקְרָא שְׁמוֹ מֹשֶׁה וַתֹּאמֶר</td><td>And she named him Moses, *for she*</td></tr>
<tr><td dir="rtl">כִּי מִן־הַמַּיִם מְשִׁיתִהוּ</td><td>*said:* 'Because I drew him out of the water' (Exod. 2.10).</td></tr>
</table>

(iii) *Pluperfect* (rare)

וַיְדַבֵּר אֲלֵהֶם אֲבִיהֶם אֵי־זֶה הַדֶּרֶךְ הָלָךְ וַיִּרְאוּ בָנָיו אֶת־הַדֶּרֶךְ	And their father said to them, 'Which way did he go?' His sons *had seen* the way (1 Kgs 13.12).

(iv) *Simultaneous events (relatively rare)*

וַיִּתֵּן אֶת־קֹלוֹ בִּבְכִי וַיִּשְׁמְעוּ מִצְרַיִם וַיִּשְׁמַע בֵּית פַּרְעֹה:	And he wept aloud, so that the Egyptians heard it, *and the household of Pharaoh heard it* (Gen. 45.2).

§21.3. *Waw Consecutive + Perfect*

A distinction must be drawn between waw consecutive + perfect as analogous to waw consecutive + imperfect and cases where waw consecutive + perfect is simply a perfect with a conjunction, a waw copulative (waw cop.) with a perfect. The latter cases occur seldom. The so-called waw copulative + perfect can be distinguished from the waw consecutive + perfect by the fact that the final syllable of the latter construction carries the accent.

עַבְדְּךָ יֵלֵךְ וְנִלְחַם עִם־הַפְּלִשְׁתִּי הַזֶּה	Your servant will go *and fight* with this Philistine (1 Sam. 17.32).

Over and against this the accent in waw cop. + perfect falls on the penultimate syllable.

וְלֹא־שָׁאַלְתָּ לְךָ יָמִים רַבִּים וְשָׁאַלְתָּ לְךָ הָבִין לִשְׁמֹעַ מִשְׁפָּט	And you did not ask for a long life, ... but *have asked* for yourself understanding to discern what is right (1 Kgs 3.11).

It is possible that at a very early stage of BH, that is before the waw consecutive + imperfect began to fulfil this function, the waw copulative + perfect was the usual form of referring to narratives in the past. However, in the later books waw consecutive + imperfect again loses this role and waw copulative + perfect occurs in places where one would have expected waw consecutive + imperfect. (Cf. Joüon–Muraoka §119z.)

Waw consecutive + perfect does not necessarily follow a clause with an imperfect as a main verb. It often follows commands too. Although this happens less frequently, waw consecutive + perfect can also follow a clause that has a perfect, a participle or infinitive as a main verb. It may sometimes follow a nominal clause. The waw consecutive + perfect, however, does not simply continue the meaning of the preceding verb, but is to be understood as follows:

1. *Waw consecutive + perfect refers to the same temporal spheres and aspects as imperfect forms. However, it also has 'progression' as a characteristic.*

(i) The following *temporal spheres and aspects* may be distinguished:

a. Events in the future

עַבְדְּךָ יֵלֵךְ וְנִלְחַם עִם־הַפְּלִשְׁתִּי הַזֶּה	Your servant will go and *fight* with this Philistine (1 Sam. 17.32).

b. Habitual actions

וּמְעִיל קָטֹן תַּעֲשֶׂה־לּוֹ אִמּוֹ וְהַעֲלְתָה לוֹ מִיָּמִים יָמִימָה	And his mother used to make for him a little robe and *take* it to him each year (1 Sam. 2.19).

c. Modality (or non-indicative)
Possibility

וּבַמֶּה נוּכַל לוֹ וַאֲסַרְנֻהוּ לְעַנֹּתוֹ	And by what means we may overpower him, that we *may bind* him to subdue him (Judg. 16.5).

Direct directive

בֹּא אֶל־פַּרְעֹה וְאָמַרְתָּ אֵלָיו	Go to Pharao *and say* to him (Exod. 7.26).

(ii) The following *types of progression* may be distinguished:

a. Sequence in time (most common)

וְהָרִית וְיָלַדְתְּ בֵּן	And you shall conceive *and bear* a son (Judg. 13.3).

b. Logical sequence

אֲנִי יְהוָה וְהוֹצֵאתִי אֶתְכֶם ... וְגָאַלְתִּי אֶתְכֶם ...	I am the Lord, and I *will bring you out* ... and I *will deliver you* ... (Exod. 6.6).

2. *Waw consecutive + perfect can indicate the backbone of one or other discourse type*

(i) Waw consecutive + perfect indicates the *backbone of a predictive discourse*. This applies especially in dialogue.

אֲנִי יְהוָה וְהוֹצֵאתִי אֶתְכֶם ... וְגָאַלְתִּי אֶתְכֶם ...	I am the Lord, and I *will bring you out* ... and I *will deliver you* ... (Exod. 6.6).

(ii) Waw consecutive + perfect indicates the *backbone of a sequence of habitual actions in a descriptive section of a narrative.*

וּמְעִיל קָטֹן תַּעֲשֶׂה־לּוֹ אִמּוֹ	And his mother *used to make for* him a
וְהַעַלְתָה לוֹ מִיָּמִים יָמִימָה	little robe and *take* it to him each
וּבֵרַךְ עֵלִי	year... *Then* Eli *would bless* (1 Sam. 2.19-20).

(iii) Waw consecutive + perfect is used to link a *series of directives* with one another in a prescriptive text. The waw consecutive + perfect is used only in cases where *the execution of one command is dependent on the execution of a prior one directed to the same person(s)* (usually an imperative and only sometimes a jussive or cohortative).

בֹּא אֶל־פַּרְעֹה וְאָמַרְתָּ אֵלָיו	Go to Pharao *and say* to him (Exod. 7.26).
עֲלֵה ... וַאֲכַלְתֶּם	Go up ... *and eat* (1 Sam. 9.19).
וְנִקְרְבָה בְּאַחַד הַמְּקֹמֹת וְלַנוּ	Let us draw near to one of these places, *and spend the night* (Judg. 19.13).

Note the following:

(1) A waw consecutive + perfect can also sometimes be interrupted because the BH syntax necessitates this, for example, if a negative or a conjunction has to be used. The backbone of the future statement or habitual action concerned, however, is not interrupted in such cases.

(2) According to Revell (1989: 24) waw consecutive + perfect *is usually used after directives in contexts in which the speakers do not look down upon their listener(s). The directive is usually not very urgent.* In contrast to this, a string of directives (e.g. imperative + waw + imperative) is usually used when a command is urgent and the speakers are speaking to someone of a lower status.

3. *Waw consecutive + perfect can introduce the apodosis of a condition*

וְעָזַב אֶת־אָבִיו וָמֵת	And if he should leave, *his father would die* (Gen. 44.22).

4. *Waw consecutive + perfect refers to events/actions where no temporal sequence is involved*

(i) In *closer definition* (rare)

וּמֵישַׁע מֶלֶךְ־מוֹאָב הָיָה נֹקֵד
וְהֵשִׁיב לְמֶלֶךְ־יִשְׂרָאֵל כָּרִים

Now King Mesha of Moab was a sheep breeder, *who used to deliver to the king of Israel one hundred thousand lambs* (2 Kgs 3.4).

דַּבֵּר אֶל־בְּנֵי יִשְׂרָאֵל וְאָמַרְתָּ
אֲלֵהֶם

Speak to the people of Israel, and *say* to them: (Lev. 1.2).

(ii) Introducing the *protasis of a condition*

וְעָזַב אֶת־אָבִיו וָמֵת

And if he should *leave*, his father would die (Gen. 44.22).

§21.4. *Waw Copulative + Imperfect (Long Form)*

Besides linking clauses, this construction has no semantic function in itself.

תַּעְתִּיר אֵלָיו וְיִשְׁמָעֶךָ

You will make your prayer to him, *and* he *will hear* you (Job 22.27).

§21.5. *Waw Copulative + Directives (Jussive-, Imperative- and Cohortative Forms)*

Waw + a jussive, imperative or cohortative can follow any other directive or question. The following combinations are thus possible:

cohortative	+	waw	+	cohortative/imperative/jussive
imperative	+	waw	+	cohortative/imperative/jussive
jussive	+	waw	+	cohortative/imperative/jussive
question	+	waw	+	cohortative/imperative/jussive

Note that directives without waw also occur. For the semantic functions of directives, cf. §19.4.

1. *Purpose (of preceding directive, mostly with a change in person)*

(i) After an *imperative*

הַעְתִּירוּ אֶל־יְהוָה
וְיָסֵר הַצְפַרְדְּעִים מִמֶּנִּי

Entreat the Lord *so that* he *take* the frogs *away* from me (Exod. 8.4).

(ii) After a *cohortative*

אָסֻרָה־נָּא וְאֶרְאֶה

I will turn aside *so that I can see* (Exod. 3.3).

(iii) After a *jussive*

יִתְּנוּ־לִי מָקוֹם ...   Let a place be given me ..., *that* I may
וְאֵשְׁבָה שָׁם   *dwell* there (1 Sam. 27.5).

(iv) After *an imperfect* (in a question)

מַה־נַּעֲשֶׂה לָךְ וְיִשְׁתֹּק הַיָּם   What shall we do to you, *that* the sea
may quiet down? (Jon. 1.11).

2. *Consequence (of the preceding directive)*

(i) With waw + *jussive*

שְׁאַל אֶת־נְעָרֶיךָ וְיַגִּידוּ לָךְ   Ask your young men, *and* they *will*
tell you (1 Sam. 25.8).

**(ii) Where the waw+*imperative* is quite unambiguously not a directive
(e.g. the addressees can by no means carry out the order they had
received)**

זֹאת עֲשׂוּ וִחְיוּ   Do this *and* you *will live* (Gen.
42.18).

3. *Listing of urgent commands*

This occurs especially when imperatives are linked with waw and
both imply *the same addressee*. The speakers are usually addressing
someone of a lower status or someone they look down upon.

עֲלֵה אֱכֹל וּשְׁתֵה   Go up, *eat* and *drink* (1 Kgs 18.41).

4. *After some verbs of movement* (e.g. קוּם and הלך)

In such constructions the imperative forms of קוּם and הלך serve as
exhortations to execute the following waw + directive (which is
often a cohortative).

לְכוּ וְנִמְכְּרֶנּוּ לַיִּשְׁמְעֵאלִים   Come, let us *sell* him to the Ishmael-
ites (Gen. 37.27).

§22. **The Valency of Verbs**

The valency of a verb refers to the number of complements a verb
may select. (Cf. §12.3 and §33.2.) A verb may select one or more
complements, e.g.

1. *One complement: Verb + subject*

וַיָּמָת שָׁאוּל   And Saul died (Gen. 36.38).

2. *Two complements: Verb + subject + object*

כִּי הָרַג שָׁאוּל אֵת כֹּהֲנֵי יְהוָה ...   ... that Saul had killed the priests of the LORD (1 Sam. 22.21).

3. *Three complements: Verb + subject + object + indirect object*

וַיִּתֵּן יְהוֹנָתָן אֶת־כֵּלָיו אֶל־הַנַּעַר   Jonathan gave his weapons to the boy (1 Sam. 20.40).

Chapter 5

THE NOUN

§23. Introduction

The noun class (*nomen* – *nomina*) includes the following main categories:

- Nouns (substantives)
- Pronouns (*pronomina*)
- Numerals

Although adjectives correspond morphologically to the other nouns, they are normally classified in a separate category from nouns on the basis of syntactic criteria. In this grammar, however, they will be dealt with as a sub-category of the nouns.

Nouns are words that indicate the names of people, places, things or feelings. The following sub-categories of nouns may be distinguished in BH:

- Proper names
  These are the names of

Gods/gods	יהוה	Yahweh
people	דָּוִד	David
places	יְרוּשָׁלַיִם	Jerusalem
nations/groups	יִשְׂרָאֵל	Israel
happenings	פֶּסַח	Passover

- Common names/generic names
  These are common names for types of

things	שֻׁלְחָן	table
plants	עֵץ	tree
animals	עֵז	goat
people	יֶלֶד	child

- Collective nouns
  These are words that name a group consisting of members in singular form.

animals	צֹאן	sheep and goats

- Abstract nouns
  These are the names given to non-concrete things such as

qualities	אַהֲבָה	love
conditions	חֳלִי	illness
actions	עֲבוֹדָה	work

§24. The Congruency Features of Nouns

§24.1. *Morphology of Congruency Features*

Nouns (including proper nouns) are characteristically third person entities and govern a verb in the third person form as subject. They are also marked in terms of gender, i.e. masculine or feminine, and number, i.e. singular, plural or dual. The gender and number of nouns may be recognized by the following endings:

	Masculine	*Feminine*
Singular	-	הָ֞
Plural	◌ִים	וֹת
Dual	◌ַיִם	◌ָתַיִם

- The masculine singular thus has no ending—it is a zero or unmarked form.
- Other typical feminine singular endings are: ת‑, ה‑, ‑ַאת, ‑ִית, ‑וֹת, ‑וּת.
- The masculine plural ending is sometimes replaced by ‑ִין, for example, יָמִין (days).

§24.2. *Gender*

1. *Gender at morphological, syntactic and semantic level*
Gender is a feature allocated to nouns *on the basis of their form or the way they combine with other elements in a clause.* Some languages (such as English and Afrikaans) do have masculine and femi-

nine words (e.g. actor and actress), but they do not affect the constructions of phrases or clauses. Compare for example:

> The fine *actor* plays the role.
> The fine *actress* plays the role.

In other words the forms of the adjective and verb have not changed, even though the gender of the subject has changed from masculine to feminine. Most words do not even have specific masculine or feminine endings, e.g. man/wife/boy/girl. In these languages one is inclined to look at real life to determine a word's gender. Son is masculine, daughter is feminine and tree is neuter. This background creates a problem for the BH student because BH allocates a 'grammatical gender' to each noun that does not necessarily correspond to its sex in real life. When the gender of a noun is described in BH, the level of description must be indicated, namely morphological, syntactic or semantic:

(i) On the *morphological* level gender is indicated by means of an ending. (Cf. §24.1.)

(ii) On the *syntactic* level gender is indicated by means of the congruency features of words (such as adjectives and verbs), e.g.

הָעִיר הַגְּדֹלָה   the big city (Gen. 10.12)

Indicating gender at morphological and syntactic level is also known as 'grammatical gender'.

(iii) On the *semantic* level gender refers to the actual sex (in real life). In BH two genders are identified on the morphological and syntactic level, namely masculine and feminine. The result is that things that are neuter in real life must be described in terms of these two categories. Thus עִיר (city) is grammatically feminine, but מָקוֹם (place) is normally grammatically masculine. There is no logical reason for allocating gender to inanimate objects. Hebrew does not have a neuter as Latin and Greek do. On the semantic level, however, a distinction is made between masculine, feminine and neuter.

(iv) *Different combinations of* morphological, syntactic and semantic gender are possible in BH.

a. *Gender agrees at all levels.* That is, if the form is masculine, it refers to a male animal. If the word were the subject of a verb, then the verb would also be masculine. Similarly, the feminine form refers to a female animal, etc.

סוּס   stallion
סוּסָה   mare

b. *On semantic level the gender is neuter* (i.e. it does not refer to a male or female living person or animal); *nevertheless it is masculine or feminine on the morphological and syntactic level*, e.g.

הֵיכָל   a palace (masculine)
תּוֹרָה   a law (feminine)

Thus הֵיכָל has a masculine form and תּוֹרָה a feminine form (morphological gender). If these words were to be qualified by an adjective, הֵיכָל would govern the masculine form of an adjective and תּוֹרָה the feminine form, e.g.

הֵיכָל טוֹב   a good palace
תּוֹרָה טוֹבָה   a good law

c. Some words are *feminine on the semantic and syntactic level, but masculine on the morphological level*, for example, נָשִׁים (women) is a masculine form but refers to female persons. It also takes the feminine form of the adjective, e.g.

נָשִׁים טוֹבוֹת   good women

d. Some nouns are *morphologically masculine, syntactically feminine and semantically neuter*, e.g.

עִיר   a city
עִיר טוֹבָה   a good city

e. The gender of a word remains unchanged on the syntactic level, even though the *morphological form sometimes varies*, for example, מָקוֹם which is masculine in the singular on the morphological and syntactic level, becomes feminine in the plural on the morphological level (מְקוֹמוֹת), but remains masculine on the syntactic level.

f. Some words may be syntactically masculine or feminine in the singular, for example, דֶּרֶךְ. The plural of דֶּרֶךְ, however, is always masculine.

The most important combinations are summarized in the following table:

Hebrew forms	Morphological gender	Syntactic gender	Semantic gender
אִישׁ / אֲנָשִׁים	m.	m.	m.
מַלְכָּה / מְלָכוֹת	f.	f.	f.
עִיר /עָרִים	m.	f.	neuter
אֶרֶץ / אֲרָצוֹת	sing. m. / pl. f.	f.	neuter
חֲלוֹם / חֲלוֹמוֹת	sing. m. / pl. f.	m.	neuter
אָב / אָבוֹת	sing. m. / pl. f.	m.	m.
אִשָּׁה / נָשִׁים	sing. f. / pl. m.	f.	f.
דֶּרֶךְ / דְּרָכִים	m.	sing. m. or f. / pl. m.	neuter
יָד / יָדַיִם / יָדוֹת	sing. m. / du. m./ pl. f.	f.	neuter
יוֹם / יוֹמַיִם / יָמִים	m.	m.	neuter
רֶגֶל / רִגְלַיִם / רִגְלִים	m.	f.	neuter
קֹהֶלֶת	f.	m.	m.

2. Gender features of inanimate objects

(i) Nouns with a *masculine form* (i.e. morphologically masculine nouns).

Most nouns that are morphologically masculine are also masculine on the syntactic level. There are, however, exceptions.

a. Nouns with a *spatial reference* are usually syntactically feminine, even though they lack feminine endings.

אֶרֶץ   earth
חֵבֶל   world
עִיר   city

b. Nouns that refer to *natural elements and forces* are usually syntactically feminine, even though they lack feminine endings.

אֶבֶן   stone
רוּחַ   wind
אֵשׁ   fire

c. Nouns that refer to *implements* are usually syntactically feminine, even though they lack feminine endings.

חֶרֶב	sword
כּוֹס	cup
נַעַל	shoe

d. Nouns that refer to *dual parts of the body* are usually syntactically feminine, even though they lack feminine endings.

אֹזֶן	ear
עַיִן	eye
יָד	hand

An exception is שַׁד (breast) which is masculine on the syntactic level.

e. With *place names* gender on the syntactic level is often not determined by the proper noun itself, but by the presumed generic term associated with it.

- בֵּית־לֶחֶם and בֵּית־אֵל are morphologically and syntactically masculine because בַּיִת is morphologically and syntactically masculine.
- יְהוּדָה, בָּבֶל and יְרוּשָׁלַיִם are syntactically feminine because מַמְלָכָה (kingdom), אֶרֶץ (country) and עִיר (city) are syntactically feminine.
- פְּרָת (the Euphrates river) is syntactically masculine even though פְּרָת is morphologically feminine. The reason for this is that the generic term נָהָר (river) is syntactically masculine.

f. When words are used *figuratively* their gender may sometimes vary from that of their literal use on the syntactic level.
- עַיִן (literally '*eye*', feminine, but figuratively '*engraving surface*', masculine).

(ii) Nouns that have a *feminine form* (i.e. morphologically feminine nouns)

a. *Abstract* nouns are morphologically feminine.

גְּבוּרָה	power
יִשְׁרָה	sincerity
נְדִיבוֹת	noble things (plural)

An exception is חַיִל (power), which is morphologically masculine.

b. *Collective* nouns are often also morphologically feminine.

אָרְחָה	caravan
דַּלָּה	(the) poor
אֹיֶבֶת	enemy

c. A single member of a *collective* is often also morphologically feminine.

אֳנִיָּה	ship

as opposed to

אֳנִי	fleet

Compare, however, the following exception:

דָּגָה	fish (collective)

as opposed to

דָּג	a fish

d. When an *infinitive* is used as a noun, it is often regarded as morphologically feminine.

דַּעַת	knowledge, to know

e. A noun used *figuratively* is often morphologically feminine.

יוֹנֶקֶת	a young shoot, sapling

as opposed to

יוֹנֵק	suckling/child

Most nouns with feminine forms are also feminine on the level of syntax and semantics.

(iii) *Gender doublets*

Some nouns that refer to inanimate objects sometimes have masculine and feminine forms with the same meaning—this applies to abstract concepts as well as concrete things.

אָשָׁם / אַשְׁמָה	debt
מַתָּן / מַתָּנָה	gift

3. *Characteristics of gender in animate objects*

(i) *Natural pairs*

a. Sometimes there is no morphological indication of the gender of the elements in semantically marked opposite gender pairs.

אָב	father
אֵם	mother

b. The gender of some semantically related pairs is marked morphologically by a *masculine and a feminine form* of the same word.

פַּר	bull, ox
פָּרָה	cow

(ii) *Epicene nouns*

a. Some words bear semantic reference to a mixed gendered group, but are either morphologically masculine or feminine.

כֶּלֶב	dog (masculine form refers to both male and female)
יוֹנָה	dove (feminine form refers to both male and female)

b. Some epicene nouns that have a masculine form are syntactically feminine.

גְּמַלִּים מֵינִיקוֹת	nursing camels

c. The word for god(s)/godess(es) אֱלֹהִים is also regarded as an epicene noun.

(iii) *Precedence of the masculine gender on syntactic level*

When masculine and feminine word forms are combined, the masculine gender is accorded precedence on the syntactic level. (Cf. §35/(viii).)

זָכָר וּנְקֵבָה בָּרָא אֹתָם	Male and female he created them (m.) (Gen. 1.27).

This syntactic precedence is possibly due to the function of the masculine form as an unmarked gender, especially in the plural for mixed groups.

§24.3. *Number*[29]

1. *Number as a grammatical and extra-linguistic concept*

Number is a *grammatical (morphological and syntactic) characteristic* of nouns, but also refers to the extra-linguistic reality (the semantic aspect of number). Morphologically, nouns in BH have singular, plural and dual forms. The dual forms in BH are mainly reserved for objects that occur in pairs (such as parts of the body) and for certain indications of time.

---

29. Cf. Waltke and O'Connor §7.

(i) *Morphological characteristics of number in general*

a. *Some words have all three forms of number.*

יָד, יָדַיִם, יָדוֹת   hand, hands

b. *Others have only a singular and dual form*—the dual form is then used for the plural.

אֹזֶן, אָזְנַיִם   ear, ears

c. Some words have *only a dual form*.

מָתְנַיִם   hips

(ii) *Syntactic characteristics of number in general*

a. Syntactically a singular noun in subject position takes a singular form of the verb. (Cf. §35.)

וַיַּשְׁכֵּם אֲבִימֶלֶךְ בַּבֹּקֶר   And *Abimelech rose early* in the morning (Gen. 20.8).

b. A plural subject takes a plural verb.

וַיִּירְאוּ הָאֲנָשִׁים מְאֹד   And *the men were* very much *afraid* (Gen. 20.8).

c. There are *exceptions*, for example, when a noun with a plural form has a singular meaning.

וַיֹּאמֶר אֱלֹהִים ...   And *God said* ... (Gen. 1.3).

d. *Dual subjects take plural verbs because BH verbs have no dual forms.*

אַל־יִרְפּוּ יָדֶיךָ   Let not *your hands* (dual form) grow weak (Zeph. 3.16).

וְעֵינֵי אֲדֹנִי־הַמֶּלֶךְ רֹאוֹת   While *the eyes of my lord the king* see it (2 Sam. 24.3).

(iii) *The semantics of number in general*

Number is a grammatical feature of nouns that does not always correspond to extra-linguistic reality. For example, collective nouns are singular nouns that refer to more than one object, e.g. עוֹף (birds) and הָעָם (the people). On the other hand, Hebrew also makes use of the plural noun פָּנִים to refer to the singular 'face'. In the case of the latter type, the morphological number *sometimes* corresponds to the syntactic number *and sometimes does not*.

פָּנַי יֵלֵכוּ וַהֲנִחֹתִי לָךְ:	My presence (lit. my face) will go with you, and I will give you rest (Exod. 33.14).
וְיָדְעוּ הָעָם כֻּלּוֹ	And all *the people will know* (Isa. 9.8).

Furthermore, the allocation of grammatical number to concepts differs from language to language.

2. *Syntactic and semantic aspects of the singular form*

(i) With nouns referring to countable objects, the singular refers to *one example of many* (the so-called numerical singular).

אִישׁ	a man
בַּיִת	a house

(ii) With collective nouns the singular is used to refer to *a group* (the so-called collective singular).

צֹאן	sheep
אָדָם	people, humanity
עוֹף	birds
דָּגָה	fish

Collective nouns in subject positions may govern the singular or plural form of the verb. Compare §35 for possible reasons.

יֹאכְלוּ עוֹף הַשָּׁמָיִם	The birds of heaven shall eat (1 Kgs 14.11).
עוֹף הַשָּׁמַיִם יוֹלִיךְ אֶת־הַקּוֹל	The birds of heaven *will carry* your voice [lit. the voice] (Eccl. 10.20).

a. Some nouns are used *almost exclusively in the singular* as collective nouns.

פְּרִי	fruit
דֶּשֶׁא	grass
רֶמֶשׂ	creeping things
בְּהֵמָה	animals
טַף	children
רֶכֶב	war-chariots

b. Nouns that often occur in the plural form can, however, also sometimes be used *in the singular collective*.

אִישׁ	men
אִשָּׁה	women
עֵץ	trees

(iii) The singular noun occurring after cardinal numbers, after כֹל and other words indicating quantity, *refers to a class or a group*. Gentilic nouns (names of people or groups) are also often used in the singular.

וּשְׁלֹשִׁים וּשְׁנַיִם מֶלֶךְ	32 kings (1 Kgs 20.1)
כָּל־זְכוּרְךָ	all your *males* (Exod. 34.23)
וְלָרֹאוּבֵנִי ... אָמַר יְהוֹשֻׁעַ	And to the *Reubenites* ... Joshua said (Josh. 1.12)

(iv) When the same noun is repeated in the singular—with or without the conjunction וֹ or with a preposition—it has a *distributive sense*. (Cf. §29.3/(viii).)

שָׁנָה שָׁנָה	*year by* year (Deut. 14.22)
דּוֹר־וָדוֹר	*all* generations / *every* generation (Deut. 32.7)
שָׁנָה בְשָׁנָה	*year by* year (Deut. 15.20)
בַּבֹּקֶר בַּבֹּקֶר	*morning by* morning (Exod. 16.21)

(v) When the same noun is repeated syndetically in the singular (i.e. with a conjunction), it expresses *diversity*.

בְּלֵב וָלֵב יְדַבֵּרוּ	They speak with a *double* heart [= deceitfully] (Ps. 12.3).

(vi) Repetition of the same noun can also indicate *exclusivity* or *intensity*. (Cf. §29.3/(ix).)

זָהָב זָהָב	*pure* gold (2 Kgs 25.15)
בַּדֶּרֶךְ בַּדֶּרֶךְ אֵלֵךְ	I will go *only* by the road (Deut. 2.27).

3. *Syntactic and semantic aspects of the plural form*

(i) With nouns referring to countable objects the plural indicates more than one or two specimens (the so-called *numerical plural*).

אֲנָשִׁים	men
מְלָכִים	kings

(ii) The repetition of the same noun in the plural indicates *intensification*.

עָשֹׂה הַנַּחַל הַזֶּה גֵּבִים גֵּבִים I will make this wadi (dry river bed) *full of pools* (2 Kgs 3.16).

(iii) The plural form of a singular collective noun indicates *a disruption or processing of the collective*. With nouns referring to crops it often indicates the processed state.

דָּם blood
דָּמִים blood*shed*
שְׂעֹרָה barley (in the fields)
שְׂעֹרִים *cooked* barley

(iv) The plural forms of some nouns indicate that the referent of the noun is *large, complex or manifold* (the so-called plurals of extension).

מַיִם water
אֹהָלִים camp, dwelling
as opposed to
אֹהֶל tent (often a religious use)

Some nouns that refer to *body parts* are used only in the plural as plurals of extension.

פָּנִים face

(v) The plural form of some nouns indicates *a repeated series of actions or a habit*. It can have an abstract meaning.

זְנוּנִים prostitution
כּוֹס תַּנְחוּמִים cup of consolation (Jer. 16.7)

(vi) With abstract nouns the plural often refers to a *characteristic or condition*.

בִּינוֹת understanding
בְּחֻרִים youth
זְקֻנִים old age

(vii) The plural form of some nouns refers to a *special or exalted person*, or superior deity or person, the so-called *honorific plural* (*pluralis majestatis*).

הָאֱלֹהִים gods/God

a. The plural forms of *participles* are also sometimes used as honorific plurals in reference to God or people.

עֹשָׂי   my Maker (Job 35.10)

b. The plural form of some nouns that refer to animals is sometimes used as an honorific plural to designate *a whole species*.

וְעַל־עַיִר בֶּן־אֲתֹנוֹת   and on a colt, the foal of an ass (Zech 9.9)

c. The honorific plural is also used in reference to *people*.

בְּעָלִים   boss, master
אֲדֹנִים   lord

The word אֲדֹנָי (Lord, as the name of the God of Israel) must be distinguished from both אֲדֹנִי (my master) and אֲדֹנַי (my lord), which refer to people.

4. *Syntactic and semantic aspects of the dual form*

(i) The dual occurs especially in nouns referring to *body parts* that occur in pairs.

אָזְנַיִם   two ears
עֵינַיִם   two eyes

a. The dual is also used for *nouns* that refer to objects that usually occur in pairs.

נַעֲלַיִם   a pair of sandals

b. The plural form of nouns that have dual forms referring to body parts is often used *metaphorically*.

יָדַיִם   two hands
        but
יָדוֹת   handles

(ii) The dual form of nouns is also used for *measurable time and measuring units*.

אַמָּה	cubit	אַמָּתַיִם	2 cubits	אַמּוֹת	cubits
יוֹם	day	יוֹמַיִם	2 days	יָמִים	days

(iii) Although מַיִם and שָׁמַיִם *look like dual forms*, they should be regarded as plural forms.

(iv) Some nouns have dual forms without there being any obvious reason for this.

צָהֳרִים	midday (12 o'clock)
מִצְרַיִם	Egypt
יְרוּשָׁלַיִם	Jerusalem

§24.4. *Definiteness (Status Determinatus)*

Definiteness may be regarded as a congruency feature of nouns. In English a distinction is made between the definite article *the* and the indefinite article *a*. BH has an equivalent only for the definite article. When a common noun occurs without a definite article it is regarded as indefinite.

1. *The way in which indefiniteness/definiteness is expressed in BH*
The indefiniteness or definiteness of BH nominal forms is morphologically determined as follows:

(i) A noun is *indefinite* if:

a. an article or pronominal suffix is not affixed to it and it is not followed by a definite noun in a construct relation. (Cf. §25.3.)

b. אֶחָד or אַחַת is used, however, to mark a certain or specific someone or something.

אִישׁ אֶחָד	a *certain* man (Judg. 13.2)

(ii) A noun is *definite* if:

a. it is definite in itself
   a proper name

וַיְבַקֵּשׁ לַהֲרֹג אֶת־מֹשֶׁה	And he sought to kill *Moses* (Exod. 2.15).

   a pronoun

וַיֵּשֶׁב בַּמְּעָרָה הוּא וּשְׁתֵּי בְנֹתָיו	*And he* dwelt in a cave with his two daughters [lit. he dwelt in a cave, *he* and *his* two daughters] (Gen. 19.30).

   a title

וַיַּמְלִכוּ כָל־יִשְׂרָאֵל אֶת־עָמְרִי שַׂר־צָבָא עַל־יִשְׂרָאֵל	And all Israel made Omri, *the commander of the army*, king over Israel (1 Kgs 16.16).

a common noun that has acquired the value of a proper noun

וַיָּ֫שֶׁת עֲלֵיהֶם תֵּבֵל   And on them he has set *the world* (1 Sam. 2.8).

b. it has the definite article הַ or

c. a pronominal suffix affixed to it

d. it is in *status constructus* and followed by a definite noun

הָשֵׁב אֵשֶׁת־הָאִישׁ   Restore the man's wife [lit. *the wife of the man*] (Gen. 20.7).

Note the following:

   (1) BH differs from English in its use of the definite article. The function of the article must thus be determined carefully, especially in translation.

   (2) The use of the article is a relatively recent phenomenon in Semitic languages and is therefore often omitted in poetic sections.

2. *The form of the article*

The basic form of the article is הַ. The article is directly attached to the front of the relevant noun resulting in the doubling of the first consonant of that word.

הַ + מֶ֫לֶךְ   the + king
הַמֶּ֫לֶךְ   the king

The following exceptions occur:[30]

(i) The gutturals (א, ה, ח, ע) and ר (as a rule) cannot be doubled. (Cf. §4.2/4(i).) When a definite noun begins with one of these consonants, the / ַ / of the *article changes or lengthens to compensate* for the doubling that can no longer occur.

These changes may be presented systematically as follows:

The first vowel is not a qāmeṣ.			*The first vowel is a qāmeṣ.*		
אִישׁ	א		אָדָם	א	הֶ
רֹאשׁ	ר	הָ	רָשָׁע	ר	
עִיר	ע		עָפָר	ע	
הֵיכָל	ה	הַ	הָרִים	ה	הֶ
חֶ֫רֶב	ח		חָכָם	ח	

30. Cf. Waltke and O'Connor §13.3.

(ii) As well as with the gutturals, and usually with ר, the first consonant of the noun also *does not double* in the following instance:

a. In words beginning with י or מ the doubling usually falls away. (Cf. §8.2/5.)

הַיְלָדִים   the children

b. If the י is followed by a ה or ע the doubling does occur.

הַיְהוּדִים   the Jews

c. If the מ is followed by a ה, ע or ר the doubling does occur.

הַמְרֵעִים   the mischief-makers

(iii) The *vocalization of some nouns changes* when the article is added to them.

הָאָרֶץ   the land
הָאָרוֹן   the ark

(iv) When *the bound prepositions* (בְּ, כְּ and לְ) appear before the article, the prepositions and the article *combine* to form a single syllable, e.g. -בַּ instead of -בְּהַ, -לַ instead of -לְהַ, -כַּ instead of -כְּהַ.

בַּמֶּלֶךְ   by the king
לַמֶּלֶךְ   for the king
כַּמֶּלֶךְ   like the king

3. *Syntactic functions of the article*[31]

(i) The article is sometimes used in the construction of the vocative to designate *a specific addressee*. (Cf. §34.4.)

חֵי־נַפְשְׁךָ הַמֶּלֶךְ

As your soul lives, *O king* (1 Sam. 17.55).

It may be *omitted*.

לֵךְ־אֶל־נְמָלָה עָצֵל

Go to the ant, *O sluggard* (Prov. 6.6).

(ii) The article is used in the place of a relative pronoun to construct a *relative clause*.

a. With *a finite verb* (rare and usually in Late BH)

עַמְּךָ הַנִּמְצְאוּ־פֹה

your people who *are present* here (1 Chron. 29.17).

---

31. Cf. Waltke and O'Connor §13.5.2.

b. Apparently with a *participle* (Cf. §20.3/3.)

לַיהוָה הַנִּרְאֶה אֵלָיו

to the Lord *who had appeared to him* (Gen. 12.7).

(iii) The article is used to construct *the superlative.*

כִּי־אַתֶּם הַמְעַט מִכָּל־הָעַמִּים

For you were the *fewest* of all peoples (Deut. 7.7).

(iv) It *marks* an adjective or demonstrative pronoun as *grammatically congruent* with a noun.

וַנֵּלֶךְ אֵת כָּל־הַמִּדְבָּר הַגָּדוֹל ...

And we went through all that *great* desert ... (Deut. 1.19).

4. *Semantic functions of the article*[32]

(i) The article makes a *demonstrative* semantic contribution when used with nouns referring to time.

הַיּוֹם

today [lit. this day] (Gen. 4.14)

(ii) The definite noun focuses attention on the referent's *identity.* The following constructions are important here:

a. A common noun with an article can refer to a *unique referent* (i.e. there is only one of its kind).

הַשֶּׁמֶשׁ

the sun

b. A common noun with an article can refer to a specific referent that has, for example, *been mentioned before. This contributes towards creating a coherent text.* To put this in another way, if there were no indication that a particular referent had already been mentioned, that text would seem awkward (or incoherent).

וַיִּקַּח בֶּן־בָּקָר ...
וַיִּקַּח חֶמְאָה וְחָלָב
וּבֶן־הַבָּקָר

And he took a calf ... then he took curds, and milk, and *the calf* (Gen. 18.7-8).

c. Things that are *implied by the context* take the article, even if they have not been mentioned before.

וַתְּעַר כַּדָּהּ אֶל־הַשֹּׁקֶת

And she emptied her jar into *the trough* (Gen. 24.20).

---

32. Cf. Waltke and O'Connor §13.5.1.

d. The article is used *generically to designate* a class of persons or things that are definite in themselves.

... אַךְ אֶת־זֶה לֹא תֹאכְלוּ אֶת־הַגָּמָל ... וְאֶת־הַשָּׁפָן	But you shall not eat these ... the *camel* ... and the *rock badger* (Lev. 11.4-5).
הַכּוֹכָבִים	*the stars* (Gen. 15.5)
הַכְּנַעֲנִי	*the Canaanite(s)*
בָאֵשׁ	with *the fire* (Josh. 11.9)
בַּסַּנְוֵרִים	with *(the) blindness* (Gen. 19.11)

This construction is used particularly in comparisons, e.g.

כְּלֵב הָאַרְיֵה	like the heart of *a (the) lion* (2 Sam. 17.10)

e. The article is used to mark a common noun as a *proper noun*.

הַיְאֹר	*The River* = the Nile River

§25. **The Declension of the Noun**

§25.1. *Cases in BH. The Construct State*

1. *General*

Unlike most Semitic languages, BH no longer has noun cases. A BH noun thus does not 'decline' as a Greek or Latin noun; i.e. it does not have different endings for the nominative, vocative, accusative, genitive, dative and ablative cases.

The closest BH comes to having cases is in the personal pronoun.

	Subject	Direct Object	Possessive	Indirect Object
	'Nominative'	'Accusative'	'Genitive'	'Dative'
1 sing.	אֲנִי	אוֹתִי	־ִי	לִי
	I	me	my	to me
3 m. sing.	הוּא	אוֹתוֹ	־וֹ	לוֹ
	he	him	his	to him

2. Terminology: the status absolutus (st. abs.), status constructus (st. cs.) and postconstructus (pcs.)

BH has adopted other strategies to compensate for the loss of noun cases. There is, for example, a specific construction for the 'genitive' in BH. This construction which is, in a sense, the only morphological indicator of a 'case' in BH, is called a *construct relation*. It is a linguistic phenomenon in BH that involves two nouns that could be expressed in English as follows:

The horse of the king.

In its simplest form it consists of a *status constructus* form of the noun and a *status absolutus* form.

St. cs.	*St. abs. and pcs.*
the horse	of the king
the God	of the heavens

The *status absolutus* is the normal form of the word. It may occur in any syntactic position, e.g. subject, direct object, indirect object (with a preposition), etc. It is also called the נִפְרָד. The *status constructus* is a special form of the word that is used to indicate that that particular word and the word following it form a possessive construction (in the broadest sense of the word). This is called the *construct relationship* or סְמִיכוּת (support). The *status constructus* is also called the נִסְמָךְ (supported) and the word that follows it the סֹמֵךְ (supporter). The סֹמֵךְ is the equivalent of the genitive in Greek and Latin and other Semitic languages. The סֹמֵךְ can also be called the *postconstructus*. The *postconstructus* has the normal form of the word (*status absolutus*), unless it is itself in the *status constructus* and followed by a *postconstructus*. A whole series of constructs can be thus formed. This is called a *construct chain*.

לֵב רָאשֵׁי עַם־הָאָרֶץ The *heart* of the *chiefs* of the *people* of the earth (Job 12.24)

Note the following:

(1) BH grammars do not normally distinguish between the *status absolutus* and what has been called the *postconstructus* in this grammar. This distinction is important for the following reason: even though the forms of the *status absolutus* and the *post constructus* are often identical, this is not the case in a construct chain (as in Job 12.24).

(2) The *status constructus* has different endings from the *status absolutus* in all the numbers and genders, except the masculine singular (which has no endings) and the feminine plural where it is the same as the absolute. The masculine dual *status constructus* ending and masculine plural *status constructus* endings look the same. (Cf. the second table in §25.2.)

(3) A *status constructus* form loses its main accent and this is why vowel reduction often occurs, for example, דָּבָר becomes דְּבַר. (Cf. §7.3.)

(4) Sometimes the *status constructus* is joined to the *postconstructus* with the maqqēf, for example, בֶּן־. (Cf. §9.1.)

(5) The Masoretic accents (cf. §9.5) can also indicate the distinction between the *status absolutus* and the *status constructus*. A conjunctive accent can indicate a construct relationship, but a disjunctive accent indicates that the word is in the *status absolutus*.

§25.2. *Morphology of the Status Absolutus, Postconstructus and Status Constructus*

BH nouns can have the following endings:

	Masculine		Feminine	
	st. abs.	*st. cs.*	*st. abs.*	*st. cs.*
singular	-	-	־ָה	־ַת
plural	־ִים	־ֵי	־וֹת	־וֹת
dual	־ַיִם	־ֵי	־ָתַיִם	־ָתֵי

If endings are 'added' to unchangeable nouns, the results are:

	Masculine		Feminine	
	st. abs.	*st. cs.*	*st. abs.*	*st. cs.*
singular	סוּס stallion	סוּס stallion of	סוּסָה mare	סוּסַת mare of
plural	סוּסִים stallions	סוּסֵי stallions of	סוּסוֹת mares	סוּסוֹת mares of
dual	סוּסִים 2 stallions	סוּסֵי 2 stallions of	סוּסָתַיִם 2 mares	סוּסָתֵי 2 mares of

Vowel reduction or other changes also occur in most nouns—the relevant rules and paradigms will be dealt with in §26 and 27. Not all the forms below occur, but they have been theoretically reconstructed in order to form a complete paradigm.

§25.3. *The Noun in Construct Relationships*

1. *Syntactic features*

(i) A noun in the *postconstructus* state can be found with or without the article הַ and is accordingly definite or indefinite.

(ii) A noun in the *status constructus never takes the article* הַ. The definiteness of the *postconstructus* also applies to the *status constructus* (with certain exceptions, especially in poetry). Where the definiteness of the elements does differ, a construction with the preposition לְ is used, e.g.

מִזְמוֹר לְדָוִד   a psalm *of David*

(iii) A construct relationship is *usually inseparable*. The only element that can normally stand between the *status constructus* and the *postconstructus* is the article.

Other parts of speech do sometimes come between the two elements. In such a case one speaks of a *broken* construct relationship. Such elements include (*inter alia*) the following:

a. the *he locale* (Cf. §28.)

וַיָּבֵא הָאִישׁ אֶת־הָאֲנָשִׁים   And the man brought the men to
בֵּיתָה יוֹסֵף   *Joseph's house* (Gen. 43.17).

b. *prepositions*

אֶת־אַחַד מֵהַנְּעָרִים   one *of the servants* (1 Sam. 9.3).

c. אֵת

לְיֵשַׁע אֶת־מְשִׁיחֶךָ   for the salvation *of your anointed*
(Hab. 3.13)

d. *certain verb forms (rare)*

דֶּרֶךְ יְרַצְּחוּ־שֶׁכְמָה   They murder on the *way to/of*
Shechem (Hos. 6.9)

e. the so-called enclitic *mem.*[33]

יְהֹוָה־אֱלֹהִי־ם צְבָאוֹת   Lord, God *of hosts* (Ps. 59.6)
(MT reads אֱלֹהִים)

(iv) *Additional syntactic features of the construct relationship*

a. *Usually two constructs cannot occur with one postconstructus.* Where this does occur, the construction is broken up and the *post-constructus* is replaced by a pronominal suffix.

אֶל־תְּפִלַּת עַבְדְּךָ   to the prayer of *your servant and to*
וְאֶל־תְּחִנָּתוֹ   *his supplication* [= *to the prayer and supplication of your servant*] (1 Kgs 8.28)

There are, however, some *exceptions.*

מִבְחַר וְטוֹב־לְבָנוֹן   the *choice and best* of Lebanon (Ezek. 31.16)

b. *One status constructus cannot usually govern two postconstructa either.* Where this does occur, the *status constructus* is usually repeated.

אֱלֹהֵי הַשָּׁמַיִם וֵאלֹהֵי הָאָרֶץ   *the God* of the heaven and *the God* of the earth [= the God of the heaven and the earth] (Gen. 24.3)

In some cases the *status constructus* is not repeated, especially if the two *postconstructa* are closely related.

בְּעֵינֵי אֱלֹהִים וְאָדָם   in the sight *of God and man* (Prov. 3.4)

c. *A prepositional phrase or verb phrase sometimes follow a noun in the status constructus.*

יֹשְׁבֵי בְּאֶרֶץ צַלְמָוֶת   those who dwelt *in the land* of deep darkness (Isa. 9.1)

כָּל־יְמֵי הִתְהַלַּכְנוּ אִתָּם   all the days *that we went with them* [lit. all the days *of our going with them*] (1 Sam. 25.15)

33. Cf. Waltke and O'Connor §9.8 and §28a.

d. *A pronominal suffix that belongs to the status constructus 'jumps' to the next possible position*, i.e. *the postconstructus*. It must, however, be translated as a part of the *status constructus*. In order to determine the element to which the pronominal suffix belongs, the textual context needs to be taken into account.

הַר קָדְשִׁי   *my* mountain of holiness (= *my* holy mountain) (Isa. 11.9)

e. The noun in the *status constructus* can fulfil any syntactic function, while the noun in the *postconstructus can only be an adjectival qualification of the status constructus*.

2. *Possible combinations in construct relationship (and other 'posses-sive constructions' with the preposition* לְ*)*

(i) *Instances where definiteness agrees*

סוּסַת מַלְכָּה   *a* mare of *a* queen
סוּסַת הַמַּלְכָּה   *the* mare of *the* queen

a. In a construct chain all the members of the chain are in the *status constructus* except the last. A word can thus be a *postconstructus* and at the same time stand in the *status constructus*. The last member, however, always stands in the ordinary form or the *status absolutus*. The definiteness or indefiniteness of the last part also applies to all the other parts.

יִרְאַת סוּסַת מַלְכָּה   *a* fear of *a* mare of *a* queen
יִרְאַת סוּסַת הַמַּלְכָּה   *the* fear of *the* mare of *the* queen

b. The *status constructus* and/or the *postconstructus* can be singular or plural.

דְּבַר הַנָּבִיא   the word of the prophet
דְּבַר הַנְּבִיאִים   the word of the prophets
דִּבְרֵי הַנָּבִיא   the words of the prophet
דִּבְרֵי הַנְּבִיאִים   the words of the prophets

c. The *status constructus* can be a participle.

שֹׁמֵר הַתּוֹרָה   *the guardian* (participle) of the law

d. The *status constructus* can be an adjective.

טוֹבַת הַנָּשִׁים   *the good* (adjective) of the women

(ii) Should the *status constructus* and the *postconstructus differ in definiteness*, the construct relationship cannot be used, but the preposition לְ is used to express the 'possesssive construction'.

סוּסָה לַמַּלְכָּה	a mare of the queen
הַסּוּסָה לְמַלְכָּה	the mare of a queen
הַסּוּסָה הַגְּדוֹלָה לְמַלְכָּה	the large mare of a queen
סוּסָה גְדוֹלָה לַמַּלְכָּה	a large mare of the queen

(iii) The *preposition* לְ can also be used in cases where there is *no difference in definiteness*. In such cases it can assist in determining which element is being qualified. The following constructions are thus possible:

סוּסַת הַמַּלְכָּה הַגְּדוֹלָה	*the large mare* of the queen
or	
הַסּוּסָה הַגְּדוֹלָה לַמַּלְכָּה	
סוּסַת הַמַּלְכָּה הַגְּדוֹלָה	the mare of *the large queen*
or	
הַסּוּסָה לַמַּלְכָּה הַגְּדוֹלָה	
סוּסַת מַלְכָּה גְדוֹלָה	*a large mare* of a queen
or	
סוּסָה גְדוֹלָה לְמַלְכָּה	
סוּסַת מַלְכָּה גְדוֹלָה	a mare of *a large queen*
or	
סוּסָה לְמַלְכָּה גְדוֹלָה	

§25.4. *Syntactic-Semantic Relationships in Construct Relationships*

The *status constructus* is used to express many other relationships beside that of possession-possessor.

The *status constructus* and *postconstructus* can occur in the following relationships:[34]

---

34. Cf. Kroeze 1991: 129-143 for a discussion of the problems in analysing *status constructus* relationships. Cf. Kroeze 1993: 68-88 for a syntax-based classification of constructs and Kroeze 1994a: 231-314 for a purely semantic approach.

1. *Relationships of Possession*
(i) Possession (concrete object)–possessor

בֵּית הַמֶּלֶךְ   the house of the king

(ii) Possession (body part)–possessor

שִׂפְתֵי הַמֶּלֶךְ   the lips of the king

(iii) Possession (characteristic)–possessor

הֲדְרַת־הַמֶּלֶךְ   the majesty of the king

(iv) Kinship/relationship–possessor

בְּנֵי הַמֶּלֶךְ   the sons of the king

(v) Possessor–possession

בַּעַל הַבַּיִת   the owner of the house

2. *Subject and object relations*
(i) Verbal notion–subject

בִּרְכַּת יהוה   the blessing of (or by) the Lord

(ii) Verbal notion (passive)–agent

הֲרוּגֵי הָאִשָּׁה   the murdered (ones) of the woman

(iii) Verbal notion–object

יִרְאַת יהוה   the fear of (for) Lord

3. *Partitive relationships*
(i) Part–divided whole

בְּנֵי הַנְּבִיאִים   the members of (among) the
prophet guild

(ii) Superlative part–divided whole

טוֹב הַבָּנִים   the best (good) of (among) the sons

(iii) Part–undivided whole

כָּל־הַבָּנִים   all of the sons (all the sons)

4. *Equalizing relationships*
(i) Entity–synonym

שִׂמְחַת גִּיל   joy of (viz.) happiness

(ii) Entity–class (genus)

כְּסִיל אָדָם   a fool of (viz.) a person

(iii) Entity–type (species)

זִבְחֵי שְׁלָמִים   sacrifices of (viz.) peace offerings

(iv) Entity–name

נְהַר פְּרָת   the river of (viz.) the Euphrates

(v) Entity–characteristic (description, attribute, quality)

אִמְרֵי בִינָה   words of (with) insight

5. *Adverbial relationships*
(i) Entity–aim, goal or result

אַבְנֵי־קֶלַע   stones of (meant for) a sling

(ii) Entity–manner

אוֹצְרוֹת רֶשַׁע   riches of (acquired through) injustice

(iii) Entity–cause or reason

מְזֵי רָעָב   exhausted (ones) of (due to) hunger

(iv) Entity–means (instrument)

חַלְלֵי־הַחֶרֶב   the wounded (ones) of (by means of) the sword

(v) Entity–duration of time

בֶּן־שָׁנָה   a son of a year (a one year old)

(vi) Entity–direction

יוֹרְדֵי בוֹר   the (ones) going down (into the) pit

(vii) Entity–origin

שְׁלַל הֶעָרִים   the loot of (from) the cities

6. *Other relationships*
(i) Product–material

כְּלֵי כֶסֶף   vessels of silver

(ii) Product–author, creator, source, origin

סֵפֶר הָאִישׁ   the book of (by) the man

(iii) Characteristic–with regard / respect to (specification)

אֱוִיל שְׂפָתַיִם   foolish of (with respect to) lips

(iv) Entity–interested (favoured/injured) party

מוֹקֵשׁ הָאָדָם   the trap of (for, to the detriment of)
a person

(v) Container–content

חֵמַת מַיִם   a bag of (full of) water

§26. The Noun with Pronominal Suffixes

§26.1. *Morphology of Nouns with Pronominal Suffixes*

1. *General*

Suffixes are elements added to the end of a word. BH has different types of suffixes:

- Finite *verbs* have suffixes that designate the person, gender and number of the subject. (Cf. §15.) In addition, *object suffixes* may also be affixed to them. (Cf. §17.)
- With *nouns* the distinction between the singular, plural and dual, masculine and feminine, *status absolutus* and *status constructus* is also expressed by means of suffixes. (Cf. §24 and §25.) These suffixes are called *endings*. In contrast to the classical languages, however, *person suffixes* also occur with nouns. These *pronominal suffixes/enclitic personal pronouns* may be regarded as the possessive equivalent of the separate personal pronoun. One could even speak of *genitive* suffixes here as morphologically distinguishable endings do indeed occur. *Whenever further reference is made to 'suffixes' here the possessive pronominal suffixes are understood.*

The following distinctions must be maintained in the declension of nouns:

- Words with masculine forms and words with feminine forms
- Words in the singular, plural or dual

There are six unique sets of pronominal suffixes (cf. Table 21):

Set 1 is used with *masculine singular* nouns.
Set 2 is used with *feminine singular* nouns.

Set 3 is used with *masculine plural* nouns.

Set 4 is used with *feminine plural* nouns.

Set 5 is used with *masculine dual* nouns.

Set 6 is used with *feminine dual* nouns.

The consonant and vowel pattern of a noun influences the declension.

Note the following: The characteristics of nouns with suffixes may be systematized as follows (*always compare the full declension of a noun in Table 21*):

(1) The endings of the *status absolutus* and *status constructus* in the singular, dual and plural of nouns with masculine and feminine forms are unique. (Cf. §25.2.)

(2) The pronominal suffixes occurring with masculine singular nouns constitute the so-called *basic paradigm* in BH.

(3) The *heavy suffixes* are כֶם-, כֶן-, הֶם- and הֶן-. All other pronominal suffixes are *light suffixes*.

(4) If a closed syllable has developed from an open syllable, for example, after applying the rule of šᵉwā', the syllable is considered half-closed and the *begadkefat* letter following it does not get a dāgēsh, for example, when the heavy suffixes are added to singular nouns. (Cf. Table 21, e.g. תּוֹרַתְכֶם.)

(5) Masculine dual nouns use the same set of suffixes that is used with plural, masculine nouns.

(6) The suffixes used with feminine nouns can be deduced from the suffixes used with masculine nouns as follows:

Singular: *status absolutus* הָ- becomes תָ- before light suffixes

status constructus ת- appears before heavy suffixes

Dual: *status absolutus* (תַיִם-) // the form תָ- before the light suffixes (which look just like the suffixes in masculine plural nouns)

status constructus (תֵי-) // the form תֵ- before the heavy suffixes (which look just like those used with masculine plural nouns)

Plural: *status absolutus* = *status constructus* (וֹת-) = the form occurring before all suffixes (which look just like those used with masculine plural nouns)

The complete declension is as follows:

2. Table 21. *The complete declension of the noun*

MASCULINE SINGULAR			FEMININE SINGULAR		
st. abs.			st. abs.		הָ-
st. cs.			st. cs.		ת-
with sing. suffix	1 c.	-ִי	with sing. suffix	1 c.	תִ-י
	2 m.	-ְךָ		2 m.	תְֽךָ-
	2 f.	-ֵךְ		2 f.	תֵֽךְ-
	3 m.	-ֹו, -הֹו, -ֹו		3 m.	תֹ-ו
	3 f.	-ָהּ, -ָהּ		3 f.	תָהּ-
with pl. suffix	1 c.	-ֵנוּ	with pl. suffix	1 c.	תֵנוּ-
	2 m.	-ְכֶם		2 m.	תְכֶם-
	2 f.	-ְכֶן		2 f.	תְכֶן-
	3 m.	-ָהֶם, -ָם		3 m.	תָם-
	3 f.	-ָן, -ָהֶן		3 f.	תָן-
MASCULINE DUAL			FEMININE DUAL		
st. abs.		-ַים	st. abs.		תַיִם-
st. cs.		-ֵי	st. cs.		תֵי-
with sing. suffix	1 c.	-ַי	with sing. suffix	1 c.	תַי-
	2 m.	-ֶיךָ		2 m.	תֶיךָ-
	2 f.	-ַיִךְ		2 f.	תַיִךְ-
	3 m.	-ָיו, -ָו, -ָיהוּ		3 m.	תָיו-
	3 f.	-ֶיהָ		3 f.	תֶיהָ-
with pl. suffix	1 c.	-ֵינוּ	with pl. suffix	1 c.	תֵינוּ-
	2 m.	-ֵיכֶם		2 m.	תֵיכֶם-
	2 f.	-ֵיכֶן		2 f.	תֵיכֶן-
	3 m.	-ֵיהֶם, -ֵימוֹ		3 m.	תֵיהֶם-
	3 f.	-ֵיהֶן		3 f.	תֵיהֶן-

MASCULINE PLURAL			FEMININE PLURAL		
st. abs.		־ִים	st. abs.		־וֹת
st. cs.		־ֵי	st. cs.		־וֹת
with sing. suffix	1 c.	־ַי	with sing. suffix	1 c.	־וֹתַי
	2 m.	־ֶיךָ		2 m.	־וֹתֶיךָ
	2 f.	־ַיִךְ		2 f.	־וֹתַיִךְ
	3 m.	־ָיו, ־ֵיהוּ, ־ָיְ		3 m.	־וֹתָיו
	3 f.	־ֶיהָ		3 f.	־וֹתֶיהָ
with pl. suffix	1 c.	־ֵינוּ	with pl. suffix	1 c.	־וֹתֵינוּ
	2 m.	־ֵיכֶם		2 m.	־וֹתֵיכֶם
	2 f.	־ֵיכֶן		2 f.	־וֹתֵיכֶן
	3 m.	־ֵיהֶם		3 m.	־וֹתֵיהֶם
	3 f.	־ֵיהֶן		3 f.	־וֹתֵיהֶן

§26.2. *Syntactic and Semantic Functions of the Pronominal Suffixes*

The pronominal suffixes fulfil the syntactic function of an adjectival qualification occurring with a noun—*in the same way as does the second element* (the *postconstructus*) *of a construct relationship.* Like the *postconstructus*, pronominal suffixes are used to express many underlying syntactic and semantic relations. Because a pronominal suffix can replace any noun, almost all the distinctions made with the *status constructus* are possible here. (Cf. §25.4.)

§27. Noun Patterns and Suffixes

Nouns can be divided into various groups on the basis of the vowel changes that occur with declensions. The endings and suffixes given above lead to systematized vowel changes in each group. The general sound rules remain valid, namely the rule of šᵉwâ (§8.1), the rules of gutturals (§4.2/4(i)) and the *begadkefat* rules (§8.2).

§27.1. The Declension of Nouns with Unchangeable Vowels[35]

1. Table 22. *Nouns with Unchangeable Vowels*

The endings and suffixes are added to the simplest form of the word with no further changes. תּוֹרָה serves as the example for the feminine forms of this group.

MASCULINE SINGULAR			FEMININE SINGULAR		
Gloss		horse	*Gloss*		law
st. abs.		סוּס	st. abs.		תּוֹרָה
st. cs.		סוּס	st. cs.		תּוֹרַת
with sing. suffix	1 c.	סוּסִי	with sing. suffix	1 c.	תּוֹרָתִי
	2 m.	סוּסְךָ		2 m.	תּוֹרָתְךָ
	2 f.	סוּסֵךְ		2 f.	תּוֹרָתֵךְ
	3 m.	סוּסוֹ		3 m.	תּוֹרָתוֹ
	3 f.	סוּסָהּ		3 f.	תּוֹרָתָהּ
with pl. suffix	1 c.	סוּסֵנוּ	with pl. suffix	1 c.	תּוֹרָתֵנוּ
	2 m.	סוּסְכֶם		2 m.	תּוֹרַתְכֶם
	2 f.	סוּסְכֶן		2 f.	תּוֹרַתְכֶן
	3 m.	סוּסָם		3 m.	תּוֹרָתָם
	3 f.	סוּסָן		3 f.	תּוֹרָתָן
MASCULINE DUAL			FEMININE DUAL		
st. abs.		סוּסִים	st. abs.		תּוֹרָתַיִם
st. cs.		סוּסֵי	st. cs.		תּוֹרָתֵי
with sing. suffix	1 c.	סוּסַי	with sing. suffix	1 c.	תּוֹרָתַי
	2 m.	סוּסֶיךָ		2 m.	תּוֹרָתֶיךָ
	2 f.	סוּסַיִךְ		2 f.	תּוֹרָתַיִךְ
	3 m.	סוּסָיו		3 m.	תּוֹרָתָיו
	3 f.	סוּסֶיהָ		3 f.	תּוֹרָתֶיהָ
with pl. suffix	1 c.	סוּסֵינוּ	with pl. suffix	1 c.	תּוֹרָתֵינוּ
	2 m.	סוּסֵיכֶם		2 m.	תּוֹרָתֵיכֶם

---

35. Cf. Lambdin, 1980: xvii.

MASCULINE DUAL			FEMININE DUAL		
with pl. suffix	2 f.	סוּסֵיכֶן	with pl. suffix	2 f.	תּוֹרֹתֵיכֶן
	3 m.	סוּסֵיהֶם		3 m.	תּוֹרֹתֵיהֶם
	3 f.	סוּסֵיהֶן		3 f.	תּוֹרֹתֵיהֶן
MASCULINE PLURAL			FEMININE PLURAL		
st. abs.		סוּסִים	st. abs.		תּוֹרוֹת
st. cs.		סוּסֵי	st. cs.		תּוֹרוֹת
with sing. suffix	1 c.	סוּסַי	with sing. suffix	1 c.	תּוֹרֹתַי
	2 m.	סוּסֶיךָ		2 m.	תּוֹרֹתֶיךָ
	2 f.	סוּסַיִךְ		2 f.	תּוֹרֹתַיִךְ
	3 m.	סוּסָיו		3 m.	תּוֹרֹתָיו
	3 f.	סוּסֶיהָ		3 f.	תּוֹרֹתֶיהָ
with pl. suffix	1 c.	סוּסֵינוּ	with pl. suffix	1 c.	תּוֹרֹתֵינוּ
	2 m.	סוּסֵיכֶם		2 m.	תּוֹרֹתֵיכֶם
	2 f.	סוּסֵיכֶן		2 f.	תּוֹרֹתֵיכֶן
	3 m.	סוּסֵיהֶם		3 m.	תּוֹרֹתָם \ ־ֵיהֶם
	3 pl.	סוּסֵיהֶן		3 f.	תּוֹרֹתָן \ ־ֵיהֶן

§27.2. *The Declension of Nouns with Changeable Long Vowels* ־ָ *and* ־ֵ

1. *Form of the declensions*

The rules regarding vowel changes in this group may be summarized by means of the following scheme. The first column indicates the position of the changeable long vowel in a word and the others indicate the changes that this vowel undergoes:

EXAMPLE	NOUN SING.	NOUN SING.	NOUN PL.	ALL OTHER
	st. abs.	st. cs. or	st. cs. or	sing. or pl.
		heavy suffix	heavy suffix	
פָּקִיד	a. ־ ־ָ	־ ־ְ	־ ־ְ	־ ־ְ
מִדְבָּר	b. ־ְ ־ָ	־ְ ־ַ	־ְ ־	־ָ ־
שֹׁמֵר	c. ־ ־ֵ	־ ־ֶ / ־ְ	־ְ ־	־ְ ־

EXAMPLE	NOUN SING.		NOUN SING.	NOUN PL.	ALL OTHER
	st. abs.		*st. cs. or*	*st. cs. or*	*sing. or pl.*
			heavy suffix	heavy suffix	
	d. (ii)	(i)			
דָּבָר	ָ	ָ			
זָקֵן	ֵ	ָ			
לֵבָב	ָ	ֵ			
(i) Treated like the ָ of a.					
(ii) Treated like the ָ of b (where the ֵ of b is retained, the ָ in d is also retained).					

2. *Forms of nouns with changeable long vowels*

(i) Nouns with ֵ in the penultimate (second-last) syllable

    Cf. Table 23a   פָּקִיד

(ii) Nouns with ֵ in the final syllable

    Cf. Table 23b   מִדְבָּר

(iii) Nouns with ֹ in the final syllable

    Cf. Table 23c   שֹׁמֵר

(iv) Nouns with ָ in the last two syllables

    Cf. Table 24a   דָּבָר

(v) Nouns with ֵ in the final and ָ in the penultimate syllable

    Cf. Table 24b   זָקֵן

(vi) Nouns with ָ in the final and ֵ in the penultimate syllable

    Cf. Table 24c   לֵבָב

(vii) Feminine nouns with ָ in the last two syllables

    Cf. Table 25   שָׁנָה

(viii) Trisyllabic feminine nouns with a šᵉwā in the first, ָ in the second and with the feminine ending הָ in the final syllable

    Cf. Table 26   צְדָקָה

(ix) Nouns with gutturals in this group

    Cf. Table 27

(x) Monosyllabic nouns with a changeable vowel

Cf. Table 28

3. Table 23. *Nouns with changeable long vowels*

		Table 23a	Table 23b	Table 23c
		Nouns with ָ in the penultimate syllable	*Nouns with ָ in the final syllable*	*Nouns with ֵ in the final syllable*
		פָּקִיד	מִדְבָּר	שֹׁמֵר
Gloss		commissioner/ officer	desert	guardian/guard
SINGULAR				
st. abs.		פָּקִיד	מִדְבָּר	שֹׁמֵר
st. cs.		פְּקִיד	מִדְבַּר	שֹׁמֵר
with sing. suffix	1 c.	פְּקִידִי	מִדְבָּרִי	שֹׁמְרִי
	2 m.	פְּקִידְךָ	מִדְבָּרְךָ	שֹׁמֶרְךָ
	2 f.	פְּקִידֵךְ	מִדְבָּרֵךְ	שֹׁמְרֵךְ
	3 m.	פְּקִידוֹ	מִדְבָּרוֹ	שֹׁמְרוֹ
	3 f.	פְּקִידָהּ	מִדְבָּרָהּ	שֹׁמְרָהּ
with pl. suffix	1 c.	פְּקִידֵנוּ	מִדְבָּרֵנוּ	שֹׁמְרֵנוּ
	2 m.	פְּקִידְכֶם	מִדְבַּרְכֶם	שֹׁמֶרְכֶם
	2 f.	פְּקִידְכֶן	מִדְבַּרְכֶן	שֹׁמֶרְכֶן
	3 m.	פְּקִידָם	מִדְבָּרָם	שֹׁמְרָם
	3 f.	פְּקִידָן	מִדְבָּרָן	שֹׁמְרָן
PLURAL				
st. abs.		פְּקִידִים	מִדְבָּרִים	שֹׁמְרִים
st. cs.		פְּקִידֵי	מִדְבְּרֵי	שֹׁמְרֵי
with sing. suffix	1 c.	פְּקִידַי	מִדְבָּרַי	שֹׁמְרַי
	2 m.	פְּקִידֶיךָ	מִדְבָּרֶיךָ	שֹׁמְרֶיךָ
	2 f.	פְּקִידַיִךְ	מִדְבָּרַיִךְ	שֹׁמְרַיִךְ
	3 m.	פְּקִידָיו	מִדְבָּרָיו	שֹׁמְרָיו
	3 f.	פְּקִידֶיהָ	מִדְבָּרֶיהָ	שֹׁמְרֶיהָ
with pl. suffix	1 c.	פְּקִידֵינוּ	מִדְבָּרֵינוּ	שֹׁמְרֵינוּ
	2 m.	פְּקִידֵיכֶם	מִדְבְּרֵיכֶם	שֹׁמְרֵיכֶם

		Table 23a	Table 23b	Table 23c
		Nouns with ֵ in the penultimate syllable	*Nouns with ֵ in the final syllable*	*Nouns with ֵ in the final syllable*
		PLURAL		
	2 f.	פְּקִידֵיכֶן	מְדַבְּרֵיכֶן	שֹׁמְרֵ^cיכֶן
	3 m.	פְּקִידֵיהֶם	מְדַבְּרֵיהֶם	שֹׁמְרֵיהֶם
	3 f.	פְּקִידֵיהֶן	מְדַבְּרֵיהֶן	שֹׁמְרֵיהֶן

4. Table 24. *Nouns with changeable long vowels (continued 1)*

		Table 24a	Table 24b	Table 24c
		Nouns with ָ in the final and second last syllable	*Nouns with ֵ in the final and ָ in the second last syllable*	*Nouns with ֵ in the final and ֵ in the penultima*
		דָּבָר	זָקֵן	לֵבָב
Gloss		thing, word	old man/elder	heart
		SINGULAR		
st. abs.		דָּבָר	זָקֵן	לֵבָב
st. cs.		דְּבַר	זְקַן	לְבַב
with sing. suffix	1 c.	דְּבָרִי	זְקֵנִי	לְבָבִי
	2 m.	דְּבָרְךָ	זְקֵנְךָ	לְבָבְךָ
	2 f.	דְּבָרֵךְ	זְקֵנֵךְ	לְבָבֵךְ
	3 m.	דְּבָרוֹ	זְקֵנוֹ	לְבָבוֹ
	3 f.	דְּבָרָהּ	זְקֵנָהּ	לְבָבָהּ
with pl. suffix	1 c.	דְּבָרֵנוּ	זְקֵנֵנוּ	לְבָבֵנוּ
	2 m.	דְּבַרְכֶם	זְקַנְכֶם	לְבַבְכֶם
	2 f.	דְּבַרְכֶן	זְקַנְכֶן	לְבַבְכֶן
	3 m.	דְּבָרָם	זְקֵנָם	לְבָבָם
	3 f.	דְּבָרָן	זְקֵנָן	לְבָבָן
		PLURAL		
st. abs.		דְּבָרִים	זְקֵנִים	לְבָבוֹת
st. cs.		דִּבְרֵי	זִקְנֵי	
with sing. suffix	1 c.	דְּבָרַי	זְקֵנַי	
	2 m.	דְּבָרֶיךָ	זְקֵנֶיךָ	

		Table 24a	Table 24b	Table 24c
		Nouns with - in the final and second last syllable	*Nouns with - in the final and - in the second last syllable*	*Nouns with - in the final and - in the penultimate*
PLURAL				
with sing. suffix	2 f.	דְּבָרַיִךְ	זְקֵנַיִךְ	
	3 m.	דְּבָרָיו	זְקֵנָיו	
	3 f.	דְּבָרֶיהָ	זְקֵנֶיהָ	
with pl. suffix	1 c.	דְּבָרֵינוּ	זְקֵנֵינוּ	
	2 m.	דִּבְרֵיכֶם	זִקְנֵיכֶם	
	2 f.	דִּבְרֵיכֶן	זִקְנֵיכֶן	...
	3 m.	דִּבְרֵיהֶם	זִקְנֵיהֶם	
	3 f.	דִּבְרֵיהֶן	זִקְנֵיהֶן	לִבְבֶהֶן

5. Table 25 *Nouns with changeable long vowels (continued 2)*

			Feminine nouns with - in the final two syllables	
	St. abs.	*St. cs.*	Light suffix 1 sing.	Heavy suffix 2 m. pl.
Gloss	year			
Sing.	שָׁנָה	שְׁנַת	שְׁנָתִי	שְׁנַתְכֶם
Pl.	שָׁנוֹת/שָׁנִים	שְׁנוֹת/שְׁנֵי	שְׁנוֹתַי	שְׁנוֹתֵיכֶם

6. Table 26. *Nouns with changeable long vowels (continued 3)*

		Trisyllabic feminine nouns with a šᵉwâ in the first, a - in the second and with the feminine ending הָ- in the final syllable
		צְדָקָה
Gloss		righteousness/justice
SINGULAR		
st. abs.		צְדָקָה
st. cs.		צִדְקַת
with sing. suffix	1 c.	צִדְקָתִי
	2 m.	צִדְקָתְךָ

		Trisyllabic feminine nouns with a šᵉwâ in the first, a ֽ in the second and with the feminine ending ה ֽ in the final syllable
		SINGULAR
	2 f.	צִדְקָתֵךְ
	3 m.	צִדְקָתוֹ
	3 f.	צִדְקָתָהּ
with pl. suffix	1 c.	צִדְקָתֵנוּ
	2 m.	צִדְקַתְכֶם
	2 f.	צִדְקַתְכֶן
	3 m.	צִדְקָתָם
	3 f.	צִדְקָתָן
		PLURAL
st. abs.		צְדָקוֹת
st. cs.		צִדְקוֹת
with sing. suffix	1 c.	צִדְקוֹתַי
	2 m.	צִדְקוֹתֶיךָ
	2 f.	צִדְקוֹתַיִךְ
	3 m.	צִדְקוֹתָיו
	3 f.	צִדְקוֹתֶיהָ
with pl. suffix	1 c.	צִדְקוֹתֵינוּ
	2 m.	צִדְקוֹתֵיכֶם
	2 f.	צִדְקוֹתֵיכֶן
	3 m.	צִדְקוֹתֵיהֶם
	3 m.	צִדְקוֹתָם
	3 f.	צִדְקוֹתֵיהֶן
	3 f.	צִדְקוֹתָן

7. Table 27. *Nouns with changeable long vowels (continued 4)*

	Nouns with gutturals			
	St. abs.	*St. cs.*	Light suffix 1 sing.	Heavy suffix 2 m. pl.
Gloss	land, country			
Sing.	אֲדָמָה	אַדְמַת	אַדְמָתִי	
Pl.	אֲדָמוֹת			

Nouns with gutturals			
	St. abs.	*St. cs.*	Light suffix 1 sing.	Heavy suffix 2 m. pl.

	St. abs.	*St. cs.*	Light suffix 1 sing.	Heavy suffix 2 m. pl.
Gloss	wise (adjective)			
Sing.	חָכָם	חֲכַם	חֲכָמִי	חֲכַמְכֶם
Pl.	חֲכָמִיםחֲכָמוֹת	חַכְמֵי/חַכְמוֹת	חֲכָמַי	חַכְמֵיכֶם
Gloss	village			
Sing.	חָצֵר	חֲצַר	חֲצֵרִי	
Pl.	חֲצֵרִים/חֲצֵרוֹת	חַצְרֵי/חַצְרוֹת	חֲצֵרַי	חַצְרֵיכֶם
Gloss	meeting, meeting place			
Sing.	מוֹעֵד	מוֹעֵד	מוֹעֲדִי	
Pl.	מוֹעֲדִים	מוֹעֲדֵי	מוֹעֲדַי	מוֹעֲדֵיכֶם
Gloss	messenger			
Sing.	מַלְאָךְ	מַלְאַךְ	מַלְאָכִי	
Pl.	מַלְאָכִים	מַלְאֲכֵי	מַלְאָכַי	
Gloss	river, stream			
Sing.	נָהָר	נְהַר	נְהָרִי	נַהַרְכֶם
Pl.	נְהָרִים/נְהָרוֹת	נַהֲרֵי/נַהֲרוֹת	נְהָרַי	נַהֲרֵיכֶם
Gloss	meeting, gathering			
Sing.	עֵדָה	עֲדַת	עֲדָתִי	
Gloss	grapes			
Sing.	עֵנָב			
Pl.	עֲנָבִים	עִנְבֵי		
Gloss	riches			
Sing.	עָשִׁיר			
Pl.	עֲשִׁירִים	עֲשִׁירֵי	עֲשִׁירֵי	
Gloss	side			
Sing.	צֵלָע	צֶלַע/צֵלַע	צַלְעִי	
Pl.	צְלָעוֹת/צְלָעִים	צַלְעוֹת		
Gloss	hair			
Sing.	שֵׂעָר	שַׂעַר/שְׂעַר	שְׂעָרִי	
Pl.	none	none	none	

8. Table 28. *Nouns with changeable long vowels (continued 5)*

	St. abs.	St. cs.	Light suffix 1 sing.	Heavy suffix 2 m. pl.
	Monosyllabic nouns with changeable vowels			
Gloss	son			
Sing.	בֵּן	בֵּן/בֶּן	בְּנִי	בִּנְכֶם
Pl.	בָּנִים	בְּנֵי	בָּנַי	בְּנֵיכֶם
Gloss	blood			
Sing.	דָּם	דַּם	דָּמִי	דִּמְכֶם
Pl.	דָּמִים	דְּמֵי	דָּמַי	דְּמֵיכֶם
Gloss	hand			
Sing.	יָד	יַד	יָדִי	יֶדְכֶם
Pl.	יָדוֹת	יְדוֹת	יְדוֹתַי	
Gloss	tree			
Sing.	עֵץ	עֵץ	עֵצִי	
Pl.	עֵצִים	עֲצֵי	עֵצַי	

§27.3. *The Declension of Segholate Nouns*

1. *Introduction*

The segholates are nouns that have a characteristic s°gōl in their final syllable. Most segholates have two syllables in the singular *status absolutus*. The first syllable may have a ֶ , ִ or ֵ as vowel. Segholates originally had one syllable, which is called the stem form. The vowel of the stem is ֶ , ִ or ֻ / ֹ. The stem form recurs in large sections of the declension.

2. *Forming the declensions*

(i) *Singular status constructus, masculine and feminine*

a. masculine *status absolutus* = masculine *status constructus* (Tables 29a-c).

     מֶלֶךְ   and   מֶלֶךְ

b. feminine *status absolutus* = feminine *status constructus*,
  • BUT the feminine ending הָ becomes תַ (Table 32).

     מַלְכָּה   to   מַלְכַּת

- With trisyllabic segholates the following changes occur: הַָ֑ becomes הַַ֑ (Table 33).

מַמְלָכָה   to   מַמְלֶכֶת

(ii) *Plural status absolutus, masculine and feminine*

a. All three types (בֹּקֶר, סֵפֶר, מֶלֶךְ) take on a stem form that has the same appearance, for example, מְלָכִים. (Tables 29a-c). The latter form corresponds with the plural of דָּבָר. (Cf. Table 24a.)

מֶלֶךְ	and	מְלָכִים
סֵפֶר	and	סְפָרִים
בֹּקֶר	and	סְפָרִים

b. The same stem form also occurs with the feminine words where *only* the ending differs.

מְלָכוֹת   or   מַלְכָּה

- The feminine plural words such as מְלָכוֹת were probably formed by analogy with the masculine plural forms. (Cf. also Joüon-Muraoka §97Ab.)

מְלָכוֹת   such as   מְלָכִים

(iii) *Plural status constructus, masculine and feminine*

a. Here the original stem form recurs before the ending and the first syllable is half closed. (Cf. also §8.1/3.)

מַלְכ	in	מַלְכֵי
סִפְר	in	סִפְרֵי
בָּקְר	in	בָּקְרֵי

b. The feminine plural *status constructus* forms were probably formed by analogy with the masculine plural

מַלְכוֹת   as   מַלְכֵי

(iv) *Dual status absolutus and status constructus, masculine and feminine*

Here the original stem form returns before the ending, BUT the first syllable is fully closed, e.g. בִּרְכַּיִם

(v) Segholate forms with pronominal suffixes

MASCULINE	*FEMININE*
Singular	*Singular*
stem (closed) + all suffixes	stem (closed) + all suffixes
Dual	*Dual*
stem (closed) + all suffixes	stem (closed) + all suffixes
Plural	*Plural*
st. abs. (lengthened form like דְּבָרִים) + light suffixes	*st. abs.* (lengthened form)
st. cs. (stem, half closed) + heavy suffixes	*st. cs.* (stem, half-closed) + all suffixes

PLUS application of sound rules (Cf. §4.2/4, 5.2 and Table 31.)

PLUS contraction of the fricatives ו and י as *middle* consonant: with the singular *status constructus* and before all suffixes as well as with the plural *status constructus* and before heavy or all suffixes (Cf. §4.2/4, 5.1/2 and Table 34.)

Note also the following:

There are some exceptions:

(1) With words that have י as final consonant, the lengthened form occurs throughout in the plural (Cf. Table 34.)

גְּדִי   and   גְּדָיִים

(2) as well as with words that have ו as final consonant, where the stem form occurs thoughout in the plural (Cf. Table 34.).

שָׂלוּ   and   שְׂלָוִים

3. *Forms of the segholate nouns*

(i) Words with an original short ַ (a-stem) that acquired a ֶ in both syllables

Cf. Table 29a   מֶלֶךְ

(ii) Words with an original short ִ (i-stem) that became ֵ and have a ֶ in the second syllable

Cf. Table 29b   סֵפֶר

(iii) Segholates with an original short ֻ (u-stem) or ָ (o-stem), and with a ֶ in the second syllable

Cf. Table 29c   בֹּקֶר

(iv) Segholates that look just like the a-stems in the singular *status absolutus* and *status constructus*, but nevertheless conjugate further like the i-stems´

Cf. Table 30   קֶבֶר

(v) Segholate nouns with gutturals

Cf. Table 31   עֶבֶד

(vi) Feminine segholate nouns

Cf. Table 32   מַלְכָּה

(vii) Trisyllabic segholate nouns

Cf. Table 33   מִשְׁמֶרֶת

(viii) Nouns with a fricative י or ו as middle or final consonant

Cf. Table 34   חַיִל

4. Table 29. *Segholate nouns*

		Table 29a	Table 29b	Table 29c
		Segholates with an original short ֶ	*Segholates with an original short* ִ	*Segholates with an original short* ֻ *or* ָ *(o)*
		מֶלֶךְ	סֵפֶר	בֹּקֶר
Gloss		king	book (scroll)	morning
		SINGULAR		
st. abs.		מֶלֶךְ	סֵפֶר	בֹּקֶר
st. cs.		מֶלֶךְ	סֵפֶר	בֹּקֶר
with sing. suffix	1 c.	מַלְכִּי	סִפְרִי	בָּקְרִי
	2 m.	מַלְכְּךָ	סִפְרְךָ	בָּקְרְךָ
	2 f.	מַלְכֵּךְ	סִפְרֵךְ	בָּקְרֵךְ
	3 m.	מַלְכּוֹ	סִפְרוֹ	בָּקְרוֹ
	3 f.	מַלְכָּהּ	סִפְרָהּ	בָּקְרָהּ
with pl. suffix	1 c.	מַלְכֵּנוּ	סִפְרֵנוּ	בָּקְרֵנוּ
	2 m.	מַלְכְּכֶם	סִפְרְכֶם	בָּקְרְכֶם

		Table 29a	Table 29b	Table 29c
		Segholates with an original short $\bar{\;}$	*Segholates with an original short* $\;$	*Segholates with an original short* $\;$ *or* $\;$ *(o)*
SINGULAR				
	2 f.	מַלְכְּכֶן	סִפְרְכֶן	בְּקָרְכֶן
	3 m.	מַלְכָּם	סִפְרָם	בְּקָרָם
	3 f.	מַלְכָּן	סִפְרָן	בְּקָרָן
PLURAL				
st. abs.		מְלָכִים	סְפָרִים	בְּקָרִים
st. cs.		מַלְכֵי	סִפְרֵי	בָּקְרֵי
with sing. suffix	1 c.	מְלָכַי	סְפָרַי	בְּקָרַי
	2 m.	מְלָכֶיךָ	סְפָרֶיךָ	בְּקָרֶיךָ
	2 f.	מְלָכַיִךְ	סְפָרַיִךְ	בְּקָרַיִךְ
	3 m.	מְלָכָיו	סְפָרָיו	בְּקָרָיו
	3 f.	מְלָכֶיהָ	סְפָרֶיהָ	בְּקָרֶיהָ
with pl. suffix	1 c.	מְלָכֵינוּ	סְפָרֵינוּ	בְּקָרֵינוּ
	2 m.	מַלְכֵיכֶם	סִפְרֵיכֶם	בְּקָרֵיכֶם
	2 f.	מַלְכֵיכֶן	סִפְרֵיכֶן	בְּקָרֵיכֶן
	3 m.	מַלְכֵיהֶם	סִפְרֵיהֶם	בְּקָרֵיהֶם
	3 f.	מַלְכֵיהֶן	סִפְרֵיהֶן	בְּקָרֵיהֶן

5. Table 30. *Segholate nouns (continued 1)*

Segholates that look like the a-stems in the singular status absolutus and status constructus, but decline like the i-stems			
	St. abs.	*St. cs.*	Light suffix 1 sing.	Heavy suffix 2 m. pl.
Gloss	grave			
Sing.	קֶבֶר	קֶבֶר	קִבְרִי	קִבְרְכֶם
Pl.	קְבָרִים	קִבְרֵי	קְבָרַי	קִבְרֵיכֶם

6. Table 31. *Segholate nouns (continued 2)*

	St. abs.	St. cs.	Light suffix 1 sing.	Heavy suffix 2 m. pl.
	Segholates with gutturals			
Gloss	seed, posterity			
Sing.	זֶרַע	זֶרַע	זַרְעִי	זַרְעֲכֶם
Pl.	זְרָעִים	זְרָעֵי	זְרָעַי	זַרְעֵיכֶם
Gloss	month, new moon			
Sing.	חֹדֶשׁ	חֹדֶשׁ	חָדְשִׁי	חָדְשְׁכֶם
Pl.	חֳדָשִׁים	חָדְשֵׁי	חֳדָשַׁי	חָדְשֵׁיכֶם
Gloss	young boy, servant			
Sing.	נַעַר	נַעַר	נַעֲרִי	נַעַרְכֶם
Pl.	נְעָרִים	נַעֲרֵי	נְעָרַי	נַעֲרֵיכֶם
Gloss	eternity			
Sing.	נֶצַח	נֶצַח	נִצְחִי	נִצְחֲכֶם
Pl.	נְצָחִים	נִצְחֵי	נְצָחַי	נִצְחֵיכֶם
Gloss	slave, servant			
Sing.	עֶבֶד	עֶבֶד	עַבְדִּי	עַבְדְּכֶם
Pl.	עֲבָדִים	עַבְדֵּי	עֲבָדַי	עַבְדֵּיכֶם
Gloss	valley, lowlands			
Sing.	עֵמֶק	עֵמֶק	עִמְקִי	עִמְקְכֶם
Pl.	עֲמָקִים	עִמְקֵי	עֲמָקַי	עִמְקֵיכֶם
Gloss	deed, (handi)work			
Sing.	פֹּעַל	פֹּעַל	פָּעֳלִי	פָּעָלְכֶם
Pl.	פְּעָלִים	פָּעֳלֵי	פְּעָלַי	פָּעֳלֵיכֶם
Gloss	spear			
Sing.	רֹמַח	רֹמַח	רָמְחִי	רָמְחֲכֶם
Pl.	רְמָחִים	רָמְחֵי	רְמָחַי	רָמְחֵיכֶם

7. Table 32. *Segholate nouns (continued 3)*

	St. abs.	St. cs.	Light suffix 1 sing.	Heavy suffix 2 m. pl.
Feminine segholates				
Gloss	queen			
Sing.	מַלְכָּה	מַלְכַּת	מַלְכָּתִי	מַלְכַּתְכֶם
Pl.	מְלָכוֹת	מַלְכוֹת	מַלְכוֹתַי	מַלְכוֹתֵיכֶם
Gloss	baldness			
Sing.	קָרְחָה	קָרַחַת	קָרְחָתִי	קָרַחְתְכֶם
Pl.	קָרָחוֹת	קָרְחוֹת	קָרְחוֹתַי	קָרְחוֹתֵיכֶם
Gloss	joy, gladness			
Sing.	שִׂמְחָה	שִׂמְחַת	שִׂמְחָתִי	שִׂמְחַתְכֶם
Pl.	שְׂמָחוֹת	שִׂמְחוֹת	שִׂמְחוֹתַי	שִׂמְחוֹתֵיכֶם

8. Table 33. *Segholate nouns (continued 4)*

With trisyllabic segholate nouns the first syllable is unchangeable and the last two syllables decline like the other segholates.

	St. abs.	St. cs.	Light suffix 1 sing.	Heavy suffix 2 m. pl.
Trisyllabic segholate nouns				
Gloss	skull			
Sing.	גֻּלְגֹּלֶת	גֻּלְגֹּלֶת	גֻּלְגָּלְתִּי	גֻּלְגָּלְתְּכֶם
Pl.	גֻּלְגָּלוֹת	גֻּלְגְּלוֹת	גֻּלְגְּלוֹתַי	גֻּלְגְּלוֹתֵיכֶם
Gloss	(wet-)nurse			
Sing.	מֵינֶקֶת	מֵינֶקֶת	מֵינִקְתִּי	מֵינִקְתְּכֶם
Pl.	מֵינִקוֹת		מֵינִקוֹתַי	
Gloss	kingdom			
Sing.	מַמְלָכָה	מַמְלֶכֶת	מַמְלַכְתִּי	מַמְלַכְתְּכֶם
Pl.	מַמְלָכוֹת	מַמְלְכוֹת	מַמְלְכוֹתַי	מַמְלְכוֹתֵיכֶם
Gloss	guard			
Sing.	מִשְׁמֶרֶת	מִשְׁמֶרֶת	מִשְׁמַרְתִּי	מִשְׁמַרְתְּכֶם
Pl.	מִשְׁמָרוֹת	מִשְׁמְרוֹת	מִשְׁמְרוֹתַי	מִשְׁמְרוֹתֵיכֶם

9. Table 34. *Segholate nouns (continued 5)*

Some nouns with a fricative ʾ or ו as middle or final consonant do not look like segholates in the singular *status absolutus* and *status constructus*, but in the rest of the declension it is clear that they decline in the same way.

	St. abs.	St. cs.	Light suffix 1 sing.	Heavy suffix 2 m. pl.
Nouns with a fricative ʾ or ו as middle or final consonant				
Gloss	lion			
Sing.	אֲרִי	אֲרִי	אֲרִיי	אֲרִיכֶם
Pl.	אֲרָיִים	אֲרָיֵ	אֲרָיֵי	אֲרֵייכֶם
Gloss	kid/goat			
Sing.	גְּדִי	גְּדִי	גְּדִיי	גְּדִיכֶם
Pl.	גְּדָיִים	גְּדָיֵ	גְּדָיֵ	גְּדָייכֶם
Gloss	olive			
Sing.	זַיִת	זֵית	זֵיתִי	זֵיתְכֶם
Pl.	זֵיתִים	זֵיתֵי	זֵיתַי	זֵיתֵיכֶם
Gloss	power, strength			
Sing.	חַיִל	חֵיל	חֵילִי	חֵילְכֶם
Pl.	חֲיָלִים	חֵילֵי	חֲיָלַי	חֵילֵיכֶם
Gloss	death			
Sing.	מָוֶת	מוֹת	מוֹתִי	מוֹתְכֶם
Pl.	מוֹתִים	מוֹתֵי	מוֹתַי	מוֹתֵיכֶם
Gloss	sickness			
Sing.	חֳלִי	חֳלִי	חָלְיִי	חָלְיְכֶם
Pl.	חֳלָיִים	חֳלָיֵ	חֳלָיַ	חֳלָיֵכֶם
Gloss	prosperity			
Sing.	שָׁלוּ	שָׁלוּ	שַׁלְוִי	שַׁלְוְכֶם
Pl.	שְׁלָוִים	שַׁלְוֵי	שַׁלְוַי	שַׁלְוֵיכֶם

§27.4. *The Declension of Monosyllabic Nouns with Double Final Consonants*

1. *Formation of the declensions*

Some monosyllabic nouns originally had two identical final consonants. The double final consonants recur when a suffix is added to the noun.

(i) *Forming the singular status constructus (masculine)*

Status absolutus singular = *status constructus* singular

(ii) *Forming the plural status absolutus and status constructus and the form of the word (singular and plural) with all pronominal suffixes*

a. The stem vowel has shortened where possible (־ becomes ־, ־ becomes ־ and ־ becomes ־)

חֵץ	becomes	חִצִי
עֹז	becomes	עֻזִי

b. The final consonant doubles when endings or pronominal suffixes are added.

חֵץ   and   חִצִי

With stems ending in a guttural or resh no doubling occurs. Accordingly compensation occurs in the preceding syllable.

שַׂר   but   שָׂרִי

c. With bisyllabic words that have the characteristics of mono-syllabic nouns, the changeable vowel changes in the first syllable if a suffix is added.

נָמָל   but   גְמַלִי

2. *Forms of monosyllabic nouns with double final consonants*

(i) Monosyllabic words with a ־ (a-stems) and where the final consonant was originally double

    Cf. Table 35a   עַם

(ii) Monosyllabic words with a ־ (i-stems) and where the final consonant was originally double

    Cf. Table 35b   חֵץ

(iii) Monosyllabic words with a ־ (u-stems) and where the final consonant was originally double

    Cf. Table 35c   עֹז

(iv) Monosyllabic words that originally had their final consonants doubled and gutturals

Cf. Table 36   חֹר

(v) Bisyllabic words with the characteristics of monosyllabic words (rare)

Cf. Table 37   גָּמָל

(vi) Monosyllabic words with feminine endings in the plural

Cf. Table 38   אֵם

3. Table 35. *Monosyllabic nouns*

		Table 35a	Table 35b	Table 35c
		Monosyllabic words with a ִ (a-stems)	*Monosyllabic words with a ִ (i-stems)*	*Monosyllabic words with a ִ (u-stems)*
		עַם	חֵץ	עֹז
		people/nation	arrow	strength, power
SINGULAR				
st. abs.		עַם	חֵץ	עֹז
st. cs.		עַם	חֵץ	עֹז/עָז
with sing. suffix	1 c.	עַמִּי	חִצִּי	עֻזִּי
	2 m.	עַמְּךָ	חִצְּךָ	עֻזְּךָ
	2 f.	עַמֵּךְ	חִצֵּךְ	עֻזֵּךְ
	3 m.	עַמּוֹ	חִצּוֹ	עֻזּוֹ
	3 f.	עַמָּהּ	חִצָּהּ	עֻזָּהּ
with pl. suffix	1 c.	עַמֵּנוּ	חִצֵּנוּ	עֻזֵּנוּ/עוֹזֵנוּ
	2 m.	עַמְּכֶם	חִצְּכֶם	עֻזְּכֶם
	2 f.	עַמְּכֶן	חִצְּכֶן	עֻזְּכֶן
	3 m.	עַמָּם	חִצָּם	עֻזָּם
	3 f.	עַמָּן	חִצָּן	עֻזָּן
PLURAL				
st. abs.		עַמִּים	חִצִּים	עֻזִּים
st. cs.		עַמֵּי	חִצֵּי	עֻזֵּי
with sing. suffix	1 c.	עַמַּי	חִצַּי	עֻזַּי
	2 m.	עַמֶּיךָ	חִצֶּיךָ	עֻזֶּיךָ

		Monosyllabic words with a ־ַ (a-stems)	Monosyllabic words with a ־ִ (i-stems)	Monosyllabic words with a ־ֻ (u-stems)
		PLURAL		
with sing. suffix	2 f.	עֲמַיִךְ	חִצַּיִךְ	עֻזַּיִךְ
	3 m.	עֲמָיו	חִצָּיו	עֻזָּיו
	3 f.	עֲמֶיהָ	חִצֶּיהָ	עֻזֶּיהָ
with pl. suffix	1 c.	עֲמֵינוּ	חִצֵּינוּ	עֻזֵּינוּ
	2 m.	עֲמֵיכֶם	חִצֵּיכֶם	עֻזֵּיכֶם
	2 f.	עֲמֵיכֶן	חִצֵּיכֶן	עֻזֵּיכֶן
	3 m.	עֲמֵיהֶם	חִצֵּיהֶם	עֻזֵּיהֶם
	3 f.	עֲמֵיהֶן	חִצֵּיהֶן	עֻזֵּיהֶן

4. Table 36. *Monosyllabic nouns (continued 1)*

Monosyllabic words that originally had their final consonants doubled and gutturals				
	St. abs.	St. cs.	Light suffix 1 sing.	Heavy suffix 2 m. pl.
Gloss	cave, hole			
Sing.	חֹר	חֹר	חֹרִי	חֹרְכֶם
Pl.	חֹרִים	חֹרֵי	חֹרֵי	חֹרֵיכֶם
Gloss	chief/leader			
Sing.	שַׂר	שַׂר	שָׂרִי	שַׂרְכֶם
Pl.	שָׂרִים	שָׂרֵי	שָׂרֵי	שָׂרֵיכֶם

5. Table 37. *Monosyllabic nouns (continued 2)*

Bisyllabic words with the characteristics of monosyllabic words that have a double final consonant (rare)				
	St. abs.	St. cs.	Light suffix 1 sing.	Heavy suffix 2 m. pl.
Gloss	camel			
Sing.	גָּמָל	גְּמַל	גְּמַלִּי	גְּמַלְּכֶם
Pl.	גְּמַלִּים	גְּמַלֵּי	גְּמַלֵּי	גְּמַלֵּיכֶם
Gloss	people, nation			
Sing.	לְאֹם	לְאֹם	לְאֻמִּי	לְאֻמְכֶם
Pl.	לְאֻמִּים	לְאֻמֵּי	לְאֻמֵּי	לְאֻמֵּיכֶם

Bisyllabic words with the characteristics of monosyllabic words that have a double final consonant (rare)				
	St. abs.	St. cs.	Light suffix 1 sing.	Heavy suffix 2 m. pl.
Gloss	fortress			
Sing.	מָעוֹז	מָעוֹז	מָעֻזִּי	מָעֻזְכֶם
Pl.	מָעֻזִּים	מָעֻזֵּי	מָעֻזַּי	מָעֻזֵּיכֶם

6. Table 38. *Monosyllabic nouns (continued 3)*

Monosyllabic words with original double final consonant that have feminine endings in the plural				
	St. abs.	St. cs.	Light suffix 1 sing.	Heavy suffix 2 m. pl.
Gloss	mother			
Sing.	אֵם	אֵם	אִמִּי	אִמְּכֶם
Pl.	אִמּוֹת	אִמּוֹת	אִמֹּתַי	אִמֹּתֵיכֶם

§27.5. *The Declension of Nouns That End in* הָ‍-

1. *Introduction*

The characteristic feature of nouns in this group is that they end in הָ‍-
in the singular *status absolutus.* They are usually bisyllabic and the
first syllable can have a changeable or unchangeable vowel.

2. *Forming the declensions*

a. Forming the singular *status constructus* (masculine).
   - הָ‍- (מִקְנֶה) becomes הֵ‍- (מִקְנֵה). (Cf. Table 39.)

b. Forming the plural *status absolutus* and *status constructus* and the
   form of the word (singular and plural) with all pronominal suffixes.
   - The ending הָ‍- is dropped and the endings and pronominal suffixes
     are added to the stem, e.g. מִקְנֵי.
   - The 3 masculine singular and 3 feminine singular suffixes in the
     singular noun differ from those of the other main groups.

מִקְנֵהוּ	instead of	מִקְנוֹ
מִקְנֶהָ	instead of	מִקְנָהּ

c. With words in which the vowel of the first syllable is changeable
   (e.g. קָצֶה), vowel reduction occurs in the singular *status constructus*

(קָצֶה) and plural *status constructus* and also before heavy suffixes with the plural noun (קְצֵיכֶם).

3. *Forms of nouns that end in* הָ-

(i) Bisyllabic nouns that end in הָ- and have a closed first syllable

   Cf. Table 39a   מִקְנֶה

(ii) Bisyllabic nouns that end in הָ- and have a ָ in an open first syllable

   Cf. Table 39b   קָצֶה

4. Table 39. *Nouns that end in* הָ-

		Table 39a	Table 39b
		Bisyllabic nouns that end in הָ- which have a closed first syllable	*Bisyllabic nouns that end in הָ- which have a ָ in first syllable that is open*
		מִקְנֶה	קָצֶה
Gloss		stock	end, border
SINGULAR			
st. abs.		מִקְנֶה	קָצֶה
st. cs.		מִקְנֵה	קְצֵה
with sing. suffix	1 c.	מִקְנִי	קָצִי
	2 m.	מִקְנְךָ	קָצְךָ
	2 f.	מִקְנֵךְ	קָצֵךְ
	3 m.	מִקְנֵהוּ	קָצֵהוּ
	3 f.	מִקְנָהּ	קָצָהּ
with pl. suffix	1 c.	מִקְנֵנוּ	קָצֵנוּ
	2 m.	מִקְנְכֶם	קְצְכֶם
	2 f.	מִקְנְכֶן	קְצְכֶן
	3 m.	מִקְנָם	קָצָם
	3 f.	מִקְנָן	קָצָן
PLURAL			
st. abs.		מִקְנִים	קָצִים
st. cs.		מִקְנֵי	קְצֵי
with sing. suffix	1 c.	מִקְנַי	קָצַי
	2 m.	מִקְנֶיךָ	קָצֶיךָ
	2 f.	מִקְנַיִךְ	קָצַיִךְ

		Table 39a	Table 39b
		Bisyllabic nouns that end in ה- which have a closed first syllable	*Bisyllabic nouns that end in ה- which have a ֵ in first syllable that is open*
	PLURAL		
with sing. suffix	3 m.	מִקְנָיו	קָצָיו
	3 f.	מִקְנֶיהָ	קָצֶיהָ
with pl. suffix	1 c.	מִקְנֵינוּ	קָצֵינוּ
	2 m.	מִקְנֵיכֶם	קָצֵיכֶם
	2 f.	מִקְנֵיכֶן	קָצֵיכֶן
	3 m.	מִקְנֵיהֶם	קָצֵיהֶם
	3 f.	מִקְנֵיהֶן	קָצֵיהֶן

§27.6. *The Declension of Irregular Nouns*

Even though these nouns are classified as irregular, several repeated patterns occur. The greatest irregularity lies in the fact that these words cannot be classified in one specific group—precisely because they often have the characteristics of more than one group.

1. Table 40. *Irregular nouns*

Irregular nouns				
	St. abs.	*St. cs.*	*Light suffix* 1 sing.	*Heavy suffix* 2 m. pl.
Gloss	father			
Sing.	אָב	אֲבִי	אָבִי	אֲבִיכֶם
Pl.	אָבוֹת	אֲבוֹת	אֲבוֹתַי	אֲבוֹתֵיכֶם
Gloss	brother			
Sing.	אָח	אֲחִי	אָחִי	אֲחִיכֶם
Pl.	אַחִים	אֲחֵי	אַחַי	אֲחֵיכֶם
Gloss	sister			
Sing.	אָחוֹת	אֲחוֹת	אֲחוֹתִי	אֲחוֹתְכֶם
Pl.	אֲחָיוֹת	אַחְיוֹת	אַחְיוֹתַי	אַחְיוֹתֵיכֶם
Gloss	man			
Sing.	אִישׁ	אִישׁ	אִישִׁי	אִישְׁכֶם
Pl.	אֲנָשִׁים	אַנְשֵׁי	אֲנָשַׁי	אַנְשֵׁיכֶם

	St. abs.	St. cs.	Light suffix 1 sing.	Heavy suffix 2 m. pl.
	Irregular nouns			
Gloss	woman			
Sing.	אִשָּׁה	אֵשֶׁת	אִשְׁתִּי	אֶשְׁתְּכֶם
Pl.	נָשִׁים	נְשֵׁי	נָשַׁי	נְשֵׁיכֶם
Gloss	beast			
Sing.	בְּהֵמָה	בֶּהֱמַת	בְּהֶמְתִּי	בְּהֶמְתְּכֶם
Pl.	בְּהֵמוֹת	בַּהֲמוֹת		
Gloss	house			
Sing.	בַּיִת	בֵּית	בֵּיתִי	בֵּיתְכֶם
Pl.	בָּתִּים	בָּתֵּי	בָּתַּי	בָּתֵּיכֶם
Gloss	son			
Sing.	בֵּן	בֶּן־וּבֶן־	בְּנִי	בִּנְכֶם
Pl.	בָּנִים	בְּנֵי	בָּנַי	בְּנֵיכֶם
Gloss	daughter			
Sing.	בַּת	בַּת	בִּתִּי	בִּתְּכֶם
Pl.	בָּנוֹת	בְּנוֹת	בְּנוֹתַי	בְּנוֹתֵיכֶם
Gloss	sin			
Sing.	חַטָּאת	חַטַּאת	חַטָּאתִי	חַטַּאתְכֶם
Pl.	חַטָּאוֹת	חַטֹּאת	חַטֹּאתַי	חַטֹּאתֵיכֶם
Gloss	day			
Sing.	יוֹם	יוֹם	יוֹמִי	יוֹמְכֶם
Pl.	יָמִים	יְמֵי	יָמַי	יְמֵיכֶם
Gloss	container, vessel, implement			
Sing.	כְּלִי	כְּלִי	כֶּלְיִי	כֶּלְיְכֶם
Pl.	כֵּלִים	כְּלֵי	כֵּלַי	כָּלֵיכֶם
Gloss	tunic			
Sing.	כֻּתֹּנֶת	כְּתֹנֶת	כֻּתָּנְתִּי	כֻּתָּנְתְּכֶם
Pl.	כֻּתֳּנֹת	כָּתְנֹת	כֻּתֳּנֹתַי	
Gloss	water			
Pl.	מַיִם	מֵימֵימֵי	מֵימַי	מֵימֵיכֶם
Gloss	city			
Sing.	עִיר	עִיר	עִירִי	עִירְכֶם
Pl.	עָרִים	עָרֵי	עָרַי	עָרֵיכֶם

	St. abs.	St. cs.	Light suffix 1 sing.	Heavy suffix 2 m. pl.
Irregular nouns				
Gloss	tree			
Sing.	עֵץ	עֵץ	עֵצִי	עֶצְכֶם
Pl.	עֵצִים	עֲצֵי	עֵצַי	עֲצֵיכֶם
Gloss	mouth			
Sing.	פֶּה	פִּי	פִּי	פִּיכֶם
Pl.	פֵּיוֹת וּ פִּיּוֹת	פִּפִיּוֹת		
Gloss	head, chief			
Sing.	רֹאשׁ	רֹאשׁ	רֹאשִׁי	רֹאשְׁכֶם
Pl.	רָאשִׁים	רָאשֵׁי	רָאשַׁי	רָאשֵׁיכֶם
Gloss	ear of grain			
Sing.	שִׁבֹּלֶת			
Pl.	שִׁבֳּלִים	שִׁבֳּלֵי		
Gloss	name			
Sing.	שֵׁם	שֵׁם / שֶׁם־	שְׁמִי	שִׁמְכֶם
Pl.	שֵׁמוֹת	שְׁמוֹת	שְׁמוֹתַי	שְׁמוֹתֵיכֶם
Gloss	heaven			
Pl.	שָׁמַיִם	שְׁמֵי	שָׁמַי	שְׁמֵיכֶם

§28. The He *Locale* and Enclitic Mem

The enclitic mem is a suffix affixed to the end of a word. In the vocalization of the Hebrew Bible it was sometimes confused with the masculine plural ending ־ים, the suffix 3 masculine plural ־ם or the preposition מִן. It occurs with virtually all word types. The meaning of this mem is, however, unknown.

Some scholars believe that in the following case the enclitic mem has been confused with the plural ending. (Cf. §25.3/1(iii).)

יְהוָה־אֱלֹהִים (אֱלֹהֵי־ם read) Yahweh *the God of* hosts (Ps. 59.6)
צְבָאוֹת

The he *locale* (or locative he) is formed by adding the suffix ־ָה to a place name and some common nouns to indicate the goal of a movement. It can occur with or without the article in the latter case.

It also occurs with directional adverbs. This ending is never accented and is thereby distinguished from the feminine ending ָה‎ , e.g.

אֶרֶץ‎	earth	אַרְצָה‎	to the earth, to the ground
יְרוּשָׁלַיִם‎	Jerusalem	יְרוּשָׁלַיְמָה‎	to Jerusalem
שָׁם‎	there	שָׁמָּה‎	(to) there

§29. Nouns in Appositional Relationships[36]

An appositional relationship means that two elements in a particular clause have the same referent. The second element qualifies the first in some way. Together the two elements form a construction that can function as a clause constituent (i.e. subject, object, etc.). They usually agree in number and gender, but not necessarily in person. The first element is the head of the construction. Apposition has a wider use in BH than in English. A word in apposition may often be better translated with an adjective or prepositional phrase.

§29.1. *Types of Appositional Contructions*

(i) A *proper name* can stand in apposition to *another noun.*

הָאָרֶץ כְּנַעַן‎   the country *Canaan*

(ii) A noun with *pronominal suffix* can stand in apposition to *a proper name.*

שָׂרָה אִשְׁתּוֹ‎   Sarah, *his wife* (Gen. 20.2)

(iii) *One noun* can stand in apposition to *another noun.*

אִשָּׁה אַלְמָנָה‎   a woman, *a widow* (1 Kgs 7.14)

(iv) A *lexicalized noun* can also stand in apposition to a *pronominal suffix.*

וַתִּרְאֵהוּ אֶת־הַיֶּלֶד‎   And she saw him, the child (Exod. 2.6).

(v) The same element can be *repeated* in apposition. (Cf. 24.3/2(iv).)

a. *Two identical nouns* may occur directly after each other.

זַרְעֶךָ הַיֹּצֵא הַשָּׂדֶה שָׁנָה שָׁנָה‎   your seed which comes forth from the field every year *(year by year)* (Deut. 14.22)

---

36. Cf. Waltke and O'Connor §12.

b. In a similar construction a *preposition* can occur with the second
noun.

לִפְנֵי יְהוָה אֱלֹהֶיךָ תֹּאכְלֶנּוּ
שָׁנָה בְשָׁנָה

You shall eat it before the Lord your
God every year [lit. year *on year*]
(Deut. 15.20).

c. An identical *adverb* can also be repeated in apposition.

אַל ... תְּדַבְּרוּ גְּבֹהָה גְבֹהָה

Talk no more so *very proudly*
(1 Sam. 2.3).

(vi) A *prepositional phrase* can also stand in apposition to a noun or
phrase that has a noun as its head.

וְאַרְבַּע־מֵאוֹת אִישׁ עִמּוֹ

and four hundred men *with him* (Gen.
32.7).

§29.2. *Syntactic Functions of Nouns in Apposition*

Syntactically speaking such an appositional element is always an
adjectival qualification. It thus functions on the same level as attributive adjectives (§30), *postconstructa* (§25) and relative clauses.

§29.3. *Semantic Functions of Nouns in Apposition*

The second member of the phrase *elucidates* the first in one of the
following ways:

(i) The second member designates *the role/capacity* of the first member.

שָׂרָה אִשְׁתּוֹ

Sarah, *his wife* (Gen. 20.2)

(ii) The second member specifies the *status* of the first member.

אִשָּׁה אַלְמָנָה

a woman, *a widow* (1 Kgs 7.14)

(iii) The second member reveals *a characteristic/quality* of the first
member.

אֲמָרִים אֱמֶת

words, truth [true words] (Prov.
22.21)

(iv) The second member specifies *the material* from which the first
member is made.

הַבָּקָר הַנְּחֹשֶׁת

the cattle, *the bronze* [the cattle made
of bronze] (2 Kgs 16.17)

(v) The second member specifies *the substance, a measuring unit or number* of the first member.

סְאָה־סֹלֶת ... וְסָאתַיִם שְׂעֹרִים   a measure of *fine meal* ... and two measures *of barley* (2 Kgs 7.1)

(vi) The second member specifies *the place* where the first member is to be found.

וְאַרְבַּע־מֵאוֹת אִישׁ עִמּוֹ   and four hundred men *with him* (Gen. 32.7)

(vii) The second member specifies *the pronominal reference* of the first member.

וַתִּרְאֵהוּ אֶת־הַיֶּלֶד   She saw him, the child (Exod. 2.6).

(viii) When the same word is repeated, the construction indicates *distribution*. (Cf. also §24.3/2(iv).)

זַרְעֶךָ הַיֹּצֵא הַשָּׂדֶה שָׁנָה שָׁנָה   your seed which comes forth from the field *every* year (year *by year*) (Deut. 14.22)

(ix) When the same word is repeated, the construction implies the *high degree–positive or negative–of intensity* of a referent or a quality referred to. (Cf. also §24.3/2(vi).)

זָהָב זָהָב   *pure* gold (2 Kgs 25.15)

(x) When the same word is repeated (with the waw copulative), the construction indicates *diversity*. (Cf. §24.3/2(v).)

אֶבֶן וָאָבֶן   two *kinds of* weights (Deut. 25.13)

§30. Qualification of the Noun by the Adjective

§30.1. *Morphology of the Adjective*

Like the construct and appositional constructions, the use of the adjective is but one of the ways in which nouns may be described. Adjectives describe or qualify nouns by qualifying their *state*. (Cf. 11.3.)

1. *The declension of the adjective*
The basic paradigm for the declension of adjectives is as follows:

	Masculine	Feminine
	st. abs.	st. abs.
Singular	טוֹב	טוֹבָה
Plural	טוֹבִים	טוֹבוֹת

Additional vowel reductions and consonantal changes can also occur in the stem.[37]

	Singular		Plural	
	masculine	*feminine*	*masculine*	*feminine*
good	טוֹב	טוֹבָה	טוֹבִים	טוֹבוֹת
great	גָּדוֹל	גְּדוֹלָה	גְּדוֹלִים	גְּדוֹלוֹת
wise	חָכָם	חֲכָמָה	חֲכָמִים	חֲכָמֹת
many	רַב	רַבָּה	רַבִּים	רַבּוֹת
bitter	מַר	מָרָה	מָרִים	מָרֹת
bad	רַע	רָעָה	רָעִים	רָעוֹת
beautiful	יָפֶה	יָפָה	יָפִים	יָפוֹת
small	קָטֹן	קְטַנָּה	קְטַנִּים	קְטַנּוֹת

Note the following:

(1) Qualification by an adjective can be *attributive* (e.g. the *good* king, §30.2) or *predicative* (e.g. the king is *good*, §30.3).

(2) Adjectives do not bear an indication of person. The same form is used in apposition or predicatively with subjects of the first, second or third person.

(3) Adjectives are either masculine or feminine

(4) Adjectives can only be singular or plural. The plural is used in the qualification of a dual noun.

(5) An adjective agrees with its noun at least in number and gender.

2. *Patterns of adjectives with personal suffixes*
Since BH does not make a clear morphological distinction between nouns and adjectives, the patterns for the two groups correspond to a large extent. (Cf. §26-27.)

---

37. Cf. also Lambdin 1980:13.

§30.2. *Attributive Qualification*[38]

An attributive adjective modifies a noun and has the following *syntactic* characteristics:

1. *Subordination*
The adjectival qualification is *subordinate* to its noun and can never be one of the main elements of a clause, e.g.

כָּתַב אִישׁ טוֹב   A *good* man wrote.

אִישׁ טוֹב is the subject (constituent) with the verb כָּתַב. אִישׁ is the head of the subject phrase and טוֹב is an adjectival qualification of it.

2. *Congruency*

(i) An attributive adjective *agrees with its noun in number, gender and definiteness.*

(ii) The article of the adjective is sometimes omitted, possibly because adjectives are regarded as inherently definite, e.g. the numerals one and two, אַחֵר and רַבִּים.

הַגּוֹיִם רַבִּים   *many* nations (Ezek. 39.27)

(iii) The attributive adjective does take the article *with a noun that has no article*, but which can nevertheless be regarded as inherently definite. This also occurs with numerals.

וְיוֹם הַשְּׁבִיעִי   the *seventh* day (Exod. 20.10)

שֶׁבַע פָּרֹת הַטֹּבֹת   the seven *good* cows (Gen. 41.26)

(iv) An adjective *often agrees ad sensum* with its noun—in this way a collective singular noun may take a plural adjective and an honorific plural may take a singular adjective. (Cf. §24.3.)

צֹאן רַבּוֹת   *large* flocks (Gen. 30.43)

אֱלֹהִים צַדִּיק   *righteous* God (Ps. 7.10)

(v) As far as gender is concerned, the adjective *agrees* with *the syntactic gender of the noun regardless of its morphological form.* (Cf. §24.2.)

הַשָּׁנִים הַטֹּבֹת הַבָּאֹת הָאֵלֶּה   these *good* years that are coming (Gen. 41.35)

---

38. Cf. also Waltke and O'Connor §14.1-14.3.

(vi) *The masculine is preferred syntactically.* In a series of nouns with different genders, the adjective qualifying them is masculine. When two adjectives follow a feminine noun, the second one may be masculine.

חֻקִּים וּמִצְוֹת טוֹבִים	*good* statutes and commandments (Neh. 9.13)
בְּאֶרֶץ־צִיָּה וְעָיֵף	in a *dry and weary* land (Ps. 63.2)

(vii) An adjective *cannot qualify a proper noun directly,* but must be preceded by an appropriate common noun.

נִינְוֵה הָעִיר הַגְּדוֹלָה	Nineveh, that great city (Jon. 1.2)

(viii) The adjective does not have a dual form. *Dual nouns usually take a plural* attributive adjective.

עֵינַיִם עִוְרוֹת	*blind* eyes (Isa. 42.7)

3. *Position in relation to the noun*

(i) In BH an adjective usually *follows the noun*

מַלְכָּה טוֹבָה	a *good* queen
הַמַּלְכָּה הַטּוֹבָה	The *good* queen
מְלָכוֹת טוֹבוֹת	*good* queens
הַמְּלָכוֹת הַטּוֹבוֹת	The *good* queens

(ii) The adjective רַב sometimes *precedes the noun.*

רַבּוֹת בָּנוֹת	*many* daughters (Prov. 31.29)

(iii) An attributive adjective that qualifies a word in the *status constructus follows the entire construct phrase.* (Cf. §25.3.)

סוּסַת מַלְכָּה גְּדוֹלָה	a big mare of the queen

This sometimes means that the reader does not know whether the adjective qualifies the *status constructus* or *postconstructus* (if the gender and number of both are the same). In such cases the broader context usually makes the meaning clear.

§30.3. *Predicative Qualification*

A predicative adjective functions as a predicate and has the following syntactic characteristics:

1. *Subordination*

(i) As opposed to an attributive adjective a predicative adjective is syntactically speaking *the main element of a (nominal) clause.*

אֲדֹנִי חָכָם   My lord *has wisdom* (2 Sam. 14.20).

(ii) It is also *the head of the copulative predicate (or complement) in a clause with a copulative verb.*

וּדְבַר־יהוה הָיָה יָקָר ...   The word of the Lord *was rare* ... (1 Sam. 3.1).

2. *Congruence*

A predicative adjective agrees with its noun in number and gender, but is *always indefinite.*

3. *Position in relation to the noun*

In BH it *usually follows* the subject, but *can also precede it.* In the first case it can—if the noun is indefinite—look like the attributive construction. Here are some examples:

מַלְכָּה טוֹבָה	A queen is good/good queen
טוֹבָה מַלְכָּה	Good is a queen.
הַמַּלְכָּה טוֹבָה	The queen is good.
טוֹבָה הַמַּלְכָּה	Good is the queen
מְלָכוֹת טוֹבוֹת	Queens are good/good queens.
טוֹבוֹת מְלָכוֹת	Good are queens.
הַמְּלָכוֹת טוֹבוֹת	The queens are good.
טוֹבוֹת הַמְּלָכוֹת	Good are the queens.

§30.4. *Adjectives Used as Substantives*[39]

Adjectives can be substantivized. They then function as *nouns,* for example, זָקֵן old > old one (= old man). They consequently have the syntactic characteristics of nouns:

(i) They *can* be in the *status constructus,* act as *postconstructus* and take pronominal suffixes.

קְטֹן בָּנָיו   the *youngest* of his sons (2 Chron. 21.17)

יֵין הַטּוֹב   the wine of the *good* [the best wine] (Song 7.10)

---

39. Cf. Waltke and O'Connor §14.3.3.

(ii) When an adjective is being used as a noun, *the expected accompanying noun is omitted.* This phenomenon often occurs in poetry for the sake of metonymy (i.e. where a concept is indicated by means of something that is related to it).

עַל־קַל נִרְכָּב

We will ride upon *swift* (steeds) (Isa. 30.16).

(iii) An adjective being used as a noun can stand in apposition to another noun. In this case it *precedes the word that is being qualified* (seldom).

צַדִּיק עַבְדִּי

a righteous one, my servant (Isa. 53.11)

(iv) A substantivized adjective can sometimes act as *an adverb* describing a noun (the so-called 'accusative of specification').

יֹאכְלוּ בְנֵי־יִשְׂרָאֵל לַחְמָם טָמֵא

The people of Israel shall eat their bread *unclean* (Ezek. 4.13).

§30.5. *Degrees of Comparison*[40]

In addition to the positive degree, for example, 'I am big', languages usually also make provision for a comparative degree, for example, 'I am bigger than you' and a superlative degree, for example, 'I am the biggest'. In BH the positive degree is expressed with a predicative adjective (cf. §30.3) or stative verb (cf. §16.2/2).

The adjective in BH has no forms to indicate the degrees of comparison. The semantic effect normally created by the degrees of comparison is effected by means of other constructions, namely:

1. *The comparative degree*
The preposition מִן is used to indicate *the standard* against which an object is being compared. (Cf. §39.14.)

חָכָם אַתָּה מִדָּנִאֵל

You are wiser *than Daniel* (Ezek. 28.3).

40. Cf. Waltke and O'Connor §14.5.

2. *The superlative degree*

(i) The *absolute superlative*, which manifests the outstanding feature, condition or state of something or someone can be expressed by:

a. A *singular noun in the status constructus preceding* the indefinite plural form of the same word.

הֲבֵל הֲבָלִים   vanity of vanities = *utmost* vanities (Eccl. 1.2)

b. The same construction as above, for example, expressed *through synonyms.*

שִׂמְחַת גִּילִי   my exceeding joy (Ps. 43.4)

c. The *adverbial qualifications* מְאֹד or עַד־מְאֹד following the adjective.

וְהַנַּעֲרָה יָפָה עַד־מְאֹד   The maiden was *very beautiful* (1 Kgs 1.4)

d. The use of *divine or royal terms* in a construct relationship.

נְשִׂיא אֱלֹהִים   a *mighty* prince [lit. a prince of gods] (Gen. 23.6)

בֵּית זְבֻל   an *exalted* house [lit. a house of a prince] (1 Kgs 8.13)

e. The use of מוּת (die), מָוֶת (death) and שְׁאֹל (underworld) (for absolute superlatives in a negative sense).

כִּי־עַזָּה כַמָּוֶת אַהֲבָה   For love is strong as death [*enormously strong*] (Song 8.6).

(ii) The *comparative superlative* refers to an individual or object that surpasses all the others in the group in some way. The group can sometimes be omitted or assumed. This is expressed by:

a. A *definite article* with the adjective

הִנֵּה בִתִּי הַגְּדוֹלָה   Here is my *eldest* [largest] daughter (1 Sam. 18.17).

b. An adjective made definite by *a suffix or construct relationship*

מִקְּטַנָּם וְעַד־גְּדוֹלָם   from the *least* to the *greatest* [lit. from their small to their large] (Jer. 6.13)

c. A definite adjective preceding *a prepositional phrase with* בְּ (rare)

הַיָּפָה בַּנָּשִׁים   *the fairest* among women (Song 1.8)

d. A singular noun *in the status constructus followed by a definite plural form of the same word*

שִׁיר הַשִּׁירִים

the most beautiful song (Song of Songs) [lit. the song of the songs] (Song 1.1)

e. A *status constructus with* מִכֹּל preceding the *postconstructus*

וְהַנָּחָשׁ הָיָה עָרוּם מִכֹּל חַיַּת הַשָּׂדֶה

Now the serpent was *most subtle* of all the wild creatures (Gen. 3.1).

f. *Definite abstract terms* for features/qualities like רֵאשִׁית, מִבְחָר, טוּב

וּמִבְחַר שָׁלִשָׁיו

and his *choice* officers [lit. *the chosen* of his officers] (Exod. 15.4)

§31. Co-ordination of the Noun

Co-ordination can be defined as the addition of a second element at the same level as the first element.

§31.1. *Forms of Co-ordination*

1. *The conjunction* ו *(Cf. §40.8.)*

(i) The *morphology* of ו

The conjunction ו is the most common co-ordinating conjunction. ו takes the following forms before nouns:[41]

a. It is *affixed to the next word.*

אִישׁ וְסוּס

a man and a horse

b. Before בּ, ו, מ, פּ it becomes וּ.

סוּס וּפָרָשׁ

a horse and a rider

c. Before a syllable with an audible šᵉwâ it also becomes וּ.

וּסְדֹם

and Sodom

d. It combines with the syllable יְ to form וִ.

וִירִיחוֹ

in Jericho (יְרִיחוֹ)

e. With concepts that *are closely related* (provided the first syllable of the second word is stressed), it becomes וָ.

יוֹם וָלַיְלָה

day and night

---

41. Cf. Gemser 1975: 23.

f. Before a syllable with a ḥāṭēp vowel וֹ acquires the corresponding full vowel.

וַאֲרִי   and a lion

(ii) The *syntax* of וֹ (Cf. also §40.8.)

וֹ has the following distribution:

a. In a series of conjunctions וֹ *can be repeated before each element.*

וַיְהִי־לוֹ צֹאן־וּבָקָר וַחֲמֹרִים	And he had sheep *and* oxen *and* he-
וַעֲבָדִים וּשְׁפָחֹת וַאֲתֹנֹת	asses *and* menservants *and* maidser-
וּגְמַלִּים:	vants *and* she-asses *and* camels
	(Gen. 12.16)

b. In some cases וֹ may occur *before the last element of a list only.*

מִן־הָאֱמֹרִי הַחִתִּי הַפְּרִזִּי	of the Amorites, the Hittites, the
הַחִוִּי וְהַיְבוּסִי	Perizzites, the Hivites, *and* the
	Jebusites (1 Kgs 9.20)

c. In a series of pairs וֹ can also occur *among the pairs.*

נֹתְנֵי לַחְמִי וּמֵימַי צַמְרִי	who give me my bread *and* my water,
וּפִשְׁתִּי שַׁמְנִי וְשִׁקּוּיָי	my wool *and* my flax, my oil *and* my
	drink (Hos. 2.7)

d. In a series of entities וֹ can also *be omitted entirely* (asyndetic).

בִּימֵי עֻזִּיָּה יוֹתָם אָחָז	in the days of Uzziah, Jotham, Ahaz,
יְחִזְקִיָּה	and Hezekiah (Hos. 1.1)

e. In a word chain וֹ can sometimes be *affixed to the first and second element* (rare).

וּבְיִשְׂרָאֵל וּבָאָדָם	*both* in Israel *and* among all mankind
	(Jer. 32.20)

2. *The conjunction* אוֹ *(or). (Cf. §40.3.)*

אוֹ usually occurs between elements of a word chain. (Cf. אִם on the other hand, §40.5.)

וְכִי־יִגַּח שׁוֹר אֶת־אִישׁ	When an ox gores a man *or* a woman
אוֹ אֶת־אִשָּׁה וָמֵת	to death (Exod. 21.28)

3. *Double conjunctions*

(i) וֹ ... וֹ (Cf. §40.8.)

וּבְיִשְׂרָאֵל וּבָאָדָם	*both* in Israel *and* among all mankind
	(Jer. 32.20)

(ii) אוֹ (וֹ) ... אוֹ (Cf. §40.3.)

כִּי־פָשָׂה הַנֶּגַע בַּבֶּגֶד אוֹ־בַשְׁתִי אוֹ־בָעֵרֶב אוֹ בָעוֹר	If the disease has spread in the garment *or* in the warp, *or* in the woof, *or* in the skin (Lev. 13.51).

(iii) אִם (וֹ) ... אִם (Cf. §40.5.)

זֹבְחֵי הַזֶּבַח אִם־שׁוֹר אִם־שֶׂה	those offering a sacrifice, *whether* it be ox *or* sheep (Deut. 18.3)

(iv) גַּם ... גַּם (Cf. §41.4/5.)

גַּם־תֶּבֶן גַּם־מִסְפּוֹא רַב עִמָּנוּ	We have *both* straw and provender enough (Gen. 24.25).

§31.2. *Syntactic Functions of Co-ordinating Nouns*

Syntactically a noun phrase with co-ordinating nouns forms a unit. It is also referred to as a *word chain*, because it chains together entities. As a whole it can (like apposition and attributive constructions) fulfil any syntactic function within a clause, e.g., subject, direct object, indirect object, adjunct, copulative predicate, etc. In the word chain itself the co-ordinating elements are placed on the same level. As opposed to construct, attributive and appositional constructions, it is impossible to single out one unit as the head of the word chain and identify the others as the qualifications.

For the *semantic functions* of co-ordinating conjunctions, cf. §40.

§32. **The Noun as Complement of Prepositions**

§32.1. *Syntactic Characteristics of Prepositions*

Prepositions are words that designate the relationships between verbs and nouns or between nouns themselves. *They precede the nouns they govern.* (For the morphological processes that can occur when prepositions are affixed to nouns, cf. §39.1.) The noun accompanying the preposition is the preposition's *complement*. The preposition and its complement together form a *prepositional phrase* (the abbreviation PP is commonly used to refer to this phrase).

Prepositions may *also take pronominal suffixes* in the place of nouns as complements. (Cf. §39.1.)

Should a preposition govern more than one complement, it is *normally repeated before each complement*. There are, however, cases where the preposition is written before the first complement only.

לֶךְ־לְךָ מֵאַרְצְךָ וּמִמּוֹלַדְתְּךָ וּמִבֵּית אָבִיךָ	Go *from* your country and *from* your kindred and *from* your father's house (Gen. 12.1).
הַחֵפֶץ לַיהוָה בְּעֹלוֹת וּזְבָחִים	Has the Lord as great delight *in burnt offerings and sacrifices?* (1 Sam. 15.22).

For the *semantic functions* of prepositions, cf. §39.

§32.2. *Syntactic Functions of Prepositional Phrases*

Prepositional phrases are used in a variety of syntactic positions. (Cf. §39.1/3.)

1. *A prepositional phrase can function as predicate (as adverbial qualification that may not be omitted) of a nominal clause.*

אֲרִי בֵּין הָרְחֹבוֹת	A lion is *in (between) the streets* (Prov. 26.13).

2. *A prepositional phrase can function as complement of a verb (cf. §32.1):*

(i) As *direct object* (prepositional object)
The prepositions לְ, אֶל־ and בְּ can mark the direct object.

וַיִּבְחַר בָּכֶם	He chose *you* (Deut. 7.7).

(ii) As *indirect object*
The prepositions לְ, אֶל־, אֶת, עַל can mark the indirect object.

לְזַרְעֲךָ אֶתֵּן אֶת־הָאָרֶץ הַזֹּאת	*To your descendants* I will give this land (Gen. 12.7).

(iii) As *complement of a prepositional verb*

וְהוּא נִלְחַם בְּמֶלֶךְ מוֹאָב הָרִאשׁוֹן	And he had fought *against the former king of Moab* (Num. 21.26).

3. *A prepositional phrase can function as an adjunct. (Cf. §32.1.)*
(i) As *optional adverbial modifier*

וַיִּזְבַּח יַעֲקֹב זֶבַח בָּהָר	And Jacob offered a sacrifice *on the mountain* (Gen. 31.54).

(ii) As the *agent of a passive verb*. It can be marked by בְּ, לְ, מִן.

שֹׁפֵךְ דַּם הָאָדָם בָּאָדָם	Whoever sheds the blood of man—*by*
דָּמוֹ יִשָּׁפֵךְ	man shall his blood be shed (Gen. 9.6).

4. *A prepositional phrase can function as an adjectival qualification.*

אִישׁ מִבֵּית לֶחֶם יְהוּדָה	A man of Bethlehem in Judah (Ruth 1.1)

§33. The Noun as Complement/Adjunct of Verbs

§33.1. *Introduction: A Terminological Orientation*

Verbs may govern nouns directly, i.e. without the help of prepositions. In other words, they are nominal elements of the verb phrase that can be complements or adjuncts. (Cf. §12.3.) *Complements* cannot be omitted without changing the meaning of the clause or without making the clause ungrammatical.[42] Direct objects are examples of complements. *Adjuncts*, however, add information to the core of the clause and may be omitted without changing the basic meaning of the clause. Direct objects and adjuncts especially may also be expressed by prepositional phrases.

In some of the other Semitic languages complements and adjuncts are marked by the *accusative*.[43] The accusative expresses the direct object and the so-called adverbial accusative. By analogy some BH grammars speak of the accusative.

In contrast to the languages referred to above, BH does not have cases. (Cf. §25.1.) The reader is thus dependent on clause analysis to determine what the syntactic function of the ordinary form of the word is. Even though word order is not absolutely rigid in BH, it can sometimes help in determining these functions. The direct object and adjunct will usually follow the verb and subject. If the direct object is definite, it is usually preceded by the object marker אֵת/אֶת. Nominal adjuncts can also be marked by it, but this occurs more rarely.

---

42. The complement of a verb may be omitted, but then only when it can be inferred from the context of the sentence. This phenomenon is referred to as *ellipsis*.

43. Cf. also Waltke and O'Connor §10.1-2.

Nouns that are governed directly by verbs thus have two possible *syntactic functions*: complement (direct object and other complements) and adjunct.

§33.2. *Complements*

The number and type of complements in a clause is determined, or more technically speaking 'selected', by the verb of the clause. (Cf. §22.) The following types and combinations of nominal complements occur in BH.

1. *One object*

The direct object is the complement of a transitive verb. It is the receiver of the action of the transitive verb. It could have one of the following *semantic functions* (*inter alia*):

(i) The direct object is *the patient* of an action.

a. An *affected* patient exists before and apart from the action.

וַיִּקַּח יְהוָה אֱלֹהִים
אֶת־הָאָדָם

And the Lord God took *the man* (Gen. 2.15).

b. The *effected* patient is the product or result of the action. It thus comes into being through the action concerned and did not exist before that action occurred. Upon completion of the action it exists as a concrete object apart from the action.

נִלְבְּנָה לְבֵנִים

Let us make *bricks* (Gen. 11.3).

c. Sometimes the noun, which apparently functions as object, has the same root as the verb (the so-called internal object). However, the related entity in most cases is an adjunct. (Cf. §33.3/(v).)

זְקֵנֵיכֶם חֲלֹמוֹת
יַחֲלֹמוּן

Your old men shall dream *dreams* (Joel 3.1).

שָׁם פָּחֲדוּ פָחַד

There they feared *(with) a fear* (Ps. 14.5).

(ii) The direct object is *the interested party* with respect to the action.

וְאָיַבְתִּי אֶת־אֹיְבֶיךָ וְצַרְתִּי
אֶת־צֹרְרֶיךָ

And I will be an *enemy to your enemies* (interested party—put at disadvantage) and an adversary *to your adversaries* (Exod. 23.22).

(iii) The direct object is *the person addressed* by the action.

וַיִּקְרָא אֶת־עֵשָׂו

And he called *Esau* (Gen. 27.1).

(iv) The direct object is *the agent* of the action (rare).

לֹא תִנָּשֵׁנִי

You will not be forgotten *by me* (Isa. 44.21).

Note the following:

    (1)   Verbs that are transitive in BH are not necessarily so in English, and *vice versa*.

    (2)   Some verbs may govern their direct objects either directly or by a preposition. The latter are called prepositional objects. Both constructions sometimes occur with the same verb, sometimes with different nuances.

וַיִּבְחַר בְּזַרְעָם אַחֲרֵיהֶם

And he chose *their descendants* after them (Deut. 10.15).

וַיִּבְחַר־לוֹ לוֹט אֵת כָּל־כִּכַּר
הַיַּרְדֵּן

So Lot chose for himself *all the Jordan valley* (Gen. 13.11).

2. *Two objects*

Where verbs govern two complements as objects, they may have the following semantic functions (*inter alia*):

(i) With verbs of address one direct object is the person addressed and the other *the patient*.

וַיְצַוֵּם אֵת כָּל־אֲשֶׁר דִּבֶּר
יְהוָה אִתּוֹ

And he gave (or commanded) *them / all that the Lord had spoken to him* (Exod. 34.32).

(ii) With verbs of giving or taking one of the direct objects is *the receiver* and the other is *the patient*.

וְנָתַתִּי אֶת־חֵן הָעָם־הַזֶּה

And I will give *this people / favor* (Exod. 3.21).

וְאֶת־צַדִּיקִים יְשַׁלֶּם־טוֹב

He will reward *the righteous / (with) prosperity* (Prov. 13.21).

(iii) With verbs where the status, role or name of someone is changed, one *object is the old and the other is the new status, role or name.*

וַיָּשֶׂם אֶת־בָּנָיו שֹׁפְטִים

He made his *sons / judges* (1 Sam. 8.1).

וַיִּקְרְאוּ שְׁמוֹ עֵשָׂו

So they called his *name / Esau* (Gen. 25.25).

(iv) *Causative and factitive* verbs also take two objects. *The one is the object of the causative idea (let), and the other is the object of the action.*

וְהַרְאֵיתִי גוֹיִם מַעְרֵךְ   And I will let *nations* / look on *your nakedness* (Nah. 3.5).

3. *Other nominal complements (non-objects)*

Nouns that are non-objects may also act as complements with the following verbs:

(i) With *verbs of abiding*

וְהוּא יֹשֵׁב פֶּתַח־הָאֹהֶל   And he sat *at the door of his tent* (Gen. 18.1).

(ii) With *verbs of movement*

וַיָּבֹאוּ אֶרֶץ כְּנַעַן   And they came *to the land of Canaan* (Gen. 45.25).

(iii) With stative verbs that refer to *a condition of being full or covered*

יְדֵיכֶם דָּמִים מָלֵאוּ   Your hands are full of *blood* (Isa. 1.15).

§33.3. *Adjuncts*

Adjuncts are optional, non-verbal parts of the verb phrase. Nouns can act as adjuncts. Nominal adjuncts in BH take the ordinary form of the noun. They are sometimes (very rarely) marked with the object marker אֵת/אֶת־. They can perform several semantic functions, such as indicating time, place, manner and specification. (In other Semitic languages with case endings these are referred to as the *adverbial accusative*.)

Nominal adjuncts can fulfil the following semantic functions (*inter alia*):

(i) Indicate *time*

a. *Specific point(s) in time*

הַשָּׁנָה אַתָּה מֵת   *This very year* you shall die (Jer. 28.16).

b. *Duration*

שֵׁשֶׁת יָמִים תַּעֲבֹד   *Six days* (long) you shall labour (Exod. 20.9).

(ii) Indicate *means/method*

וְהִכֵּיתִי אֶת־הָאָרֶץ חֵרֶם   I shall smite the land *with a curse* (Mal. 3.24).

(iii) Indicate *specification*

רַק לְעֵת זִקְנָתוֹ חָלָה אֶת־רַגְלָיו   Except that in his old age he was diseased *in his feet* (1 Kgs 15.23).

(iv) Indicate *material*

עַמּוּדָיו עָשָׂה כֶסֶף   He made its posts of *silver* (Song 3.10).

(v) *Repeating the verbal idea*

This occurs with a noun that is directly governed by a verb and which has either the same root or approximately the same meaning as the verb. The so-called internal adjunct (often referred to as the internal object, *schema etymologicum* or *figura etymologica*) normally has *no semantic meaning*.

וַיַּחֲלֹם יוֹסֵף חֲלוֹם   Joseph had a dream. (Gen. 37.5).

The internal adjunct is sometimes used to describe the *intensity* of the verbal idea by means of an adjective.

וַיִּצְעַק צְעָקָה גְּדֹלָה וּמָרָה עַד־מְאֹד   He cried out with an *exceedingly great and bitter* cry (Gen. 27.34).

וְקָרְאוּ בְאָזְנַי קוֹל גָּדוֹל   They cry in my ears *with a loud voice* (Ezek. 8.18).

§33.4. *The 'Object Marker'* אֵת/אֶת־[44]

1. *Morphology of the marker*

The marker has the form אֵת when it is written apart from the subsequent word and אֶת־ if it is affixed to the noun with a maqqēf. Pronominal suffixes may be added to the marker. (Cf. §36.1.) The paradigm is set out as follows:

Person	Singular		Plural	
1 m./f.	אֹתִי	me	אֹתָנוּ	us
2 m.	אֹתְךָ	you	אֶתְכֶם	you
2 f.	אֹתָךְ	you	אֶתְכֶן	you

44. For a fuller discussion of אֵת/אֶת־, cf. Waltke and O'Connor §10.3.

3 m.	אֹתוֹ	him	אֹתָם	them
3 f.	אֹתָהּ	her	אֹתָן	them

2. The syntax (= distribution) of the marker

(i) It marks *the definite direct object* of *transitive* verbs. This is also why it is called the *object marker*.

וַיַּעַשׂ אֱלֹהִים אֶת־חַיַּת הָאָרֶץ   And God made *the beasts of the earth* (Gen. 1.25).

(ii) *Indefinite objects are usually unmarked.*

וְנוֹדִיעָה אֶתְכֶם דָּבָר   And we will show you *a thing* (1 Sam. 14.12).

(iii) There are *exceptions*, however. Sometimes definite direct objects are not marked, while indefinite direct objects are marked.

וְהַדֶּלֶת סָגַר אַחֲרָיו   And he shut *the door* after him (Gen. 19.6).

אִם־נָשַׁךְ הַנָּחָשׁ אֶת־אִישׁ   If the serpent bit *any man* (Num. 21.9).

(iv) In a list of definite direct objects אֵת/אֶת־ is usually repeated before each one, but it can also *sometimes be affixed to the first one only* (when they are regarded as a group).

וַיַּכּוּ אֶת־הַכְּנַעֲנִי וְאֶת־הַפְּרִזִּי   and defeated *the Canaanites and the Perizzites* (Judg. 1.5)

וַיִּתֵּן יְהוָה אֶת־הַכְּנַעֲנִי וְהַפְּרִזִּי בְּיָדָם   and the Lord gave *the Canaanites and the Perizzites* into their hand (Judg. 1.4)

(v) אֵת/אֶת־ can also be used to distinguish a *group within a list.*
In such cases אֵת/אֶת־ can stand, for example, before the first two units of a word chain, but not before the third because the second and third units form a group. Compare 1 Sam. 8.14 as opposed to 1 Sam. 8.16.

וְאֶת־שְׂדוֹתֵיכֶם וְאֶת־כַּרְמֵיכֶם וְזֵיתֵיכֶם הַטּוֹבִים יִקָּח   And he will take your fields and *your best vineyards and olive orchards* (1 Sam. 8.14).

וְאֶת־עַבְדֵיכֶם וְאֶת־שִׁפְחוֹתֵיכֶם וְאֶת־בַּחוּרֵיכֶם הַטּוֹבִים וְאֶת־חֲמוֹרֵיכֶם יִקָּח וְעָשָׂה לִמְלַאכְתּוֹ׃   He will take your menservants and maidservants, and *your best young men* and your asses, and put them to his work (1 Sam. 8.16).

(vi) With *other complements and adjuncts* אֶת/אֵת occurs less frequently, but it is used, for example, *after verbs of movement and of fullness as well as with an adjunct referring to a duration in time.*

הֵם יָצְאוּ אֶת־הָעִיר	They left *the city* (Gen. 44.4).
וַיִּמָּלֵא אֶת־הַחָכְמָה	And he was full of *wisdom* (1 Kgs 7.14).
מַצּוֹת יֵאָכֵל אֵת שִׁבְעַת הַיָּמִים	Unleavened bread shall be eaten *for seven days* (Exod. 13.7).

(vii) אֶת/אֵת is even used to mark *subjects* (rare).

a. In *clauses with a verb*

וְאֶת־הַבַּרְזֶל נָפַל אֶל־הַמָּיִם	*The iron* fell into the water (2 Kgs 6.5).

b. In *nominal clauses* (rare)

הַמְעַט־לָנוּ אֶת־עֲוֺן פְּעוֹר	Have we not had enough *of the sin at Peor?* (Josh. 22.17).

§34. The Noun as Subject, Predicate, Vocative and Dislocated Constituent[45]

§34.1. *The Noun as Subject of Verbal Clauses*

A noun can act as the subject of a clause. If the clause has a verb, its person, number and gender are determined by the subject. Since finite verbs have affixes which indicate the person, number and gender of the subject, one could also say that an explicit subject is a repetition or more precise specification of the 'built-in' subject.

... וַתֹּאמֶר רָחֵל	And *she* said, *Rachel* said ... (Gen. 30:8).

The position of the subject in a verbal clause is as follows (cf. also §46):

(i) With asyndetic verbal clauses and with consecutive clauses the subject usually *follows the verb directly.*

דָּבְקָה נַפְשִׁי אַחֲרֶיךָ	*My soul* clings to you (Ps. 63.9).

---

45. Cf. Waltke and O'Connor §8.3 for a more traditional discussion of the so-called nominative function.

(ii) If *the complement of the verb is a preposition plus a pronominal suffix*, it usually stands between the verb and the subject. (Cf. §46.1/2(ii).)

וַיִּבְחַר־לוֹ לוֹט אֵת כָּל־כִּכַּר
הַיַּרְדֵּן

So Lot chose *for himself* all the Jordan valley (Gen. 13.11).

(iii) With so-called *split subjects* the word chain that specifies the subject may stand at the *end of a clause*. (Cf. also §36.1/2(iii).)

וַיֵּלֶךְ אִישׁ מִבֵּית לֶחֶם יְהוּדָה ...
הוּא וְאִשְׁתּוֹ וּשְׁנֵי בָנָיו

And a certain man of Bethlehem in Judah went ..., *he and his wife and his two sons* (Ruth 1.1).

(iv) If the subject precedes the verb, this construction may express specific semantic and pragmatic functions. (Cf. §47.)

§34.2. *The Noun as Subject of Nominal Clauses*

1. *The subject usually stands first in the clause.*
Nominal clauses may have the following structure:
(i) Noun + *adjective*

וִידֵי מֹשֶׁה כְּבֵדִים

And Moses' hands grew weary (Exod. 17.12).

(ii) Noun + *prepositional phrase*

וַאֲדָמָה עַל־רֹאשׁוֹ

And earth is upon his head (2 Sam. 15.32).

(iii) Noun + *predicator of existence*

וּפֹתֵר אֵין אֹתוֹ

And there is no *one who can interpret* it (Gen. 41.15).

2. *If the subject does not precede the predicate, specific semantic-pragmatic functions may be involved*
For the functions of word order in nominal clauses, cf. §47.3.

§34.3. *The Noun as Predicate of Nominal Clauses*

In such clauses, which consist of two noun phrases, the semantic functions *identification or classification* can be realized.

(i) In *an identifying clause* both the subject and the predicate are definite.

אָנֹכִי עֵשָׂו

I am Esau (Gen. 27.19).

(ii) In *a classifying clause* the subject is definite and the predicate indefinite.

גּוּר אַרְיֵה יְהוּדָה

Judah is *a lion's whelp* (Gen. 49.9).

§34.4. *The Noun as Vocative (Form of Address)*

The addressee is usually designated by the ordinary form of the noun with the article. (Cf. §24.4/3(i).) The 'vocative' occurs only in direct speech. It often stands in apposition to a pronoun in the second person or with the built-in subject of an imperative. In other respects it is syntactically separate from the rest of the clause. Syntactically it can be regarded as an adjunct.

בֶּן־מִי אַתָּה הַנַּעַר

Whose son are you, *young man*? (1 Sam. 17.58).

הַחֵרְשִׁים שְׁמָעוּ

Hear, *you deaf* (Isa. 42.18).

§34.5. *The Noun as Dislocated (Pendensed) Constituent*

A noun or noun phrase can be taken from its normal position in the clause and placed at the beginning of the clause. This dislocated constituent often refers to the matter which the clause is about. For more details about this construction, cf. §46.1/2(i).

§35. **Congruence between the Subject and Predicate in BH Clauses**

Congruence between the subject and predicate of clauses in BH has the following characteristics:

(i) *Normally* the subject determines the person, gender and number of the predicate. (In the example below the subjects are italicized.)

וַיִּבְחַר־לוֹ לוֹט אֵת כָּל־כִּכַּר הַיַּרְדֵּן

Lot chose for himself all the Jordan valley (Gen. 13.11).

(ii) If the *subject is dual, the predicate* is in the plural.

אַל־יִרְפּוּ יָדֶיךָ

Let not *your hands* (dual) grow weak (Zeph. 3.16).

(iii) If the subject is a *collective* singular noun, the predicate can be either *singular or plural*.

וְיָדְעוּ הָעָם כֻּלּוֹ

And *all the people* will know (Isa. 9.8).

יֹאכְלוּ עוֹף הַשָּׁמָיִם

The birds of heaven shall eat (1 Kgs 14.11).

עוֹף הַשָּׁמַיִם יוֹלִיךְ אֶת־הַקּוֹל   *The birds* of heaven will carry your [lit. the] voice (Eccl. 10.20).

(iv) Plural subjects that refer to people can take a singular predicate if the statement bears upon the individual members of the group. This is called the *distributive or individualizing* singular.

מְבָרֲכֶיךָ בָרוּךְ   Blessed be *every one who blesses you* (Num. 24.9).

(v) Plural nouns with a singular meaning, such as *royal plurals, often govern the predicate in the singular.*

וַיֹּאמֶר אֱלֹהִים ...   And *God* said: ... (Gen. 1.3).

(vi) If *the predicate precedes the subject* (usually in an asyndetic clause), the *simplest* form of the predicate is often used.

חָזַק מִמֶּנּוּ הַמִּלְחָמָה   *The battle* became too heavy for him [i.e. was going against him] (2 Kgs 3.26).

(vii) *If the subject in the status constructus precedes a postconstructus, the verb is sometimes congruent with the postconstructus if it is the actual topic of the clause (constructio ad sensum).*

נֶגַע צָרַעַת כִּי תִהְיֶה בְּאָדָם   When a man is afflicted with [the plague of] *leprosy* (Lev. 13.9).

(viii) If a subject consisting of more than one word precedes the predicate, the predicate is in the plural. *If one part of the subject is masculine and the other part feminine, the predicate will be masculine.*

וְאַבְרָהָם וְשָׂרָה זְקֵנִים   *Abraham and Sarah* were old (Gen. 18.11).

(ix) If a subject consisting of more than one word follows the predicate, the predicate *can be congruent with the first word of the compound subject.* If such a predicate is followed by *additional predicates,* they will be in the *plural.*

וַתַּעַן רָחֵל וְלֵאָה וַתֹּאמַרְנָה   Then *Rachel* answered, as well as Leah, and *they* said: (Gen. 31.14).

If a preposition with pronominal suffix occurs between the predicate and the compound subject, the predicate often agrees with the compound subject, i.e. the predicate is in the plural.

וַיֵּרְדוּ אֵלָיו מֶלֶךְ יִשְׂרָאֵל   And *the king of Israel, Jehoshaphat*
וִיהוֹשָׁפָט וּמֶלֶךְ אֱדוֹם: and *the king of Edom* went down to
    him (2 Kgs 3.12).

(x) If the compound subject consists of a pronoun and a noun, *the pronoun is often expressed separately,* even if the verb has the appropriate
form.

וַיֵּרֶד הוּא וְנַעֲרוֹ   Then *he and his servant* went down
    (Judg. 7.11).

§36. **Pronouns**

Pronouns are a closed class of words (lexemes) that can be used in
the place of a noun or noun phrase within a certain context. (Cf.
§11.2.) By using pronouns languages avoid the unnecessary repetition of nouns or noun phrases, for example, not 'Jacob loved Joseph.
Jacob made *Joseph* a cloak with long sleeves', but 'Jacob loved
Joseph. *He* made *him* a cloak with long sleeves'. The person or
object to which a pronoun refers can only be determined in the
context in which the pronoun occurs. The sentence in which a pronoun appears is thus always part of a larger whole.

§36.1. *Personal Pronouns*

A personal pronoun usually refers to a person or thing that has
already been mentioned. This person or thing is called the *antecedent* of the pronoun. In BH a distinction need to be made between
independent personal pronouns and enclitic pronouns. The latter are
not separate words, but in the form of pronominal suffixes affixed to
verbs, nouns and other word types. (Cf. §17, 26 and 27.)

I. *Independent Personal Pronouns*

1. *Forms*

The following independent personal pronouns occur in BH:

Person	Singular		Plural	
1 m./f.	אָנֹכִי / אֲנִי	I	אֲנַחְנוּ	we
2 m.	אַתָּה	you	אַתֶּם	you
2 f.	אַתְּ	you	אַתֵּן	you
3 m.	הוּא	he	הֵם / הֵמָּה	they
3 f.	הִוא / הִיא	she	הֵנָּה	they

2. *The syntax of independent personal pronouns*[46]

(i) Function as the *subject of a nominal clause* or a clause in which *the verb is not marked for person*

וַיֹּאמֶר אַבְרָהָם אֶל־שָׂרָה אִשְׁתּוֹ אֲחֹתִי הִוא	And Abraham said of Sarah his wife: *She* is my sister (Gen. 20.2).
הֵמָּה עֹלִים בְּמַעֲלֵה הָעִיר	As *they* went up the hill to the city (1 Sam. 9.11).

(ii) Precede a *finite verb* or follow a constituent that is *already marked for person*

אָנֹכִי נָתַתִּי שִׁפְחָתִי בְּחֵיקֶךָ	I *myself* gave my maid to your embrace (Gen. 16.5).
בִּי־אֲנִי אֲדֹנִי הֶעָוֹן	*Upon me alone*, my lord, be the guilt (1 Sam. 25.24).

The independent personal pronoun follows the verb only in cases where a waw consecutive + imperfect or waw consecutive + perfect makes it impossible for the independent pronoun to precede the verb.

וְזָכַרְתִּי אֲנִי אֶת־בְּרִיתִי אוֹתָךְ	And *I* will remember my covenant with you (Ezek. 16.60).

(iii) The third person masculine singular independent personal pronoun is used *between the subject and predicate of a nominal clause* with three constituents.

הֲלֹא אַתָּה־הוּא יְהוָה אֱלֹהֵינוּ	Are you not the Lord our God? (Jer. 14.22).

(iv) Function as *part of the extention of a constituent*, for example, the subject

וַיַּעַל אַבְרָם מִמִּצְרַיִם הוּא וְאִשְׁתּוֹ	So *Abram* went up from Egypt, *he* and his wife (Gen. 13.1).

(v) Indicate *the syntactic domain of some focus particles* (Cf. §41.4/5.1.)

כִּי אָמַר פֶּן־יָמוּת גַּם־הוּא כְּאֶחָיו	for he feared that *he too* would die like his brothers.(Gen. 38.11).
וַתְּהִי עָלָיו גַּם־הוּא רוּחַ אֱלֹהִים	And the Spirit of God came *upon him also* (1 Sam. 19.23).

---

46. This section benefitted much from Naudé 1996.

3. *The semantic-pragmatic functions of independent pronouns*

The use of the independent personal pronoun is often syntactically motivated. However, apart from cases where they function as part of the extention of a constituent and *introduce or activate new characters that are anchored to one of the prominent characters in a narrative* (cf. §36.1/I.2(iv)), independent personal pronouns are predominately used to express semantic-pragmatic functions. This happens in particular in those cases where the pronouns appear to be used superfluously and correlate syntactically with those where fronting is involved. (Cf. §46.1/1-2.) Fronting by means of an apparently superfluous pronoun can be used as follows (Cf. §47.2.):

(i) It indicates the focus of an utterance *confirming the personal or exclusive role of the referent of the pronoun in an event*

אָנֹכִי נָתַתִּי שִׁפְחָתִי בְּחֵיקֶךָ   *I myself* gave my maid to your embrace (Gen. 16.5).

This use of the pronoun often occurs in *contexts where speakers boasts* about what *they* have done.

אֲנִי הֶעֱשַׁרְתִּי אֶת־אַבְרָם   *I (and nobody else)* have made Abram rich (Gen. 14.23).

The construction is also used in cases where *pledges or promises* are made, or where someone is being *confronted* with what he or she has done.

וַיֹּאמֶר אָנֹכִי אֲשַׁלַּח גְּדִי־עִזִּים   And he said: *I* will (*personally*) send you a kid (Gen. 38.17).

When the third person masculine singular form of the pronoun is used between the subject and predicate of a nominal clause, it apparently also indicate the focus of the utterance. It confirms the identification of a referent as a particular somebody or something.

הֲלֹא אַתָּה־הוּא יְהוָה אֱלֹהֵינוּ   Are *you* (and nobody else) not the Lord our God? (Jer. 14.22).

(ii) It reactivates entities (e.g. characters) that are *compared* or *contrasted*. (Cf. §47/2(ii)e.)

הוּא יְשׁוּפְךָ רֹאשׁ וְאַתָּה תְּשׁוּפֶנּוּ עָקֵב   *He (on the one hand)* shall bruise your head, and *you (on the other hand)* shall bite his heel (Gen. 3.15).

Both entities need not be explicitly mentioned.

וְאַתָּה תָּבוֹא אֶל־אֲבֹתֶיךָ בְּשָׁלוֹם

But *you* shall go to your fathers in peace (in contrast to the nations referred to in Gen. 15.14) (Gen. 15.15).

(iii) It signals that *an anterior construction* is involved. (Cf. §47/2(iii).) This construction has *a discourse active referent* as fronted subject and a proposition that has a pluperfect or preperfect relationship with the main line of the narration.

וַיְהִי כִּרְאוֹת מֶלֶךְ־הָעַי ...
וַיְשַׁכִּימוּ וַיֵּצְאוּ אַנְשֵׁי־הָעִיר
לִקְרַאת־יִשְׂרָאֵל לַמִּלְחָמָה ...
וְהוּא לֹא יָדַע כִּי־אֹרֵב
לוֹ מֵאַחֲרֵי הָעִיר

And when the king of Ai saw this ... the men of the city went out early to to meet Israel in battle ...; but *he* did not know that there was an ambush against him behind the city (Josh. 8.14).

(iv) It signals a *specific type of temporal construction*. This construction is used to refer to two *simultaneous* (or nearly simultaneous) *actions*.

הִנֵּה עוֹדָךְ מְדַבֶּרֶת שָׁם
עִם־הַמֶּלֶךְ וַאֲנִי אָבוֹא
אַחֲרַיִךְ

Then while you are still speaking with the king there, *I* also will come in after you (1 Kgs 1.14).

הֵמָּה בָּאוּ בְּאֶרֶץ צוּף
וְשָׁאוּל אָמַר לְנַעֲרוֹ

When *they* reached the district of Suph, Saul said to his servant: (1 Sam. 9.5).

II. *Pronominal Suffixes Added to Verbs*[47]

1. *Morphology*
Cf. §17.

2. *The syntactic-semantic functions of pronominal suffixes affixed to verbs*
Pronominal suffixes affixed to verbs function as:
(i) the *object* of the clause

וַיִּשְׁלָחֵהוּ מֵעֵמֶק חֶבְרוֹן

So he sent *him* from the valley of Hebron (Gen. 37.14).

(ii) the *indirect object* of the clause

וַהֲשִׁבֵנִי דָבָר

And bring *me* word again (Gen. 37.14).

47. Also called the 'object suffix.'

III. *Pronominal Suffixes Added to Nouns (including the infinitive construct[48])*

1. *Morphology*
Cf. §26 and §27.

2. *The syntactic-semantic functions of pronominal suffixes affixed to nouns (Cf. also §25.4.)*
Pronominal suffixes affixed to nouns function as:

(i) the *subject of* an infinitive clause

וְהָיָה בִכְזִיב בְּלִדְתָּהּ אֹתוֹ   And she was in Chezib when *she* bore him (Gen. 38.5).

(ii) the *object* in an infinitive clause

לַהֲמִיתוֹ   to kill *him* (Gen. 37.18)

(iii) the *indirect object* in an infinitive clause

וְלֹא יָכְלוּ דַּבְּרוֹ לְשָׁלֹם   And they could not speak peaceably *to him* (Gen. 37.4).

(iv) Pronominal suffixes indicate *possession*.

וְהִנֵּה קָמָה אֲלֻמָּתִי   Suddenly *my* sheaf arose (Gen. 37.7).

IV. *Pronominal Suffixes Added to Prepositions*

1. *Morphology*
Cf. §39.1/1.

2. *Functions*
For the syntactic functions, cf. §39.1/3.
For the semantic functions, cf. §39.1/4 and 39.2-21.

V. *Personal Pronouns Suffixes Added to* הִנֵּה

1. *Morphology*
Cf. §44.3/2.

2. *Functions*
Cf. §44.3/4.

---

48. An *infinitive form can also take the suffixes added to verbs*, but then only if the suffixes fulfil a definite syntactic function, namely as the object of the infinitive sentence. (Cf. §17.5.)

VI. *Personal Pronouns Suffixes Added to* עוֹד

1. *Morphology*
Cf. §41.2/5.

2. *Functions*
Cf. §41.2/5.

VII. *Personal Pronouns Suffixes Added to* אֵין *and* יֵשׁ

1. *Morphology*
Cf. §42.1.

2. *Functions*
Cf. §43.2-3.

VIII. *Personal Pronouns Suffixes Added to* אֵת *and* אֶת־

1. *Morphology*
Cf. §33.4/1.

2. *Functions*
Cf. §33.4/2.

Note the following:

(1) The position of the syntactic antecedent of a pronominal suffix determines the nature of the pronominal suffix. If the syntactic antecedent occurs in the same clause as the pronominal suffix, the pronominal suffix has a reflexive (anaphoric) nature and is usually translated with *self (himself, herself, etc.)*.

אֶת־בְּנֵיכֶם יִקָּח וְשָׂם לוֹ	He will take your sons and *he* will appoint them for *himself* (1 Sam. 8.11).

(2) If the syntactic antecedent does not function in the same clause as the pronominal suffix, the pronominal suffix has a pronominal nature and is usually translated with *him/her/them*.

וְהִמְלַכְתָּ לָהֶם מֶלֶךְ	And appoint a king *over them* (1 Sam. 8.22).

§36.2. *Demonstrative Pronouns*

1. *Morphology*

Demonstrative pronouns are deictic or 'showing' words that can take the place of a noun or a noun phrase (NP), for example, 'Here is the document; *this* is what you must read'. Like adjectives they can also qualify an NP, for example, 'You must help *this* child'. A distinction is usually drawn between *near* and *distant* demonstrative pronouns. Distinctions are also drawn between masculine and feminine, and the singular and the plural of the demonstrative pronouns. In BH the following sets of pronouns are distinguished:

	Near	*Distant*
	this	that
m. sing.	זֶה, זוּ, זֹה	הוּא
f. sing.	זֹאת	הִיא
m. pl.	אֵלֶּה	הֵם / הֵמָּה
f. pl.	אֵלֶּה	הֵנָּה

The BH 'distant' demonstrative pronouns above are, however, called quasi-demonstrative pronouns because they cannot stand in every syntactic position, for example, הוּא cannot be used as the object of a clause. Yet זֶה can be used as the object, for example, קְרָא נָא־זֶה 'Read *that*' (Isa. 29.11).[49]

2. *The syntactic and semantic functions of the 'near' demonstrative pronouns* זֶה, זֹה, זוּ, זֹאת *and* אֵלֶּה

(i) The demonstrative pronoun can stand *in the place of an NP*.

שְׁלְחוּ־נָא אֶת־זֹאת מֵעָלַי   Send *this* woman out of my presence (2 Sam. 13.17).

---

49. For a more exhaustive discussion, cf. Waltke and O'Connor §17.3 and Joüon-Muraoka §143j.

(ii) A demonstrative pronoun can *qualify a noun*. It can be used *attributively or predicatively.*

a. The demonstrative pronoun is used just like the adjective. In other words, it usually *follows* the noun and *agrees* with it in definiteness, gender and number. In such cases the demonstrative pronoun is used *attributively.*

כִּי־אֹתְךָ רָאִיתִי צַדִּיק לְפָנַי
בַּדּוֹר הַזֶּה

For I have seen that you are righteous before me in *this* generation (Gen. 7.1).

When an independent pronoun is defined by both an adjective and a demonstrative pronoun, the adjective *precedes* the demonstrative pronoun.

הַגּוֹי הַגָּדוֹל הַזֶּה

this great nation (Deut. 4.6)

b. Sometimes the demonstrative pronoun *precedes* the noun and does not agree with it in *definiteness.*

כִּי־זֶה מֹשֶׁה הָאִישׁ
אֲשֶׁר הֶעֱלָנוּ

as for *this* Moses, the man who brought us up (Exod. 32.1)

c. The predicative use of the demonstrative pronoun corresponds with the predicative use of the adjective; in other words it can be placed before the noun and it agrees with it in gender and number.

וְאֵלֶּה תּוֹלְדֹת אַהֲרֹן

And *these* are the generations of Aaron (Num. 3.1).

d. Sometimes people are qualified in such a way that the nuance of *belonging to a group* is expressed.

כִּי־קָרָא יְהוָה לִשְׁלֹשֶׁת
הַמְּלָכִים הָאֵלֶּה

For the Lord has called *these* three kings (2 Kgs 3.10).

(iii) The demonstrative pronoun can function like a *relative pronoun.* (Cf. §36.3.)

הַר־צִיּוֹן זֶה שָׁכַנְתָּ בּוֹ

Mount Zion, *where* you came to dwell (Ps. 74.2).

(iv) Demonstrative pronouns (usually in pairs) function as *reciprocal pronouns.*

וְקָרָא זֶה אֶל־זֶה

And one called to *another* (Isa. 6.3).

(v) The demonstrative pronoun is sometimes used *tautologically after* הִנֵּה.

וְהִנֵּה־זֶה מַלְאָךְ נֹגֵעַ בּוֹ	And look, an angel touched him (1 Kgs 19.5).

(vi) Demonstrative pronouns combined with interrogative pronouns sometimes express the *surprise or amazement of a speaker* about a state of affairs in the form of a rhetorical question. (Cf. also §43.3/2(i).)

מַה־זֹּאת עֲשִׂיתֶם	*What is this* you have done?! (Judg. 2.2).

Sometimes זֶה is used to emphasize the frequency of an event or action.

וַיְנַסּוּ אֹתִי זֶה עֶשֶׂר פְּעָמִים	And yet they have put me to the proof *these* ten times (Num. 14.22).

3. *The syntactic and semantic functions of the 'distant' demonstrative pronoun* הַהוּא[50]

(i) The demonstrative pronoun can *qualify a noun*.

וְהֵבֵאתִי עַל־הָאָרֶץ הַהִיא	And I will bring upon *that* land (Jer. 25.13).

It is used especially to refer to *a specific point in time* in the future or the past.

בַּיּוֹם הַהוּא יָסִיר אֲדֹנָי	In *that* day the Lord will take away (Isa. 3.18).
בַּיּוֹם הַהוּא כָּרַת יְהוָה אֶת־אַבְרָם בְּרִית	On *that* day the Lord made a covenant with Abram (Gen. 15.18).

(ii) In contrast to the 'near' demonstrative pronouns, the *'distant' pronoun is only used attributively.*

§36.3. *Relative Pronouns*

The following relative pronouns occur in BH: אֲשֶׁר and שֶׁ. The latter is found especially in the later books of the Bible (e.g. Ezra and Ecclesiastes). It also occurs in early texts, e.g. Judges 5:7. In the intermediate period, however, שֶׁ is not used. Other syntactic units which are not primarily relative pronouns, but still function as such

---

50. The quasi-demonstrative pronoun occurs mainly in this form.

are: זֶה, זֹה and זוּ and the article הַ A feature of all the relative pronouns in BH is that they do not decline.

1. אֲשֶׁר

(i) אֲשֶׁר where the antecedent is *the subject* of the subordinate clause

הָעֵץ אֲשֶׁר בְּתוֹךְ־הַגָּן

The tree *which* is in the midst of the garden (Gen. 3:3).

The so-called *independent* relative clauses suppress the antecedent. In such clauses this antecedent is always the subject or object (cf. Num. 22.6) of the subordinate clause.

... וַיֹּאמֶר לַאֲשֶׁר עַל־בֵּיתוֹ

He said to *him* who was over his house: ... (Gen. 43.16).

(ii) אֲשֶׁר where the antecedent is *the object* of the subordinate clause

אֱלֹהִים אֲחֵרִים אֲשֶׁר לֹא יָדַעְתָּ

other gods *which* you have not known (Deut. 13.7)

Sometimes the antecedent of אֲשֶׁר is also referred to by means of a pronominal suffix which occurs later in the subordinate clause.

הַנָּבִיא אֲשֶׁר־שְׁלָחוֹ יְהוָה

the prophet *which* the Lord has sent (Jer. 28.9)

(iii) אֲשֶׁר where the antecedent is *the time* at which the events in the subordinate clause took place

בַּיּוֹם הַהוּא אֲשֶׁר תָּבֹא

on that day *when* you go (1 Kgs 22.25)

(iv) אֲשֶׁר where the antecedent is *the place where* the events in the subordinate clause took place.

הָאָרֶץ אֲשֶׁר אַתָּה שֹׁכֵב עָלֶיהָ

the land *on which* you lie (Gen. 28.13)

(v) אֲשֶׁר where the antecedent is *the place to which, along which or from which* the subject in the subordinate clause moves.

אֶת־הָאֲדָמָה אֲשֶׁר לֻקַּח מִשָּׁם

the ground *from which* he was taken (Gen. 3.23)

2. שֶׁ־

(i) שֶׁ where the antecedent is *the subject* of the subordinate clause

כַּחוֹל שֶׁעַל־שְׂפַת הַיָּם

as the sand *which* is upon the sea-shore (Judg. 7.12)

שֶׁ where a *hidden* antecedent is resumed by means of a pronominal suffix in a subordinate clause

אַשְׁרֵי שֶׁאֵל יַעֲקֹב בְּעֶזְרוֹ

Happy is he *whose* help is the God of Jacob (Ps. 146.5).

(ii) שֶׁ where the antecedent is *the place to which, along which or from which* the subject in the subordinate clause moves

שֶׁשָּׁם עָלוּ שְׁבָטִים

to which the tribes go up (Ps. 122.4)

3. זֶה/זוֹ/זִי/זוּ

(i) זֶה where the antecedent is *the subject* of the subordinate clause

שְׁמַע לְאָבִיךָ זֶה יְלָדֶךָ

Listen to your father *who* begot you (Prov. 23.22).

(ii) זֶה where the antecedent is *the object* of the subordinate clause

וְעֵדֹתִי זוֹ אֲלַמְּדֵם

and my testimonies *which* I shall teach them (Ps. 132.12)

זֶה where a *hidden* antecedent is the object in a subordinate clause

וְזֶה־אָהַבְתִּי נֶהְפְּכוּ־בִי

and those *whom* I loved have turned against me (Job 19.19)

(iii) זֶה where the antecedent is *the place in which* the events in the subordinate clause take place (with resumption by means of a pronominal suffix)

הַר־צִיּוֹן זֶה שָׁכַנְתָּ בּוֹ

Mount Zion, where you came to dwell.(Ps. 74.2)

4. הַ

The article הַ began to act as a relative pronoun before finite verbs and particularly perfect forms in the later books. Note that it can be argued that the הַ which sometimes precedes participles should not be understood as a relative pronoun, compare, for example, Gen. 12.7 where הַ occurs and Ezek. 1.4 where it is absent. The equivalent of *that* is thus due to the participial construction and not to הַ.

לַיהוָה הַנִּרְאֶה אֵלָיו

to the Lord, *who* had appeared to him (Gen. 12.7)

סְעָרָה בָּאָה מִן־הַצָּפוֹן

a stormy wind which came out of the north (Ezek. 1.4)

(i) הַ before a perfect where the antecedent is *the subject* of a subordinate clause

וְכֹל אֲשֶׁר בֶּעָרֵינוּ הַהֹשִׁיב נָשִׁים נָכְרִיּוֹת   all those in our cities *who* have taken foreign wives (Ezra 10.14)

(ii) הַ before a perfect where the antecedent is *the object* of a subordinate clause

וְכֹל הַהִקְדִּישׁ שְׁמוּאֵל   and all *that* Samuel had dedicated (1 Chron. 26.28)

§36.4. *Interrogative Pronouns*

Cf. §43.3.

§36.5. *Indefinite Pronouns*

Indefinite pronouns can be expressed by means of the following elements or in the following ways:

1. כֹּל + *noun (without* הַ*)*

כָּל־הֹרֵג קַיִן   *anyone* who slays Cain (Gen. 4.15)

2. מַה

מַה־תֹּאמַר נַפְשְׁךָ וְאֶעֱשֶׂה־לָּךְ   *Whatever you say*, I will do for you (1 Sam. 20.4).

3. מִי

מִי־יָרֵא וְחָרֵד יָשֹׁב   *Whoever* is fearful and trembling, let him return (Judg. 7.3).

Sometimes מִי is followed by אֲשֶׁר or even הָאִישׁ אֲשֶׁר.

מִי אֲשֶׁר חָטָא־לִי אֶמְחֶנּוּ מִסִּפְרִי   *Whoever* has sinned against me, him will I blot out of my book (Exod. 32.33).

מִי־הָאִישׁ אֲשֶׁר בָּנָה בַיִת־חָדָשׁ   *everyone* that has built a new house (Deut. 20.5)

4. אִישׁ

אִם־יוּכַל אִישׁ לִמְנוֹת ...   If *one* could count ... (Gen. 13.16).

לְכוּ אִישׁ לְעִירוֹ   Go, *every man* to his city (1 Sam. 8.22).

5. אָדָם

אָדָם כִּי־יַקְרִיב מִכֶּם קָרְבָּן
לַיהוָה ...
When *any man* of you brings an offering to the Lord ... (Lev. 1.2).

6. נֶפֶשׁ

נֶפֶשׁ כִּי־תֶחֱטָא ...
If *any one* sins, ... (Lev. 4.2).

7. *The participle as subject of a finite verb with the same stem*

כִּי־יִפֹּל הַנֹּפֵל מִמֶּנּוּ ...
If *any one* fall from it, ... (Deut. 22.8).

8. *An unspecified third person verb ending*

וַיְהִי אַחֲרֵי הַדְּבָרִים הָאֵלֶּה
וַיֹּאמֶר לְיוֹסֵף ...
And then, after this *somebody* told Joseph: ... (Gen. 48.1).

9. דָּבָר

הֲיִפָּלֵא מֵיְהוָה דָּבָר
Is *anything* too hard for the Lord? (Gen. 18.14).

10. מְאוּמָה

וְאַל־תַּעַשׂ לוֹ מְאוּמָה
Do not do *anything* to him (Gen. 22.12).

§37. Numerals

§37.1. *Introduction*

Numerals express numbers and are dealt with as a separate word type on that basis. Numbers in the BH text are always written out in full.

On the basis of form and combination with other words, two kinds of numerals may be distinguished: cardinals and ordinals.

§37.2. *Cardinals*

1. *Form of the cardinals*
The numerals 1 to 19 have different forms when qualifying masculine and feminine words.

(i) *The numerals 1 to 10*
Status absolutus and *status constructus* forms may be differentiated with the numerals 1 to 10.

	With a masculine noun		With a feminine noun	
	St. abs.	*St. cs.*	*St. abs.*	*St. cs.*
1	אֶחָד	אַחַד	אַחַת	אַחַת
2	שְׁנַיִם	שְׁנֵי	שְׁתַּיִם	שְׁתֵּי
3	שְׁלֹשָׁה	שְׁלֹשֶׁת	שָׁלוֹשׁ	שְׁלֹשׁ
4	אַרְבָּעָה	אַרְבַּעַת	אַרְבַּע	אַרְבַּע
5	חֲמִשָּׁה	חֲמֵשֶׁת	חָמֵשׁ	חֲמֵשׁ
6	שִׁשָּׁה	שֵׁשֶׁת	שֵׁשׁ	שֵׁשׁ
7	שִׁבְעָה	שִׁבְעַת	שֶׁבַע	שְׁבַע
8	שְׁמֹנָה	שְׁמֹנַת	שְׁמֹנֶה	שְׁמֹנֶה
9	תִּשְׁעָה	תִּשְׁעַת	תֵּשַׁע	תְּשַׁע
10	עֲשָׂרָה	עֲשֶׂרֶת	עֶשֶׂר	עֶשֶׂר

(ii) *The numerals 11 to 19*

a. The numerals 11 to 19 are simply combinations of the unit (1-9) and a form for 10 (as in English, thirteen, seventeen, etc.).

b. The first component of the combination, the unit, takes a shortened form which usually looks like the *status constructus*.

	With a masculine noun	With a feminine noun
11	אַחַד עָשָׂר	אַחַת עֶשְׂרֵה
11	עַשְׁתֵּי עָשָׂר	עַשְׁתֵּי עֶשְׂרֵה
12	שְׁנַיִם עָשָׂר	שְׁתֵּים עֶשְׂרֵה
12	שְׁנֵי עָשָׂר	שְׁתֵּי עֶשְׂרֵה
13	שְׁלֹשָׁה עָשָׂר	שְׁלֹשׁ עֶשְׂרֵה
14	אַרְבָּעָה עָשָׂר	אַרְבַּע עֶשְׂרֵה
15	חֲמִשָּׁה עָשָׂר	חֲמֵשׁ עֶשְׂרֵה
16	שִׁשָּׁה עָשָׂר	שֵׁשׁ עֶשְׂרֵה
17	שִׁבְעָה עָשָׂר	שְׁבַע עֶשְׂרֵה
18	שְׁמֹנָה עָשָׂר	שְׁמֹנֶה עֶשְׂרֵה
19	תִּשְׁעָה עָשָׂר	תְּשַׁע עֶשְׂרֵה

(iii) *The tens*

The tens look like (masculine) plural forms of singular numbers.

20	עֶשְׂרִים	60	שִׁשִּׁים
30	שְׁלֹשִׁים	70	שִׁבְעִים

| 40 | אַרְבָּעִים | 80 | שְׁמֹנִים |
| 50 | חֲמִשִּׁים | 90 | תִּשְׁעִים |

(iv) *Larger units (100, 1000 and 10,000)*

The numerals for larger units have distinct singular, dual and plural forms. In the case of the singular and plural forms for 100 and 1000 there is also a *status constructus* form in addition to the normal *status absolutus* form. The word for 10,000 is not used much and there is no distinction between a *status absolutus* and a *status constructus* form.

		St. abs.	St. cs.
100		מֵאָה	מְאַת
200	dual	מָאתַיִם	
	plural	מֵאוֹת	מְאוֹת
1000		אֶלֶף	אֶלֶף
2000	dual	אַלְפַּיִם	
	plural	אֲלָפִים	אַלְפֵי
10,000		רִבּוֹ or רִבּוֹא or רְבָבָה	
20,000	dual	רִבּוֹתַיִם	
	plural	רִבּוֹת or רִבּוֹאת	

(v) *Compound numbers*

Compound numbers are expressed by combinations of the above-mentioned cardinals. When a numeral between 3 and 10 combines with מֵאָה or רְבָבָה, it takes the form it would take with a feminine noun, and when it combines with אֶלֶף, it takes the form it would take with a masculine noun. There is no rigid sequence for the different elements within the compound number. The following numbers will serve as examples:

31	שְׁלֹשִׁים וְאַחַת	2 Kgs 22.1
33	שָׁלוֹשׁ וּשְׁלֹשִׁים	Ezek. 41.6
150	מֵאָה וַחֲמִשִּׁים	1 Chron. 8.40
212	מָאתַיִם וּשְׁנַיִם עָשָׂר	1 Chron. 9.22
250	חֲמִשִּׁים וּמָאתַיִם	2 Chron. 8.10
675	שֵׁשׁ מֵאוֹת חָמֵשׁ וְשִׁבְעִים:	Num. 31.37
2700	אֲלָפִים וּשְׁבַע מֵאוֹת	1 Chron. 26.32

42,360	אַרְבַּע רִבּוֹא אֲלָפִים שְׁלֹשׁ־מֵאוֹת וְשִׁשִּׁים	Neh. 7.66
44,760	אַרְבָּעִים וְאַרְבָּעָה אֶלֶף וּשְׁבַע־מֵאוֹת וְשִׁשִּׁים	1 Chron. 5.18

2. *Syntax of the cardinals*[51]

The cardinals can combine with nouns in the following ways:

(i) *One*

a. The number *one* acts syntactically as an adjective. The numeral follows the noun and agrees with it in gender, number and definiteness. This *attributive* construction occurs only with the cardinal אֶחָד.

מָנָה אַחַת   *one* part (1 Sam. 1.5)

הַטּוּר הָאֶחָד   the *first* row (Exod. 39.10)

b. The numeral in the *status constructus* can also stand before a noun in the *status absolutus* (as *postconstructus*). Only in the case of the numeral אֶחָד does the noun that follows a numeral in the *status constructus* take the article.

אַחַד הֶהָרִים   *one* of the mountains (Gen. 22.2)

c. The numeral אֶחָד in the *status absolutus* can also *follow a noun in the status constructus*. This combination is, however, rare.

מִשְׁפַּט אֶחָד   *one* judgement (Lev. 24.22)

(ii) *Two*

a. The number two acts as *a noun* and can be placed before or after the plural noun.

b. The gender of the numeral two agrees with the gender of the noun with which it stands. This construction has all the characteristics of an *appositional* relationship. (Cf. §29.)

יָמִים שְׁנַיִם   *two* days (2 Sam. 1.1)[52]

---

51. For a more exhaustive explanation of the syntax of numerals, see Richter 1979: 26.

52. Joüon–Muraoka §142c remarks: 'This number (i.e. two, Van der Merwe *et al.*) has a nature which is less adjectival than that of אֶחָד, but more so than that of the other numbers.'

c. If the numeral two is placed before the noun, it can also occur in the *status constructus* form.

שְׁנֵי בָנִים   *two* sons

The numeral two can also combine with a pronominal suffix.

שְׁנֵיהֶם   the *two* of them (Est. 2.23)

(iii) *3-10*

The numbers 3-10 act as nouns and can be placed before or after the plural form of the noun.

a. *Reversed gender:* The numerals for the numbers 3 to 10 take the characteristic feminine ending (הָ‑) if the noun is masculine.

שְׁלֹשָׁה בָנִים   *three* sons (Gen. 29.34)

If the noun is feminine, the numeral has no ending (as is normally the case with masculine nouns).

b. *Appositional relationship:* The numeral and a noun—both in the *status absolutus*—stand next to each other and have the form of an *appositional relationship*. Although the numeral *usually* precedes the noun, it often *also follows* the noun.

שְׁלֹשָׁה בָנִים   *three* sons (Gen. 29.34)

עָרִים אַרְבַּע   *four* cities (Josh. 21.18)

c. *Construct relationship:* The cardinals 3-10 in the *status constructus* can also stand before a noun in the *status absolutus*. The rules for agreement in gender between the numeral and the noun (as set out above) still apply. The noun is usually in the plural.

וּשְׁנֵי לְאֻמִּים   *two* nations (Gen. 25.23)

שְׁלֹשֶׁת יָמִים   *three* days (Josh. 2.16)

(iv) *11-19*

Reversed gender: With the numbers 11 to 19 the teens as well as the units (1-2) always have the same gender as the noun, while the units (3-9) have the opposite gender.

עָרִים שֵׁשׁ־עֶשְׂרֵה   *sixteen* cities (Josh. 15.41)

(v) *Tens*

a. The tens (20, 30, 40, etc.) are used with masculine and feminine nouns *without changing the form of the numerals.*

שְׁלֹשִׁים וּשְׁנַיִם מֶלֶךְ   *thirty-two* kings (1 Kgs 20.1)

עָרִים אַרְבָּעִים וּשְׁמֹנֶה   *forty-eight* cities (Josh. 21.41)

b. With double-figure numbers *the units (1-9) or the tens (20, 30, 40 etc.) can be written first.*

c. The tens *look like masculine plural forms of the singular numbers* and are used with masculine and feminine nouns without distinction.

(vi) *100 and 1000*

a. מֵאָה (100) acts as *a feminine noun and* אֶלֶף (1000*) as a masculine noun.* They do not change form according to the gender of the accompanying noun. *These numerals always precede the noun.*

מֵאָה פְעָמִים   *a hundred* times (2 Sam. 24.3)

וּמֵאָה צֹאן   a *hundred* sheep (1 Kgs 5.3)

אֶלֶף פְּעָמִים   a *thousand* times (Deut. 1.11)

אֶלֶף גֶּפֶן   a *thousand* vines (Isa. 7.23)

b. The cardinal 100 *in the status constructus can also stand before a noun in the status absolutus.* The rules for congruency in gender between the numeral and the noun (as set out above) still apply.

בֶּן־מְאַת שָׁנָה   a *hundred* years old (Gen. 11.10)

Note the following:

(1) With numerals having a semantic value greater than 1 the noun is usually in the plural. The collective use of nouns with numerals is, however, common—especially with words such as שֶׁקֶל, זָהָב, לֶחֶם, בָּקָר, עִיר, יוֹם, חֹדֶשׁ, שָׁנָה, נֶפֶשׁ, אִישׁ and אַמָּה. There are thus several examples of nouns in the singular with numerals greater than 1. Compare also the following two cases:

שְׁלֹשׁ־עֶשְׂרֵה עָרִים   *thirteen* cities (Josh. 21.19)

שְׁלֹשׁ־עֶשְׂרֵה עִיר   *thirteen* cities (Josh. 21.33)

(2) In constructions including numeral the noun is usually indefinite, although there are exceptions.

שְׁלֹשׁ־מֵאוֹת הַשּׁוֹפָרוֹת	the *three hundred* trumpets (Judg. 7.22)
וַחֲמֵשׁ עָשָׂר בָּנָיו	his *fifteen* sons (2 Sam. 19.18)

(3)   With compound numbers the noun is often *repeated*.

שְׁתַּיִם וְשִׁשִּׁים שָׁנָה וּמְאַת שָׁנָה	hundred and sixty-two years (Gen. 5.18)
שְׁתַּיִם וּשְׁמוֹנִים שָׁנָה וּשְׁבַע מֵאוֹת שָׁנָה	seven hundred and eight-two years (Gen. 5.26)

3. *Semantic function of the cardinals*
Cardinals can fulfil various semantic functions.

(i) The most common use is indicating *a specific number or quantity*.

שִׁבְעַת בָּנָיו	his *seven* sons (1 Sam. 16.10)
אַרְבָּעָה מְלָכִים אֶת־הַחֲמִשָּׁה	*four* kings against *five* (Gen. 14.9)

(ii) The numeral אֶחָד is often used to mark an indefinite noun as *a certain specific someone/something*. (Cf. §24.4.)

אִישׁ אֶחָד מִן־הָרָמָתַיִם	*a certain* man of Ramathaim (1 Sam. 1.1)

(iii) Cardinals are often used to *express priority*.
In the case of numerals greater than 10 priority can only be expressed by means of the cardinals as BH does not have separate ordinals for these numbers. If cardinals are used to express priority, they precede the noun. The numeral אֶחָד is an exception to this rule as it can stand in an attributive relationship to the noun.

הַטּוּר הָאֶחָד	the *first* row (Exod. 39.10)
וַיְהִי בְּאַרְבָּעִים שָׁנָה בְּעַשְׁתֵּי־עָשָׂר חֹדֶשׁ בְּאֶחָד לַחֹדֶשׁ	in the fortieth year, on the *first* day of the eleventh month [lit. in the eleventh month on the first day] (Deut. 1.3)

(iv) Cardinals are often used to *express multiples*—whether with the ordinary form of the numeral, or through a form of the numeral that looks like a dual.

פַּעַם וּשְׁתָּיִם	once or *twice* (Neh. 13.20)
וְאֶת־הַכִּבְשָׂה יְשַׁלֵּם אַרְבַּעְתָּיִם	And he shall restore the lamb *four-fold* (2 Sam. 12.6).

(v) Cardinals are also used to express *distribution* by means of the following constructions (Cf. §24.3/2(iv) and §29.3/(viii).):

a. *repetition* of the numeral (and the noun)

שְׁנַיִם שְׁנַיִם   *two by two* (Gen. 7.9)

b. by joining two numerals *with the conjunction* וֹ (Cf. §24.3/2(iv).)

וְאֶצְבְּעֹת יָדָיו וְאֶצְבְּעֹת רַגְלָיו   *six* fingers on *each* hand, and *six* toes
שֵׁשׁ וָשֵׁשׁ   on *each* foot (2 Sam. 21.20)

c. or with the *preposition* לְ (Cf. §39.11/4.)

אַחַת לְשָׁלֹשׁ שָׁנִים   *once every three* years (1 Kgs 10.22)

§37.3. *Ordinals*

1. *Form of the ordinals*

Only the first ten numbers have separate forms for ordinals. Except for the ordinal 'first' all the other ordinals end in characteristically masculine and feminine forms.

	Masculine	*Feminine*
first	רִאשׁוֹן	רִאשׁוֹנָה
second	שֵׁנִי	שֵׁנִית
third	שְׁלִישִׁי	שְׁלִישִׁית
fourth	רְבִיעִי	רְבִיעִית
fifth	חֲמִישִׁי	חֲמִישִׁית
sixth	שִׁשִּׁי	שִׁשִּׁית
seventh	שְׁבִיעִי	שְׁבִיעִית
eighth	שְׁמִינִי	שְׁמִינִית
ninth	תְּשִׁיעִי	תְּשִׁיעִית
tenth	עֲשִׂירִי	עֲשִׂירִית

2. *Syntax of the ordinals*

Ordinals act as attributive adjectives. They follow the noun and agree with it in gender and definiteness.

בַּשָּׁנָה הַתְּשִׁיעִית בַּחֹדֶשׁ הָעֲשִׂירִי   In the *ninth* year, in the *tenth* month
(Ezek. 24.1)

3. *Semantics of the ordinals*

Ordinals always express sequence or priority.

Chapter 6

THE OTHER WORD CLASSES

§38. Introduction

Apart from nominals and verbs traditional grammars also distinguish a third main word class, namely particles. Particles represent a class of words with diverse features. Most *traditional grammars* distinguish the following particles:

- prepositions,
- conjunctions,
- adverbs and
- interjections.

Since prepositions form a clearly determined class and are considered as a distinct word class, this grammar would rather refer to 'other word classes' than to particles. The *other word classes* include the following:

- prepositions
- conjunctions
- adverbs
- predicators of existence (existential words)
- interrogatives
- discourse markers
- interjections

For the purposes of this grammar the application of semantic and pragmatic criteria in distinguishing the different classes is useful. The different classes then provide the reader with a clear indication of the type of function that can be fulfilled by lexemes that belong to a certain class. The term 'function' is used here in preference to 'meaning' because the latter term suggests a specific lexical meaning. The lexical meaning of most particles is usually very generic (general) and can be used by speakers to fulfil a variety of semantic or pragmatic functions.

§39. Prepositions

§39.1. *Introduction*

1. *Morphology: prepositions plus pronominal suffixes*

When BH employs a pronoun in a prepositional phrase, e.g. to *you*, under *her*, then the pronoun is affixed to the preposition as a pronominal suffix. This may be accomplished by the addition of the suffixes that are normally attached either to singular or to plural nouns. The following classes are distinguished on the basis of the suffixes and the morphological patterns of the prepositions + suffixes:

(i) Prepositions with the pronominal suffixes of *singular* nouns:

a. The prepositions בְּ, לְ, כְּ, אֵת, עִם, אֵצֶל, נֶגֶד and בַּעַד decline with the suffixes attached to singular nouns.

Person	Singular		Plural	
1 m./f.	לִי	to me	לָנוּ	to us
2 m.	לְךָ	to you	לָכֶם	to you
2 f.	לָךְ	to you	לָכֶן	to you
3 m.	לוֹ	to him	לָהֶם	to them
3 f.	לָהּ	to her	לָהֶן	to them

b. Before the suffixes the prepositions כְּ, אֵת and עִם become כְּמוֹ-, אֵת- and עִמָּ- respectively.

c. In certain cases the linking vowel between the preposition and the suffixes is a qāmeṣ, e.g. לָכֶם as opposed to אֶתְכֶם.

d. The bisyllabic prepositions such as אֵצֶל and נֶגֶד do not decline exactly like segholate nouns with / ֶ / as stem vowel, for example, נֶגְדִּי. (Cf. §27.3.) However, בַּעַד declines like a segholate noun with / ֶ / as stem vowel (i.e. an a-stem) and a guttural as middle consonant. (Cf. §27.3/6, Table 31.)

(ii) Prepositions with the pronominal suffixes of *plural* nouns

The prepositions אֶל, עַל, עַד, תַּחַת, אַחַר and סָבִיב decline with the suffixes attached to plural nouns.

Person	Singular		Plural	
1 m./f.	אֵלַי	to me	אֵלֵינוּ	to us
2 m.	אֵלֶיךָ	to you	אֲלֵיכֶם	to you
2 f.	אֵלַיִךְ	to you	אֲלֵיכֶן	to you
3 m.	אֵלָיו	to him	אֲלֵיהֶם	to you
3 f.	אֵלֶיהָ	to her	אֲלֵיהֶן	to you

a. Before the suffixes the above prepositions become אֶל-, עַל- and עַד- respectively.

b. Before the suffixes, תַּחַת and אַחַר react like segholate words with a / ִ / as stem vowel and a guttural as middle consonant, for example, אַחֲרֵי. (Cf. §27.3/6, table 31.) In some cases the šᵉwâ under the guttural is not replaced by a ḥāṭēp vowel, e.g. תַּחְתִּי.

c. סָבִיב reacts like a noun with a variable vowel in the first syllable, e.g. סְבִיבַי. (Cf. §27.2/3, Table 23a.)

(iii) *The preposition בֵּין with pronominal suffixes*

The preposition בֵּין has a variable declension pattern in that it utilizes the suffixes of both singular and the plural nouns, e.g. בֵּינִי and בֵּינָיו.

(iv) *The preposition מִן with pronominal suffixes*

The preposition מִן declines with the suffixes affixed to singular nouns.

Person	Singular		Plural	
1 m./f.	מִמֶּנִּי	from me	מִמֶּנּוּ	from us
2 m.	מִמְּךָ	from you	מִכֶּם	from you
2 f.	מִמֵּךְ	from you	מִכֶּן	from you
3 m.	מִמֶּנּוּ	from him	מֵהֶם	from them
3 f.	מִמֶּנָּה	from her	מֵהֶן	from them

2. *Morphology: prepositions prefixed to other words*

(i) The prepositions בְּ, לְ and כְּ are *joined directly* to the subsequent word.

a. If the word begins with י, the two audible šᵉwâs combine to form בִּי, כִּי or לִי. (Cf. §8.1/1.)

בִּיהוּדָה   =   בְּ   plus   יְהוּדָה

b. If the word begins with any consonant other than י which is followed by a šᵉwâ, the two audible šᵉwâs combine to form a single closed syllable. (Cf. §8.1/1.)

כִּשְׁמוּאֵל   =   כְּ   plus   שְׁמוּאֵל

c. If the noun begins with a guttural, which is followed by a ḥāṭēp vowel, the preposition takes the corresponding full vowel. (Cf. §8.1/1.)

בַּחֲלוֹם   =   בְּ   plus   חֲלוֹם

d. The prepositions לְ and בְּ are sometimes vocalized with a / ַ /. This happens especially with words in which the first syllable is accented:

לָתֵת   =   לְ   plus   תֵת
בָּזֶה   =   בְּ   plus   זֶה
לָבֶטַח   =   לְ   plus   בֶטַח

(ii) If a *definite* article is prefixed to the noun, *the preposition and the article combine.* (Cf. §24.4/2.)

הַ = לַ (not לְהַ)   plus   לְ

(iii) *The preposition* מִן may be attached directly to or written apart from the subsequent word. If it is attached directly to the subsequent word, the following rules apply:

a. The nun assimilates with the first consonant of the subsequent word. (Cf. §4.2/4(ii).) This consonant then doubles accordingly:

מִמֶּלֶךְ   =   מִן   plus   מֶלֶךְ

b. If מִן is attached to a word beginning with a guttural or resh, the guttural cannot double. Compensatory lengthening then occurs. The / ִ / of מִן changes to / ֵ / (cf. §8.2/2):

מֵעִיר   =   מִן   plus   עִיר

c. If מִן is attached to a word beginning with a י, then מִן and י combine to form מִי:

מִיהוּדָה = מִן plus יְהוּדָה

3. *Syntax*

Prepositional phrases may be used in several syntactic positions. (Cf. §32.2.)

(i) Prepositional phrases may function as *predicates* of nominal clauses.

אֲרִי בֵּין הָרְחֹבוֹת	There is a lion *in (between)* the streets (Prov. 26.13).

(ii) Prepositional phrases can function as *complements*. (Cf. §32.2.)

a. As *direct objects* (prepositional objects).
The prepositions לְ, אֶל־ and בְּ can mark the direct object.

וַיִּבְחַר בָּכֶם	He chose *you* (Deut. 7.7).

b. As *indirect objects*
The prepositions לְ, אֶל־, אֶת, עַל can mark the indirect object.

לְזַרְעֲךָ אֶתֵּן אֶת־הָאָרֶץ הַזֹּאת	*To your descendants* I will give this land (Gen. 12.7).

c. As *complements of prepositional verbs*

וְהוּא נִלְחַם בְּמֶלֶךְ מוֹאָב הָרִאשׁוֹן	And he fought against the former king of Moab (Num. 21.26).

(iii) Prepositional phrases can function as *adjuncts*. (Cf. §32.2.)

a. As *optional adverbial modifier*

וַיִּזְבַּח יַעֲקֹב זֶבַח בָּהָר	And Jacob offered a sacrifice *on the mountain* (Gen. 31.54).

b. As *agents of a passive verb*. This can be marked by בְּ, לְ, מִן.

שֹׁפֵךְ דַּם הָאָדָם בָּאָדָם דָּמוֹ יִשָּׁפֵךְ	Whoever sheds the blood of man—*by man* shall his blood be shed (Gen. 9.6).

(iv) Prepositional phrases can function as *adjectival qualifications*.

אִישׁ מִבֵּית לֶחֶם יְהוּדָה	a certain man *of Bethlehem, Judah* (Ruth 1.1)

4. *Semantics*

Not all languages have prepositions like BH. The semantic relationships that are expressed by prepositions in BH are expressed by other means in other languages, e.g. Xhosa. In BH the semantic relationship indicated by אֶל can also be expressed by the so-called *he locale*. (Cf. §28.)

הַשְׁלִיכוּ אֹתוֹ אֶל־הַבּוֹר הַזֶּה	Cast him *into this pit* (Gen. 37.22).
וַיַּשְׁלִכוּ אֹתוֹ הַבֹּרָה	And they cast him *into the pit* (Gen. 37.24).

BH prepositions have the following semantic features:

(i) The relationships expressed by BH prepositions are limited. They usually express *spatial* relationships. Most of these could also apply to *temporal* relationships.

(ii) Three *degrees of semantic specialization* can be distinguished (Jenni 1992: 18):

a. Very general, e.g.

בְּ, לְ and כְּ.

b. Less general with (especially spatial) oppositional pairs. e.g.

עַל	on	תַּחַת	under
לִפְנֵי	before	אַחֲרֵי	after/behind
מִן	from	אֶל	to

c. More specialized

עַד	until
אֵצֶל	next to

Compound prepositions consisting of more than one preposition are also usually more specialized, e.g.

מִמַּעַל לְ   at the top of

Note the following:

(1) The predominantly semantic description of the prepositions offered here is in no way complete. It should cover about 80% of the cases in the Hebrew Bible. A dictionary should be used in conjunction with this grammar.[53]

(2) Some semantic functions that are attributed to prepositions are largely due to the verbs that govern those prepositions.

---

53. The works by Jenni (1992 and 1994) are a very useful source of information on the less specialized prepositions such as בְּ, לְ and כְּ.

This feature of some prepositions has not been dealt with systematically.

§39.2. אַחַר *and* אַחֲרֵי

1. *Indicate spatial positioning (= localization)*
The translation of the spacial equivalent of the preposition אַחֲרֵי is '*behind* or *after* x'. It usually stands in opposition to לִפְנֵי ('*before* x').

a. Locative: *behind*

הִנֵּה־זֶה עוֹמֵד אַחַר כָּתְלֵנוּ׃   Behold, there he stands *behind* our wall (Song 2.9).

b. Metaphoric locative: *after*

וַיֵּלֶךְ אַחַר חַטֹּאת יָרָבְעָם   And followed *(after)* the sins of Jeroboam (2 Kgs 13.2).

c. Localize a specific direction: *western side* (rare)
BH speakers sometimes express direction by referring to persons' left or right side, or back or front as reference to the four wind directions. The 'persons' concerned are facing east. Their backs thus face west and their left indicates north.

וַיִּנְהַג אֶת־הַצֹּאן אַחַר הַמִּדְבָּר   And he led his flock *to the west side* of the wilderness (Exod. 3.1).

2. *Indicate temporal positioning: after*

אַחַר הַדְּבָרִים הָאֵלֶּה   *After these things* the word of the
הָיָה דְבַר־יְהוָה אֶל־אַבְרָם   Lord came to Abram (Gen. 15.1).

§39.3. אֶל

1. *Localizes the goal of a movement or process (usually with reference to a specific person or place).*[54]
The translation of the spacial equivalent of the preposition אֶל is '*to* x'. It usually stands in opposition to מִן '*from* x'.

a. Goal of some type of movement: *to, within*

וַתָּשָׁב אֵלָיו אֶל־הַתֵּבָה   And she returned *to* him to the ark (Gen. 8.9).

---

54. For a discussion of the difference between אֶל and לְ, cf. Jenni 1992: 21-24.

b. Goal of movement in a metaphorical sense

לִהְיוֹת עֵינֶךָ פְתֻחוֹת
אֶל־הַבַּיִת הַזֶּה

that your eyes may be open *toward* this house (1 Kgs 8.29).

c. Goal of a giving process: *for, to*

וְנָתַן אֵלֶיךָ אוֹת

and gives *to* you a sign (Deut. 13.2).

d. Goal of a saying process: *to*

וְרִבְקָה אָמְרָה אֶל־יַעֲקֹב בְּנָהּ

Then Rebekah said *to* her son Jacob (Gen. 27.6).

e. Goal of an emotional process: *against*

לִסְפּוֹת עוֹד עַל חֲרוֹן
אַף־יְהוָה אֶל־יִשְׂרָאֵל

to increase still more the fierce anger of the Lord *against* Israel (Num. 32.14).

2. Indicates the *joining together of entities (comitative)* (rare)

(i) Indicates *accompaniment: together with*

וְלֹא־חָטְאוּ לַיהוָה לֶאֱכֹל
אֶל־הַדָּם

And do not sin against the Lord by eating (it) *with* the blood. (1 Sam. 14.34).

(ii) Indicates *addition to: to, with*

הוֹסַפְתָּ חָכְמָה וָטוֹב
אֶל־הַשְּׁמוּעָה אֲשֶׁר שָׁמָעְתִּי

Your wisdom and prosperity surpass the report which I have heard [lit. you have added wisdom and prosperity *to* the report which I have heard] (1 Kgs 10.7).

3. *Indicates spatial positioning: at* (rare)

וַיִּשְׁחָטוּהוּ אֶל־מַעְבְּרוֹת הַיַּרְדֵּן

And slew him *at* the fords of the Jordan (Judg. 12.6).

4. *Gives the ground (motivational reason) upon which a certain process is based (like עַל)*

כִּי־הִתְאַבֵּל שְׁמוּאֵל אֶל־שָׁאוּל

but Samuel grieved *over* Saul (1 Sam. 15.35).

§39.4. אֵצֶל

Indicates *spatial positioning: beside*
The translation of the spatial equivalent of the preposition אֵצֶל is
'beside x'.

<table>
<tr><td>וְשָׂמוֹ אֵצֶל הַמִּזְבֵּחַ:</td><td>And put them *beside* the altar (Lev. 6.3).</td></tr>
</table>

§39.5. אֵת

1. *Indicates spatial positioning: proximity to something else*
The translation of the spacial equivalent of the preposition אֵת is
'with' or '*together with* x'.

(i) Indicates *accompaniment*

<table>
<tr><td>וְאַתָּה וּבָנֶיךָ אִתָּךְ</td><td>And you and your sons *with* you (Num. 18.2)</td></tr>
</table>

The 'accompaniment' sometimes has the connotation of *besides* x or
alongside x.

<table>
<tr><td>לֹא תַעֲשׂוּן אִתִּי אֱלֹהֵי כֶסֶף</td><td>You shall not make *alongside* me gods of silver (Exod. 20.23).</td></tr>
</table>

(ii) Indicates *localization: proximity, nearness*

<table>
<tr><td>וְהוּא שָׁב מִן־הַפְּסִילִים אֲשֶׁר אֶת־הַגִּלְגָּל</td><td>But he himself turned back at the sculptured stones *near* Gilgal (Judg. 3.19).</td></tr>
</table>

(iii) Indicates *possession*

<table>
<tr><td>מָה אִתָּנוּ</td><td>What have we? [lit. What is *with* us?] (1 Sam. 9.7).</td></tr>
</table>

2. *Occurs after verbs that refer to processes during which people are
dealt with*

<table>
<tr><td>כְּכֹל אֲשֶׁר עָשָׂה אִתְּכֶם בְּמִצְרַיִם לְעֵינֵיכֶם</td><td>Just as he did *for* you in Egypt before your eyes (Deut. 1.30).</td></tr>
<tr><td>דִּבֶּר הָאִישׁ ... אִתָּנוּ קָשׁוֹת</td><td>The man ... spoke roughly *to* us (Gen. 42.30).</td></tr>
</table>

§39.6. בְּ

Approximately 60% of the cases where this preposition is used in the
Hebrew Bible have a locative connotation while 15% have a tempo-

ral connotation. The examples below, however, attest to the fact that בְּ in BH has a more general meaning than '*in*' or '*within*'. It is a preposition that is not very specialized semantically. (Cf. Jenni 1992 for further details.)

1. *Indicates localization*
The translation of the spacial equivalent of the preposition בְּ is more or less '*in* x'.

(i) Indicates *spatial localization*—the so-called *beth locale*

a. *In* or *at* a place

וּשְׁמוּאֵל שֹׁכֵב בְּהֵיכַל יְהוָה

And Samuel was lying down *in* the temple of the Lord (1 Sam. 3.3).

b. *On* a place

וַיִּזְבַּח יַעֲקֹב זֶבַח בָּהָר

And Jacob offered a sacrifice *on* the mountain (Gen. 31.54).

c. *Within* a spatial area

וְאָכַלְתָּ בָשָׂר ... בְּכָל־שְׁעָרֶיךָ

And you may eat flesh ... *in* any of your towns (Deut. 12.15).

d. Indicates the *route* of a verb of movement: *through*

וַיַּעֲבֹר בְּאֶרֶץ־שָׁלִשָׁה
וְלֹא מָצָאוּ

And they [uncommon singular] passed *through* the land of Shalishah, but they did not find them (1 Sam. 9.4).

(ii) Indicates *localization within a group*

אוֹדְךָ בָעַמִּים אֲדֹנָי

I will praise you, O Lord, *among* the nations (Ps. 57.10).

(iii) Localizes through: *indicating contact with an x*

a. Material contact: *person or thing*

אַל־תְּהִי יָדִי בּוֹ
וּתְהִי־בוֹ יַד־פְּלִשְׁתִּים

Let not my hand be *upon* him, but let the hand of the Philistines be *upon* him (1 Sam. 18.17).

b. *Social contact (often with verbs of 'ruling')*

אִם־מָשׁוֹל תִּמְשֹׁל בָּנוּ

Or are you indeed to have dominion *over* us? (Gen. 37.8).

c. *Spiritual contact*

וְגַם־בְּךָ יַאֲמִינוּ לְעוֹלָם   And may they also believe *in* you for ever (Exod. 19.9).

d. Contact with *part of a whole–partitive* (rare)

וְנָשְׂאוּ אִתְּךָ בְּמַשָּׂא הָעָם   And they will help you to bear [*some of*] the burden of the people (Num. 11.17).

2. *Indicates a temporal frame*

Indicates a time frame in which an event or state of affairs needs to be positioned: *in*

וּדְבַר־יְהוָה הָיָה יָקָר בַּיָּמִים הָהֵם   And the word of the Lord was rare *in* those days (1 Sam. 3.1).

The preposition בְּ + infinitive construct often refers to events that provide the temporal frame of an event or events referred to in a subsequent sentence. (Compare in contrast the preposition כְּ + infinitive construct in §39.10/2.)

בְּלֶכְתְּךָ הַיּוֹם מֵעִמָּדִי ...   *When you depart from me today* you will meet two men ... (1 Sam. 10.2).
וּמָצָאתָ שְׁנֵי אֲנָשִׁים ...

3. Realizes an action by indicating one of the following:

(i) *Instrument*—the so-called *beth instrumenti*
a. *Non-human* instrument

בַּשֵּׁבֶט יַכּוּ עַל־הַלְּחִי   *With* a rod they strike upon the cheek
אֵת שֹׁפֵט יִשְׂרָאֵל: the ruler of Israel (Mic. 4.14).

b. Human instrument or *agent*

שֹׁפֵךְ דַּם הָאָדָם   Whoever sheds the blood of man,
בָּאָדָם דָּמוֹ יִשָּׁפֵךְ   *by* man shall his blood be shed (Gen. 9.6).

(ii) *Price*—the so-called *beth pretii*

תְּנָה־לִּי אֶת־כַּרְמְךָ בְּכֶסֶף   Give me your vineyard *for* money (1 Kgs 21.6).

(iii) *Joining together (comitative)*—the so-called *beth comitantiae*

וַתָּבֹא יְרוּשָׁלַ͏ְמָה   And she came to Jerusalem *with* a
בְּחַיִל כָּבֵד מְאֹד   very great retinue (1 Kgs 10.2).

(iv) *Cause*—the so-called *beth causa*

וְשָׂמַחְתָּ בְכָל־הַטּוֹב אֲשֶׁר נָתַן־לְךָ
יְהוָה אֱלֹהֶיךָ

And you shall rejoice *in* (or: *because of*) all the good which the Lord your God has given to you (Deut. 26.11).

כִּי כַפֵּיכֶם נְגֹאֲלוּ בַדָּם

For your hands are defiled *with* blood (Isa. 59.3).

(v) *Manner* (rare)

בֹּכִים בְּקוֹל גָּדוֹל

(They) wept aloud [lit. with a large voice] (Ezra 3.12).

§39.7. בֵּין

I. בֵּין

The translation of the spatial equivalent of the preposition בֵּין is '*between* x'.

Indicates *localization in a space: between two or more points*

וְהִנֵּה תַנּוּר עָשָׁן וְלַפִּיד אֵשׁ אֲשֶׁר
עָבַר בֵּין הַגְּזָרִים הָאֵלֶּה

And behold, a smoking fire pot and a flaming torch passed *between* these pieces (Gen. 15.17).

II. בֵּין ... בֵּין

1. *Indicates localization in a space: between two or more points*

בֵּין בֵּית־אֵל וּבֵין הָעָי

between Bethel and Ai (Gen. 13.3)

2. *Distinguishes different parties that are each actively involved in a process*

בְּרִית בֵּינִי וּבֵינֶךָ בֵּין אָבִי
וּבֵין אָבִיךָ

a covenant *between* me *and* you, as *between* my father *and* your father (1 Kgs 15.19)

III. בֵּין ...לְ

Distinguishes different objects

וְהִבְדַּלְתֶּם בֵּין־הַבְּהֵמָה הַטְּהֹרָה
לַטְּמֵאָה

You shall therefore make a distinction *between* the clean beast *and* the unclean (Lev. 20.25).

§39.8. בְּעַד

1. *Indicates localization*

(i) After verbs that refer to a *process of closure*

וַיִּסְגְּרוּ בַּעֲדָם And shut themselves *in* (Judg. 9.51).

Sometimes the reference is metaphorical.

כִּי־סָגַר יְהוָה בְּעַד רַחְמָהּ because the Lord had closed her womb (1 Sam. 1.6).

(ii) After verbs that refer to *movement through an opening: through*

וַתּוֹרִדֵם בַּחֶבֶל בְּעַד הַחַלּוֹן And she let them down by a rope *through* the window (Josh. 2.15).

2. *Indicates benefit to: for the sake of, for (after verbs of supplication).*

כִּי־נָבִיא הוּא וְיִתְפַּלֵּל בַּעַדְךָ For he is a prophet, and he will pray *for* you (Gen. 20.7).

§39.9. בַּעֲבוּר

1. *Indicates grounds (motive)*

אֲרוּרָה הָאֲדָמָה בַּעֲבוּרֶךָ Cursed is the ground *because of* you (Gen. 3.17).

2. *Indicates purpose: in order to*

(i) As a *preposition*

הֲלוֹא בַּעֲבוּר חֲקוֹר
אֶת־הָעִיר וּלְרַגְּלָהּ וּלְהָפְכָהּ
שָׁלַח דָּוִד אֶת־עֲבָדָיו אֵלֶיךָ Has not David sent his servants to you *to* search the city, and to spy it out, and to overthrow it? (2 Sam. 10.3).

(ii) Also functions as *conjunction* (Cf. §40.7.)

§39.10. כְּ

The preposition כְּ indicates agreement and has no spatial connotation.

1. *Indicates general agreement with respect to the following categories:*
(i) *Sort or type*

וִהְיִיתֶם כֵּאלֹהִים יֹדְעֵי טוֹב וָרָע And you will be *like* God, knowing good and evil (Gen. 3.5).

(ii) *Manner or norm*

חָנֵּנִי אֱלֹהִים כְּחַסְדֶּךָ	Have mercy on me, O God, *according to* your steadfast love (Ps. 51.3).

(iii) *Quantity*

וְהֵמָּה כִּשְׁלֹשִׁים אִישׁ	They were *about* thirty persons (1 Sam. 9.22).

2. *Indicates corresponding or precise agreement.*
The preposition is often repeated before the corresponding entities in order to indicate precise agreement.

מוֹת יוּמָת ... כַּגֵּר כָּאֶזְרָח	He shall be put to death; the sojourner *as well* the citizen ... (Lev. 24.16).

3. *Indicates a precise point on the time-line (temporal use)*
כְּ + infinitive construct is used to indicate that an event referred to in the main clause following the temporal clause with the כְּ + infinitive construct, *immediately follows it in time*. This use of כְּ + infinitive construct can be compared with בְּ+ infinitive construct that provides the temporal frame of a subsequent event. (Cf. 39.6/2.)

וַיְהִי כְּהַזְכִּירוֹ אֶת־אֲרוֹן הָאֱלֹהִים וַיִּפֹּל מֵעַל־הַכִּסֵּא	*The moment that he mentioned the ark of God*, Eli fell ... from his seat (1 Sam. 4.18).

§39.11. לְ

The preposition לְ has a very unspecialized meaning. It is a preposition that indicates a very general relationship between two entities that can at best be described as 'x *as far as* y *is concerned*'.

Syntactically a distinction is drawn between לְ plus nouns or pronouns and לְ plus infinitive contruct forms.

לְ thus does not necessarily have a spatial function expressing 'to'. This function is used metaphorically so often that לְ has virtually lost its original meaning. The wide variety of relations in which לְ is used is evidence of this. It is also typical that a preposition with such unspecialized content is used to mark relationships that are indicated in other languages by case markers/indicators. In BH לְ is used especially to characterize relationships that are marked by the dative form in Latin and Greek. It is only in Late BH, under the influence of

Aramaic, that אֶל was supplanted by לְ and עַל as the spatial locative 'to'.

I. לְ *plus nouns or pronouns*

1. *Indicates the goal of a process*

The following distinctions can be made on the basis of the process being referred to:

a. Indicates the goal of a process of *movement towards*: *to*

וַיָּשָׁב לִמְקֹמוֹ וְגַם־בָּלָק
הָלַךְ לְדַרְכּוֹ

And he went back *to* his place; and Balak also went his way (Num. 24.25).

b. Indicates the goal of a process where something has been *transferred to*

אֶת־הַמָּנָה אֲשֶׁר נָתַתִּי לָךְ

the portion I gave *to* you (1 Sam. 9.23)

c. Indicates the goal of a process during which a *new role* has been given to an entity (The opposite of מִן.) (Cf. §39.14/3.)

וַיִּתֶּן־לוֹ אֶת־רָחֵל בִּתּוֹ
לוֹ לְאִשָּׁה

Then he gave him his daughter Rachel *as* wife (Gen. 29.28).

d. Indicates the destination of a process of *saying*

אוּלַי יַגִּיד לָנוּ

Perhaps he can tell [*for*] us (1 Sam. 9.6).

e. Indicates the direction of an emotional process

כִּי־נִכְסֹף נִכְסַפְתָּה לְבֵית
אָבִיךָ

because you longed greatly *for* your father's house (Gen. 31.30).

f. Indicates the terminal point in time of a process

וְלֹא־יָלִין מִן־הַבָּשָׂר
... לַבֹּקֶר

Nor shall any of the flesh be kept overnight ... *until* the morning (Deut. 16.4).

2. *Indicates specification*

The following things are specified:

(i) *Topic* of an expression

וְלָאֲתֹנוֹת הָאֹבְדוֹת לְךָ הַיּוֹם
שְׁלֹשֶׁת הַיָּמִים
אַל־תָּשֶׂם אֶת־לִבְּךָ לָהֶם

As for your asses that were lost three days ago, do not set your mind on them (1 Sam. 9.20).

לֹא־רָאִיתִי כָהֵנָּה בְּכָל־אֶרֶץ מִצְרַיִם לָרֹעַ	Such as I had never seen in all the land of Egypt, *concerning* their ugliness (Gen. 41.19).
אִמְרִי־לִי אָחִי הוּא	Say *of* me: He is my brother (Gen. 20.13).

(ii) *Norm*

וְעַתָּה הִתְיַצְּבוּ לִפְנֵי יְהוָה לְשִׁבְטֵיכֶם	Now therefore present yourselves before the Lord *according to* your tribes (1 Sam. 10.19).

(iii) *Detail*

עַל־כָּל־הָאָרֶץ לְמַלְכֵי יְהוּדָה לְשָׂרֶיהָ לְכֹהֲנֶיהָ וּלְעַם הָאָרֶץ	against the whole land, *against* the kings of Judah, *against* its princes, *against* its priests, and *against* the people of the land (Jer. 1.18)

3. *Indicates the possessor in a relationship of possession*

a. In a *phrase* (Cf. §25.3.)

וַתֹּאבַדְנָה הָאֲתֹנוֹת לְקִישׁ אֲבִי שָׁאוּל ...	When the asses *of* Kish, Saul's father, were lost ... (1 Sam. 9.3).

b. In a *clause*

כַּסְפְּךָ וּזְהָבְךָ לִי־הוּא	Your silver and your gold are mine [lit. *to* me it is] (1 Kgs 20.3).

4. *Indicates the greater whole in terms of which a distribution occurs*

אַחַת לְשָׁלֹשׁ שָׁנִים תָּבוֹא אֳנִי תַרְשִׁישׁ	Once *every three years* the fleet of ships of Tarshish used to come (1 Kgs 10.22).
אִישׁ אֶחָד לְמַטֶּה אֲבֹתָיו תִּשְׁלָחוּ	*From each* tribe of their fathers shall you send a man (Num. 13.2).

5. *Indicates the semantic roles of an expression*

(i) The *agent* of a passive verb

הֲלוֹא נָכְרִיּוֹת נֶחְשַׁבְנוּ לוֹ	Are we not regarded *by* him as foreigners? (Gen. 31.15).

(ii) The *patient* of an active verb

לְשַׁחֵת לָעִיר בַּעֲבוּרִי	to destroy *the city* on my account (1 Sam. 23.10).

(iii) The *reflexive element of an agent* (the so-called ethical dative or *dativus ethicus*)

פְּנוּ וּלְכוּ לָכֶם לְאָהֳלֵיכֶם

Turn and go (*yourselves*) to your tents (Josh. 22.4).

II. לְ *plus infinitive*

Should לְ precede an infinitive, it often bears the connotation of *purpose*. (Cf. §20.1.)

§39.12. לְמַעַן

1. *Indicates purpose: for the sake of, so that*

(i) As *preposition*

וְאוֹתָנוּ הוֹצִיא מִשָּׁם
לְמַעַן הָבִיא אֹתָנוּ לָתֶת לָנוּ
אֶת־הָאָרֶץ אֲשֶׁר נִשְׁבַּע לַאֲבֹתֵינוּ

He brought us out from there, *so that* he might bring us in and give us the land which he swore to give our ancestors (Deut. 6.23).

(ii) Also as *conjunction* (Cf. §40.13.)

2. *Indicates consequence—usually as conjunction (Cf. §40.13.)*

§39.13. לִפְנֵי

1. *Indicates spatial positioning*

The translation of the spacial equivalent of the preposition לִפְנֵי is '*before* x'. It often stands in opposition to אַחֲרֵי '*after/behind* x'. The preposition נֶגֶד is sometimes used as an alternative for לִפְנֵי.

וַיִּשְׁתַּחוּ אַבְרָהָם
לִפְנֵי עַם־הָאָרֶץ

Then Abraham bowed down *before* the people of the land (Gen. 23.12).

2. *Indicates temporal positioning*

וְאֹכֵלָה וַאֲבָרֶכְכָה לִפְנֵי יְהוָה
לִפְנֵי מוֹתִי

that I may eat it, and bless you before the Lord *before* I die (Gen. 27.7).

§39.14. מִן

1. *Indicates spatial positioning: source*

The basic spatial function of the preposition מִן is movement '*away from* x'. It usually stands in opposition to אֶל '*to* x'.

a. *Place from where* an action is undertaken

| וַיַּעֲלוּ מִשָּׁם | And they have gone up *from* there (1 Kgs 1.45). |

b. *Person from whom* something has come

| כִּי מֵיהוָה הָיְתָה לֹּו | For it came to him *from* the Lord [lit. For *from* the Lord it was for him] (1 Kgs 2.15). |

c. Sometimes a fixed expression is formed with לְ which is translated as: *at* the northern side of. Literally it means '*from* the north for'.

| וַיָּשִׂימוּ הָעָם אֶת־כָּל־הַמַּחֲנֶה אֲשֶׁר מִצְּפוֹן לָעִיר | So they stationed the forces, the main encampment which was north *of* the city (Josh. 8.13). |

2. *Indicates temporal positioning: a point in time since when something happened*

| מִיּוֹם דַּעְתִּי אֶתְכֶם | *From* the day that I knew you (Deut. 9.24). |

3. *Indicates alienation—a so-called privative*

a. Alienation of a role (opposite of לְ) (Cf. 39.11/1.)

| וַיִּמְאָסְךָ מִמֶּלֶךְ | He has rejected you *from* being king (1 Sam. 15.23). |

b. Alienation of a process (usually a threat)

| וְאֵין נִסְתָּר מֵחַמָּתוֹ | And there is nothing hid *from* its heat (Ps. 19.7). |

c. Alienation of an object

After verbs of fear or awe (usually before objects that pose some form of threat)

| וּמִמִּשְׁפָּטֶיךָ יָרֵאתִי | And I stand in awe *of* your decrees (Ps. 119.120). |

4. *Indicates material from which something is made*

| וַיִּצֶר יְהוָה אֱלֹהִים מִן־הָאֲדָמָה כָּל־חַיַּת הַשָּׂדֶה | So *out of* the ground the Lord God formed every beast of the field (Gen. 2.19). |

5. *Indicates cause of a situation*

לֹא מֵרֻבְּכֶם מִכָּל־הָעַמִּים חָשַׁק יְהוָה בָּכֶם	It was not *because* you were more in number than any other people that the Lord set his love upon you (Deut. 7.7).

6. *Indicates instrument*

a. Non-human *instrument*

וְלֹא־יִכָּרֵת כָּל־בָּשָׂר עוֹד מִמֵּי הַמַּבּוּל	All flesh shall not be cut off *by* the waters of a flood (Gen. 9.11).

b. Human instrument or *agent*

וְאִשָּׁה גְּרוּשָׁה מֵאִישָׁהּ לֹא יִקָּחוּ	Neither shall they marry a woman divorced *by* her husband (Lev. 21.7).

7. *Indicates part of a greater whole (partitive)*

יָצְאוּ מִן־הָעָם לִלְקֹט	*Some of the* people went out to gather (Exod. 16.27).
הַטּוֹב וְהַיָּשָׁר מִבְּנֵי אֲדֹנֵיכֶם	the best and fittest *of* your master's sons (2 Kgs 10.3)

8. *Indicates a comparison*

The adjective in BH does not have comparative and superlative forms. (Cf. §30.5.) The comparative degree is expressed by the preposition מִן. Stative verbs are often used in the place of adjectival nouns.

The following distinctions can be made with respect to comparisons:

(i) *Positive comparison (more than, greater than)*

חָכָם אַתָּה מִדָּנִאֵל	You are wiser *than* Daniel (Ezek. 28.3).

The *adjective* on which the comparative מִן is logically dependent is *sometimes omitted* and must then be assumed from the context.

יָשָׁר מִמְּסוּכָה	The best of them is worse *than* a briar (Mic. 7.4).

(ii) *Comparison of abilities*

הֲיִפָּלֵא מֵיהוָה דָּבָר	Is anything too hard *for* the Lord? (Gen. 18.14).

(iii) *Exclusive comparison*

צָדְקָה מִמֶּנִּי	She is more righteous *than* I (Gen. 38.26).

§39.15. מִפְּנֵי

1. *Indicates spatial positioning: away from someone's immediate presence*

The translation of the spacial equivalent of the compound preposition מִפְּנֵי is '*away from the immediate presence of* x'.

וַיִּסַּע עַמּוּד הֶעָנָן מִפְּנֵיהֶם	The pillar of cloud moved *from before* them (Exod. 14.19).

2. *Indicates a cause*

כִּי־מָלְאָה הָאָרֶץ חָמָס מִפְּנֵיהֶם	For the earth is filled with violence *through* them (Gen. 6.13).

3. *Indicates alienation*

After verbs of fear the object usually holds *an immediate* threat to the subject of the verb.

וַיִּרְאוּ מִפְּנֵי פְלִשְׁתִּים	They were afraid *of* the Philistines (1 Sam. 7.7).

§39.16. נֶגֶד

Indicates spatial positioning

The spatial translation equivalent of the preposition נֶגֶד is '*before or against* x'.

וַיִּחַן־שָׁם יִשְׂרָאֵל נֶגֶד הָהָר	And there Israel encamped *before* the mountain (Exod. 19.2).

§39.17. סָבִיב

Indicates spatial positioning

The translation of the spacial equivalent of the preposition סָבִיב is '*around* x'.

תִּהְיֶינָה הֶעָרִים הָאֵלֶּה עִיר עִיר וּמִגְרָשֶׁיהָ סְבִיבֹתֵיהָ	These cities had each its pasture lands *round* it (Josh. 21.42).

§39.18. עַד

1. *Indicates spatial positioning: Marks a point up to which a movement occurs*

The translation of the spacial equivalent of the preposition עַד is '*up to* x' (a so-called allative).

וַיָּבֹאוּ עַד־חָרָן

They came *to* Haran (Gen. 11.31).

2. *Indicates temporal positioning: a point in time up to which events occur*

שֵׁם־הָעִיר בְּאֵר שֶׁבַע עַד הַיּוֹם הַזֶּה

The name of the city is Beersheba *to* this day (Gen. 26.33).

3. *Indicates the extent of an event*

לֹא נִשְׁאַר עַד־אֶחָד

Not *even* a single man was left (Judg. 4.16).

4. *Indicates the goal of a process* (rare)

וְעָדֵיכֶם אֶתְבּוֹנָן

I gave *you* my attention (Job 32.12).

§39.19. עַל

1. *Indicates spatial positioning*

The translation of the spacial equivalent of the preposition עַל is '*on* x' or '*above* x'. It usually stands in opposition to תַּחַת '*under* x'. The following distinctions may be drawn:

(i) *Singular* locative: *on, on top of*

שְׁכַב עַל־מִשְׁכָּבְךָ

Lie down *on* your bed (2 Sam. 13.5).

(ii) *Comprehensive* locative: *above*

תְּנָה הוֹדְךָ עַל־הַשָּׁמָיִם

You have set your glory *above* the heavens (Ps. 8.2).

(iii) *Contingent* locative: *at, next to* (rare)

וּשְׁנֵיהֶם עָמְדוּ עַל־הַיַּרְדֵּן

And they both were standing *by* the Jordan (2 Kgs 2.7).

(iv) *Metaphorical locative*

וְיוֹאָב בֶּן־צְרוּיָה עַל־הַצָּבָא

And Joab the son of Zeruiah was *over* the army (2 Sam. 8.16).

וְעָלַי לָתֵת לְךָ עֲשָׂרָה כֶּסֶף

It was/would have been my responsibility [lit. *on* me it would have been to give ...] to give you ten pieces of silver (2 Sam. 18.11).

2. *Indicates the goal of a process* (rare)

עַל is in some of these cases a variant form of אֶל.

וַיִּקְצֹף פַּרְעֹה עַל שְׁנֵי סָרִיסָיו

And Pharaoh was angry *with* his two officers (Gen. 40.2).

3. *Indicates the joining together of entities*

(i) Indicates *accompaniment* (rare)

וַיָּבֹאוּ הָאֲנָשִׁים עַל־הַנָּשִׁים

The men came *along with* the women (Exod. 35.22).

(ii) Indicates *addition to* (rare)

כִּי־יָסַפְנוּ עַל־כָּל־חַטֹּאתֵינוּ רָעָה

For we have added this evil *to* all our sins (1 Sam. 12.19).

4. *Indicates specification*

The following are specified:

(i) *Topic*

וַאֲנִי שָׁמַעְתִּי עָלֶיךָ

And I myself have heard it said *of* you (Gen. 41.15).

וְעַל הִשָּׁנוֹת הַחֲלוֹם
אֶל־פַּרְעֹה פַּעֲמָיִם
כִּי־נָכוֹן הַדָּבָר מֵעִם הָאֱלֹהִים

And *concerning* the fact that Pharaoh's dream was repeated twice; it is because the matter has been established by God (Gen. 41.32).

(ii) *Norm* (rare)

הַבְּרִית אֲשֶׁר כָּרַת יְהוָה עִמָּכֶם
עַל כָּל־הַדְּבָרִים הָאֵלֶּה

The covenant which the Lord has made with you *in accordance with* all these words (Exod. 24.8).

5. *Indicates cause*

הִנְּךָ מֵת עַל־הָאִשָּׁה אֲשֶׁר־לָקָחְתָּ

Behold, you are a dead man, *because of* the woman whom you have taken (Gen. 20.3).

§39.20. עִם

1. *Indicates the joining together of entities (comitative)*

The translation of the spacial equivalent of the preposition עִם is 'with x'.

(i) Indicates *accompaniment*

וַיֹּאכְלוּ וַיִּשְׁתּוּ הוּא וְהָאֲנָשִׁים
אֲשֶׁר־עִמּוֹ

And he and the men who were *with* him ate and drank (Gen. 24.54).

(ii) Indicates *addition to*

עִם־עָרֵיהֶם הֶחֱרִימָם יְהוֹשֻׁעַ

Joshua utterly destroyed them *with* their cities (Josh. 11.21).

2. *Indicates the direction of an action*

וַעֲשֵׂה־חֶסֶד עִם אֲדֹנִי אַבְרָהָם

And show steadfast love *to* my master Abraham (Gen. 24.12).

3. *Indicates spatial positioning*

The following distinctions can be made:

(i) *Proximity to*

וַיֵּשֶׁב יִצְחָק עִם־בְּאֵר לַחַי רֹאִי

And Isaac dwelt *at* Beer-lahai-roi (Gen. 25.11).

(ii) Metaphorical use of the locative: *in*

וְיָדַעְתָּ עִם־לְבָבֶךָ

Know then *in* your heart (Deut. 8.5).

§39.21. תַּחַת

1. *Indicates spatial positioning*

The spatial translation equivalent of the preposition תַּחַת is '*under* x'. It usually stands in opposition to עַל '*on top of* x'.

(i) *Under*

וַיְכֻסּוּ כָּל־הֶהָרִים הַגְּבֹהִים
אֲשֶׁר־תַּחַת כָּל־הַשָּׁמָיִם

So that all the high mountains *under* the whole heaven were covered (Gen. 7.19).

(ii) Metaphorical use of the locative: *under*

וְיִצְבְּרוּ־בָר תַּחַת יַד־פַּרְעֹה

And let them store up grain *under* the authority of Pharaoh (Gen. 41.35).

(iii) *On the spot* (rare)

וְעָמַדְנוּ תַחְתֵּינוּ

Then we will stand still *in* our place (1 Sam. 14.9).

2. *Indicates substitution*

וְנָתַתָּה נֶפֶשׁ תַּחַת נָפֶשׁ

Then you shall give life *for* life (Exod. 21.23).

§40. **Conjunctions**

§40.1. *Introduction*

There are two classes of conjunctions, namely, co-ordinating and subordinating conjunctions. (Cf. 11.5.)

- *Co-ordinating conjunctions* are conjunctions that link syntactically equal entities, whether they be clauses, or parts of a word chain. (Cf. §31.2.) In BH only וְ, וּ and אוֹ can be regarded as fully co-ordinating conjunctions. אִם and כִּי are only sometimes used in a co-ordinating way.

- *Subordinating conjunctions* are conjunctions that introduce clauses, which as a rule, cannot be used to carry out a speech act. A distinction can be made between (1) complementary conjunctions, which introduce clauses, for example, an object clause, and (2) supplementary conjunctions. In BH subordinate clauses often have the same syntactic structure as co-ordinating clauses. It is thus sometimes difficult to distinguish between co-ordinating conjunctions and subordinating conjunctions.

§40.2. אֲבָל

1. *Marks opposition (adversative)*

Indicates the opposite of an expectation *raised by an immediately preceding expression* (co-ordinating conjunction)

וְהָאֲנָשִׁים אֲשֶׁר הָיוּ עִמִּי לֹא
רָאוּ אֶת־הַמַּרְאָה אֲבָל חֲרָדָה
גְדֹלָה נָפְלָה עֲלֵיהֶם

The men who were with me did not see the vision, *but* a great trembling fell upon them (Dan 10.7).

2. *Also functions sometimes as a modal word (Cf. §41.3/2.)*

§40.3. אוֹ

1. *Lists alternatives (co-ordinating conjunction)*

The alternatives are usually *nominal entities*. When alternative *actions* are involved אִם is used more often. (Cf. §40.5/3.) The distribution of אוֹ is as follows:

(i) אוֹ precedes *the second alternative only*.

וְכִי־יִגַּח שׁוֹר אֶת־אִישׁ אוֹ	When an ox gores a man *or* a woman
אֶת־אִשָּׁה וָמֵת	to death (Exod. 21.28)

(ii) אוֹ precedes *all the alternatives*. It then functions as a double conjunction. (Cf. §31.1/3(ii).)

A speaker uses this double conjunction in order to specify that *all the alternatives* preceded by אוֹ are of particular importance in the context in which they occur. (Cf. §41.4/5.2(ii).)

כִּי־פָשָׂה הַנֶּגַע בַּבֶּגֶד אוֹ־בַשְּׁתִי	If the disease has spread in the gar-
אוֹ־בָעֵרֶב אוֹ בָעוֹר	ment, or in warp, *or* in the woof, *or*
	in the skin, (Lev. 13.51)

§40.4. אָז/אֱזַי

1. *Introduce the apodosis of a condition (subordinating conjunctions)* (rare)

אַחֲלֵי אֲדֹנִי לִפְנֵי הַנָּבִיא אֲשֶׁר	Would that my lord were with the
בְּשֹׁמְרוֹן אָז יֶאֱסֹף אֹתוֹ מִצָּרַעְתּוֹ	prophet who is in Samaria! *Then* he
	would cure him of his leprosy (2 Kgs 5.3).

2. *Introduce a clause that refers to events that are a logical implication of what was referred to in a preceding clause*

יָשַׁנְתִּי אָז יָנוּחַ לִי	I would be asleep; *then* I would be at rest (Job 3.13).

3. *Function usually as an ordinary adverb with a deictic character (Cf. §41.2/1.)*

§40.5 אִם

1. *Introduces a real condition (subordinating conjunction)*

אִם־אֶמְצָא בִסְדֹם חֲמִשִּׁים	*If* I find at Sodom fifty righteous in
צַדִּיקִם בְּתוֹךְ הָעִיר	the city, I will spare the whole place
וְנָשָׂאתִי לְכָל־הַמָּקוֹם בַּעֲבוּרָם	for their sake (Gen. 18.26).

2. *Introduces a concession (subordinating conjunction)*

אִם־צָדַקְתִּי לֹא אֶעֱנֶה   *Though* I am innocent, I cannot answer him (Job 9.15).

3. *Introduces an alternative (co-ordinating conjunction)*

(i) *Only the second alternative is preceded by* אִם

הֲתָבוֹא לְךָ שֶׁבַע שָׁנִים רָעָב   Shall three years of famine come to
בְּאַרְצֶךָ וְאִם־שְׁלֹשָׁה חֳדָשִׁים נֻסְךָ   you in your land? *Or* will you flee
לִפְנֵי־צָרֶיךָ   three months before your foes while they pursue you? (2 Sam. 24.13).

(ii) אִם precedes *both alternatives*. It then functions as a double conjunction. (Cf. §31.1/3(iii).)

A speaker uses this double conjunction to indicate that *both alternatives* preceded by אִם are of particular importance in the context in which they occur. (Cf. §41.4/5.2(ii).)

זֹבְחֵי הַזֶּבַח אִם־שׁוֹר אִם־שֶׂה   Those offering a sacrifice, *whether* it be ox *or* sheep (Deut. 18.3).

4. *Also functions as a modal word (Cf. §41.3/6.)*

(i) Marks a process *that will not occur* (primarily in a *sworn oath*)

חַיְךָ וְחֵי נַפְשְׁךָ   As you live, and as your soul lives, I
אִם־אֶעֱשֶׂה אֶת־הַדָּבָר הַזֶּה   *will* not do this thing! (2 Sam. 11.11).

(ii) With לֹא marks a process *that will occur* (primarily in a *sworn oath*)

וַיִּשָּׁבַע מֹשֶׁה בַּיּוֹם הַהוּא   And Moses swore on that day, say-
לֵאמֹר אִם־לֹא הָאָרֶץ אֲשֶׁר   ing, *Surely* the land on which your
דָּרְכָה רַגְלְךָ בָּהּ לְךָ תִהְיֶה   foot has trodden shall be an inheri-
לְנַחֲלָה וּלְבָנֶיךָ עַד־עוֹלָם   tance for you and your children for ever (Josh. 14.9).

§40.6. אֲשֶׁר

1. *Functions normally as a relative pronoun (Cf. §36.3.)*

וּמִפְּרִי הָעֵץ אֲשֶׁר בְּתוֹךְ־הַגָּן   from the fruit of the tree *which* is in the midst of the garden (Gen. 3.3)

2. *Introduces an object clause, especially after verbs of observation and mental processes (rare) (subordinating conjunction)*

וַיַּרְא שָׁאוּל אֲשֶׁר־הוּא מַשְׂכִּיל מְאֹד   And when Saul saw *that* he had great success (1 Sam. 18.15).

3. *Introduces a result (rare) (subordinating conjunction)*

הִנֵּה נָתַתִּי לְךָ לֵב חָכָם וְנָבוֹן
אֲשֶׁר כָּמוֹךָ לֹא־הָיָה לְפָנֶיךָ

Look, I give you a wise and discerning mind [lit. heart], *so that* there has been none like you before you (1 Kgs 3.12)

4. *Introduces a purpose (rare) (subordinating conjunction)*

וְשָׁמַרְתָּ אֶת־חֻקָּיו וְאֶת־מִצְוֹתָיו
אֲשֶׁר אָנֹכִי מְצַוְּךָ הַיּוֹם אֲשֶׁר
יִיטַב לְךָ וּלְבָנֶיךָ אַחֲרֶיךָ

Therefore you shall keep his statutes and his commandments, which I command you this day, *that* it may go well with you, and with your children after you (Deut. 4.40).

5. *Indicates a cause (rare) (subordinating conjunction)*

נָתַן אֱלֹהִים שְׂכָרִי
אֲשֶׁר־נָתַתִּי שִׁפְחָתִי לְאִישִׁי

God has rewarded me *because* I gave my maid to my husband (Gen. 30.18).

6. *Introduces a motivation (rare) (subordinating conjunction)*

מֵעֲמָלֵקִי הֱבִיאוּם אֲשֶׁר חָמַל
הָעָם עַל־מֵיטַב הַצֹּאן וְהַבָּקָר

They have brought them from the Amalekites; *for* the people spared the best of the sheep and of the oxen (1 Sam. 15.15).

7. *Introduces a real condition (rare) (subordinating conjunction)*

אֲשֶׁר תִּשְׁמְעוּ אֶל־מִצְוֹת יְהוָה
אֱלֹהֵיכֶם אֲשֶׁר אָנֹכִי מְצַוֶּה
אֶתְכֶם הַיּוֹם

If you obey the commandments of the Lord your God, which I command you this day (Deut. 11.27)

8. *Introduces direct speech (rare) (subordinating conjunction)*

וַיֹּאמֶר שָׁאוּל אֶל־שְׁמוּאֵל
אֲשֶׁר שָׁמַעְתִּי בְּקוֹל יְהוָה

And Saul said to Samuel: I have obeyed the voice of the Lord (1 Sam. 15.20).

§40.7. בַּעֲבוּר

1. *Introduces a purpose*
As subordinating conjunction

בַּעֲבוּר תֵּדַע כִּי אֵין כָּמֹנִי
בְּכָל־הָאָרֶץ

that you may know that there is none like me in all the earth (Exod. 9.14).

2. *Also functions as a preposition (Cf. §39.9.)*

§40.8. וְ

Only the so-called waw copulative will be dealt with here. Compare §21 for the waw consecutive. When וְ is affixed to a word it sometimes takes on variant forms. (Cf. §31.1/1.)

1. *Joins syntactic similar entities, that is, words, constituents or clauses (co-ordinating conjunction)*

(i) *Joins entities in a list: and*

a. *Every entity (or only the last entity in the list) may be preceded by* וְ

כִּי אָנֹכִי נָתַתִּי לָהּ הַדָּגָן וְהַתִּירוֹשׁ וְהַיִּצְהָר	that I gave her the grain, the wine, *and* the oil (Hos. 2.10)
כָּל־מְשׂוֹשָׂהּ חַגָּהּ חָדְשָׁהּ וְשַׁבַּתָּהּ וְכֹל מוֹעֲדָהּ	all her mirth, her feasts, her new moons *and* her sabbaths, *and* all her appointed feasts (Hos. 2.13)

b. Sometimes *both the first and the second* entity of a word chain are preceded by וְ. It is then regarded as *a double conjunction*. (Cf. §31.1/3.)

A speaker uses this double conjunction to indicate that *both* the entities preceded by וְ are of particular importance in the context in which they occur. (Cf. §41.4/5.2.)

וּבְיִשְׂרָאֵל וּבָאָדָם	*both* in Israel *and* among humanity (Jer. 32.20)

c. Sometimes two words form a type of fixed compound. (If the words that is preceded by וְ is short then וָ is used instead of וְ.)

טוֹב וָרָע	good and evil (Gen. 2.17)

(ii) Joins *alternatives* in a list: *or*

לֹא־תַעֲשֶׂה כָל־מְלָאכָה אַתָּה וּבִנְךָ־וּבִתֶּךָ עַבְדְּךָ וַאֲמָתְךָ וּבְהֶמְתֶּךָ וְגֵרְךָ אֲשֶׁר בִּשְׁעָרֶיךָ	You shall not do any work, you, *or* your son, *or* your daughter, your manservant, *or* your maidservant, *or* your cattle, *or* the sojourner who is within your gates (Exod. 20.10).

(iii) Joins clauses that refer to events that will occur one after the other, in other words it *links sequential events*. (rare)

וְכָל־הָעָם יִשְׁמְעוּ וְיִרָאוּ	And all the people shall hear, *and* fear (Deut. 17.13).

(iv) Joins clauses in which the content of the clause with ו is *contrasted* with that of the other: *but*

נִחַמְתִּי כִּי עֲשִׂיתִם
וְנֹחַ מָצָא חֵן בְּעֵינֵי יְהוָה

I am sorry that I have made them. *But* Noah found favour in the eyes of the Lord (Gen. 6.7-8).

(v) Links two entities in a word chain that form *a hendiadys* (rare)

הַבְּרִית וְהַחֶסֶד

the covenant of grace (Deut. 7.9)

2. *Joins dissimilar clauses (subordinating conjunction)*

(i) Joins clauses in which the content of the clause with ו refers to the *purpose* of the content of the preceding clause (Cf. also §21.5.)

אָסֻרָה־נָּא וְאֶרְאֶה אֶת־הַמַּרְאֶה
הַגָּדֹל הַזֶּה

I must go across *to see* this great sight (Exod. 3.3).

(ii) Joins clauses in which the content of the clause with ו alludes to the *result* of the content of the preceding clause

זֹאת עֲשׂוּ וִחְיוּ

Do this *and* you will live (Gen. 42.18).

(iii) Joins clauses in which the content of the clause with ו refers to *circumstances* that prevailed at the same time as those described in the other clause

רִבְקָה יֹצֵאת ... וְכַדָּהּ עַל־שִׁכְמָהּ

Rebekah came out ... with her water jar upon her shoulder (Gen. 24.15).

(iv) Joins clauses in which the content of the clause with ו refers to *a motivation* for the other

וְגֵר לֹא תִלְחָץ וְאַתֶּם יְדַעְתֶּם
אֶת־נֶפֶשׁ הַגֵּר

You shall not oppress a stranger *for* you know the heart of a stranger (Exod. 23.9).

(v) Joins clauses in which the content of the clause with ו refers to *background information* necessary for understanding the other one better

גְּאַל־לְךָ אַתָּה אֶת־גְּאֻלָּתִי
כִּי לֹא־אוּכַל לִגְאֹל:
וְזֹאת לְפָנִים בְּיִשְׂרָאֵל
עַל־הַגְּאוּלָּה

Take my right of redemption yourself, for I cannot redeem it. *Now* this was the custom in former times in Israel concerning redeeming (Ruth 4.6-7).

(vi) Joins clauses in which the content of the clause with וְ refers to a *comparison* with the other clause (rare)

| הַדֶּלֶת תִּסּוֹב עַל־צִירָהּ | As a door turns on its hinges, *so* does |
| וְעָצֵל עַל־מִטָּתוֹ | a sluggard on his bed (Prov. 26.14). |

(vii) Joins clauses in which the content of the clause with וְ *describes more fully* the content of the preceding one (the so-called epexegetical waw)

| כִּי־גוֹי אֹבַד עֵצוֹת הֵמָּה | For they are a nation void of counsel, |
| וְאֵין בָּהֶם תְּבוּנָה | there is no understanding in them (Deut. 32.28). |

3. *The apparently superfluous use of* וְ *(rare)*

| וַתֵּשֶׁב תָּמָר וְשֹׁמֵמָה | So Tamar dwelt, a desolate woman (2 Sam. 13.20). |

§40.9. כִּי

I. כִּי + *Main Clause*

1. *Introduces the protasis of a condition and may then be translated* if *(subordinating conjunction)*

| וְכִי־יִגַּח שׁוֹר אֶת־אִישׁ אוֹ | *If* an ox gores a man or a woman to |
| אֶת־אִשָּׁה וָמֵת סָקוֹל יִסָּקֵל הַשּׁוֹר | death, the ox shall be stoned (Exod. 21.28). |

In legal texts כִּי often does not stand at the beginning of the clause.

| אִשָּׁה כִּי תַזְרִיעַ וְיָלְדָה | *If* a woman conceives, and bears a |
| זָכָר וְטָמְאָה שִׁבְעַת יָמִים | male child, then she shall be unclean seven days (Lev. 12.2). |

כִּי and אִם are sometimes apparently used as synonyms. However, כִּי normally precedes the *general conditions* and אִם *the details* of these general conditions.

2. *Introduces a temporal clause that refers to a process occurring simultaneously with the main clause (subordinating conjunction). In such cases* כִּי *may be translated* when.

The distinction between a temporal clause and a conditional clause is sometimes vague. A temporal clause is one that usually refers to a process that has a good chance of being realized.

כִּי יְבִיאֲךָ יְהוָה אֱלֹהֶיךָ   *When* the Lord your God brings you
אֶל־הָאָרֶץ ... וְהִכִּיתָם   into the land ... and you defeat them,
הַחֲרֵם תַּחֲרִים אֹתָם   then you must utterly destroy them
     (Deut. 7.1-2).

3. Introduces the cause[55] *of a condition or process (subordinating conjunction)*

כִּי עָשִׂיתָ זֹּאת אָרוּר אַתָּה   *Because* you have done this, cursed
     are you (Gen. 3.14).

The reason that the clause referring to the cause comes first in the clause is that the speaker/narrator wishes to remove any doubt about the specific cause of a situation.

II. *Main clause* + כִּי

1. Introduces an object clause after the following verbs: רָאָה, שָׁמַע, יָדַע, אָמַן, זָכַר, נָגַד, שָׁבַע *and* עוֹד. *It may then be translated* that *(subordinating conjunction).*

דַּע כִּי־מוֹת תָּמוּת   Know *that* you shall surely die (Gen.
     20.7).

2. Marks a clause that provides a reason (co-ordinating conjunction)

(i) Provides the reason for a state of affairs by marking the *actual reason* with כִּי. The causal relation is due to natural laws. כִּי may be translated *because*.

וְכֹל שִׂיחַ הַשָּׂדֶה טֶרֶם   When no plant of the field was yet in
יִהְיֶה בָאָרֶץ וְכָל־עֵשֶׂב הַשָּׂדֶה   the earth and no herb of the field had
טֶרֶם יִצְמָח כִּי לֹא הִמְטִיר   yet sprung up, *for* the Lord God had
יְהוָה אֱלֹהִים עַל־הָאָרֶץ   not caused it to rain upon the earth
     (Gen. 2.5).

---

55. In some contexts it is not clear whether a temporal or causal relation is involved, e.g. Judg. 2.18 and Ps. 32.3. Sometimes כִּי is preceded by יַעַן (1 Kgs 13.21), תַּחַת (Deut. 4.37) or עֵקֶב (Amos 4.12) to confirm that a causal relation is indeed involved.

(ii) Provides the reason for a preceding expression or expressions by marking with כִּי the *motivation given by speakers* to explain something they have said. The causal relation is thus not due to natural laws but is due to the speaker's own reasoning. כִּי can usually also be translated *for*.

a. Speakers base their motivation for an *assertion* on *their interpretation* of events.

וַיֹּאמֶר נָתָן אֲדֹנִי הַמֶּלֶךְ	And Nathan said, 'My lord the king,
אַתָּה אָמַרְתָּ אֲדֹנִיָּהוּ יִמְלֹךְ	have you said, 'Adonijah shall reign
אַחֲרַי וְהוּא יֵשֵׁב עַל־כִּסְאִי׃	after me, and he shall sit upon my
כִּי יָרַד הַיּוֹם וַיִּזְבַּח שׁוֹר	throne'? *For* he has gone down this
וּמְרִיא־וְצֹאן לָרֹב וַיִּקְרָא	day, and has sacrificed oxen, fatlings,
לְכָל־בְּנֵי הַמֶּלֶךְ וּלְשָׂרֵי	and sheep in abundance, and has
הַצָּבָא וּלְאֶבְיָתָר הַכֹּהֵן	invited all the king's sons, the commanders of the army, and Abiathar the priest' (1 Kgs 1.24-25).

b. Speakers base their motivation for a *directive action* (request, command, summons, exhortation, etc.) on *what they or someone else is doing, has done or will do.*

וַיֹּאמֶר יְהוָה אֶל־מֹשֶׁה	But the Lord said to Moses, 'Do not
אַל־תִּירָא אֹתוֹ	fear him; *for* I have given him into
כִּי בְיָדְךָ נָתַתִּי אֹתוֹ	your hand' (Num. 21.34).

c. *Speakers motivate a whole argument or series of statements* by means of כִּי. In such cases translators are inclined to leave כִּי untranslated because it does not entirely make sense on a grammatical level. In Ps. 1 the psalmist gives the reason in verse 6 for what is said in verses 1-5. In this way the psalmist *provides evidence* for the assertions made in verses 1-5.

כִּי־יוֹדֵעַ יְהוָה דֶּרֶךְ	*For* the Lord knows the way of the
צַדִּיקִים וְדֶרֶךְ רְשָׁעִים	righteous, but the way of the wicked
תֹּאבֵד׃	will perish (Ps. 1.6).

In cases where it is clear that speakers consider the grounds on which they base their motivation are difficult to contest, thus suggesting *the force of their conviction*, one can translate כִּי '*in fact, the fact of the matter*'.

וְעַתָּה הָשֵׁב אֵשֶׁת־הָאִישׁ	Now then restore the man's wife; *in*
כִּי־נָבִיא הוּא וְיִתְפַּלֵּל בַּעַדְךָ	*fact,* he is a prophet, and he will pray for you (Gen. 20.7).

If speakers believe that their motivation contains information that is generally known, כִּי may be translated *after all*, for example, Jer 1.6, 'I cannot speak for, after all, I am too young'. In a secondary communication situation such as the one in which modern interpreters of the Hebrew Bible find themselves, however, it is very difficult to track down such pragmatic information.

3. *Expresses a counter-statement after a negative statement. Then* כִּי *may be translated as* but *(co-ordinating conjunction)*

שָׂרַי אִשְׁתְּךָ לֹא־תִקְרָא	As for Sarai your wife, you shall not
אֶת־שְׁמָהּ שָׂרָי כִּי שָׂרָה שְׁמָהּ	call her name Sarai, *but* Sarah shall
	be her name (Gen. 17.15).

כִּי אִם is sometimes used instead of כִּי. With כִּי אִם the speakers make it very clear that not only is an alternative involved, but that it is *the only possible alternative*.

לֹא יַעֲקֹב יֵאָמֵר עוֹד שִׁמְךָ	Your name shall no more be called
כִּי אִם־יִשְׂרָאֵל	Jacob, *but* Israel (Gen. 32.29).

4. *Introduces a clause that follows a question that asks about the background to events referred to by the clause introduced by* כִּי *(subordinating conjunction)*

וּמֶה־חָטָאתִי לָךְ כִּי־הֵבֵאתָ עָלַי	And how have I sinned against you,
חֲטָאָה גְדֹלָה ...	*that* you have brought upon me ... a
	great sin? (Gen. 20.9).

5. *Functions as a modal word (Cf. §41.3/9.)*
כִּי expresses confirmation (primarily in a context of swearing an oath). In these instances it may be translated *indeed, truly, surely*.

חֵי פַרְעֹה כִּי מְרַגְּלִים אַתֶּם	By the life of Pharaoh, *surely* you are
	spies (Gen. 42.16).

§40.10. לוּ

Introduces an unreal condition (i.e. an unlikely situation) (subordinating conjunction)

לוּ חָפֵץ יְהוָה לַהֲמִיתֵנוּ	*If* the Lord had meant to kill us, he
לֹא־לָקַח מִיָּדֵנוּ עֹלָה וּמִנְחָה	would not have accepted a burnt
	offering and a cereal offering at our
	hands (Judg. 13.23).

§40.11. לוּלֵי

Introduces a negative unreal condition (subordinating conjunction)

כִּי לוּלֵי פְּנֵי יְהוֹשָׁפָט מֶלֶךְ־יְהוּדָה אֲנִי נֹשֵׂא אִם־אַבִּיט אֵלֶיךָ	*If* I did not have regard for Jehoshaphat the king of Judah, I would neither look at you, nor see you (2 Kgs 3.14).

§40.12. לָכֵן

1. *Introduces after a statement or statements of grounds, a declaration or command.*

לָכֵן הַמִּטָּה אֲשֶׁר־עָלִיתָ שָּׁם לֹא־תֵרֵד מִמֶּנָּה	*Therefore* you shall not come down from the bed to which you have gone (2 Kgs 1.6).

Whether לָכֵן is indeed a conjunction, is not certain. Scholars agree that it is made up out of the preposition לְ and the deictic adverb כֵּן. Furthermore, it can often be understood as a *discourse marker* because it relates two contents with one another which are not necessarily referred to only by means of two successive sentences, but also clusters of sentences, e.g. 1 Kgs 14.10. (Cf. §44.1.)

2. *In a conversation, in response to an objection,* לָכֵן *is used 'to state the ground upon which the answer is made' (Brown, Driver and Briggs 1907: 487)*

וַתֹּאמֶר לָהּ הַמְעַט קַחְתֵּךְ אֶת־אִישִׁי וְלָקַחַת גַּם אֶת־דּוּדָאֵי בְּנִי וַתֹּאמֶר רָחֵל לָכֵן יִשְׁכַּב עִמָּךְ תַּחַת דּוּדָאֵי בְנֵךְ	But she said to her, 'Is it a small matter that you have taken away my husband? Would you take away my son's mandrakes also?' Rachel said, '*That being so*, he may lie with you tonight for your son's mandrakes' (Gen. 30.15).

§40.13. לְמַעַן

לְמַעַן often indicates the purpose or result of a sequence of utterances.
1. *Indicates purpose: so that, for the sake of*
   (i) As *subordinating conjunction*

וְכָתַבְתָּ עֲלֵיהֶן אֶת־כָּל־דִּבְרֵי הַתּוֹרָה הַזֹּאת בְּעָבְרֶךָ לְמַעַן אֲשֶׁר תָּבֹא אֶל־הָאָרֶץ אֲשֶׁר־יְהוָה אֱלֹהֶיךָ נֹתֵן לָךְ	And you shall write upon them all the words of this law, *so that* you can pass over to enter the land which the Lord your God gives you (Deut. 27.3).

(ii) Also functions as a *preposition* (Cf. §39.12.)

2. *Indicates result (subordinating conjunction)*

יְבִאֻהוּ בַּמְּצֹדוֹת לְמַעַן לֹא־יִשָּׁמַע קוֹלוֹ עוֹד	They brought him into custody, *so that* his voice should no more be heard (Ezek. 19.9).

§40.14. פֶּן

Indicates negative purpose (subordinating conjunction)
On the basis of its meaning, פֶּן could also be classified as a *negative* particle. (Cf. §41.5/9.)

וַיֹּאמֶר אֵלָיו אַבְרָהָם הִשָּׁמֶר לְךָ פֶּן־תָּשִׁיב אֶת־בְּנִי שָׁמָּה	Abraham said to him, 'See to it *that* you do *not* take my son back there' (Gen. 24.6).
וְלֹא תִגְּעוּ בּוֹ פֶּן־תְּמֻתוּן	You shall not touch it, *lest* you die (Gen. 3.3).

§40.15. עַל־כֵּן

Introduces after the statement of grounds, a fact (co-ordinating conjunction)

עַל־כֵּן לֹא־נְתַתִּיךָ לִנְגֹּעַ אֵלֶיהָ:	*Therefore* I did not let you touch her (Gen. 20.6).

Note that לָכֵן apparently has the same semantic value as עַל־כֵּן. However, the former tends to introduce declarations or commands, while עַל־כֵּן more often introduces facts. (Cf. §40.12.)

§41. Adverbs

§41.1. *Introduction*

Traditionally, the term 'adverb' has been accorded a very broad definition. The concept has included adverbs, modal words, negatives, questions, discourse markers and predicators of existence—which all are dealt with as distinct categories in this grammar. (Joüon–Muraoka §102 is a good example of the traditional approach.) In this grammar adverbs are also regarded as an inclusive word class that *can modify a word, a constituent or clause.* (Cf. §11.6.) Sub-classes are distinguished primarily according to the nature of the modification.

- *Ordinary adverbs*: adverbs that only modify a clause or a constituent
- *Modal words:* adverbs that modify a clause
- *Focus particles:* adverbs that can modify a word, a constituent and a clause

A semantic criterion has been adopted to distinguish a fourth class of adverbs, namely

- *Negatives*: adverbs that negate a constituent or a clause

§41.2. *Ordinary Adverbs*

(i) Ordinary adverbs *usually modify an adjective or the predicate of a clause*. BH has a few ordinary adverbs. Morphological distinctions may be drawn between the following types:

a. so-called *primitive adverbs*

כֹּה (so), פֹּה (here), כֵּן (so), שָׁם (there), and אָז (then)

b. derived adverbs *with* adverbial suffixes

with ־ָם, e.g. יוֹמָם (daily), רֵיקָם (in vain), הִנָּם (without reason)

with ־ָם, e.g. פִּתְאֹם (suddenly)

c. derived adverbs *without* adverbial suffixes

הַרְבֵּה (many), הֵיטֵב (good), הַרְחֵק (far), הַשְׁכֵּם (early) and מַהֵר (fast) which are primarily infinitive absolute forms used as adverbs

מְאֹד (many) and מְעַט (few) which were primarily nouns, but now function mostly as adverbs

מַר (bitterly) which is primarily an adjective, but can also be used as an adverb

d. derived adverbs: *nouns plus preposition*

לָרֹב (many), לְשָׁלוֹם (peacefully), לָבֶטַח (safely)

(ii) *Semantically* adverbs function as follows:

a. Adverbs that modify verbs *describe the time, place or manner* of the action to which the verb refers.

b. Adverbs that modify adjectives usually describe a *degree* of the attribute involved.

Most adverbs have a very specific lexical meaning. Only a few that occur relatively frequently are dealt with here.

1. אָז/אֲזַי

(i) Indicate the *time* of the action to which the verb refers: *afterwards, then*

<table>
<tr><td dir="rtl">אָז יִבְנֶה יְהוֹשֻׁעַ מִזְבֵּחַ לַיהוָה
אֱלֹהֵי יִשְׂרָאֵל בְּהַר עֵיבָל</td><td>*Then* Joshua built an altar on Mount Ebal to the Lord, the God of Israel (Josh. 8.30).</td></tr>
</table>

(ii) Function also as a *conjunction* (Cf. §40.4.)

2. טֶרֶם

טֶרֶם could also be classified as a *negative* on the basis of semantic considerations. (Cf. §41.5/7.)

(i) Indicates the *time* of the action to which the verb refers: *not yet*
This adverb is usually followed by an imperfect form.

<table>
<tr><td dir="rtl">טֶרֶם יִשְׁכָּבוּ ... אַנְשֵׁי
סְדֹם נָסַבּוּ עַל־הַבַּיִת</td><td>They had *not yet* lain down, ..., when the men of Sodom, gathered about the house (Gen. 19.4).</td></tr>
</table>

3. כֹּה

כֹּה usually functions as *a demonstrative adverb* and *precedes* the action that it modifies.

(i) *Refers back* to given information that *describes the nature of a process or events*: *so*

<table>
<tr><td dir="rtl">כֹּה יִהְיֶה זַרְעֶךָ</td><td>*So* shall your descendants be (Gen. 15.5).</td></tr>
</table>

(ii) *Refers in advance* to the *content of direct speech which immediately follows*: *thus*

<table>
<tr><td dir="rtl">כֹּה אָמַר אֲדֹנָי יְהוִה
לֹא תָקוּם וְלֹא תִהְיֶה:</td><td>*Thus* says the Lord God: It shall not stand, and it shall not come to pass (Isa. 7.7).</td></tr>
</table>

(iii) Indicates *spatial positioning: here* (rare)

<table>
<tr><td dir="rtl">שִׂים כֹּה נֶגֶד אַחַי</td><td>Set it *here* before my kinsmen (Gen. 31.37).</td></tr>
</table>

4. כֵּן

כֵּן usually *follows* the action that it modifies.

(i) *Refers back* to given information that describes the *nature (manner, quality, quantity or degree)* of a process or condition: *such*

לֹא בָא־כֵן עֲצֵי אַלְמֻגִּים וְלֹא נִרְאָה עַד הַיּוֹם הַזֶּה	No *such* quantities of almug wood have come or been seen, to this day (1 Kgs 10.12).

(ii) With the preposition כְּ it forms *a type of fixed expression that emphasizes the similarities between processes or conditions* (Cf. also §39.10/2.)

כְּכָל־הַמַּעֲשִׂים אֲשֶׁר־עָשׂוּ ... כֵּן הֵמָּה עֹשִׂים גַּם־לָךְ:	*According* to all the deeds which they have done (to me) ... *so* they are also doing to you (1 Sam. 8.8).

5. עוֹד

עוֹד differs from all the other ordinary adverbs in the sense that it can take a pronominal suffix. These suffixes are normally the subject of a clause.

Person	Singular		Plural	
1 m./f.	עוֹדִי / עוֹדֶנִּי	Yet, I		Yet, us
2 m.	עוֹדְךָ	Yet, you		Yet, you
2 f.	עוֹדֵךְ	Yet, you		Yet, you
3 m.	עוֹדֶנּוּ	Yet, he	עוֹדָם	Yet, them
3 f.	עוֹדֶנָּה / עוֹדָהּ	Yet, she	עוֹדֵינוּ	Yet, them

Indicates the *time* of the action to which the verb refers: *still or yet*

הִנֵּה עוֹדָךְ מְדַבֶּרֶת שָׁם עִם־הַמֶּלֶךְ	Then while you are *still* speaking with the king (1 Kgs 1.14).

6. וְעַתָּה

(i) Indicates the *time* of the action to which the verb refers: *now*
In most cases in which עַתָּה and not וְעַתָּה is used, it is an adverb of time.

וְאַל־תַּעַשׂ לוֹ מְאוּמָה כִּי עַתָּה יָדַעְתִּי כִּי־יְרֵא אֱלֹהִים אַתָּה	Do not do anything to him; for *now* I know that you fear God (Gen. 22.12).

However, when וְעַתָּה fulfils an adverbial function it usually indicates a contrast between 'then' and 'now'.

בְּשִׁבְעִים נֶפֶשׁ יָרְדוּ אֲבֹתֶיךָ מִצְרָיְמָה	Your fathers went down to Egypt
וְעַתָּה שָׂמְךָ יְהוָה אֱלֹהֶיךָ	seventy persons; *but now* the Lord
כְּכוֹכְבֵי הַשָּׁמַיִם לָרֹב	your God has made you as the stars
	of heaven for multitude (Deut.
	10.22).

(ii) Functions mostly as *a discourse marker* (Cf. §44.6.)

§41.3. *Modal Words*

1. *Introduction*

As opposed to ordinary adverbs, modal adverbs usually relate to an entire clause. In fact, an outstanding feature of modal words is that they involve the speaker in the content of a clause. They refer to a speaker's understanding of the *probability (certainty to uncertainty)* of the state of affairs or events to which a clause refers.

2. אֲבָל

(i) Indicates *the denial of an expectation or view* that a speaker thinks a listener holds: *indeed, but.*

וַיֹּאמֶר אֱלֹהִים אֲבָל שָׂרָה	God said: *No, but* (contrary to what
אִשְׁתְּךָ יֹלֶדֶת לְךָ בֵּן	you believe) Sarah your wife shall
	bear you a son (Gen. 17.19).

(ii) Functions mostly as a *conjunction*. (Cf. §40.2.)

3. אַךְ

(i) Expresses the *conviction as to the correctness of an observation*: *certainly, surely*

וַיְהִי בְּבוֹאָם וַיַּרְא אֶת־אֱלִיאָב	When they came, he looked on Eliab
וַיֹּאמֶר אַךְ נֶגֶד יְהוָה מְשִׁיחוֹ	and thought: *Surely* the Lord's
	anointed is before him. (1 Sam.
	16.6).

(ii) Functions mostly as a *focus particle* (Cf. §41.4/2.)

4. אָכֵן

Expresses a *strong conviction* that the content of a statement is true: *truly, undoubtedly*

וַיֹּאמֶר אָכֵן יֵשׁ יְהוָה בַּמָּקוֹם הַזֶּה	And he said: *Truly* the Lord is in this
וְאָנֹכִי לֹא יָדָעְתִּי	place; and I did not know it (Gen.
	28.16).

Sometimes it is used to deny, with great conviction, the implications of an expression that directly preceeds it. אָכֵן can then be translated *nevertheless*.

וַאֲנִי אָמַרְתִּי לְרִיק יָגַעְתִּי לְתֹהוּ וְהֶבֶל כֹּחִי כִלֵּיתִי אָכֵן מִשְׁפָּטִי אֶת־יְהוָה וּפְעֻלָּתִי אֶת־אֱלֹהָי	But I said: I have laboured in vain, I have spent my strength for nothing and vanity! *Nevertheless* my justice is with the Lord, and my recompense with my God (Isa. 49.4).

5. אֻלַי

Expresses uncertainty: *maybe* or *perhaps*

אוּלַי יָקֵל אֶת־יָדוֹ מֵעֲלֵיכֶם	*Maybe* he will lighten his hand from off you (1 Sam. 6.5).

6. אִם

(i) Functions in taking an *oath*

a. With אִם a speaker expresses commitment that a process shall *not* take place.

חַיֶּךָ וְחֵי נַפְשֶׁךָ אִם־אֶעֱשֶׂה אֶת־הַדָּבָר הַזֶּה	As you live, and as your soul lives, I will *surely not* do this thing! (2 Sam. 11.11).

b. With אִם לֹא a speaker expresses commitment that a process *will take* place.

וַיִּשָּׁבַע מֹשֶׁה בַּיּוֹם הַהוּא לֵאמֹר אִם־לֹא הָאָרֶץ אֲשֶׁר דָּרְכָה רַגְלְךָ בָּהּ לְךָ תִהְיֶה לְנַחֲלָה וּלְבָנֶיךָ עַד־עוֹלָם	And Moses swore on that day, saying: *Surely* the land on which your foot has trodden shall be an inheritance for you and your children for ever (Josh. 14.9).

(ii) Functions mostly as a *conjunction* (Cf. §40.5.)

7. אָמְנָה

Expresses a speaker's *commitment to the truth* of a statement: *really, truly, indeed* (rare).

וְגַם־אָמְנָה אֲחֹתִי בַת־אָבִי הִוא	What is more, she is *indeed* my sister, the daughter of my father (Gen. 20.12).

8. אָמְנָם

A speaker uses אָמְנָם to enquire about how a state of affairs *correlates with the truth*: *truly* (rare).

כִּי הַאָמְנָם יֵשֵׁב אֱלֹהִים עַל־הָאָרֶץ	But will God *indeed* dwell on the earth? (1 Kgs 8.27).

9. כִּי

(i) Expresses *confirmation* of something the speaker has already said, an assumption or conviction (mostly in a sworn oath). In such instances it may be translated *indeed, truly* or *yes*.

חֵי פַרְעֹה כִּי מְרַגְּלִים אַתֶּם	By the life of Pharaoh, *surely* you are spies (Gen. 42.16).

(ii) Functions mostly as a *conjunction* (Cf. §40.9.)

10. רַק

(i) Expresses *conviction as to the correctness of an observation*

וַיֹּאמֶר אַבְרָהָם כִּי אָמַרְתִּי רַק אֵין־יִרְאַת אֱלֹהִים בַּמָּקוֹם הַזֶּה וַהֲרָגוּנִי עַל־דְּבַר אִשְׁתִּי	Abraham said: I did it because I thought, there is *certainly* [lit. I *just/only* thought there is] no fear of God at all in this place, and they will kill me because of my wife (Gen. 20.11).

(ii) Functions mostly as *a focus particle* (Cf. §41.4/7.)

§41.4. *Focus Particles*

1. *Introduction*

Focus particles are a group of adverbs that can modify a word (as part of a word chain or of a constituent), a constituent or a clause. They are called focus particles because they place a particular focus on the entity or clause that follows them. An outstanding feature of focus particles is that their meaning always indicates that the referent to which they refer *is an addition to or limitation of another refer-ent*. This is why some people prefer to call these adverbs *quantifiers*.

2. אַךְ

(i) Indicates a *limitation: only, just*

a. In the limitation/exclusion of *something or someone* in the preceding context

וְהַנַּעַר לֹא־יָדַע מְאוּמָה	But the lad knew nothing; *only*
אַךְ יְהוֹנָתָן וְדָוִד יָדְעוּ	Jonathan and David knew the matter
אֶת־הַדָּבָר׃	(1 Sam. 20.39).
וַאֲדַבְּרָה אַךְ־הַפַּעַם	Let me speak again *only* this once (Gen. 18.32).

b. In placing a *limiting condition* (the domain of אַךְ is the *protasis* of the condition)

אַךְ־בְּזֹאת נֵאוֹת לָכֶם אִם	*Only* on this condition will we con-
תִּהְיוּ כָמֹנוּ לְהִמֹּל לָכֶם	sent to you: that you will become as
כָּל־זָכָר	we are and every male of you be cir-cumcised (Gen. 34.15).

c. In placing a *limitation* with respect to the *content of an expression directly preceding* it

וַיַּעַן אָכִישׁ וַיֹּאמֶר אֶל־דָּוִד	And Achish answered David: I know
יָדַעְתִּי כִּי טוֹב אַתָּה בְּעֵינַי	that you are as blameless in my sight
כְּמַלְאַךְ אֱלֹהִים אַךְ שָׂרֵי	as an angel of God; *nevertheless* the
פְלִשְׁתִּים אָמְרוּ לֹא־יַעֲלֶה	commanders of the Philistines have
עִמָּנוּ בַּמִּלְחָמָה	said, He shall not go up with us to the battle (1 Sam. 29.9).

(ii) Also functions as a *modal word* (Cf. §40.3.)

3. אַף

Indicates *addition*

This particle is used predominantly in poetic texts. As opposed to גַּם, אַף does not necessarily directly precede its syntactic domain.

a. A speaker/narrator uses אַף to indicate very clearly that *an entity must be added to another.*

לְךָ יוֹם אַף־לְךָ לָיְלָה	Yours is the day, yours is *also* the night (Ps. 74.16).
וְאַף לַאֲמָתְךָ תַּעֲשֶׂה־כֵּן	And *also* to your maidservant you shall do likewise (Deut. 15.17).

Sometimes the entity that is added or need to be added is *an extreme case.* It is an entity that one would not have expected to

be added to a particular group. In such cases אַף is usually translated as *even*.

אַף־עַל־זֶה פָּקַחְתָּ עֵינֶךָ   *Even* upon such a one do you open
your eyes (Job 14.3).

b. A speaker/narrator uses אַף to indicate very clearly that the content of
one clause must be added to that of another as *an additional confirmation of the preceding statement.*

חֲבָלִים נָפְלוּ־לִי בַּנְּעִמִים   The lines have fallen to me in
אַף־נַחֲלָת שָׁפְרָה עָלָי   pleasant places; *indeed,* my heritage
is beautiful to me (Ps. 16.6).

c. A speaker/narrator uses אַף to *introduce a rhetorical question* that
must be joined to a preceding statement. By using אַף כִּי the speaker
indicates that what has been suggested in the rhetorical question *can
only be confirmed* in the light of a preceding situation. As with גַּם an
argument that has been added to another is involved. The second
argument is then the one bearing persuasive power.

וַיֹּאמְרוּ אַנְשֵׁי דָוִד אֵלָיו הִנֵּה   But David's men said to him: Behold,
אֲנַחְנוּ פֹה בִיהוּדָה יְרֵאִים   we are afraid here in Judah; *how
וְאַף כִּי־נֵלֵךְ קְעִלָה   much more* then if we go to Keilah
אֶל־מַעַרְכוֹת פְּלִשְׁתִּים   against the armies of the Philistines?
(1 Sam. 23.3).

4. אֶפֶס

(i) Indicates *limitation: only, nevertheless*

a. In limiting the *implications arising from the content* of an expression
directly preceding it. *Usually in the form:* אֶפֶס כִּי. As opposed to אַף
and רַק the domain of אֶפֶס כִּי is *always* a clause. אֶפֶס is used without
כִּי in the few instances where its domain is a constituent.

אֶפֶס כִּי לֹא יִהְיֶה־בְּךָ אֶבְיוֹן   *However,* there shall be no poor
among you (Deut. 15.4).

b. In limiting/excluding *something or someone* in the (usually preceding) context (rare)

וְאֶפֶס אֶת־הַדָּבָר אֲשֶׁר־   But *only* the word which I bid you,
אֲדַבֵּר אֵלֶיךָ אֹתוֹ תְדַבֵּר   that shall you speak (Num. 22.35).

(ii) Also functions as a *common noun*
a. *ends* (of the earth)

יְהוָה יָדִין אַפְסֵי־אָרֶץ   The Lord will judge the *ends* of the
earth (1 Sam. 2.10).

b. *expressing non-existence: nothing*

וְכָל־שָׂרֶיהָ יִהְיוּ אָפֶס   And all its princes shall be *as nothing* (Isa. 34.12).

5. גַּם

5.1   *The syntax of* גַּם

A syntactic feature of גַּם is that it can modify a word, a constituent or a clause. גַּם (as opposed to אַף) almost always directly precedes the constituent or clause to which it refers (its domain). A pronoun is sometimes directly repeated after גַּם (usually as an independent personal pronoun) to indicate that its antecedent lies in the domain of גַּם. (Cf. §36.1/I.2(v).)

פֶּן־יָמוּת גַּם־הוּא כְּאֶחָיו   Otherwise *he too* might die, like his brothers! (Gen. 38.11).

בָּרֲכֵנִי גַם־אָנִי אָבִי   Bless me, *me also*, O my father! (Gen. 27.34).

The following syntactic configurations are found:

(i) גַּם + *entity*

a. גַּם + word in a word chain

וַיִּיטַב בְּעֵינֵי כָל־הָעָם
וְגַם בְּעֵינֵי עַבְדֵי שָׁאוּל
And this was good in the sight of all the people and *also in the sight of Saul's servants* (1 Sam. 18.5).

b. גַּם + constituent

וַיָּמֶת גַּם־אֹתוֹ   And he slew *him also* (Gen. 38.10).

c. גַּם + clause

אָמַרְתִּי רַק אֵין־יִרְאַת אֱלֹהִים
בַּמָּקוֹם הַזֶּה וַהֲרָגוּנִי עַל־דְּבַר אִשְׁתִּי
וְגַם־אָמְנָה אֲחֹתִי
I thought, there is certainly [lit. I just/only thought there is] no fear of God at all in this place, and they will kill me because of my wife. *Moreover, she is indeed my sister* (Gen. 20.11).

(ii) גַּם + *entity* // גַּם + *entity*

When גַּם has this syntactic configuration, it is also regarded as a double conjunction. (Cf. §31.1/3(iv).)

a. גַּם + word // גַּם + word

וַיַּעַל עִמּוֹ
גַּם־רֶכֶב גַּם־פָּרָשִׁים
And there went up with him *both* chariots *as well as* horsemen (Gen. 50.9).

b. גַם + clause // גַם + clause

וַיֹּאמֶר אֲבִימֶלֶךְ

לֹא יָדַעְתִּי מִי עָשָׂה אֶת־הַדָּבָר הַזֶּה

וְגַם־אַתָּה לֹא־הִגַּדְתָּ לִּי

וְגַם אָנֹכִי לֹא שָׁמַעְתִּי

בִּלְתִּי הַיּוֹם

And Abimelech said: I do not know
who has done this thing.
Neither did you tell me ...
Nor have I not heard of it until today
(Gen. 21.26).

5.2 *The semantics and pragmatics of* גַם

(i) Speakers or writers give an explicit indication to their audience *that
a specific something or someone* must be added to something or
someone referred to in the preceding context: *also, even, moreover,
even more so.*

a. If the reference to this entity occurs in a previous expression, an
   audience would find it strange if the speakers or writers did not
   indicate that the entity after גַם has to be added to the entity in the
   preceding expression. In other words, the use of גַם contributes
   toward *constituting a well formed text* or discourse.

וַיְהִי עֵר בְּכוֹר יְהוּדָה רַע

בְּעֵינֵי יְהֹוָה וַיְמִתֵהוּ יְהֹוָה:

וַיֵּרַע בְּעֵינֵי יְהֹוָה אֲשֶׁר עָשָׂה

וַיָּמֶת גַּם־אֹתוֹ:

But Er, Judah's first-born, was
wicked in the sight of the Lord; and
the Lord slew him. And what he
(Onan) did was displeasing in the
sight of the Lord, and he slew him
also (Gen. 38.7, 38.10).

b. By using גַם speakers can also give their audience an indication that
   the expression with גַם *is part of a larger discourse* that they assume
   the audience is familiar with.

הִנֵּה יָלְדָה מִלְכָּה גַם־הִוא

בָּנִים לְנָחוֹר אָחִיךָ

Behold, Milcah *also* has borne children to your brother Nahor (Gen.
22.20).

In order to make sense of Gen. 22.20 the audience must be
familiar with Gen. 11.29.

c. If the entity that has to be added is something that is possible, but
   which one *would not expect*, i.e. an extreme case, גַם is translated
   even.[56]

---

56. BH thus does not distinguish lexically between *also* and *even* as in English.
Compare Xhosa which does not have a lexical equivalent for *also* or *even*. The
Xhosa conjunction *na* (= *and*) is used for both *also* and *even*.

גַּם בְּטֶרֶם יַקְטִרוּן אֶת־הַחֵלֶב
וּבָא נַעַר הַכֹּהֵן וְאָמַר לָאִישׁ
הַזֹּבֵחַ ...

Even before the fat was burned, the priest's servant would come and say to the man who was sacrificing: ... (1 Sam. 2.15).

d. Speakers wish to indicate clearly that *an expression has to be supplemented* with the expression (sentence) after גַּם to support a specific argument. In this way the audience is left in no doubt about the connection between the two expressions. The expression after גַּם usually refers to *a more persuasive or compelling argument* than the preceding one.

כִּי אָמַרְתִּי רַק אֵין־יִרְאַת
אֱלֹהִים בַּמָּקוֹם הַזֶּה
וַהֲרָגוּנִי עַל־דְּבַר אִשְׁתִּי
וְגַם־אָמְנָה אֲחֹתִי

I thought, there is certainly [lit. I just/only thought there is] no fear of God at all in this place, and they will kill me because of my wife. *Moreover*, she is indeed my sister (Gen. 20.11).

e. The specific inclusion of the entity or entities after גַּם usually reflects *some special role* that the inclusion has played.

וַיִּיטַב בְּעֵינֵי כָל־הָעָם
וְגַם בְּעֵינֵי עַבְדֵי שָׁאוּל

And this was good in the sight of all the people and *also* in the sight of Saul's servants (1 Sam. 18.5).

(ii) Speakers make it clear that the inclusion of *both* entities preceded by גַּם *is of special importance* in a particular context: *both, as well as*.

וַיַּעַל עִמּוֹ גַּם־רֶכֶב גַּם־פָּרָשִׁים

And there went up with him *both* chariots *as well as* horsemen (Gen. 50.9).

Sometimes the entities are *two arguments* that both carry equal weight in support of a statement.

וַיֹּאמֶר אֲבִימֶלֶךְ
לֹא יָדַעְתִּי מִי עָשָׂה אֶת־הַדָּבָר הַזֶּה
וְגַם־אַתָּה לֹא־הִגַּדְתָּ לִּי
וְגַם אָנֹכִי לֹא שָׁמַעְתִּי
בִּלְתִּי הַיּוֹם

And Abimelech said: I do not know who has done this thing. *Neither* did you tell me ... *Nor* have I not heard of it until today (Gen. 21.26).

(iii) Speakers may ask their audience for a *corresponding reaction* to something someone has already done. They may also commit themselves to such a corresponding action. Narrators may describe the corresponding reaction of a referent in the syntactic domain of גַּם.

וְעַתָּה הִשָּׁבְעוּ־נָא לִי בַּיהוָה כִּי עָשִׂיתִי עִמָּכֶם חֶסֶד וַעֲשִׂיתֶם גַּם־אַתֶּם עִם־בֵּית אָבִי חֶסֶד	Swear to me by the Lord that as I have dealt kindly with you, *you also* will deal kindly with my father's house (Josh. 2.12).

6. בִּלְתִּי

(i) Indicates *exclusion: only, unless*
The events or state of affairs referred to by the expression following בִּלְתִּי are exceptions to a generalization in the preceding expression.

אֵין כֹּל בִּלְתִּי אֶל־הַמָּן עֵינֵינוּ	There is nothing at all, *only* this manna to look at (Num. 11.6).
לֹא־תִרְאוּ פָנַי בִּלְתִּי אֲחִיכֶם אִתְּכֶם	You shall not see my face, *unless* your brother is with you (Gen. 43.3).

(ii) Functions mostly as a *negative* (Cf. §41.5/6.)

7. רַק

(i) Indicates *limitation*
a. In limiting/excluding *something or someone* with respect to something or someone in the preceding context

וְהָיְתָה הָעִיר חֵרֶם הִיא וְכָל־אֲשֶׁר־בָּהּ לַיהוָה רַק רָחָב הַזּוֹנָה תִּחְיֶה	But the city and all that is within it shall be devoted to the Lord for destruction; *only* Rahab the harlot shall live (Josh. 6.17).

Sometimes the preceding context is not explicitly mentioned.

וַיַּרְא יְהוָה כִּי רַבָּה רָעַת הָאָדָם בָּאָרֶץ וְכָל־יֵצֶר מַחְשְׁבֹת לִבּוֹ רַק רַע כָּל־הַיּוֹם	The Lord saw that the wickedness of man was great in the earth, and that every imagination of the thoughts of his heart was *only* evil continually (Gen. 6.5).

b. Sets a limit with *respect to the content* of a directly preceding expression

וַעֲשׂוּ לָהֶן כַּטּוֹב בְּעֵינֵיכֶם רַק לָאֲנָשִׁים הָאֵל אַל־תַּעֲשׂוּ דָבָר	Do to them as you please; *only* do nothing to these men (Gen. 19.8).

(ii) Also functions as a *modal word* (Cf. §41.3/10.)

§41.5. *Negatives*

1. *Introduction*
This class is based predominantly on semantic considerations. A feature of all the words belonging to this class is that they *negate* a word, constituent or clause.

2. אֵין
(i) Negates the events to which *a participle* refers

אֵינֶנִּי שֹׁמֵעַ   I will *not* listen (Isa. 1.15).

(ii) Also functions as a (negative) *predicator of existence*. It denies the existence of the referent of an undetermined subject in a nominal clause. (Cf. §42.2.)

וְאָדָם אַיִן לַעֲבֹד אֶת־הָאֲדָמָה   there was *no* man to till the ground (Gen. 2.5).

3. אַל
(i) Negates *a directive*: usually applies only to a specific situation (Cf. §19.4/4.)

אַל־תֹּאכַל לֶחֶם וְאַל־תֵּשְׁתְּ מָיִם   Eat *no* bread, and drink *no* water (1 Kgs 13.22).

(ii) Negates *a desire*

כִּי אָמְרָה אַל־אֶרְאֶה בְּמוֹת הַיָּלֶד   For she said: Let me *not* look upon the death of the child (Gen. 21.16).

(iii) Indicates the *refusal of a summons*

וַיֹּאמֶר לוֹ מֶלֶךְ יִשְׂרָאֵל אַל   But the king of Israel said to him: *No,*
כִּי־קָרָא יְהוָה לִשְׁלֹשֶׁת   for the LORD has called these three
הַמְּלָכִים הָאֵלֶּה   kings (2 Kgs 3.13).

4. בַּל
Negates *a statement*. It usually occurs in poetry.

אָמַר בְּלִבּוֹ בַּל־אֶמּוֹט   He thinks in his heart: I shall *not* be moved (Ps. 10:6).

וְלִבּוֹ בַּל־עִמָּךְ   But his heart is *not* with you (Prov. 23.7).

5. בְּלִי

(i) Negates *a statement*. It usually occurs in poetry.

עַל־בְּלִי הִגִּיד לוֹ כִּי בֹרֵחַ הוּא	in that he did *not* tell him that he intended to flee (Gen. 31.20).
בְּלִי נִשְׁמָע קוֹלָם	Their voice is *not* heard (Ps. 19.4).

(ii) Negates *the referent of a noun*

אֲשֶׁר יִרְצַח אֶת־רֵעֵהוּ בִּבְלִי־דַעַת	who kills his neighbor *un*intentionally (Deut. 4.42)

6. בִּלְתִּי

(i) Negates part of the content of a *subordinate clause*

a. *Infinitive clause* where בִּלְתִּי occurs with the preposition לְ. (In a few instances בִּלְתִּי negates a finite verb, e.g. Exod. 20.20 and 2 Sam. 14.14.)

הֲמִן־הָעֵץ אֲשֶׁר צִוִּיתִיךָ לְבִלְתִּי אֲכָל־מִמֶּנּוּ אָכָלְתָּ	Have you eaten of the tree of which I commanded you *not* to eat? (Gen. 3.11).

b. *Adverbial clause* usually with the preposition עַד

וַיַּכּוּ אֹתוֹ ... עַד־בִּלְתִּי הִשְׁאִיר־לוֹ שָׂרִיד	So they slew him ... until there was *not one* survivor left to him (Num. 21.35).

(ii) Negates the referent of an *adjective* (rare)

כִּי אָמַר מִקְרֶה הוּא בִּלְתִּי טָהוֹר הוּא כִּי־לֹא טָהוֹר	For he thought: Something has befallen him; he is *not* clean, surely he is not clean (1 Sam. 20.26).

(iii) Functions also as *a focus particle* (Cf. §41.4/6.)

7. טֶרֶם

This ordinary adverb also functions as a negative. (Cf. §41.2/2.)

8. לֹא

(i) Negates *a statement*

כִּי לֹא הִמְטִיר יְהוָה אֱלֹהִים עַל־הָאָרֶץ	For the Lord God had *not* caused it to rain upon the earth (Gen. 2.5).

In a reply the other person's statement (or directive) is sometimes negated in a statement. The statement that is negated, however, is implied.

וַיֹּאמֶר אֲלֵהֶם לֹא כִּי־עֶרְוַת   He said to them: *No*, but it is the
הָאָרֶץ בָּאתֶם לִרְאוֹת   weakness of the land that you have
come to see (Gen. 42.12).

(ii) Negates *a command*. The command then acquires a generally valid character, i.e. a prohibition. (Cf. §19.3/5(iii).)

לֹא תֹאכַל מִמֶּנּוּ   Of that you *shall not* eat (Gen. 2.17).

(iii) Negates *a nominal entity* (for example, an adjective).

עַל־דֶּרֶךְ לֹא־טוֹב   on a way that is *not* good (Ps. 36.5)

9. פֶּן

This conjunction also functions as a negative. (Cf. §40.14.)

§42. **Predicators of Existence**

§42.1. *Introduction*

There are only two words in this class, יֵשׁ and אַיִן. An outstanding characteristic of these words is that they express existence or non-existence. Both of them can take a pronominal suffix.

Person	Singular		Plural	
1 m./f.	אֵינֶנִּי	not I	אֵינֶנּוּ	not us
2 m.	אֵינְךָ	not you	אֵינְכֶם	not you
2 f.	אֵינֵךְ	not you		not you
3 m.	אֵינֶנּוּ	not he	אֵינָם	not them
3 f.	אֵינֶנָּה	not she		not them

§42.2. אַיִן

1. *Indicates that an undetermined entity does not exist*

וְאָדָם אַיִן לַעֲבֹד אֶת־הָאֲדָמָה   There was *no* man to till the ground
(Gen. 2.5).

2. *Functions also as a negative (Cf. §.41.5/2.)*

Negates the events to which *a participle* refers

אֵינֶנִּי שֹׁמֵעַ   I will *not* listen (Isa. 1.15).

§42.3. יֵשׁ

Expresses existence

(i) Expresses the existence of an *undetermined or impersonal subject*

יֶשׁ־שֶׁבֶר בְּמִצְרָיִם   *There is* grain in Egypt (Gen. 42.1).

(ii) *Confirms the existence or presence* of a particular person or thing

הֲיֵשׁ בָּזֶה הָרֹאֶה: וַתַּעֲנֶינָה   Is the seer here? They answered
אוֹתָם וַתֹּאמַרְנָה יֵשׁ הִנֵּה לְפָנֶיךָ   them: He is; behold, he *is* just ahead
of you (1 Sam. 9.11-12).

§43. Interrogatives

§43.1. *Introduction*

BH has no question mark. In BH questions requiring a factual
answer (who? or what?) and questions with a yes-no reply are
marked with an interrogative. (Cf. §11.8.) Although factual questions
are usually introduced with an interrogative pronoun and should have
been dealt with in §36, they are discussed here for the sake of cov-
ering questions as a whole.

§43.2. *Yes/no Questions*

These questions are introduced as follows:

1. הֲ/הֲלֹא

(i) *Morphology*

a. The interrogative particle הֲ is attached to the most appropriate word.

הֲשָׁלוֹם לַנַּעַר לְאַבְשָׁלוֹם   Is it well with the young man
Absalom? (2 Sam. 18.32).

b. Before words that begin with a guttural, the interrogative particle is
vocalized with a / ֲ / .

הַאֵלֵךְ וְקָרָאתִי לָךְ ...   Shall I go and call you ... ? (Exod.
2.7).

c. Before words that begin with a guttural and in which the first vowel is a / ָ / or / ֳ / , the interrogative particle is vocalized with a / ַ / .

כִּי־אֶל־אֵל הֶאָמַר ...	For has any one said to God ... ? (Job 34.31).

(ii) *Semantic and pragmatic functions*

a. Mark a *yes/no question*

הֲשָׁלוֹם לַנַּעַר לְאַבְשָׁלוֹם	Is it well with the young man Absalom? (2 Sam. 18.32).

b. Mark (הֲלֹא in particular) a *rhetorical question*. In this way a statement is usually made which cannot easily be contested by the person addressed.

הֲלֹא הוּא אָמַר־לִי אֲחֹתִי הִוא	Did he not himself say to me: She is my sister? (Gen. 20.5).

A double question is usually introduced with הֲ ... (וְ) אִם.

הֲמָלֹךְ תִּמְלֹךְ עָלֵינוּ אִם־מָשׁוֹל תִּמְשֹׁל בָּנוּ	Are you indeed to reign over us? Or are you indeed to have dominion over us? (Gen. 37.8).

c. Introduce an *indirect question*

לָדַעַת הַהִצְלִיחַ יְהוָה דַּרְכּוֹ אִם־לֹא	to learn whether the Lord had prospered his journey or not (Gen. 24.21).

2. *Intonation*

Marks a yes/no question

וַיֹּאמֶר הַמֶּלֶךְ שָׁלוֹם לַנַּעַר ...	And the king said: Is it well with the young man ... ? (2 Sam. 18.29).

§43.3. *Factual (or WH-) Questions*

These questions are introduced by the following interrogatives. In a verbal question the verb follows the interrogative. In a nominal clause the predicate follows the question:

1. מִי

(i) *Enquires about the identity* of a person

מִי־הָאִישׁ הַלָּזֶה	*Who* is the man? (Gen. 24.65).

The question sometimes acquires some emotional weight by the addition of זֶה or זֹאת. One could also speak here of the speaker's *attitude* that emerges in relation to the content of the question.

בֶּן־מִי־זֶה הַנַּעַר

Whose son is this youth? (1 Sam. 17.55).

The question may sometimes be posed *indirectly*.

שְׁאַל אַתָּה בֶּן־מִי־זֶה הָעָלֶם

Inquire *whose* son the stripling is (1 Sam. 17.56).

(ii) Enquires about *the identity of a group of people* or *the name of a person*

כִּי מִי־גוֹי גָּדוֹל אֲשֶׁר־לוֹ אֱלֹהִים

For *what* great nation is there that has gods? (Deut. 4.7).

מִי שְׁמֶךָ

What is your name? (Judg. 13.17).

(iii) Introduces *a rhetorical question in which a speaker usually expresses a value judgment* about himself or someone else

וַיֹּאמֶר מִי דָוִד וּמִי בֶן־יִשָׁי

And he said: *Who* is David? *Who* is the son of Jesse? (1 Sam. 25.10).

(iv) Expresses a *wish* (rare)

וַיֹּאמֶר אַבְשָׁלוֹם מִי־יְשִׂמֵנִי
שֹׁפֵט בָּאָרֶץ

Absalom said moreover: *Oh* that I *were* judge in the land! (2 Sam. 15.4).

Sometimes a fixed expression מִי יִתֵּן is used. This construction, which acts syntactically as an interjection, expresses *a positive wish*. (Cf. §45.3.)

בַּבֹּקֶר תֹּאמַר מִי־יִתֵּן עֶרֶב

In the morning you shall say: Would it were evening! (Deut. 28.67).

(v) Functions in the fixed expression מִי יוֹדֵעַ which expresses *a wish the outcome of which is doubtful: maybe.*

אָמַרְתִּי מִי יוֹדֵעַ יְחָנַּנִי יְהוָה

I said: *Who knows maybe* the Lord will be gracious to me (2 Sam. 12.22).

(vi) Functions as *an indefinite pronoun*

מִי־יָרֵא וְחָרֵד יָשֹׁב

Whoever is fearful and trembling, let him return home (Judg. 7.3).

Sometimes מִי is followed by אֲשֶׁר or even הָאִישׁ אֲשֶׁר.

מִי אֲשֶׁר חָטָא־לִי אֶמְחֶנּוּ מִסִּפְרִי	*Whoever* has sinned against me, him will I blot out of my book (Exod. 32.33).
מִי־הָאִישׁ אֲשֶׁר בָּנָה בַיִת־חָדָשׁ	*Everyone that* has built a new house ... (Deut. 20.5).

Sometimes מִי is used absolutely, i.e. the relative clause is missing.

שִׁמְרוּ־מִי בַּנַּעַר בְּאַבְשָׁלוֹם	Protect *whoever* (you might be) the young man Absalom (2 Sam. 18.12).

Sometimes מִי is used after אֵת as the object of a clause.

בַּחֲרוּ לָכֶם הַיּוֹם אֶת־מִי תַעֲבֹדוּן	Choose this day *whom* you will serve (Josh. 24.15).

2. מָה *(Some dictionaries regard* מָה *as the basic form.)*

Morphologically מַה changes to מָה if it precedes א, ה or ר. מַה changes to מֶה if it precedes ח or ע. If מַה precedes any other consonant, no lengthening of the vowel occurs and the following consonant doubles, for example, מַה־זֹּאת. It resembles the patterns of the definite article, cf. §24.4/2.

(i) Enquires about *the nature of a thing or event*

מֶה עָשִׂיתָ	*What* have you done? (Gen. 4.10).

The question sometimes acquires emotional weight by the addition of זֶה or זֹאת. Speakers may, for example, express a degree of irritation (Cf. also §36.2/2(vi).)

וַיֹּאמֶר יְהוָה אֱלֹהִים לָאִשָּׁה מַה־זֹּאת עָשִׂית	Then the Lord God said to the woman: *What* is this that you have done? (Gen. 3.13).

The event or state of affairs that is enquired about is sometimes to *the benefit or disadvantage* of someone. In such cases מָה is followed by the preposition לְ.

מַה־לָּךְ הָגָר	*What* troubles you, Hagar? (Gen. 21.17).

(ii) Enquires sometimes about *the reason* for a state of affairs or an event

מָה אֲנַחְנוּ יֹשְׁבִים פֹּה	*Why* do we sit here? (2 Kgs 7.3).

The question sometimes acquires emotional weight by the addition of
זֶה or זֹאת. Speakers may, for example, express a degree of irritation.

מַה־זֶּה רוּחֲךָ סָרָה

Why is your spirit so vexed? (1 Kgs 21.5).

(iii) Functions as an introduction to *a rhetorical question* in which a
speaker usually expresses a *value judgment* about something or someone. This value judgment is usually *negative*.

כִּי מָה עַבְדְּךָ הַכֶּלֶב כִּי יַעֲשֶׂה
הַדָּבָר הַגָּדוֹל הַזֶּה

For *what* is your servant, who is but a
dog, that he should do this great
thing? (2 Kgs 8.13).

Sometimes the rhetorical question indicates a *strong denial*.

מַה־לָּנוּ חֵלֶק בְּדָוִד

What portion have we in David?
(1 Kgs 12.16).

(iv) Functions as an introduction to an exclamation in which a speaker
usually expresses a *value judgment* about something

מָה־אַדִּיר שִׁמְךָ בְּכָל־הָאָרֶץ

How majestic is your name in all the
earth! (Ps. 8.2).

(v) Functions also as *an indefinite pronoun* (Cf. §36.5.)

מַה־תֹּאמַר נַפְשְׁךָ וְאֶעֱשֶׂה־לָּךְ

Whatever you say, I will do for you
(1 Sam. 20.4).

3. מַה + *prepositions*

(i) לָמָה

a. Enquires as to the *reason* for a state of affairs or an action: *why?*

לָמָּה חָרָה לָךְ

Why are you angry? (Gen. 4.6).

b. Functions sometimes as an introduction to *an alternative posed with
a negative tenor: otherwise, or else*

שַׁלְּחֵנִי לָמָה אֲמִיתֶךָ

Let me go *or else* I shall kill you
(1 Sam. 19.17).

(ii) בַּמֶּה

Enquires about the *manner* in which something is to be done: *how?*

בַּמָּה אֵדַע

How am I to know? (Gen. 15.8).

(iii) עַד־מָה

Enquires about the *duration* of a state of affairs or events: *how long?*

עַד־מָה יְהוָה תֶּאֱנַף לָנֶצַח

How long, O Lord? Will you be
angry for ever? (Ps. 79.5).

(iv) עַל־מָה

Enquires about the *reason* or *motivation* for a state of affairs or action: *why?*

עַל־מָה הִכִּיתָ אֶת־אֲתֹנְךָ

Why have you struck your ass? (Num. 22.32).

4. אֵי

(i) Enquires as to the *place where* someone or something is: *where?*

אֵי הֶבֶל אָחִיךָ

Where is Abel your brother? (Gen. 4.9).

(ii) Enquires (with or without preposition) as to *the place from which or along which* movement has occurred: *from where? along which?*

אֵי־מִזֶּה בָאת

Where have you come *from*? (Gen. 16.8).

אֵי־זֶה הַדֶּרֶךְ הָלַךְ

Which way did he go? (1 Kgs 13.12).

5. אַיֵּה

Enquires about the place *in which* someone or something is: *where?*
אַיֵּה is *never* used to enquire about the place in which *an event* took place.

אַיֵּה שָׂרָה אִשְׁתֶּךָ

Where is Sarah your wife? (Gen. 18.9).

6. אֵיךְ *and* אֵיכָה *(Strictly speaking these words are not interrogative pronouns but interrogative adverbs.)*

(i) Enquire about *the manner* in which something occurred: *how?* (This apparently basic function is, however, seldom used to pose an ordinary question.)

אֵיכָה יַעַבְדוּ הַגּוֹיִם הָאֵלֶּה
אֶת־אֱלֹהֵיהֶם

How did these nations serve their gods? (Deut. 12.30).

Sometimes אֵיךְ and אֵיכָה are used in indirect questions.

הַגֶּד־נָא לָנוּ אֵיךְ כָּתַבְתָּ
אֶת־כָּל־הַדְּבָרִים הָאֵלֶּה

Tell us, *how* did you write all these words? (Jer. 36.17).

(ii) Function primarily in *rhetorical questions* (almost half the occurrences in the Hebrew Bible). In these cases the rhetorical question is used to *make it clear to listeners that some happening or state of affairs is out of the question.* אֵיךְ and אֵיכָה are then usually followed by an imperfect form.

אֵיכָה אֶשָּׂא לְבַדִּי טָרְחֲכֶם	*How* can I bear alone the weight of you? (Deut. 1.12).
הֵן אֲנִי עֲרַל שְׂפָתַיִם	Look, I am of uncircumcized lips;
וְאֵיךְ יִשְׁמַע אֵלַי פַּרְעֹה	*how* then shall Pharaoh listen to me? (Exod. 6.30).

Sometimes the rhetorical question can be used to *reproach* the person addressed.

וְאֵיךְ אָמַרְתָּ אֲחֹתִי הִוא	*How* then could you say: She is my sister? (Gen. 26.9).

(iii) Function as exclamations to introduce the nature of a particular state of affairs or events. Speakers often use such constructions to express *their disappointment, satisfaction or amazement* about a situation.

אֵיךְ נָפְלוּ גִבּוֹרִים	*How* are the mighty fallen! (2 Sam. 1.19).
אֵיכָה הָיְתָה לְזוֹנָה	*How* the (faithful city) has become a harlot! (Isa. 1.21).
אֵיךְ חַתָּה הֵילִילוּ	*How* it is broken! How they wail!
אֵיךְ הִפְנָה־עֹרֶף מוֹאָב בּוֹשׁ	*How* Moab has turned his back in shame! (Jer. 48.39).

7. אֵיפֹה

Enquires about the place *in which* someone or something is to be found or in which events occur: *where?*

אֵיפֹה שְׁמוּאֵל וְדָוִד	*Where* are Samuel and David? (1 Sam. 19.22).
אֵיפֹה לְקַטְתְּ הַיּוֹם	*Where* did you glean today? (Ruth 2.19).

8. אָן[57] *and* אָנָה

(i) Enquire about the place *to which* someone is going: *where to?*

וְאָנָה תֵלֵכִי   *Where* are you going? (Gen. 16.8).

אָן הֲלַכְתֶּם   *Where* did you go? (1 Sam. 10.14).

(ii) In exceptional cases אָנָה is used to enquire about the place *in which* an event occurred: *where?*

וְאָנָה עָשִׂית   *Where* have you worked? (Ruth 2.19).

(iii) עַד־אָנָה is used to enquire about the *duration* of events: *until when? how long still?*

עַד־אָנָה מֵאַנְתֶּם   *How* long do you refuse? (Exod. 16.28).

§44. Discourse Markers

§44.1. *Introduction*

BH speakers use discourse markers to comment on the content of a sentence *and/or* sentences from a meta-level. (Cf. §11.9.) In this way the sentence or sentences is/are anchored in the discourse in a particular way.

§44.2. הֵן

There is no essential difference between the syntactic and semantic functions of הֵן and הִנֵּה. Although it is claimed that הֵן indicates a conditional clause, the conditional function may be ascribed to the context rather than to הֵן itself.

§44.3. הִנֵּה

1. *Introduction*

The imperative form of the verb stem רָאה is sometimes used as a variant of הֵן and הִנֵּה. The word class to which הִנֵּה belongs has always been a problem for grammarians. Some have described it as an interjection while others think it is an adverb. Yet it does not really fit in either of these classes. As opposed to interjections and

---

57. אָן occurs only twice in the Hebrew Bible.

most ordinary adverbs, it can take a pronominal suffix and, as opposed to ordinary adverbs, it refers to a whole clause. In fact, it always precedes the clause upon which it has a bearing. Semantically it also differs strongly from the class *modal words* that have been identified in this grammar. It does involve the speaker in the content of the clause, but it does not refer to his opinion on the degree of probability of the events or state of affairs. It *points* to the content of the clause that follows it (hence the term sentence deictic is sometimes applied to it). In this way that content acquires a particular prominence within a larger context. In this respect הִנֵּה has the same function as the focus particles. (Cf. §41.4.)

2. *Morphology of* הִנֵּה

Pronominal suffixes can be attached to הִנֵּה. *These suffixes are usually the subject of a nominal clause.* The paradigm may be set out as follows:

Person	Singular		Plural	
1 m./f.	הִנְנִי / הִנֵּנִי	Look, I	הִנְנוּ / הִנֶּנּוּ	Look, us
2 m.	הִנְּךָ	Look, you	הִנְּכֶם	Look, you
2 f.	הִנָּךְ	Look, you		Look, you
3 m.	הִנּוֹ	Look, he	הִנָּם	Look, them
3 f.		Look, she		Look, them

3. *Syntax of* הִנֵּה

(i) הִנֵּה + *verbal clause*

וּלְשָׂרָה אָמַר הִנֵּה נָתַתִּי   And to Sarah he said: *Look*, I have
אֶלֶף כֶּסֶף לְאָחִיךְ   given your brother a thousand pieces
of silver (Gen. 20.16).

(ii) הִנֵּה *within a clause after a verb of observation*

וַיִּשָּׂא עֵינָיו וַיַּרְא וְהִנֵּה שְׁלֹשָׁה   And he lifted up his eyes and looked,
אֲנָשִׁים נִצָּבִים עָלָיו   and *look*, three men stood in front of
him! (Gen. 18.2).

(iii) הִנֵּה + *nominal clause*

a. הִנֵּה + nominal clause (with subject *and* predicate)

הִנֵּה אַרְצִי לְפָנֶיךָ   *Look*, my land is before you (Gen.
20.15).

b. הִנֵּה + nominal clause (with *predicate*)

וַיֹּאמְרוּ אֵלָיו אַיֵּה שָׂרָה אִשְׁתֶּךָ   And they said to him: Where is Sarah
וַיֹּאמֶר הִנֵּה בָאֹהֶל   your wife? And he said: *There* in the
tent (Gen. 18.9).

c. הִנֵּה + nominal clause (with *subject*)

וַיֹּאמֶר אֵלָיו אַבְרָהָם   And he said to him: Abraham! And
וַיֹּאמֶר הִנֵּנִי   he said: *Here am I* (Gen. 22.1).

4. The semantics and pragmatics of הִנֵּה

The semantic function of הִנֵּה is to *focus attention on the utterance*
that follows it.

(i) *Attention is focused on events that are surprising or unexpected for
the person addressed or the characters in a story.* It often introduces
an important change of perspective in a story.

הִנֵּה אָנֹכִי עֹשֶׂה דָבָר בְּיִשְׂרָאֵל   *Look*, I am about to do a thing in
Israel (1 Sam. 3.11).

וְהִנֵּה עוֹדֶנָּה מְדַבֶּרֶת עִם־הַמֶּלֶךְ   And *look*, while she was still
וְנָתָן הַנָּבִיא בָּא   speaking with the king, Nathan the
prophet came in (1 Kgs 1.22).

וְהִנֵּה אִישׁ מִבְּנֵי יִשְׂרָאֵל בָּא   And *look*, one of the people of Israel
וַיַּקְרֵב אֶל־אֶחָיו אֶת־הַמִּדְיָנִית   came and brought a Midianite
woman to his family (Num. 25.6).

(ii) By using הִנֵּה speakers *present* themselves, someone else or something *as available at the moment of speaking*. In other words, the
presention is performed by means of the utterance.

הִנֵּה אַרְצִי לְפָנֶיךָ   *Look*, my land is before you (Gen.
20.15).

Speaker may also present themselves as *prepared for some event.*

טָעֹם טָעַמְתִּי בִּקְצֵה הַמַּטֶּה   I tasted a little honey with the tip of
אֲשֶׁר־בְּיָדִי מְעַט דְּבַשׁ הִנְנִי אָמוּת   the staff that was in my hand; *I am
prepared to die* (1 Sam. 14.43).

Related to the above-mentioned use are instances where הִנֵּה (+ first
person pronominal suffix) is used to refer to characters' positive reaction, their reply, after someone has called them. It may be translated *yes, here I am.*

וַיִּקְרָא יהוה אֶל־שְׁמוּאֵל   And the Lord called Samuel and he
וַיֹּאמֶר הִנֵּנִי   answered (lit. said): *Yes* (1 Sam.
3.4).

§44.4. וְהָיָה

1. Precedes a sentence or an adverbial phrase (often with a temporal connotation) that *introduces a new paragraph or sub-paragraph*. By using וְהָיָה the speaker or narrator indicates that the events in the (sub) paragraph *are part of the mainstream* events belonging to the procedure being described or of the future events envisaged.

וְהָיָה כִּי־יִרְאוּ אֹתָךְ הַמִּצְרִים וְאָמְרוּ אִשְׁתּוֹ זֹאת	And if the Egyptians see you, they will say: This is his wife (Gen. 12.12).
וְהָיָה בַּיּוֹם הַהוּא שֹׁרֶשׁ יִשַׁי אֲשֶׁר עֹמֵד לְנֵס עַמִּים אֵלָיו גּוֹיִם יִדְרֹשׁוּ וְהָיְתָה מְנֻחָתוֹ כָּבוֹד	In that day the root of Jesse shall stand as an ensign to the peoples; him shall the nations seek, and his dwellings shall be glorious (Isa. 11.10).

2. *Incorporates a state of affairs* (described by means of nominal clauses) into the mainstream of the procedure being described or the future events envisaged. This is a way of preventing that state of affairs from being understood as mere background information. Semantically speaking וְהָיָה has functions that correspond with the waw consecutive + perfect form. (Cf. §21.3.)

וְהָיָה צֶדֶק אֵזוֹר מָתְנָיו וְהָאֱמוּנָה אֵזוֹר חֲלָצָיו	And *so* righteousness shall be the girdle of his waist, and faithfulness the girdle of his loins (Isa. 11.5).

3. *Functions as an ordinary verb* in the future: will be. Prerequisites for וְהָיָה to fulfil this function are the following: the subject of וְהָיָה must agree with it in number and gender and the semantic notion 'become.' must be involved. (For the functions of the waw consecutive + perfect form, cf. §21.3.)

וְהָיָה לְאוֹת בְּרִית בֵּינִי וּבֵינֵיכֶם	It *shall become* a sign of the covenant between me and you (Gen. 17.11).

§44.5. וַיְהִי

1. וַיְהִי *anchors an event, state of affairs, scene, episode or narrative to the time line.*

וַיְהִי namely signals that the event, state of affairs, scene, episode or narrative follows in time on a particular preceding event, state of affairs, scene, episode or narrative. It is therefore part of the mainstream of a greater narration. The function of וַיְהִי may be compared to the 'and then' that young children usually use to tell their stories in English. However, it is often difficult to find a suitable English equivalent of וַיְהִי. Semantically speaking וַיְהִי has functions that correspond with waw consecutive + imperfect form. (Cf. §21.2.)

The following syntactic distinctions can be made:

(i) וַיְהִי + *temporal construction*

a. In cases where the *temporal frame* of a new scene or episode is specified, וַיְהִי signals that a *new* scene or episode is subsequent to a previously mentioned scene, and that this scene is part of the mainstream of a larger episode or narrative.

וַיְהִי בָּעֵת הַהוּא ...	*And then*, at about that time
וַיֹּאמֶר אֲבִימֶלֶךְ	Abimelech said: ... (Gen. 21.22).

וַיְהִי may also signal that a scene *following some background information* is part of the mainstream of a larger episode.

וּמְפִבֹשֶׁת בֶּן־שָׁאוּל יָרַד	And Mephibosheth the son of Saul
לִקְרַאת הַמֶּלֶךְ וְלֹא־עָשָׂה	came down to meet the king; he had
רַגְלָיו וְלֹא־עָשָׂה שְׂפָמוֹ ...	neither dressed his feet, nor trimmed
וַיְהִי כִּי־בָא יְרוּשָׁלַם	his beard, ... *and then*, when he came
לִקְרַאת הַמֶּלֶךְ	from Jerusalem to meet the king, the
וַיֹּאמֶר לוֹ הַמֶּלֶךְ	king said to him: ... (2 Sam. 19.25-26).

b. In cases where *the immediate temporal proximity of two events on the time line* is involved (usually expressed by means of the preposition כְּ + infinitive construct, cf. §39.10/3) וַיְהִי allows speakers to describe the immediate temporal proximity of two events, without breaking the mainstream of events *in a scene*. These constructions are often used at the climax of a scene in order to signal what triggered a climactic event.

וַיְהִי כְּהַזְכִּירוֹ אֶת־אֲרוֹן הָאֱלֹהִים	*And then*, the moment that he
וַיִּפֹּל מֵעַל־הַכִּסֵּא	mentioned the ark of God, Eli fell ... from his seat (1 Sam. 4.18).

(ii) וַיְהִי + *state of affairs* (referred to by means of a nominal clause)

a. וַיְהִי *introduces the setting* of a new scene or episode. וַיְהִי signals that the new scene or episode needs to be link to a preceding one on which this new scene or episode follows in time.

וַיְהִי אִישׁ אֶחָד מִן־הָרָמָתַיִם ...	And there was a certain man of Ramathaim ... (1 Sam. 1.1).

b. וַיְהִי occurs *in the setting* of a new episode (seldom). וַיְהִי precedes reference to a state of affairs that (apparently) plays a pivotal role in the subsequent episode.

וַיְהִי רָעָב גָּדוֹל בְּשֹׁמְרוֹן

And there was a great famine in Samaria (2 Kgs 6.25).

c. וַיְהִי occurs *in the course of a scene.* וַיְהִי signals that a state of affairs needs to be treated on par with the mainstream events of the narration, and that is not mere background information.

וַיְהִי יְהוָה אֶת־יוֹסֵף

And the Lord was with Joseph (Gen. 39.21).

d. וַיְהִי occurs *at the conclusion of a scene.* וַיְהִי signals that a state of affairs is the outcome of a preceding series of events.

וַיְהִי לְפָנָיו כְּאֶתְמוֹל שִׁלְשׁוֹם

And *so* he was in his presence as before (1 Sam. 19.7).

2. *Functions as an ordinary verb in the past tense*: became.

A prerequisite for וַיְהִי to fulfil this function is the following: the subject of וַיְהִי must agree with it in number and gender and the semantic notion 'to become' must be involved. (Cf. also §21.2.)

וַיְהִי־הֶבֶל רֹעֵה צֹאן
וְקַיִן הָיָה עֹבֵד אֲדָמָה

Now Abel *became* a keeper of sheep, and Cain a tiller of the ground (Gen. 4.2).

§44.6. וְעַתָּה

1. *Indicates a logical conclusion: in the light of, therefore*

וַיֹּאמֶר אֵלָיו הָאֱלֹהִים בַּחֲלֹם
גַּם אָנֹכִי יָדַעְתִּי כִּי בְתָם־לְבָבְךָ
עָשִׂיתָ זֹּאת וָאֶחְשֹׂךְ גַּם־אָנֹכִי
אוֹתְךָ מֵחֲטוֹ־לִי ...
וְעַתָּה הָשֵׁב אֵשֶׁת־הָאִישׁ

Then God said to him in the dream: Yes, I know that you have done this in the integrity of your heart, and it was I who kept you from sinning against me; ... *Therefore* restore the man's wife (Gen. 20.6-7).

Sometimes the grounds for a conclusion extend over several chapters of a biblical book. For example, the grounds for the conclusion reached in Deut. 4.1 are to be found in Deut. 1–3.

וְעַתָּה יִשְׂרָאֵל שְׁמַע אֶל־הַחֻקִּים
וְאֶל־הַמִּשְׁפָּטִים

Therefore, O Israel, give heed to the statutes and the ordinances (Deut. 4.1).

2. *Functions also an adverb (Cf. §41.2/6(i).)*

§45. **Interjections**

§45.1 *Introduction*

Interjections do not form part of a constituent or a clause. (Cf. 11.10.) They are also not related to a constituent or clause. Semantically interjections could be classified as follows:

- Interjections that express emotion.
- Interjections that express an attitude.
- Interjections that express the experience of a threat.
- Interjections related to addressing someone.

§45.2. *Expression of Emotion*

(i) הֶאָח

Expresses *joy or pleasure*

הֶאָח חַמּוֹתִי רָאִיתִי אוּר   *Aha*, I am warm, I have seen the fire (Isa. 44.16).

(ii) אֲהָהּ

Expresses *sorrow*

אֲהָהּ בִּתִּי הַכְרֵעַ הִכְרַעְתִּנִי   *Oh*, my daughter! You have brought me very low (Judg. 11.35).

§45.3. *Expression of an Attitude*

(i) אַחֲלַי and אַחֲלֵי

Express a positive wish

אַחֲלֵי אֲדֹנִי לִפְנֵי הַנָּבִיא   *Would* that my lord were with the
אֲשֶׁר בְּשֹׁמְרוֹן   prophet who is in Samaria! (2 Kgs 5.3).

(ii) מִי יִתֵּן

Expresses a positive wish (Cf. §43.3/1(iv).)

וּמִי יִתֵּן אֶת־הָעָם הַזֶּה בְּיָדִי   *Would* that this people were under my hand! (Judg. 9.29).

(iii) חֲלִילָה

a. Expresses a speaker's refusal to accept a state of affairs or course of
   events

וַיֹּאמֶר לוֹ חָלִילָה לֹא תָמוּת   And he said to him: *Far from it!* You
                                                      shall not die (1 Sam. 20.2).

b. A speaker uses the expression to distance himself from a situation or
   action. This expression is more commonly the predicate of a nominal
   clause, i.e. syntactically speaking it is not an interjection.

וַיֹּאמֶר חָלִילָה לִי
מֵעֲשׂוֹת זֹאת   But he said: *Far be it* from me that I
                                                           should do so! (Gen. 44.17).

§45.4. *Expression of the Experience of a Threat*

(i) הוֹי (usually *followed by a participle*)

הוֹי אֹמֵר לְאָב מַה־תּוֹלִיד   *Woe* to him who says to a father:
                                                 What are you begetting? (Isa. 45.10).

22 of the 50 instances in which this interjection is used in the
Hebrew Bible occur in the book of Isaiah.

(ii) אוֹי (usually *followed by* לְ *plus suffix*)

וַיֹּאמְרוּ אוֹי לָנוּ כִּי לֹא הָיְתָה
כָּזֹאת אֶתְמוֹל שִׁלְשֹׁם: And they said: *Woe* to us! For nothing
                                                                                   like this has happened before (1 Sam.
                                                                                   4.7).

§45.5. *Interjections Used in an Address*

Requests

(i) ־נָא

Expresses a polite request: *please*. (Cf. §19.4/4.)

נַעְבְּרָה־נָּא בְאַרְצֶךָ   Now *please* let us pass through your
                                              land (Num. 20.17).

(ii) אָנָּה/אָנָּא

Expresses an urgent request: *I/we beg you*

אָנָּא שָׂא נָא פֶּשַׁע אַחֶיךָ   Forgive, *I beg you*, the transgression
                                                  of your brothers (Gen. 50.17).

(iii) בִּי (always followed by אֲדֹנִי or אֲדֹנָי)

Expresses a request to be excused: *pardon/excuse me/us*

בִּי אֲדֹנִי מָה אֹמַר   *Excuse me* Lord, but what can I say
                                           (Josh. 7.8).

Chapter 7

§46. The Syntax of Word Order

§46.1. *Verbal Clauses*

1. *Introduction*

Statistically speaking most clauses in the Hebrew Bible commence with a verb. The reasons for this are the following:

- In the perfect and imperfect forms of BH verbs person (first, second or third person) is not marked by means of an independent personal pronoun as it is in most European languages. In other words, BH has no direct equivalent for '*I* wrote the book'. The morpheme that marks person is part of the verbal conjugation, for example, כָּתַבְתִּי אֶת־הַסֵּפֶר. (Cf. also §15.)
- The waw consecutive + perfect and waw consecutive + imperfect constructions that are frequently used in BH do not allow a constituent (e.g. subject or object) to precede the verb.

It is therefore understandable that BH is often regarded as a so-called VSO ('Verb-Subject-Object') language. (Cf. §47.1/(d).) As their name suggests, the most common word order in VSO languages is one in which the verb takes the initial position and is followed by the subject and object. If the verb is, however, preceded by the subject or any other constituent, the word order of that clause is regarded as marked. In most BH grammars the semantic function of 'emphasis' is attributed to this so-called marked construction. No semantic function is normally attached to the order of the constituents following the verb, for example, when the indirect object precedes the direct object.

In this grammar it is assumed that a more nuanced view of BH word order is possible. For this reason the following considerations are deemed important:[58]

(a) A distinction must be made between the preverbal field ('Vorfeld') and main field ('Hauptfeld') of a BH verbal clause. The principles governing the order of constituents in the main field are relatively complex.

(b) When the preverbal field is occupied by a constituent, this phenomenon is referred to as the *fronting* of a constituent. Note that fronting is not the function of a BH syntactic construction. It is the name of a phenomenon in which (a) constituent(s) (e.g. subject or object) precede(s) the verb of a BH clause. Fronting may have a variety of functions. (Cf. §47.2.)

(c) In the main field of a clause, that is the section of the clause that is introduced by its verb, fronting is, of course, impossible.

(d) In the main field a variety of constituents may occur. As a rule they appear in a specific order, also referred to as the unmarked order of the clause. *The movement of these constituents to the left* (under specific circumstances) is associated with only one function (in contrast to fronting). (Cf. §47.3.) In these instances one may regard the construction as a marker of that function. Hence the term marked word order.

(e) A distinction must be made between instances where a particular order of constituents is obligatory (mostly due to syntactic considerations) and instances where speakers have a choice in their ordering of constituents.

2. The preverbal field

The preverbal field refers to that section of a BH clause that *precedes the verb*.

58. Many of the views put forward here are based on the results of a major research project on the function of BH word order conducted by Walter Gross at the University of Tübingen. Some of these findings have been published, cf. Gross (1987a, 1987b, 1988, 1991, 1993a, 1993b and 1996). However, this grammar is by no means an exhaustive representation of the views of Gross. It also does not represent an uncritical acceptance of his linguistic terms of reference and research findings, for example, the term 'fronting' is preferred to his term 'topicalization.' His more nuanced distinctions of constituents, referred to as syntagms, are also not used.

(i) *General features*

a. The preverbal field may be vacant.

וַיָּשֻׁבוּ הַמַּלְאָכִים
אֶל־יַעֲקֹב לֵאמֹר
בָּאנוּ אֶל־אָחִיךָ אֶל־עֵשָׂו

And the messengers returned to Jacob, saying, We came to your brother Esau (Gen. 32.7).

b. It may contain one member.
This constituent may be one word.

אֹתִי שָׁלַח יְהוָה לִמְשָׁחֲךָ לְמֶלֶךְ

The Lord sent *me* to anoint you king (1 Sam. 15.1).

The constituent may be a word chain.

בֵּיתְךָ וּבֵית אָבִיךָ
יִתְהַלְּכוּ לְפָנַי עַד־עוֹלָם

Your house and the house of your father should go in and out before me for ever (1 Sam. 2.30).

The constituent may be modified by one or more phrases.

כָּל־הָעָם הַיֹּצֵא מִמִּצְרַיִם
הַזְּכָרִים כֹּל אַנְשֵׁי הַמִּלְחָמָה
מֵתוּ בַמִּדְבָּר בַּדֶּרֶךְ

All the people who came out of Egypt, the males, all the men of war, had died on the way in the wilderness (Josh. 5.4).

c. It may be occupied by more than one constituent.
It happens only seldom that both constituents are complements. In most cases one is an adjunct of time.

וְהַנִּשְׁאָרִים הֶרָה נָּסוּ׃

and *the rest* fled *to the mountain* (Gen. 14.10).

Note the following:

(1) Subordinated conjunctions and discourse markers (in the following order: וְ[וְ]הִנֵּה לָכֵן עַתָּה) can occupy the right-hand margin of the preverbal field. They govern the entire sentence and for this reason stand at its right-hand margin. As a rule they do not influence the function of fronting.

וְעַתָּה לֹא־אַתֶּם שְׁלַחְתֶּם
אֹתִי הֵנָּה ...

So it was not you who sent me here, (Gen. 45.8).

(2) Negatives and infinitive absolutes (in a verbal construction) are part of the verbal constituent of a clause. Also when they precede the verb of a clause, they are part of the verbal constituent, and not part of the preverbal field.

כִּי־בָרֵךְ אֲבָרֶכְךָ

I will bless you richly (Gen. 22.17).

(3) The so-called *dislocated construction (pendens construction)* should not be mistaken for fronting. In the case of the former a constituent stands at the beginning of a clause *and* is taken up again later in the clause by a constituent of the clause (called the resumptive), for example, '*That big house*, I am still going to buy *it* for us.' A dislocated phrase is not part of the subsequent clause, but a construction occurring at the outer edge of a BH clause. It is usually followed by a complete sentence with or without a fronted constituent.

הַמִּטָּה אֲשֶׁר־עָלִיתָ
שָׁם לֹא־תֵרֵד מִמֶּנָּה

The bed to which you have gone, you shall not come down from *it* (2 Kgs 1.4).

שְׁכֶם בְּנִי
חָשְׁקָה נַפְשׁוֹ בְּבִתְּכֶם

Shechem my son, his soul longs for your daughter (Gen. 34.8).

The function of the above type of dislocated construction is usually to *(re-)activate an identifiable referent* that is talked about.

(4) In BH an *adjunct of time* often precedes the waw consecutive + perfect or waw consecutive + imperfect form of the verb. This *type of dislocated construction* serves a purpose that differs from the above-mentioned. In most instances it is used to provide the temporal *point of orientation* of the subsequent event(s). This construction is often preceded by וַיְהִי. For the function of וַיְהִי, cf. §44.5/1.

This type of dislocated construction differs also syntactically from those mentioned above. It does not have a resumptive element. It is, however, regarded as a dislocated construction because the dislocated element is separated from the rest of the sentence by means of a waw.

וַיְהִי בַבֹּקֶר
וַיִּקַּח בָּלָק אֶת־בִּלְעָם
וַיַּעֲלֵהוּ בָּמוֹת בָּעַל

And on the morrow Balak took Balaam and brought him up to Bamothbaal (Num. 22.41).

(5) In a clause where the verb is *a participle* the subject normally precedes the verb.

הִנֵּה אָנֹכִי עֹשֶׂה דָבָר
בְּיִשְׂרָאֵל

Look, I *am about to do* a thing in Israel (1 Sam. 3.11).

(6) In poetic texts fronting can fulfil the same functions as in non-poetic texts. Yet one must take into account the fact that poets can sometimes use the order of elements to create formal patterns, for example, a *chiastic pattern* ABBA (verb + clause X + clause X + verb).

לֹא־יָבוֹא עוֹד שִׁמְשֵׁךְ	Your sun shall no more go down, nor
וִירֵחֵךְ לֹא יֵאָסֵף	your moon withdraw itself (Isa. 60.20).

(ii) *Obligatory entities in the preverbal field*

a. An *interrogative* (introducing a factual question) as a rule occurs in the preverbal position. The same applies to the constituent that provides the answer to the question.

מִי יַעֲלֶה־לָּנוּ אֶל־הַכְּנַעֲנִי	*Who* shall go up first for us against
בַּתְּחִלָּה לְהִלָּחֶם בּוֹ׃	the Canaanites, to fight against them?
וַיֹּאמֶר יְהוָה יְהוּדָה יַעֲלֶה	The Lord said, *Judah* shall go up (Judg. 1.1-2).

b. The demonstrative (deictic) adverb in the *messenger formula*, '*Thus* speak the Lord,' as a rule occurs in the preverbal position.

לָכֵן כֹּה אָמַר אֲדֹנָי יְהוִה	Therefore *thus* says the Lord God: (Ezek. 5.8).

c. When the subject of a clause is realized by means of *an independent personal pronoun*, as rule, it occupies the preverbal field, unless prohibited by other syntactic considerations. (Cf. 36.1/I.2(ii).)

וְלֹא תֹאמַר	Lest you should say, *I* have made
אֲנִי הֶעֱשַׁרְתִּי אֶת־אַבְרָם	Abram rich (Gen. 14.23).

3. *The main field*

(i) *General features*

The main field is always introduced by a verbal constituent. The verbal constituent may be one of the following:

a. Verb

אֹתִי שָׁלַח יְהוָה לִמְשָׁחֲךָ לְמֶלֶךְ	Me the Lord *sent* to anoint you king (1 Sam. 15.1).

b. Negative + verb

הַמִּטָּה אֲשֶׁר־עָלִיתָ שָּׁם לֹא־תֵרֵד מִמֶּנָּה	The bed to which you have gone, you *shall not come down* from it (2 Kgs 1.4).

c. Infinitive absolute + verb

אָמוֹר אָמַרְתִּי בֵּיתְךָ וּבֵית אָבִיךָ יִתְהַלְּכוּ לְפָנַי עַד־עוֹלָם	I *promised* that your house and the house of your father should go in and out before me for ever (1 Sam. 2.30).

While the preverbal field as a rule is not occupied by more than two constituents, the main field is often occupied by more than two constituents.

אֹתִי (1) שָׁלַח יְהוָה (2) (3) לִמְשָׁחֲךָ לְמֶלֶךְ (4)	The Lord sent me to anoint you king over his people Israel (1 Sam. 15.1)

(ii) *Obligatory order of constituents in the main field*

a. *Shorter constituents* with a deictic function stand close to the verb, e.g. constituents that are expressed by means of a *preposition + pronominal suffix* or אֵת + *pronominal suffix* stand as close to the verb as possible.

וַיֹּאמֶר אֵלָיו הָאֱלֹהִים ...	Then God said to *him*: ... (Gen. 20.6).

Exception: If the subject consists of a *status constructus* relationship and the pronominal suffix refers to the referent of the *post-constructus*, the preposition + pronominal suffix cannot precede the subject.

וַתֵּלֶד אֵשֶׁת־גִּלְעָד לוֹ בָּנִים	And *Gilead's* wife also bore *him* sons (Judg. 11.2).

Constituents that are expressed by means of *deictic adverbs* also stand as close to the verb as possible. However, as a rule they follow the preposition + pronominal suffix (if it too occurs).

וַיַּכֵּם שָׁם דָּוִד	And David defeated them *there* (2 Sam. 5.20).
הַמָּקוֹם אֲשֶׁר דִּבֶּר אִתּוֹ שָׁם אֱלֹהִים	the place *where* God had spoken with him (Gen. 35.15)

As a rule the *adverb* עוֹד stands as close to the verb as possible.

כִּי לוֹא־יַעֲשֶׂה עוֹד עַבְדְּךָ עֹלָה וָזֶבַח לֵאלֹהִים אֲחֵרִים	For your servant will not offer *again* burnt offering or sacrifice to other gods (2 Kgs 5.17).

b. *Long constituents* tend to occur at the end of a BH clause, e.g. constituents expressed by means of *a preposition + infinitive construct*.

אֲשֶׁר הִכָּה מֹשֶׁה וּבְנֵי יִשְׂרָאֵל בְּצֵאתָם מִמִּצְרָיִם:	whom Moses and the children of Israel defeated *when they came out of Egypt* (Deut. 4.46)

Constituents expressed by means of *a relative pronoun + clause*

כִּי־לָקַח מֶלֶךְ בָּבֶל מִנַּחַל מִצְרַיִם עַד־נְהַר־פְּרָת כֹּל אֲשֶׁר הָיְתָה לְמֶלֶךְ מִצְרָיִם:	for the king of Babylon had taken all *that belonged to the king of Egypt* from the Brook of Egypt to the river Euphrates (2 Kgs 24.7).

Constituents expressed by means of *a word chain*

וְנָתַן לַכֹּהֵן הַזְּרֹעַ וְהַלְּחָיַיִם וְהַקֵּבָה:	And they shall give to the priest *the shoulder and the two cheeks and the stomach* (Deut. 18.3).

Exception: If the word chain is the subject (and in a few cases the object) of the clause, it tends not to stand at the end of the clause.

וַתָּשַׁר דְּבוֹרָה וּבָרָק בֶּן־אֲבִינֹעַם בַּיּוֹם הַהוּא	Then sang *Deborah and Barak* the son of Abinoam on that day: (Judg. 5.1).

(iii) *Unmarked and marked word order in the main field*
Lexicalized and pronominalized constituents are marked according to the same principles. Differences between clauses where these two types are used are due to the fact that pronominalized constituents occur as close to the verb as possible. (Cf. §46.1/2(ii)a.)

a. The *unmarked order* when *all the constituents are lexicalized* is:

Subject + object + indirect object + prepositional object + other complement/adjunct + complement/adjunct (place) + adjunct (time)

b. *Marked order* is indicated when:

A constituent stands further away from the verb than usual, e.g.

The lexicalized object stands in a marked position; it follows the indirect object.

יָדַעְתִּי אֵת אֲשֶׁר־תַּעֲשֶׂה לִבְנֵי יִשְׂרָאֵל רָעָה	I know what you will do to the people of Israel is *evil* (2 Kgs 8.12).

The above-mentioned principle implies that *if a pronominalized constituent is involved*, the *marked order* would be indicated by the pronominalized constituent standing *not close to the verb*, but later in the clause (i.e. where it would have stood as lexicalized constituent).[59]

The pronominalized complement of place does not stand as close to the verb as possible, e.g.

וְאָשִׁיבָה כָל־הָעָם אֵלֶיךָ   And I will bring all the people back *to you* (2 Sam. 17.3).

A marked position for the *adjunct of time*[60] and *complement/ adjunct of time*, both of which normally occur at the end of the clause, is the following: When they are lexicalized they stand closer to the verb than usual. When they are pronominalized, or have a deictic character, they do not stand close to the verb, but at the end of the clause; in other words, the place that they would have occupied as lexicalized constituents, for example.

The lexicalized adjunct of time does not stand at the end of the clause, but closer to the verb (and before the complement of place).

וָאוֹלֵךְ אֶתְכֶם
אַרְבָּעִים שָׁנָה בַּמִּדְבָּר   And I have led you *forty years* in the wilderness (Deut. 29.4).

The deictic adjunct of time does not stand as close to the verb as possible, but at the end of the clause.

וְלֹא־יָדַע אִישׁ אֶת־קְבֻרָתוֹ
עַד הַיּוֹם הַזֶּה   But no man knows the place of his burial *to this day* (Deut. 34.6).

§46.2. *Nominal Clauses*

1. *In a nominal clause the unmarked word order is:*

Subject + Predicate

הָאִישׁ מֹשֶׁה גָּדוֹל   The man Moses was very *great* (Exod. 11.3).

2. *In a nominal clause the marked word order is:*

Predicate + subject

מְרַגְּלִים אַתֶּם   *Spies* are you (Gen. 42.9).

---

59. The indirect object does not always comply with this rule.

60. Temporal adjuncts of frequency, duration and point(s) in time are here treated as a syntactically homogenous group.

§47. The Semantic-Pragmatic Functions of Word Order

1. *Introduction*

The *semantic function* of word order refers to the contribution that the order of constituents makes to the interpretation of a *clause*. Often there is no one-to-one correlation between the order of constituents and the function that is expressed by means of it. Its function can only be determined if the communicative context in which the clause was uttered, is taken into consideration. For this reason we rather refer to the *semantic-pragmatic function of word order* than merely to its semantic function. In order to determine which particular semantic-pragmatic function is involved, the following general remarks need to be taken into consideration:

(a) Participants in a communicative situation, i.e. the interlocutors, each have a cognitive world of their own. This world, among other things, consists of mental representations of *persons, things, places (entities)* and *states of affairs and events (propositions)*. These mental representations make up their *knowledge of the world*.

(b) When two parties communicate they are normally not conscious of their entire knowledge of the world. At a particular point in a conversation, only a part of it is, or can be, activated. This is because the short-term memory of humans has a limited capacity. In the case of a narrative, characters, things, places, states of affairs and events may be introduced or activated in the course of the narrative. However, only those in the short-term memory of the interlocutors are active at a particular point of a narrative. They are referred to as being *discourse active*.

(c) When one analyses the utterances of a narrative it is as a rule evident that most of the utterances are about somebody or something that is already discourse active. Now, the entity or entities about which an utterance says something is referred to as the *topic* of that utterance. A *discourse active* topic is normally referred to by means of *a pronoun* that is the subject of the sentence involved, e.g.

וַיַּשְׁכִּמוּ בַבֹּקֶר	*They* rose early in the morning
וַיִּשְׁתַּחֲווּ לִפְנֵי יְהוָה	and worshipped before the LORD (1 Sam. 1.19).

(d)   What is said about the discourse active topic of an utterance
      presents the most salient information conveyed by a particu-
      lar utterance. This section of the utterance is referred to as
      the *focus of the utterance*. In the case of 1 Sam. 1.19 it is
      'They *rose early in the morning* and (they) *worshipped
      before the* LORD'. In these utterances the predicates are the
      focus of the utterances. Across languages, utterances with
      predicate focus are those that are the *most unmarked* as far
      as the sequence of clause constituents is concerned, e.g. in
      English it is the sequence subject-verb-object (SVO) and in
      BH and Arabic it is verb-subject-object (VSO). (Cf. also
      §46.1/1.)

(e)   The *focus* of an utterance is considered to be that section of
      an utterance that carries the most salient information in that
      utterance, relative to all the information provided by that
      utterance in a given context. The focus of an utterance is also
      defined as that event (e.g. They *worshipped before the
      LORD*), that aspect of an event (e.g. *At exactly four o'clock,
      we* completed the race), that entity (e.g. *Peter* did it) or that
      attribute of an entity (e.g. The *old* dog did it, not the young
      one) that *represents a particular choice in a context where
      more than one alternative is possible.*

(f)   From the above-mentioned definition of focus it is obvious
      that not only its predicate may be the focus of an utterance.
      When an event or state of affairs is discourse active, the ref-
      erent (or attribute of the referent) of one of a sentence's com-
      plements (i.e. subject, object, indirect object) or adjuncts (i.e.
      adverbial of time, place or manner) may also be the focus of
      that utterance. The most obvious instances of this type of
      focus are in the answers to questions. For example, the ques-
      tion 'What were you singing?' may be anwered in English as
      follows: (1) 'OB-LA-DI-OB-LA-DA'; (2) 'We were singing
      OB-LA-DI-OB-LA-DA'; (3) 'What we were singing was,
      OB-LA-DI-OB-LA-DA' or (4) 'It was OB-LA-DI-OB-LA-
      DA that we were singing'. Significant is that in each case a
      special or marked construction is involved. In BH *fronting* is
      one of the constructions used to signal that an entity or an
      attribute of an entity is the focus of an utterance.

(g) The focus of an utterance does not only convey *the identity* of an entity or event. It may also *confirm* it, e.g. 'Did SHE tell you?' 'Yes, SHE HERSELF told me'.

(h) An utterance cannot have more than one topic, but may have more than one focus. For example, in the utterance '*At this very moment tomorrow, I will send a Benjamamite to you*' both the adjunct of time '*At this very moment tomorrow* and predicate '*will send a Benjamamite to you*' are the *foci* of the utterance.[61] The utterance has only one topic, viz. 'I'.

(i) When the topic of an utterance is discourse active, it is normally referred to by means of a pronoun or other unmarked construction (see (c) above). However, when the topic of an utterance is not discourse active, and needs to be newly introduced, or reactivated, a special construction may be involved again. In English, the phrase 'as far as TOPIC is concerned...' may be used. Left-dislocation may also be used, e.g. 'That TOPIC, I love it'. In BH a dislocated construction may be used. (Cf. §46.1/2 note 3.) *Fronting*, however, is more frequently used to *introduce or (re-) activate the topic of an utterance* that is not discourse active.[62]

(j) One or two *already discourse active topics* are sometimes 'apparently unnecessarily' reactivated as topics. However, the reactivation is required in order *to compare or contrast two different topics*, e.g. 'HE (topic a) STAYED in the hills, but SHE (topic b) LEFT for town'.

2. Semantic-pragmatic functions of fronting

(i) The fronting signals that an entity, an aspect of an entity or an event is *the focus of an utterance*.

a. Providing the *identity* of an entity (e.g. a character) of a discourse active event or state of affairs. Since the answer to a factual question (who? or what?) provides the identity of somebody or something, the reference to it is normally fronted. (Cf. §46.1/2(ii)a.)

---

61. In such cases the event involved is not necessarily discourse active as in the cases referred to in (f).

62. With the exception of those cases referred to in (j) where a discourse active event is negated (e.g. 'THE CHILDREN may go, but THE MEN may not go'), the events involved are as a rule not discourse active.

מִי יַעֲלֶה־לָּנוּ אֶל־הַכְּנַעֲנִי	Who shall go up first for us against
בַּתְּחִלָּה לְהִלָּחֶם בּוֹ:	the Canaanites, to fight against them?
וַיֹּאמֶר יְהוָה יְהוּדָה יַעֲלֶה	The Lord said, *Judah* shall go up
	(Judg. 1.1-2).

b. Confirming *the personal or exclusive role* of a specific discourse active entity in an event

אֹתִי שָׁלַח יְהוָה לִמְשָׁחֳךָ לְמֶלֶךְ	*Me (and no-one else)* has the Lord sent to anoint you as king (1 Sam. 15.1).

c. Confirming a *particular quality* of a discourse active event or state of affairs

בְּתָם־לְבָבִי וּבְנִקְיֹן כַּפַּי	*In the integrity of my heart and the innocence of my hands* I have done this
עָשִׂיתִי זֹאת	(Gen. 20.5).

d. Confirming *the quantity of a referent* of a discourse active event or state of affairs

וְכָל־אַנְשֵׁי בֵיתוֹ	and *all* the men of his house, those born
יְלִיד בָּיִת וּמִקְנַת־כֶּסֶף מֵאֵת	in the house and those bought with
בֶּן־נֵכָר נִמֹּלוּ אִתּוֹ	money from a foreigner, were circumcized with him (Gen. 17.27).

Note the following:

(1) Fronting is not the only way of marking the focus of an utterance. (Cf. §47.3 below and focus particles, §41.4.)

(2) Clauses with a so-called obligatory order of constituents are not necessarily without a focused constituent. (Cf. §46.2/2(i) and (ii))

(ii) The fronted complement or adjunct signals that an entity is *introduced, activated or reactivated* to function as the topic of an utterance. The event referred to by means of the predicate of that utterance is not discourse active.[63]

a. Introducing *a new character* to be the topic of an utterance:

at the beginning *of a new episode*

---

63. The process involved is also referred to as the *focus of topicalization*. It is argued that focus is involved since a topic is either picked from a universe of possible topics, or delineated from other topics. In other words, the new or (re-)activated topic represents a particular choice in a context where more than one alternative was possible. Cf. Van der Merwe 1990: 41.

וּבֶן־הֲדַד מֶלֶךְ־אֲרָם קָבַץ
אֶת־כָּל־חֵילוֹ

And Benhadad the king of Syria gathered all his army together (1 Kgs 20.1).

or at the beginning a subparagraph that refers to *background information*.

וַיָּמָת אֱלִישָׁע וַיִּקְבְּרֻהוּ
וּגְדוּדֵי מוֹאָב יָבֹאוּ
בָאָרֶץ בָּא שָׁנָה:
וַיְהִי ...

So Elisha died, and they buried him. Now bands of Moabites used to in-vade the land in the spring of the year. And as ... (2 Kgs 13.20-21).

b. Activating an *identifiable character or characters* to be the topic of an utterance at the *beginning of a new scene*.

מֹשֶׁה עֶבֶד־יְהוָה וּבְנֵי יִשְׂרָאֵל
הִכּוּם

Moses, the servant of the Lord, and the Israelites defeated them (Josh. 12.6).

c. Reactivating entities to be the topics of utterances that are the *sum-mary* of a paragraph, episode or narrative.

וַיִּשְׂמַח כָּל־עַם־הָאָרֶץ
וְהָעִיר שָׁקָטָה
וְאֶת־עֲתַלְיָהוּ הֵמִיתוּ בַחֶרֶב

So all the people of the land rejoiced; and the city was quiet and Athaliah they had killed by the sword (2 Kgs 11.20).

d. Reactivating an identifiable entity in order to comment on different entities that are *involved in the same situation*.

וַתִּקַּח תָּמָר אֵפֶר עַל־רֹאשָׁהּ
וּכְתֹנֶת הַפַּסִּים אֲשֶׁר עָלֶיהָ קָרָעָה

Tamar put ashes on her head, and the long robe that she was wearing, she tore (2 Sam.13.19).

Often the different utterances, each with a different topic, have the character of a *list*.

אָנֹכִי נֹתֵן אֶת־כֻּלָּם חֲלָלִים
לִפְנֵי יִשְׂרָאֵל אֶת־סוּסֵיהֶם
תְּעַקֵּר וְאֶת־מַרְכְּבֹתֵיהֶם
תִּשְׂרֹף בָּאֵשׁ

I will give over all of them, slain, to Israel; their horses you shall ham-string, and their chariots you shall burn with fire (Josh. 11.6).

e. Reactivating characters (or entities) that are *compared* or *contrasted*.

וַיַּעַל הָאִישׁ אֶלְקָנָה ...
וְחַנָּה לֹא עָלָתָה ...

The man, Elkana went up .... But, Hannah did not go up ... (1 Sam. 1.22).

וָאָבִיא אֶת־אֲגַג מֶלֶךְ עֲמָלֵק
וְאֶת־עֲמָלֵק הֶחֱרַמְתִּי

And I have brought Agag the king of Amalek, but the Amalekites I have utterly destroyed (1 Sam. 15:20).

(iii) The *fronted subject* signals that a so-called *anterior construction* is involved. This construction refers to events that happened, relative to a temporal sequence of events, 'in the meanwhile'.

This construction will have *a discourse active referent as fronted subject* and a proposition that has a pluperfect or preperfect relationship with the main line of the narration.[64]

וַיֹּאמֶר לוֹ הִנְּךָ מֵת עַל־הָאִשָּׁה ...	and said to him, You are about to die
וַאֲבִימֶלֶךְ לֹא קָרַב אֵלֶיהָ	... [4] *Now Abimelech had not*
וַיֹּאמַר אֲדֹנָי ...	*approached her,* so he said, Lord ...
	(Gen. 20.3-4).

(iv) The *fronted subject* signals a *special type of temporal construction* where *immediately simultaneous* or *nearly simultaneous* actions are involved.

In this type of construction, fronting of the subject may occur in both the temporal and the main clause. In some cases only the subject of the main clause occupies the preverbal field. (Cf. also §36.1/I.3(iv).)

הֵמָּה בָּאוּ בְּאֶרֶץ צוּף	*When they came to the land of Zuph,*
וְשָׁאוּל אָמַר לְנַעֲרוֹ אֲשֶׁר־עִמּוֹ	Saul said to his servant who was with
לְכָה וְנָשׁוּבָה	him, Come, let us go back ... (1 Sam.
	9.5).

Note the following:

- When an apparently superfluous independent personal pronoun occupies the preverbal field, it is also fronting that is involved. The semantic-pragmatic functions that can be expressed do not differ from those listed above. (Cf. also §36.1/I.3.)
- When a fronted constituent refers to God, sometimes not one of the above-mentioned functions can be attributed to the construction. It might be a BH sociolinguistic convention that we do not yet understand.

3. *Semantic-pragmatic functions of marked word order in nominal clauses*

To mark an entity as the *focus* of the utterance in which it occurs. It confirms *the nature or quality* of the predicate of the nominal clause.

מְרַגְּלִים אַתֶּם	You are nothing *but spies* [lit. *Spies are you*] (Gen. 42.9).

---

64. For an exhaustive discussion of the anterior construction, cf. Zevit 1998.

4. *Semantic-pragmatic functions of marked word order in the main field*

To mark an entity as a focus of the utterance in which it occurs.

a. Confirming *the quality or nature of an event*

יָדַעְתִּי אֵת אֲשֶׁר־תַּעֲשֶׂה לִבְנֵי יִשְׂרָאֵל רָעָה	I know what you will do to the people of Israel is *evil* (2 Kgs 8.12).
הִנֵּה יָמִים בָּאִים נְאֻם־יְהוָה וְכָרַתִּי אֶת־בֵּית יִשְׂרָאֵל וְאֶת־בֵּית יְהוּדָה בְּרִית חֲדָשָׁה:	Look, the days are coming, says the Lord, when I will make *a new covenant* with the house of Israel and with the house of Judah (Jer. 31.31).

b. Confirming the *identity of the goal* of an action

וְאָשִׁיבָה כָל־הָעָם אֵלֶיךָ	And I will bring all the people back *to you* (2 Sam. 17.3).

c. Confirming *the extent of the duration* of an event/action

וָאוֹלֵךְ אֶתְכֶם אַרְבָּעִים שָׁנָה בַּמִּדְבָּר	And I have led you *forty years* in the wilderness (Deut. 29.4).

The glossary contains the metalanguage that has not already been explained in the text and that is mainly linguistic in character. Terms that are themselves explained somewhere else in the glossary are indicated by capital letters. If a term is only necessary for a certain explanation, a definition is given in the explanation.

ABLATIVE   In languages that express grammatical relations explicitly by DECLENSIONS (inflexion) this term indicates the form of the word (normally a NOUN or pronoun). In Latin the ablative indicates the word form of the CASE that expresses the medium or instrument with which an action is carried out or which indicates a place or source. In BH the ablative is not indicated explicitly as in Latin, and similar functions are expressed by way of other constructions, especially with prepositions.

ACCUSATIVE   In languages that express grammatical relations explicitly by DECLENSIONS (inflexion) this term indicates the form of the word (normally a NOUN or pronoun). In Latin the accusative indicates the word form of the CASE that expresses the (DIRECT) OBJECT of the VERB. In BH the accusative is not indicated explicitly as in Latin, and similar functions are expressed by way of other grammatical ways.

AD SENSUM See CONSTRUCTIO AD SENSUM.

ADJUNCT   The term *adjunct* refers to an optional or secondary element in a construction. On the syntactic level adjuncts refer to optional, omissable, non-verbal elements in the PREDICATE or verb phrase (VP). It can be removed from the predicate without influencing the structural identity of the rest of the construction, for example, *yesterday* in *Yesterday John kicked the ball*. Adjuncts are adverbs and prepositional phrases (and sometimes also noun phrases) that are added to or combined with VERBS, although the verb itself does not require its presence. Adjuncts are in contrast to COMPLEMENTS which are obligatory elements in the verb phrase, for example, the DIRECT OBJECT.

ADVERBIAL ACCUSATIVE   In languages with explicit CASE endings the adverbial ACCUSATIVE indicates adverbial modifiers consisting of a NOUN in the accusative. In BH this function is fulfilled by nominal ADJUNCTS which show the normal form of the noun and which can fulfil different SEMANTIC functions, e.g. the indication of time, location, manner and regard.

AFFECTED The term *affected* refers to the entity (person or thing) that, although it does not cause the action or event indicated by the VERB, is somehow directly involved. In active CLAUSES the affected and the grammatical OBJECT normally refer to the same person or thing. The affected entity existed before the action, and it is only influenced by the action, for example, *the table* in *He broke the table*. See EFFECTED.

AFFIX An affix is a morpheme (= smallest unit of a language with independent meaning and/or grammatical function) that cannot act independently, but has to be combined with another morpheme to form one word. There are three kinds of affixes, i.e. PREFIXES, INFIXES and SUFFIXES.

AGENT The term *agent* refers to the acting person or thing that causes the action expressed by the VERB or PREDICATE. In active CLAUSES the agent and the grammatical SUBJECT normally refer to the same entity.

AGREEMENT Agreement, concord or congruency indicates the similarity of the formal element in two or more words with reference to number, gender and person (and sometimes definiteness), for example, that of the adjective with the NOUN, the demonstrative pronoun with the noun, or the VERB with the grammatical SUBJECT.

AKTIONSART *Aktionsart* (literally: kind of action) which can usually be deduced from the VERB, indicates the manner in which the structure of a situation or event is understood in relation to durativity (= durative progress, e.g. *The sun shines*), iterativity (= interrupted, consecutive, repeated moments of progress, for example, *The watch ticks continuously*), causativity (e.g. *The alarm clock wakes us in the morning*), and other similar factors.

ALLATIVE In languages that express grammatical relations explicitly by DECLENSIONS (inflexion) this term indicates the form of the word (normally a NOUN or pronoun). In Finnish the allative indicates the word form of the CASE that expresses the meaning of motion towards a location (= direction). In BH the allative function is not indicated explicitly as in Finnish, but is replaced by the use of certain prepositions, the *he locale* and nouns used adverbially.

ALLOPHONE Allophones are phonetic variants of a phoneme (phonemes are linguistically distinctive speech sounds, i.e. speech sounds that are used to contrast meaning). In English the sounds [i] and [e], respectively in *compete* and *competition*, are allophones of the phoneme /i/. In BH the PLOSIVE- and FRICATIVE-pronunciation of the *begadkefat*-letters (§4.2.2) are phonetic variants or allophones. Phoneme is analogous to constants, while allophones indicate variables.

ANAPHORA An *anaphora* is a grammatical element without any independent reference. For its reference it depends on a previous element (the ANTECEDENT) in the same structural unit (normally a CLAUSE). *Anaphoras* include

REFLEXIVE pronouns (e.g. *myself*) and RECIPROCAL pronouns (e.g. *each other*). In contrast these other pronouns refer independently (i.e. without an antecedent in the same structural unit, for example, *he* in *He is ill*.)

ANTECEDENT An antecedent is an element in a CLAUSE to which another word that follows it, refers.

AP The smallest units with which a CLAUSE is built, are words. Words are distinguished in different classes, e.g. VERB (V), NOUN (N), adjective (A) and preposition (P). Words can be grouped into larger units known as PHRASES. Phrases can again be distinguished in different classes, named according to the class of the head word in the phrase. AP refers to an adjective phrase, a phrase with A as head. The phrase *incredibly clever* in the clause *The student is incredibly clever* is the AP with the A clever as head. Other phrases are, for example, noun phrase (NP), verb phrase (VP) and prepositional phrase (PP).

APOCOPE Apocope is the cutting off or disappearance of an unaccented vowel and/or consonant at the end of a word, for example, יִבְנֶה>יִבֶן. The shortening at the end of a form usually causes the syllable structure of the word to change. See also SHORT FORM.

APODOSIS The *apodosis* is the second (*then-*) part of a condition (*if-then*). The *apodosis* is the consecutive main clause that follows the conditional sub-ordinate clause or *PROTASIS* (the *if*-part) of this construction.

APPOSITION Apposition is the juxtaposition (placing next to or opposite to) of an element (usually a NOUN or noun PHRASE) as a descriptive and/or explanatory modifier to another element (usuallly a noun or noun phrase) (the head). Nouns in apposition have the same reference and SYNTACTIC function as the head. Usually they also agree in number and gender with the head. In the CLAUSE *He called Sarah, his wife* the PHRASE *his wife* is in apposition to *Sarah*.

ASSIMILATION Assimilation indicates a process where one segment (= a discrete sound unit) adopts the characteristics of an adjacent segment and by which the two sounds become more identical. A consonant may take up the characteristics of a vowel, and a vowel may take up the characterstics of a consonant. A consonant may influence another consonant, and a vowel may influence another vowel. The equalization may be total or partial. It usually happens at the border of two morphemes (= the smallest unit of a language with independent meaning and/or grammatical function) or words. In the word *cupboard* the [p]-sound takes over the characteristics of the adjacent [b]-sound. Usually the change occurs in both the spelling and pronunciation. In the following examples the final consonant of a PREFIX adopted the characteristics of the initial consonant of the root word: *in+legal > illegal*; *in+mortal > im-mortal*. Progressive assimilation occurs when a sound adapts itself to a preceding one. Regressive assimilation occurs when a sound adapts itself to a following one.

ASYNDETIC　　Asyndetic indicates a connection of words, PHRASES or CLAUSES without the normal coordinate or subordinate conjunction, for example, *In the days of Uzziah, Jotham, Ahaz ...* instead of *In the days of Uzziah and Jotham and Ahaz...*

ATTRIBUTIVE　　The term *attributive* refers to the manner in which adjectives qualify. In English the placing of an adjective or other adjectival modifier before the qualified NOUN indicates an attributive, for example, *red* in *He sits on the red chair*. In BH an attributive adjective agrees with its noun in number, gender and definiteness, and it follows the noun, for example, הַסּוּס הַגָּדוֹל. PREDICATIVE is used in contrast to attributive.

AVERBAL CLAUSE　See NOMINAL CLAUSE.

BASE VOWEL　See STEM VOWEL.

BETH CAUSA　If the BH preposition בְּ indicates the *cause* or *reason* of an action, it is called the *beth causa*.

BETH COMITANTIAE　If the BH preposition בְּ indicates the person or entities that *accompany* the acting person, or that are joined to it, or associated with it, it is called the *beth comitantiae*. See COMITATIVE.

BETH INSTRUMENTI　If the BH preposition בְּ indicates the *instrument* or *means* with which the action is realized, it is called the *beth instrumenti*.

BETH LOCALE　If the BH preposition בְּ indicates the *place* where the action is realized, it is called the *beth locale*.

BETH PRETII　If the BH preposition בְּ indicates the *price* for which the action is realized, it is called the *beth pretii*.

CASE　　Case indicates a grammatical category that is used to identify the SYNTACTIC relations between words in a CLAUSE. In languages that express grammatical relations explicitly by DECLENSIONS (inflexion), case indicates the different forms of a word (normally a NOUN or pronoun). In languages like BH with abstract case (not expressed explicitly as in Latin) other grammatical means are used to mark the SYNTACTIC relations between words.

CASE MARKER　In languages with explicit CASE, case markers or endings indicate the DECLENSIONS (inflexion) of a word, thus marking the SYNTACTIC relations between words explicitly.

CASUS PENDENS　See DISLOCATION CONSTRUCTION.

CATAPHOR　A cataphor is a grammatical element that is dependent for its reference on another element occurring later in a structural unit, usually a CLAUSE. In *Here is the news* the word *here* is a cataphor for that which follows the UTTERANCE.

CAUSATIVE　A causative indicates a grammatical construction or form (usually a

VERB) that expresses cause or causality. Examples of causative verbs are *declare holy/consecrate, kindle, bring back* (= *cause to go back*).

CLAUSE A clause is considered by some to be a grammatically organized unit, smaller than a sentence, but larger than a PHRASE, for example, *who lived in Canaan* in *Jacob who lived in Canaan, loved Joseph*. In this grammar a clause is regarded as a meaningful series of words that has a subject and a predicate.

COHESION Cohesion refers to those qualities of a text that bind CLAUSES and sentences together, e.g. the cross references of pronouns and NOUNS when people and things are referred to.

COMITATIVE Comitative indicates the combining of a person or thing with another person or thing by accompanying it or by associating with it, or by causing an action in its presence.

COMPLEMENT In grammatical theory this term refers to an obligatory element in a construction. On the SYNTACTIC level complements refer to obligatory, non-omissible, non-verbal parts of the PREDICATE or verb phrase (VP). If a complement is removed from the predicate, the structural identity of the rest of the construction is affected, for example, *bread* and *sons* cannot be omitted in the sentence *John gives his sons bread*. Complements are NOUNS or prepositional phrases that are added to or combined with verbs because the VERB requires its presence. They differ from ADJUNCTS that are optional, secondary PHRASES in the verb phrase. The noun (or other element) that is obligatory after a preposition, is the complement of that preposition.

COMPLEMENT CLAUSE A complement CLAUSE is subordinate, but non-omissible, e.g. a subject and an object clause.

COMPLEX SENTENCE A complex sentence indicates the type of sentence where a clause stands in a co-ordinate relation to the so-called main clause (*John is ugly, but Mary is beautiful*), or in a subordinate relation (*When John saw Mary, he was infatuated*).

CONCORD See AGREEMENT.

CONGRUENCY See AGREEMENT.

CONJUGATION A conjugation is the collection of the different forms of a VERB. In BH verbs do not show different forms for MOODS like the INDICATIVE, SUBJUNCTIVE and OPTATIVE. Tense and mood both are expressed by the PERFECT and IMPERFECT FORMS. FINITE verbs have a STEM FORMATION, conjugation (tense/mood), person, gender and number. Non-finite verbs like the participle do not have person; the infinitive has neither person nor gender and number. The following finite conjugations are found: PERFECT, IMPERFECT, JUSSIVE, cohortative, imperative; and the following non-finite (without person) conjugations: infinitive construct, infinitive absolute, participle.

CONSONANTAL SUFFIX A consonantal SUFFIX indicates a pronominal suffix starting with a consonant.

CONSTITUENT In contrast to PHRASES which refer to the SYNTACTIC composition of a word group, e.g. noun phrase, adjective phrase, verb phrase, adverbial phrase and prepositional phrase, constituents are the word groups that
form the functional units of the CLAUSE, e.g. SUBJECT, OBJECT, INDI-
RECT OBJECT, etc.

CONSTRUCT PHRASE A construct phrase is a PHRASE consisting of a NOUN
in the *STATUS CONSTRUCTUS*, followed by a noun (or its equivalent) which is
called the *POSTCONSTRUCTUS* (or 'GENITIVE'). Usually the *postconstructus* is in the *STATUS CONSTRUCTUS*. However, it can also be in the
status constructus followed by another *postconstructus* to form a *construct
chain*. A great number of SEMANTIC relations can exist between the two
elements of a construct phrase.

CONSTRUCTIO AD SENSUM *Constructio ad sensum* refers to the forming of a
grammatical construction in accordance with the meaning rather than the
SYNTAX of the grammatical form. Usually the grammatical form of the SUB-
JECT determines the person, gender and number of the PREDICATE.
However, a plural predicate is often used with nouns that have a collective
meaning, but a singular form (thus the predicate only agrees in meaning with the
subject), for example, יָדְעוּ הָעָם (*The people knows.*).

COPULA A *copula* is that element in a NOMINAL CLAUSE which connects the
SUBJECT and the *COPULA*-PREDICATE. Together the *copula* and *copula*-
predicate form the PREDICATE of such a clause, e.g. הָיָה and בָּאֶרֶץ־עוּץ in
אִישׁ הָיָה בְּאֶרֶץ־עוּץ. In BH the *copula* is often omitted, e.g. אִיּוֹב שְׁמוֹ.

COPULA-PREDICATE A *copula*-predicate is that element in a NOMINAL
CLAUSE that is connected by the *COPULA* (if it occurs) to the SUBJECT.
Together the *copula* and *copula*-predicate form the PREDICATE of such a
clause, for example, בְּאֶרֶץ־עוּץ in אִישׁ הָיָה בְּאֶרֶץ־עוּץ.

DATIVE In languages that express grammatical relations explicitly by DE-
CLENSIONS (inflexion) this term indicates the form of the word (normally a
NOUN or pronoun). In Latin the dative indicates the word form of the CASE
that usually expresses the INDIRECT OBJECT or the receiver of something or
of an action. In BH the dative is not indicated explicitly as in Latin, and similar
functions are expressed by other grammatical ways, for example by prepositions.

DECLENSION A declension is the collection of the different forms of a NOUN.
In BH nouns do not show CASE endings, but they do have masculine and feminine forms in the singular, dual and plural; *STATUS ABSOLUTUS* and *STATUS
CONSTRUCTUS*. Singular, plural and dual nouns all can be com-bined with
pronominal SUFFIXES. Thus a word with masculine and feminine forms (like
סוּס and סוּסָה) theoretically can have 72 forms. In the declension the noun can
undergo different vowel and consonantal changes, on the basis of which five

main declension types are distinguished. Adjectives do not appear in the dual at all. Even with nouns the dual has a restricted use.

DEIXIS Deixis refers to a system of words that depends, with regard to its meaning or interpretation, on the concrete situation in which language is used (i.e. the speaker addressee, time and location), e.g. *he/she, this/that, now/then, here/there*. Thus, the meaning is relative to the situation in which it occurs.

DIRECT OBJECT A direct object refers to one of the two grammatical relations that functions as objective element in the CLAUSE structure. The other is the INDIRECT OBJECT. In English the difference between the direct object and the indirect object on the SYNTACTIC level is that the direct object cannot be marked by a preposition, for example, *I gave the book to John* and *I gave John the book*. SEMANTICALLY the direct object refers to the entity that is affected or effected by the action, for example, in the clause *John kicks the ball* the entity affected by the action is *the ball*.

DIRECTIVE A directive is a SPEECH ACT with which a person intends to cause people to do something, e.g. a command, hint or suggestion.

DISCOURSE LINGUISTICS See TEXT LINGUISTICS.

DISLOCATION CONSTRUCTION A dislocation construction consists of a grammatical element, isolated to the left or the right of the CLAUSE (the dislocated CONSTITUENT), and a main clause containing an element (the RESUMPTIVE) that refers to the dislocated constituent, e.g. *This food—I will eat it all*.

DISTRIBUTION Distribution refers to all the linguistic contexts or areas in which a grammatical element can occur.

EFFECTED The term *effected* refers to the entity (person or thing) that, although it does not cause the action or event indicated by the VERB, is somehow directly involved. In active CLAUSES the effected and the gram-matical OBJECT normally refer to the same person or thing. The effected entity did not exist before the action, but is created by the action, for example, *the table* in *He made the table*. See AFFECTED.

ENERGIC NUN The energic nun in BH refers to the INFIX-nun before (objective) pronominal SUFFIXES in certain verbal forms. The syllable in which the nun occurs, carries the accent. It has no SEMANTIC value. See SUFFIX.

EPEXEGETICAL Epexegetical refers to the function of explaining the directly preceding material.

EPICOENA *Epicoena* (NOUNS of common gender) is the phenomenon that some words which MORPHOLOGICALLY have either a masculine or feminine form, SEMANTICALLY refer to a mixed gender group. In BH the word כֶּלֶב (dog) has a masculine form although it can refer to a bitch or a male dog. The word יוֹנָה (dove) has a feminine form even when it refers to a male dove.

ERGATIVE SYSTEM An ergative system refers to languages where the DIRECT OBJECT of a TRANSITIVE verb and the SUBJECT of an INTRANSITIVE verb show the same CASE and are treated the same for grammatical aims, while the subjects of transitive VERBS are treated differently. In such a system the role of subject in an intransitive CLAUSE like *The window broke* will be the same as the role of the direct object in the transitive clause *John broke the window*. The AGENT of the action is referred to as the ergative subject.

EXTENDED SENTENCE An extended sentence is a sentence of which one CONSTITUENT is extended, for example, by a relative clause.

FACTITIVE A factitive indicates a grammatical construction or form (normally a VERB) that refers to an action or event in which a cause produces a consequence or result, for example, *makes* in *He makes wine*.

FIENTIVE A VERB that describes movement or a change of state, is called a fientive verb. In these cases the SUBJECT performs an action.

FINITE Finite refers to the grammatical classification of VERBS and CLAUSES. A finite verb is limited by person, and it can occur independently in a main clause. It allows contrasts in tense and MOOD. Non-finite verbs, however, occur only in subordinate clauses. Contrasts in time and mood are lacking. All conjugated forms of the verb are finite except infinitives and participles. Clauses with finite verbs are finite clauses.

FOCUS The focussed entity in a CLAUSE represents the most salient information in terms of the total amount of information in that clause. Usually the focussed element is specifically selected in a context where there are more than one alternative available. In BH focus can be marked by word order, or by a focus particle.

FRICATIVE This term refers to the manner of articulation of consonants that are formed by narrowing the speech canal at a certain place, thereby obstructing the outgoing breath in such a way that a clearly audible friction develops. In BH the פ, ב, ת, ד, כ and ג are fricatives when they are pronounced with friction (the so-called *begadkefat*-letters).

FRONTING If the PREVERBAL FIELD (i.e. the part of the CLAUSE that precedes the VERB) is occupied by a CONSTITUENT, this phenomenon is referred to as fronting of that constituent.

GENITIVE In languages that express grammatical relations explicitly by DECLENSIONS (inflexion) this term indicates the form of the word (normally a NOUN or pronoun). In Latin the genitive indicates the word form of the CASE that often marks the possessor. In BH the genitive is not indicated explicitly as in Latin, and the same function is expressed by way of other grammatical means like the CONSTRUCT PHRASE.

GLIDE This term refers to the manner of articulation of certain consonants that are formed when the air stream is obstructed only slightly. Glides have more in common with vowels than with consonants. Therefore, they are sometimes also called transitional sounds. In BH the consonants ה, י and ו are sometimes pronounced glidingly.

GNOMIC PERFECT   When the PERFECT FORM expresses actions, events and/or facts that are timeless or usually and always true, it is called the gno-mic PERFECT. It is usually used for general experiental verdicts where the idea of time has been moved totally to the background. In BH the VERB *keeps* in the sentence *The swallow keeps the migration period* will be in the perfect form.

HAPAX LEGOMENON   The term *hapax legomenon* (literally: read once) refers to a word or combination of words (an expression) that is known only from a single citation in a given piece of literature.

HENDIADYS   *Hendiadys* refers to the presentation of a single idea by a co-ordinate combination of words, *inter alia* two NOUNS, two VERBS or two adjectives, for example, *nice* and *warm* for *nicely warm*.

IMMINENT CONNOTATION   Imminent connotation has the quality: be on the point of happening, about to happen.

IMPERFECT   Imperfect refers to the SEMANTIC function of a verbal form (e.g. the IMPERFECT FORM in BH), i.e. an incomplete action. It usually expresses non-facts and can be translated with the future tense. Imperfect is usually contrasted with PERFECT.

IMPERFECT FORM   The imperfect form is one of the CONJUGATIONS in BH that indicates the VERB'S tense (presence/future) and/or aspect (incompleteness) and/or MOOD (non-factuality). It is also called the prefix conjugation because the Qal IMPERFECT conjugation takes PREFIXES in all its forms (SUFFIXES also appear in five of the ten forms). With reference to the imperfect 3 masculine singular of the pattern verb קטל it is also called the *yiqtol* form. The imperfect is a FINITE form having person, number and gender. It is found in all STEM FORMATIONS (*binyanim*) and is used especially for the main verb in a CLAUSE.

INDICATIVE   The indicative is a MOOD of the VERB that expresses a fact in the form of a statement or question. However, it is not expressed in BH by a separate CONJUGATION, but the PERFECT FORM (and sometimes also the IMPERFECT FORM) is often used for this.

INDIRECT OBJECT   An indirect object refers to one of the two grammatical relations that functions as objective element in the CLAUSE structure. The other is the DIRECT OBJECT. In English the difference between the indirect object and the direct object on the SYNTACTIC level is that the indirect object can be marked by a preposition, for example, *I gave the book to John* and *I gave John the book*. SEMANTICALLY the indirect object refers to the entity that receives the indirect effect of an action (cf. (*to*) *John* above).

INFIX   An infix is an AFFIX that is inserted in the ROOT of a word itself, in contrast to other affixes which are inserted before the root (PREFIX) or after the root (SUFFIX).

INGRESSIVE   The ingressive refers to the function of a verbal form that emphasizes the beginning or transitional stadium of the event indicated by the VERB.

INTERROGATIVE   An interrogative is a PARTICLE that introduces a question. Questions with yes/no answers are marked with the interrogative הֲ/הַ/הֶ. Questions with factual answers are marked by interrogative pronouns and adverbs (the so-called WH-interrogatives). There is no question mark in BH. Interrogatives can also introduce indirect questions.

INTRANSITIVE   This term indicates VERBS that do not take a DIRECT OBJECT, for example, *John walks*. See TRANSITIVE.

JUSSIVE   Jussive refers to an indirect command to the third or second person.

JUSSIVE FORM   The jussive form refers to the grammatical form that expresses the indirect command to the third or second person. In BH the SHORT FORM of the IMPERFECT FORM is often used as the jussive form.

LEXEME   Lexeme refers to the smallest, distinguishable meaningful unit in the SEMANTIC system of language. The words *wrote* and *written* are manifestations of the lexeme *write*.

LEXICAL ENTRY   Lexical entry refers to any entry of a word in a lexicon or a dictionary article. Such an entry contains distinguishable information (e.g. PHONOLOGICAL, MORPHOLOGICAL, SYNTACTIC and SEMANTIC information) of the word.

MAIN FIELD   The main field of a BH CLAUSE is that part of the clause that is introduced by the VERB. The part of the clause that precedes the verb is the PREVERBAL FIELD.

METATHESIS   *Metathesis* indicates a process where the sequence of two segments (discrete sound units) is switched. A consonant may be interchanged with a vowel, a vowel with a consonant, a consonant with another consonant, or a vowel with another vowel. It usually occurs at the border of two morphemes (smallest unit of language with independent meaning and/or grammatical function) or words, e.g. pre̲vent is pronounced as pe̲rvent. In BH the change usually occurs in the pronunciation, as well as in the spelling, for example, תִּתְשַׁכְּרִין* is written and pronounced as תִּשְׁתַּכְּרִין

MODALITY   Modality as a SEMANTIC category refers to the speaker's subjective judgement concerning the factuality of the events, for example, the possibility, potentiality, (un)desirability of events. In English modal auxiliary VERBS like *can/could, will/would, should, may, must*, etc. are used to express the subjective judgement of a speaker concerning the factuality of the events, for example, *John would have sung now*. In BH the IMPERFECT FORM is used especially to express modalities: usually the relevant events are non-factual.

MOOD   The term *mood* refers to certain CONJUGATIONS of the VERB in languages that express mood explicitly, e.g. the INDICATIVE, SUBJUNCTIVE and OPTATIVE in Greek.

MORPHOLOGY   Morphology as a component of grammar is the study of the forms of words in a language. The distinction of WORD CLASSES is part of the morphology.

NOMINAL CLAUSE   Nominal CLAUSES refer to clauses in BH that do not contain a FINITE form of the VERB and where the *COPULA is* has to be inserted in English, for example, *Jacob (is) old.*

NOMINATIVE   In languages that express grammatical relationships explicitly by DECLENSIONS (inflexion) this term indicates the form of the word (normally a NOUN or pronoun). In Latin the nominative indicates the word form of the CASE that usually expresses the SUBJECT of the VERB. In BH the nominative is not indicated explicitly as in Latin, and similar functions are expres-sed by way of other grammatical ways (or is simply unmarked).

NOUN   Noun is a term in the grammatical classification of words that tradition-ally refers to a class of words indicating persons or things. The noun includes the following main classes: SUBSTANTIVES, pronouns and numerals.

NP   The smallest units with which a CLAUSE is built, are words. Words are distinguished in different classes, e.g. VERB (V), NOUN (N), adjective (A) and preposition (P). Words can be grouped into larger units known as PHRASES. Phrases can again be distinguished in different classes, named according to the class of the head word in the phrase. NP refers to a noun phrase, a phrase with N as head. The phrase *the student* in the clause *The student is incredibly clever* is the NP with the N *student* as head. Other phrases are, for example, adjective phrase (AP), verb phrase (VP) and prepositional phrase (PP).

OBJECT   See DIRECT OBJECT.

OPTATIVE   The optative is a MOOD of the VERB that expresses non-factualities or UNREAL events and states. BH does not distinguish between the optative and SUBJUNCTIVE. See INDICATIVE.

PART OF SPEECH   Part of speech is a synonym for WORD CLASS.

PARTICLE   Particle is an umbrella term that is sometimes used for a number of parts of speech: the article, prepositions, conjunctions, adverbs, existential words, INTERROGATIVES, discourse markers and interjections.

PARTITIVE   Partitive is a SEMANTIC term that indicates part-whole relations.

PAST PERFECT   Past perfect, pluperfect or *plusquamperfectum* refers to the SEMANTIC use of the PERFECT FORM to express distant past tense, i.e. an event or state that had been completed before another in the past.

PATIENT The SEMANTIC function of the AFFECTED or EFFECTED is called patient.

PENDENS See DISLOCATION CONSTRUCTION.

PERFECT Perfect refers to the SEMANTIC function of a VERB form (the PERFECT FORM in BH), viz. a completed action, that normally expresses factualities and which can be translated with the past tense. Perfect is normally contrasted with IMPERFECT.

PERFECT FORM The perfect form is one of the CONJUGATIONS in BH that indicates the VERB'S tense (past) and/or aspect (completeness) and/or MOOD (factuality). It is also called the suffix conjugation because the Qal PERFECT conjugation only takes SUFFIXES. With reference to the perfect 3 masculine singular of the pattern verb קָטַל, it is also called the *qatal* form. The perfect is a FINITE form having person, number and gender. It is found in all STEM FORMATIONS (*binyanim*) and is used especially for the main verb in a CLAUSE.

PERFORMATIVE Performative is a term that indicates that a certain action is carried out by a linguistic UTTERANCE, for example, *He declares you holy.* The PERFECT FORM is used especially for this because it expresses factuality. See SPEECH ACT.

PERSON SUFFIX Synonym for pronominal suffix—see SUFFIX.

PHONETICS Phonetics is the study that describes the sounds of a language as they are really pronounced. It describes the acoustic and articulatory characteristics of these sounds.

PHONOLOGY Phonology is the study that explains the underlying sound structure of a language, for example, how the different forms of a language are related (like מֶלֶךְ and מַלְכָה) and how sound indicates distinctive meanings (like the difference between בָּאָה and בָּאָה) with the accent either on the first (PERFECT) or the last syllable (PARTICIPLE).

PHRASE The smallest units with that a CLAUSE is built, are words. Words are distinguished in different classes, e.g. VERB (V), NOUN (N), adjective (A) and preposition (P). Words can be grouped into larger units known as phrases. Phrases can again be distinguished in different classes, named according to the class of the head word in the phrase, e.g. noun phrase (NP), verb phrase (VP), prepositional phrase (PP) and adjective phrase (AP).

PLEONASM A pleonasm is something that is said unnecessarily, i.e. a redundancy of words, for example, tautology (to say something twice).

PLOSIVE This term refers to the manner of articulation of consonants that are formed by completely blocking the breath stream somewhere in the speech canal for an important moment, followed by the sudden release of the suppressed breath so that a light explosion is heard. In BH the sounds פ, ב, ת, ד, כ and ג are plosives or stops when they are pronounced with an occlusive sound (the so-called *begadkefat*-letters).

PLURALIS MAJESTATIS If the plural form does not express a normal numerical plural, but indicates that something or someone is mighty, big, terrible or respectable, it is called the *pluralis majestatis* or royal plural.

PLUSQUAMPERFECTUM See PAST PERFECT.

POSTCONSTRUCTUS The *postconstructus* is the second element (סָמֵךְ) of a CONSTRUCT PHRASE (סְמִיכוּת). It follows a NOUN in the *STATUS CON-STRUCTUS* (נִסְמָךְ). Following the example of other Semitic languages and the classical languages it is also called the 'GENITIVE', although CASE endings do not occur in BH. SYNTACTICALLY speaking the *postconstructus* is an attribute to the first element of the PHRASE.

PP See PHRASES.

PRECATIVE PERFECTIVE The precative perfective refers to a rare SEMANTIC use of the PERFECT FORM to make a request in prayers.

PREDICATE The predicate is that CONSTITUENT of a CLAUSE—normally a verb phrase (VP)—that combines with the SUBJECT to form a (complete) clause. The predicate of NOMINAL CLAUSES in BH is not formed by a verb phrase, but by a noun phrase (e.g. *Abraham* (*is*) *a prophet*), prepositional phrase (e.g. *Sarah* (*is*) *in the tent*) or adjective phrase (e.g. *Sarah* (*is*) *beautiful*).

PREDICATIVE The term *predicative* refers to the manner in which adjectives qualify. In English the position of an adjective or other attribute after the qualified NOUN or pronoun (and connected with it by the copulative VERB *is*) indicates the predicative, for example, *red* in *The chair is red*. In BH a predicative noun agrees with the SUBJECT in number and gender, and it is always indefinite. Usually it follows the subject (and *COPULA*), but it can precede it. ATTRIBUTIVE is used in contrast to predicative.

PREFIX A prefix is an AFFIX attached to the beginning of a ROOT, for example, the endings of the IMPERFECT FORMS that appear before the STEM CONSONANTS, in contrast to affixes which are inserted in the root itself (INFIX) or after the root (SUFFIX).

PREFIX CONJUGATION See IMPERFECT FORM.

PREFORMATIVE A preformative is a prefixed syllable or letter. In BH it occurs especially in the verbal system, for example, in the Niphal, Hithpael, Hiphil and Hophal PERFECT, as well as in the IMPERFECT of all the STEM FORMA-TIONS. The preformative is inserted before the ROOT or STEM of the VERB.

PRETERITE Preterite is a simple past tense form that is not marked for aspect, e.g. *saw, loved*.

PREVERBAL FIELD The preverbal field is that part of a BH CLAUSE that precedes the VERB. The part of the clause that is introduced by the verb, is called the MAIN FIELD.

PRIVATIVE Privative is a SEMANTIC distinction that indicates separation, loss or absence of a matter or quality.

PROCLITIC Proclitic refers to the phenomenon that, in pronunciation, a syllable is combined so closely with the following word that it loses its own accent. In BH proclisis is indicated by the maqqēf (raised hyphen between letters). Two words that are combined like this, form one accent unit, the accent being on the last part (normally on the last syllable of that part.) *Proclisis* occurs especially after monosyllabic words, for example, בֶּ֫ instead of בֶּן in בֶּן־יִשְׂרָאֵל. Words that have undergone *proclisis*, are called clitics.

PROPHETIC PERFECT The prophetic perfect is a use of the PERFECT FORM to present future events as if they have already happened. Here the use of the perfect form to express completeness and factuality is so prominent that it is even used for a future event.

PROTASIS The *protasis* is the first (*if-*) part of a condition—a subordinate, conditional clause. See *APODOSIS*.

QATAL FORM See PERFECT FORM.

REAL CONDITION A subordinate, conditional CLAUSE is real if it indicates a fact in the past, present or future, for example, *If it rains, the streets are wet.*

RECIPROCAL A construction is reciprocal if an action or relation applies mutually. The members of a plural SUBJECT carry out the action on one another, for example, *they wash each other.* In BH the Niphal STEM FORMATION is sometimes used reciprocally.

REFERENT A referent is that entity in the real or conceptual (conversational) world which is associated with a noun phrase in a specific sentence or UTTERANCE.

REFLEXIVE A construction is called reflexive when two noun PHRASES in the construction have the same REFERENT, for example, *Liza washes herself* in which *Liza* and *herself* refers to the same person.

RESUMPTIVE The resumptive is the element in a CLAUSE that repeats the concord features (number and gender) of a previous element (the ANTECE-DENT of a relative clause or a dislocated element of a DISLOCATION CON-STRUCTION), e.g. *The man, I saw him.*

ROOT See STEM.

ROYAL PLURAL See PLURALIS MAJESTATIS.

SECONDARY ACCENT In BH certain words receive a secondary accent. Words consisting of three syllables with the primary accent on the last syllable very often get secondary accentuation on the third last syllable.

SELECT Select refers to the restriction that a VERB'S lexical meaning has on the CONSTITUENTS which can or must be used with it, for example, the verb *to die* selects only a SUBJECT (*He died*). In contrast to this the verb *to give* selects a subject, DIRECT OBJECT and INDIRECT OBJECT ([*He*] gives [*the man*] [*bread*]). See VALENCY.

SEMANTICS Semantics is the study of meaning in a language. This does not only cover the meaning of words, but also the meaning of relationships expressed in CLAUSES and SENTENCES, as well as the meaning of CLAUSES and SENTENCES.

SENTENCE A sentence is regarded as the largest structural unit in terms of which the grammar of language is organized.

SHORT FORM When APOCOPE occurs at the end of a verb in the IMPERFECT FORM, that form is referred to as the short form. See also JUSSIVE FORM.

SIBILANT The term *sibilant* refers to the manner of articulation of consonants that are formed when the speech canal is narrowed and, as a result, the air stream passes through with an audible hiss. In BH the sounds ז, צ, ט, ס and שׁ are sibilants.

SPEECH ACT A speech act is an act performed by a speaker's UTTERANCE: making an assertion, asking a question, giving a command, expressing encouragement or wish, etc. See PERFORMATIVE.

SPLIT PHRASE (split SUBJECT, OBJECT, etc.) In BH a split PHRASE indicates the grammatical pattern where other CLAUSE elements are inserted between the first and other parts of a constituent. For example, *moved away* is inserted between the parts of the split subject in the clause *A man moved away, he and his wife and his sons*.

STATIVE Stative indicates a form or construction expressing a state or quality rather than an event. In the case of VERBS in BH there is a MORPHO-LOGICAL distinction between the conjugation of statives and events/actions. Stative verbs are usually used INTRANSITIVELY, and events/actions are usually TRANSITIVE.

STATUS ABSOLUTUS The *status absolutus* is the normal form of the NOUN—singular, plural or dual; masculine or feminine. It is also called the נִפְרָד. A noun in the *status absolutus* can fulfil any SYNTACTIC function. The last element of a CONSTRUCT PHRASE or chain is also in the *status absolutus*. However, the *status absolutus* should not be confused with the *POSTCONSTRUCTUS* or 'GENITIVE', because the *postconstructus* itself can again be in the *STATUS CONSTRUCTUS*, if it is followed by another *postconstructus*.

STATUS CONSTRUCTUS The form of the first element of a CONSTRUCT PHRASE is shortened where possible. This form is the *status constructus* or נִסְמָךְ. The *status constructus* is sometimes also used as a binding form before other elements like prepositions. A word in the *status constructus* often loses its own accent (see PROCLITIC). Compare CONSTRUCT PHRASE and *POSTCONSTRUCTUS*.

STEM The stem or root of a word is a theoretical abstraction containing only the basic consonants of a word, without all PREFIXES, INFIXES, SUFFIXES and STEM VOWELS. The root of the VERB in BH usually consists of three consonants.

STEM CONSONANT A stem consonant is one of the three consonants forming the abstracted STEM or root of the VERB.

STEM FORMATION Stem formation is a conjugational type of the VERB. BH distinguishes seven basic stem formations: Qal, Niphal, Piel, Pual, Hithpael, Hiphil and Hophal. Sometimes stem formations are used to express VOICE, for example, the Niphal which can be the passive or REFLEXIVE of the Qal. However, the stem formations are not in an absolutely fixed SEMANTIC relation to each other.

STEM SYLLABLE The stem syllable is that syllable of a VERB that starts with the first STEM CONSONANT. (Cf. II waw and II yod verbs.)

STEM VOWEL A stem vowel is one of the characteristic vowels of a certain CONJUGATION, for example, the vowels ָ and ַ are the stem vowels of the Qal PERFECT (כָּתַב, כָּתַבְתָּ, כָּתַבְתִּי, etc.). With reference to NOUNS the stem vowel is one of the basic vowels of the word, for example, the stem vowel of מֶלֶךְ is / ֶ / (מֶלֶךְ).

STOP See PLOSIVE.

SUBJECT The subject refers to the grammatical relation that functions as subjective element in the CLAUSE structure. On the SYNTACTIC level the subject is that part of the clause that agrees with the PREDICATE in number and gender (and person—if the verb is FINITE). SEMANTICALLY the subject refers to the one who carries out the action or who experiences the state, for example, in the clauses *John kicks the ball* and *John sleeps* the word *John* is the entity that carries out the action or experiences the state.

SUBJUNCTIVE The subjunctive is a MOOD of the VERB expressing non-factualities like a wish, expectation or possibility. However, these are not expressed in BH by a separate CONJUGATION. The IMPERFECT FORM is used to express modal functions like *can/could*, *want(ed) to*, and *may* or *have to*. See OPTATIVE.

SUBSTANTIVE   Substantive is a synonym for NOUN. If other PARTS OF SPEECH, for example, adjectives, are used as nouns, the phe-nomenon is referred to as substantivation, for example, *The poor will receive financial aid.*

SUFFIX   A suffix is an AFFIX attached to the end of a STEM/ROOT, for example, the endings of the PERFECT and the nominal endings for the singular, plural and dual; masculine and feminine; *STATUS ABSOLUTUS* and *STATUS CONSTRUCTUS.* Suffixes are in contrast to affixes which are inserted in the root itself (INFIX) or before the root (PREFIX). The possessive pronouns that are suffixed to NOUNS are called pronominal suffixes. A pronominal DIRECT OBJECT can also be expressed by a pronominal suffix to the VERB.

SUFFIX CONJUGATION   See PERFECT FORM.

SUPPLEMENT CLAUSE   A supplement CLAUSE is a subordinate clause that acts as an ADJUNCT. It can be omitted without changing the meaning of the main clause. It is also called an adverbial, subordinate clause, e.g. conditional clause, circumstantial clause, temporal clause. A speaker cannot perform a SPEEECH ACT with a supplementary clause. See also COMPLEMENT CLAUSE.

SYNDETICAL   When a CLAUSE, PHRASE or word is connected by a conjunction to another, it is connected syndetically to the first.

SYNTACTIC DOMAIN   Syntactic domain refer to the collection of objects (word, PHRASE or CLAUSE) that are modified or related by a word (e.g. focus particle or quantifier). This is called the scope of the word. For example, in BH FOCUS particles have a syntactic domain, which is sometimes indicated by an independent personal pronoun.

SYNTAGM   Syntagm is a synonym for CONSTITUENT.

SYNTAX   Syntax is the study of the structure of CLAUSES and sentences in a language, i.e. the formal connections and relations between the elements of clauses and sentences.

TEXT LINGUISTICS   Text linguistics (also referred to as discourse analysis and/ or text grammar) refers to the scientific study of the conventions in a specific language with regard to the way in which semantic relations between people and matters are brought about in a text so that it can be understood as a coherent text. It also refers to the way in which sentences in this language are organized (and depends on one another linguistically) to form texts.

TOPIC   The topic is the matter about which the sentence tells something. Usually but not necessarily, it coincides with the SUBJECT.

TRANSITIVE   This term indicates VERBS that take a DIRECT OBJECT, for example, *write a book.*

UNREAL   Unreal refers to an event or situation that is not real, or which does not really exist, or which is hypothetical or impracticable.

UTTERANCE An utterance is anything that is said in language, including anything from a single sound to a word, exclamation or a whole sentence.

VALENCY The valency of a VERB refers to the number and nature of the obligatory CONSTITUENTS required SYNTACTICALLY or SEMANTICALLY by the verb, for example, *give* has a valency of three: it SELECTS a SUBJECT, DIRECT OBJECT and INDIRECT OBJECT (semantically: AGENT, PATIENT, receiver).

VERB Verb is a term in the grammatical classification of words that traditionally refers to a class of words which expresses actions, positions, processes and states. The following subclasses are found: INTRANSITIVE, TRANSITIVE, prepositional and copulative verbs. The STEM of a BH verb normally has three consonants, and this is the dictionary form. FINITE verbs in BH have the following characteristics: STEM FORMATION, CONJUGATION (tense/ MOOD), person, gender, number. Non-finite verbs do not have person: the participle do have gender and number, and, strictly speaking, it is a verbal adjective. The infinitive has neither person nor gender and number, and, strictly speaking, it is verbal NOUN.

VERB CHAIN Verb chain refers to a sequence of finite VERBS that are each directly preceded by a WAW COPULATIVE.

VERB SEQUENCE Verb sequence refers to a specific combination of VERBS (in the PERFECT or IMPERFECT FORM) that are directly preceded by a WAW CONSECUTIVE.

VERBLESS CLAUSE See NOMINAL CLAUSE.

VOCALIC SUFFIX A SUFFIX (e.g. a verbal ending or pronominal SUFFIX) that begins with a vowel, is a vocalic suffix, for example ִ־י in סוּסִי.

VOCATIVE Vocative is the name of a CASE that occurs in certain languages like Greek and Latin. It is used to mark the addressee MORPHOLOGICALLY. In BH the addressed person is either marked by the article ־הַ or not at all.

VOICE Voice is the group of conjugated forms of a VERB that determines if the AGENT or the PATIENT will be the SUBJECT of the verb. Active, passive and REFLEXIVE forms are distinguished. In BH STEM FORMATIONS are often used to express voice.

VP (VERB PHRASE) The smallest units with which a CLAUSE is built, are words. Words are distinguished in different classes, e.g. VERB (V), NOUN (N), adjective (A) and preposition (P). Words can be grouped into larger units known as PHRASES. Phrases can again be distinguished in different classes, named according to the class of the head word in the phrase. VP refers to a verb phrase, a phrase with V as head. The phrase *gave me his paper yesterday* in the clause *The student gave me his paper yesterday* is the VP with the V *gave* as head.

WAW CONSECUTIVE The waw consecutive is a special use of the conjunction ו (and) before PERFECT and IMPERFECT FORMS. Before imperfect forms the waw consecutive has the form ו with doubling of the following consonant or compensational lengthening of the a-vowel of the ו. Before perfect forms the waw consecutive has the normal form of the conjunction ו. The waw consecutive is also called the waw conversive because it usually changes the tense of an imperfect form to past tense, and the tense of a perfect form to future. However, the waw consecutive is used more widely, mainly to express progression like temporal and logical sequence, as well as to introduce new stories and to determine the flow of a story. Normally the consecutive IMPERFECT follows a PERFECT or other consecutive imperfect, and the consecutive perfect follows an imperfect or other consecutive perfect, but there are other possibilities as well.

WAW COPULATIVE + IMPERFECT. If the normal conjunction ו is followed by the IMPERFECT FORM, the ו is used simply to combine the CLAUSES coordinately. On its own this construction has no further specific SEMANTIC value. However, following a command it often expresses an underlying relation of purpose.

WAW COPULATIVE The waw copulative is the normal conjunction ו (and) that can be prefixed to any word to connect words, PHRASES or CLAUSES coordinately. Due to the form or meaning of the word to which it is prefixed, the form can differ: ו, ו, ו, ו, ו, ו, וֹ, ו, ו. With the PERFECT FORM or IMPERFECT FORM the waw copulative has no SEMANTIC value of its own except that of 'and'. However, different underlying semantic relations between clauses can be expressed by the waw copulative on the surface.

WAYYIQTOL *Wayyiqtol* is a synonym for WAW CONSECUTIVE + IMPERFECT FORM.

WEQATAL *Weqatal* is a synonym for WAW CONSECUTIVE + PERFECT FORM.

WH-QUESTION A WH-question is an interrogative sentence with a factual answer. See INTERROGATIVE.

WORD CLASS A word class (or part of speech) is one of the categories in which words are divided, mainly on formal grounds as well as their distribution. The following word classes are distinguished in BH: i.e. VERB, NOUN, adjective, preposition, conjunction, adverb, predicator of existence, interrogative, discourse marker, interjection.

YIQTOL FORM See IMPERFECT FORM.

BIBLIOGRAPHY

Andersen, F. I.
  1974   The Sentence in Biblical Hebrew (New York: Mouton).
Bandstra, B.R.
  1992   'Word order and Emphasis in Biblical Hebrew Narrative: Syntactic Observa-
          tions on Genesis 22 from a Discourse Perspective', in Bodine 1992: 109-123.
Bauer, H., and P. Leander
  1922   Historische Grammatik der hebräische Sprache der Alten Testaments (repr.
          1962, Hildesheim: Georg Olms Verlag).
Berger, R.D. (ed.)
  1994   Biblical Hebrew and Discourse Linguistics (Dallas: Summer Institute of Lin-
          guistics).
Bergsträsser, G.
  1929   Hebräische Grammatik. Mit Benutzung der von E. Kautzsch bearbeiten 28.
          Auflage von Wilhelm Gesenius' hebräischer Grammatik (repr. 1962, Hildes-
          heim: Georg Olms Verlag).
Bodine, W. (ed.)
  1992   Linguistics and Biblical Hebrew (Winona Lake: Eisenbrauns).
Brockelmann, C.
  1908, 1913 Grundriss der vergleichenden Grammatik der semitischen Sprachen (2
          vols.; repr. 1966, Hildesheim: Georg Olms Verlag).
  1956   Hebräische Syntax (Neukirchen-Vluyn: Neukirchener Verlag).
Brown, F., S.R. Driver and C.A. Briggs
  1907   A Hebrew and English Lexicon of the Old Testament (Oxford: Clarendon
          Press).
Buth, R.
  1992   'The Hebrew Verb in Current Discussions', Journal of Translation and Text-
          linguistics 5: 91-105.
Crystal, D.
  1985   A Dictionary of Linguistics and Phonetics (Oxford: Blackwell).
Gemser, B.
  1968   Hebreeuse Spraakkuns (Pretoria: J.L. van Schaik).
Gesenius, W., E. Kautzsch and E.A. Cowley
  1910   Gesenius' Hebrew Grammar (Oxford: Blackwell, 2nd edn).
Gross, W.
  1987a   Die Pendenskonstruktion im biblischen Hebräisch (ATS, 27; St. Ottilien:
          EOS Verlag).
  1987b   'Zur Syntagm-Folge im hebräischen Verbalsatz. Die Stellung des Subjekts in
          Dtn 1-15', Biblische Notizen 40: 63-95.

1988 'Der Einfluss der Pronominalisierung auf die Syntagmem-Folgen im hebräischen Verbalsatz, untersucht an Dtn 1-25', *Biblische Notizen* 43: 49-69.

1991 'Satzfolge, Satzteilfolge und Satzart als Kriterien der Subkategorisierung hebräischer Konjunktionalsätze, am Beispiel der כ Sätze untersucht', in Gross, Irsigler and Seidl (eds.) 1991: 97-118.

1993a 'Das Vorveld als strukturell eigenständiger Bereich des hebräischen Verbalsatz. Syntaktische Erscheinungen am Satzbeginn', in Irsigler 1993: 1-24.

1993b 'Die Position des Subjekts im hebräischen Verbalsatz, untersucht an den asyndetischen ersten Redesätzen in Gen, Ex 1-19, Jos-2 Kön.', *Zeitschrift für Althebraistik* 2: 170-87.

1996 *Die Satzteilfolge im althebräischen Verbalsatz: Untersucht an den Bücher Dtn. Ri und 2Kön* (Tübingen: J.C.B. Mohr).

Gross, W., H. Irsigler and T. Siedl (eds.)

1991 *Text, Methode und Grammatik: Wolfgang Richter zum 65. Geburtstag* (St. Ottilien: EOS Verlag).

Hoftijzer, J.

1981 *A Search for Method: A Study in the Syntactical Use of the H-locale in Classical Hebrew* (Leiden: E.J. Brill).

Holladay, W. L.

1971 *A Concise Hebrew and Aramaic Lexicon of the Old Testament Based upon the Lexical Work of Ludwig Koehler and Walter Baumgartner* (Grand Rapids: Eerdmans).

Irsigler, H. (ed.)

1993 *Syntax und Text: Beiträge zur 22. Internationalen ökumenischen Hebräisch-Dozenten-Konferenz 1993 Bamberg* (ATS, 40; St. Ottilien: EOS Verlag).

Jenni, E.

1992 *Die hebräischen Präpositionen. I. Die Präposition Beth* (Stuttgart: Kohlhammer).

1994 *Die hebräischen Präpositionen. II. Die Präposition Caph* (Stuttgart: Kohlhammer).

Jongeling, K., H.L. Murre-Van den Berg and K. van Rompay (eds.)

1991 *Studies in Hebrew and Aramaic Syntax: Presented to Professor J. Hoftijzer on the Occasion of his Sixty-fifth Birthday* (Studies in Semitic Languages and Linguistics, 17; Leiden: E.J. Brill).

Joüon, P. and T. Muraoka

1991 *A Grammar of Biblical Hebrew* (Subsidia Biblica, 14; 2 vols.; Rome: Pontifical Biblical Institute).

Klein, G.L.

1990 'The "Prophetic Perfect"', *Journal of Northwest Semitic Languages*: 45-60.

König, F.E.

1881-1897 *Historisch-kritisches Lehrgebäude der hebräischen Sprache* (3 vols.; repr. 1979, Hildesheim: Georg Olm Verlag).

Kroeze, J.H.

1991 'Die Chaos van die "Genitief" in Bybelse Hebreeus', *Journal for Semitics* 3: 129-43.

1993 'Underlying Syntactic Relations in Construct Phrases of Biblical Hebrew', *Journal for Semitics* 5: 68-88.

1994a 'Semantiese Verhoudings in Constructus-Verbindings van Bybelse Hebreeus: Toegespits op Spreuke' (Unpublished dissertation, Potchefstroom: PU for CHO).

1994b 'A Three-dimensional Approach to the Gender/Sex of Nouns in Biblical Hebrew', *Literator* 15: 139-53.

Lambdin, T.O.

1971   *Introduction to Biblical Hebrew* (New York: Charles Scribner's Sons).

Lambrecht, K.

1994   *Information Structure and Sentence Form: Topic, Focus and the Mental Representations of Discourse Referents* (Cambridge Studies in Linguistics, 71; Cambridge: Cambridge University Press).

Lande, I.

1949   *Formelhafte Wendungen der Umgangsprache im Alten Testament* (Leiden: E.J. Brill).

Laubscher, F. du Toit *et al.*

1983   *'n Beknopte Grammatika van Bybelse Hebreeus* (Bloemfontein: University of the Free State).

Lyons, J.

1968   *Introduction to Theoretical Linguistics* (Cambridge: Cambridge University Press).

Miller, C.L.

1996   *The Representation of Speech in Biblical Hebrew Narrative: A Linguistic Approach* (Harvard Semitic Museum Monographs, 55; Atlanta: Scholars Press).

Mulder, M. J.

1991   'Die Partikel אֵת in biblischen Hebräisch', in Jongeling, Murre-Van den Berg and Rompay (eds.) 1991: 132-42.

Muraoka, T.

1985   *Emphatic Words and Structures in Biblical Hebrew* (Jerusalem: Magnes Press).

Naudé, J.A.

1990   'A Syntactic Analysis of Dislocations in Biblical Hebrew', *Journal of Northwest Semitic Languages* 16: 115-30.

1996   'Independent Personal Pronouns in Qumran Hebrew' (Unpublished dissertation, Bloemfontein: University of the Free State).

Quirk, R., S. Greenbaum, G. Leech and J. Svartvik

1985   *A Comprehensive Grammar of the English Language* (London: Longman).

Revell, E.J.

1989   'The System of the Verb in Standard Biblical Prose', *HUCA* 60: 1-37.

Robins, R. H.

1990   *A Short History of Linguistics* (London: Longman).

Richter, W.

1978   *Grundlagen einer althebräischen Grammatik. A. Grundfragen einer sprachwissenschaftlichen Grammatik. B. Beschreibungsebene. I. Das Wort* (ATS, 8; St. Ottilien: EOS Verlag).

1979   *Grundlagen einer althebräischen Grammatik. B. II. Die Wortfügung (Morphosyntax)* (ATS, 10; St. Ottilien: EOS Verlag).

1980   *Grundlagen einer althebräischen Grammatik. B. III. Der Satz* (ATS, 13; St. Ottilien: EOS Verlag).

Rubenstein, E.

1952   'A Finite Verb Continued by an Infinitive Absolute in Hebrew', *Vetus Testamentum* 2: 262-67.

Schneider, W.

1993   'Und es begab sich .... Anfänge von Erzählung im biblischen Hebräisch', *Biblische Notizen* 70: 62-87.

Siebesma, P.A.

1991   *The Function of the Niph'al in Biblical Hebrew* (Studia Semitica Neerlandica, 28; Assen: Van Gorcum).

Ska, J.L.

1990   *'Our Fathers Have Told Us': Introduction to the Analysis of Hebrew Narrative* (Subsidia Biblica, 13; Rome: Pontifical Biblical Institute).

Van der Merwe, C.H.J.

1987   'A Short Survey of Major Contributions to the Grammatical Description of Old Hebrew since 1800 AD', *Journal of Northwest Semitic Languages* 13: 161-90.

1990   *'The Old Hebrew Particle gam: A Syntactic-semantic Description of gam in Gn–2Kg* (ATS, 34; St. Ottilien: EOS Verlag).

1991   'The Old Hebrew "Particles" אַף and רַק (in Genesis to 2 Kings)', in Gross, Irsigler and Siedl (eds.) 1991: 297-312.

1992   'Is there any Difference between מִפְּנֵי יָרֵא, מִן יָרֵא and אֵת יָרֵא?', *Journal of Northwest Semitic Languages* 17: 177-83.

1993a   'Particles and the Interpretation of Old Testament Texts', *Journal for the Study of the Old Testament* 60: 27-44.

1993b   'The Function of Word Order in Old Hebrew—with Special Reference to Cases Where a Syntagmeme Precedes a Verb in Joshua', *Journal of Northwest Semitic Languages* 17: 129-44.

1994   'Discourse Linguistics and Biblical Hebrew Linguistics, in Berger (ed.) 1994: 13-49.

1996a   'A Biblical Hebrew Reference Grammar for Theological Students. Some Theoretical Considerations', *Journal of Northwest Semitic Languages* 22: 125-41.

1996b   'From Paradigms to Electronic Texts. New Horizons and New Tools for Interpreting the Old Testament', *Journal of Northwest Semitic Languages* 22: 167-79.

1997a   'Reconsidering Biblical Hebrew Temporal Expressions', *Zeitschrift für Althebraistik* 10: 42-62.

1997b   '"Reference time" in Some Biblical Hebrew Temporal Constructions', *Biblica* 78: 503-24.

1999   'The Elusive Biblical Hebrew term וַיְהִי. A Perspective in Terms of its Syntax, Semantics and Pragmatics in 1 Samuel', *Hebrew Studies* (submitted for publication).

Waltke, B.K., and M. O'Connor

1990   *An Introduction to Biblical Hebrew Syntax* (Winona Lake: Eisenbrauns).

Zevit, Z.

1998   *The Anterior Construction in Classical Hebrew* (Society of Biblical Literature Monograph Series, 50; Atlanta: Scholars Press).

INDEXES

INDEX OF BIBLICAL HEBREW WORDS

Page numbers in *italics* refer to those sections in the grammar where the Biblical Hebrew word involved is the topic of a paragraph or subparagraph.

A Biblical Hebrew Reference Grammar

INDEX OF SUBJECTS

Page numbers in *italics* refer to sections in the grammar where the subject referred to is the topic of a paragraph or subparagraph. The numbers in **bold** refer to subjects that are entries in the glossary.

Index of Authors